*Phil Jnhln*

# The Biochemical Basis
# of Neuropharmacology

# The Biochemical Basis
# of Neuropharmacology

SIXTH EDITION

JACK R. COOPER, Ph.D.
Professor of Pharmacology
Yale University School of Medicine

FLOYD E. BLOOM, M.D.
Chairman, Department of Neuropharmacology
The Scripps Research Institute
La Jolla, California

ROBERT H. ROTH, Ph.D.
Professor of Pharmacology and Psychiatry
Yale University School of Medicine

New York   Oxford
OXFORD UNIVERSITY PRESS
1991

Oxford University Press

Oxford  New York  Toronto
Delhi  Bombay  Calcutta  Madras  Karachi
Petaling Jaya  Singapore  Hong Kong  Tokyo
Nairobi  Dar es Salaam  Cape Town
Melbourne  Auckland

and associated companies in
Berlin  Ibadan

Copyright © 1970, 1974, 1978, 1982, 1986, 1991
by Oxford University Press, Inc.

Published by Oxford University Press, Inc.,
200 Madison Avenue, New York, New York 10016

Oxford is a registered trademark of Oxford University Press

Library of Congress Cataloging-in-Publication Data
Cooper, Jack R., 1924–
    The biochemical basis of neuropharmacology / Jack R. Cooper,
Floyd E. Bloom, Robert H. Roth.—6th ed.
    p. cm.  Includes bibliographical references and index.
    ISBN 0-19-507117-4    ISBN 0-19-507118-2 (pbk.)
    1. Neurochemistry. 2. Neuropharmacology.  I. Bloom, Floyd E.
II. Roth, Robert H., 1939–    . III. Title.
    [DNLM:  1. Nerve Tissue—chemistry.  2. Nerve Tissue—physiology.
3. Nervous System—drug effects.  4. Neuropharmacology.
5. Neuroregulators—physiology.  QV 77 C777b]
QP356.3.C66 1991  615'.78—dc20  DNLM/DLC
for Library of Congress  91-1951

9 8 7 6 5

Printed in the United States of America
of acid-free paper

This book is dedicated to the memory
of Nicholas J. Giarman, colleague and dear friend

# Preface
# to the Sixth Edition

We must confess that it is with some amazement that we find ourselves doing a sixth edition of this little book: neither we nor Jeffrey House, our editor, expected it to be that popular. With this edition we have reinstated the chapter on memory and learning, since experimentation in this field has achieved much more credibility in the past several years. The other major change is a reorganization of the chapters on the catecholamines. All other chapters have been updated, particularly with reference to the explosion of new information on peptides, receptor subtypes, and G proteins.

Despite some complaints from colleagues whose contributions we fail to cite, we still maintain our position of mainly citing recent reviews that contain useful references, rather than citing the original papers.

J.R.C.
F.E.B.
R.H.R.

*June 1991*

# Contents

# 1 | Introduction

Neuropharmacology can be defined simply as the study of drugs that affect nervous tissue. This, however, is not a practical definition since a great many drugs whose therapeutic value is extraneural can affect the nervous system. For example, the cardiotonic drug digitalis will not uncommonly produce central nervous system effects ranging from blurred vision to disorientation. For our purposes we must accordingly limit the scope of neuropharmacology to those drugs specifically employed to affect the nervous system. The domain of neuropharmacology would thus include psychotropic drugs that affect mood and behavior, anesthetics, sedatives, hypnotics, narcotics, anticonvulsants, analeptics, analgetics, and a variety of drugs that affect the autonomic nervous system.

Since, with few exceptions, the precise molecular mechanism of action of these drugs is unknown, and since recitations of their absorption, metabolism, therapeutic indications, and toxic liability can be found in most textbooks of pharmacology, we have chosen to take a different approach to the subject. We will concentrate on the biochemistry and physiology of nervous tissue, emphasizing neurotransmitters, and will introduce the neuropharmacologic agents where their action is related to the subject under discussion. Thus, a discussion of LSD is included in the chapter on serotonin, and a suggested mechanism of action of the antipsychotic drugs is found in Chapter 10.

It is not difficult to justify this focus on either real or proposed neurotransmitters since the drugs act at junctions rather than on the events that occur with axonal conduction or within the cell body. Except for local anesthetics, which interact with axonal membranes, all neuropharmacological agents whose mechanisms of action are to some extent documented seem to be involved primarily with synaptic events. This finding appears quite logical in view of the regulatory mechanisms in the transmission of nerve impulses. The extent to which a neuron is depolarized or hyperpolarized will depend largely on its excitatory and inhibitory synaptic inputs, and these inputs must obviously involve neurotransmitters, neuromodulators, or neurohormones. What is enormously difficult to comprehend is the contrast between the action of a drug on a simple neuron, which causes it either to fire or not to fire, and the wide diversity of central nervous system effects, including subtle changes in mood and behavior which that same drug will induce. As will become clearer in subsequent chapters, at the molecular level, an explanation of the action of a drug is often possible; at the cellular level, an explanation is sometimes possible; but at a behavioral level, our ignorance is abysmal. There is no reason to assume, for example, that a drug that inhibits the firing of a particular neuron will therefore produce a depressive state in an animal: there may be dozens of unknown intermediary reactions involving transmitters and modulators between the demonstration of the action of a drug on a neuronal system and the ultimate effect on behavior.

However, the fact that one can find compounds with a specific chemical structure to control a given pathological condition is an exciting experimental finding, since it suggests an approach that the neuropharmacologist can use to clarify normal as well as abnormal brain chemistry and physiology. For instance, the use of drugs that affect the adrenergic nervous system has uncovered basic and hitherto unknown neural properties such as the uptake, storage, and release of the biogenic amines. The recognition of the analogy between curare poisoning in animals and myasthenia gravis in humans led to the understanding of the cholinergic neuromuscular transmission problem in myasthenia gravis and to subsequent treatment with anticholinesterases.

We have already referred to neuroactive agents involved in synaptic transmission as neurotransmitters, neuromodulators, and neurohormones, so definitions are now in order. Although we can define these terms in a strict, rigid fashion, it will be apparent—as noted later—that it is an exercise in futility to apply these definitions to a neuroactive agent as a classification unless one both understands its activity and specifies its locus. Briefly, the traditional definition of a *neurotransmitter* states that the compound must be synthesized and released presynaptically; it must mimic the action of the endogenous compound that is released on nerve stimulation; and, where possible, a pharmacological identity is required where drugs that either potentiate or block postsynaptic responses to the endogenously released agent also act identically to the administered suspected neurotransmitter. Conventionally, based on the studies of ACh at the neuromuscular junction, transmitter action was thought to be a brief and highly restricted point-to-point process. If ones takes the word *modulation* literally, then a *neuromodulator* has no intrinsic activity but is only active in the face of ongoing synaptic activity where it can modulate transmission either pre- or postsynaptically. In many instances, however, a modulating agent does produce changes in conductance or membrane potential. Typically, modulatory effects involve a second messenger system. A *neurohormone* can be released from both neuronal and nonneuronal cells and—most important to the definition travels—in some circulation to act at a site distant from its release site. Just how far a neurohormone has to travel before it loses its neurotransmitter status and becomes a neurohormone has never been decided.

We stated earlier that while we could define these terms, it would be of little use to pigeonhole known neuroactive compounds until the site of action and the activity of the agent was specified. For example, dopamine is a certified neurotransmitter in the striatum, yet it is released from the hypothalamus and travels through the hypophyseal-portal circulation to the pituitary where it inhibits the release of prolactin. Here it obviously fits the definition of a neurohormone. Similarly, serotonin is a neurotransmitter in the raphe nuclei, yet at the facial motor nucleus it acts primarily as a neuromodulator and secondarily as a transmitter. Most peptides with their multiple activities in the brain and gut are generally considered to be neuromodulators, yet Substance P fulfills the criteria of a transmitter at sensory afferents to the dorsal horn of the spinal cord. In sum, the plethora of exceptions to the aforementioned definitions of transmitter, modulator, and hormone has generated confusion in the literature. Better to describe the activity of a neuroactive agent at a specified site rather than attempt to give a profitless definition.

The multidisciplinary aspects of pharmacology in general are particularly relevant in the field of neuropharmacology, where a "pure" neurophysiologist or neurochemist would be severely handicapped in elucidating drug action at a molecular level. The neuropharmacologist should be aware of the tools that are available for the total dissection of a biological problem. These would include morphological techniques such as electron microscopy, fluorescence microscopy, and freeze-etching, and immunological techniques as a basis for developing radioimmunoassays, immunocytochemistry, and monoclonal antibodies, as well as the classical electrophysiological and biochemical procedures. In addition, if the investigator is concerned with the action of psychotropic drugs, a prerequisite is some knowledge of the techniques and pitfalls of behavioral testing.

In science one measures something. One must know what to measure, where to measure it, and how to measure it. This sounds rather obvious, but the student should be aware that, particularly in the neural sciences, these seemingly simple tasks can be enormously difficult. For example, suppose one were interested in elucidating the presumed biochemical aberration in schizophrenia. *What* would one measure? ATP? Glucose? Ascorbic acid? Unfortunately, this problem early on had been zealously investigated by people who measured everything they could think of, generally in the blood, in their search for differences between normal individuals and schizophrenics. As could be predicted, the problem was not solved. (It may be assumed, however, that these studies produced a large population of anemic schizophrenics because of all the bloodletting.) In recent times it has been demonstrated that antidepressant drugs inhibit norepinephrine reuptake (see Chapter 9). Although this biochemical reaction takes place immediately in test tubes containing brain tissue, patients who are given antidepressant medication do now show beneficial effects for about 2 weeks. The inference, therefore, is that the drug itself and its biochemical reaction do not produce the ameliorative effect, rather it is the adaptation of the brain to the presence of the drug that is beneficial. The question then is what is this adaptation; the answer is we still don't know what to measure.

Deciding *where* to measure something in neuroscience is complicated by the heterogeneity of nervous tissue: In general, unless one has a particular axon to grind, it is preferable to use peripheral nerve rather than the CNS. Suburban neurochemists have an easier time than their CNS counterparts, since it is not only a question of which region of the brain to use for the test preparation but which of the multitude of cell types within each area to choose. If a project involved a study of amino-acid transport in nervous tissue, for example, would one use isolated nerve-ending particles (synaptosomes), glial cells, neuronal cell bodies in culture, a myelinated axon, or a ganglion cell? Up to the present time most investigators have used cortical brain slices, but the obvious disadvantage of this preparation is that one has no idea which cellular organelle takes up the amino acid.

*How* to measure something is a surprisingly easy question to answer, at least if one is dealing with simple molecules. With the recent advances in microseparation techniques and in fluorometric, radiometric, and immunological assays, there is virtually nothing that cannot be measured with a high degree of specificity and sensitivity. In this regard one should be careful not to overlook the classical bioassay, which tends to be scorned by young investigators but is in fact largely responsible for striking progress in our knowledge of both the prostaglandins and the opiate receptor with its peptide agonists. The major problem is with macromolecules. How can neuronal membranes be quantified, for example, if extraneuronal constituents are an invariable contaminant and if markers to identify unequivocally a cellular constituent are often lacking? The quantitative and spatial measurement of receptors utilizing autoradiography is also a key problem (see Chapter 5).

This harangue about measurement is meant to point out that what would on the surface appear to be the simplest part of research can in fact be very difficult. It is vital that students learn not to accept data without a critical appraisal of the procedures that were employed to obtain the results.

Finally, although the theme is not explicitly dealt with in this book, students may find it educational and often entertaining to attempt to define patterns of research design in neuropharmacology as well as current trends in research areas. One common pattern is for someone to observe something in brain tissue, trace its regional distribution in the brain, and then perform a developmental study of the phenomenon in laboratory animals from prenatal through adult life. Another common pattern is for someone to develop a technique and then search (sometimes with what appears to be desperation) for projects that will utilize the technique. Yet another somewhat simplistic idea is that of attempting to relate a behavioral effect to a changing level of a single neurotransmitter, invariably the one that a team has just learned how to measure. Current trends in the neural sciences that are related to neuropharmacology include isolating ion channels, utilizing molecular genetics to uncover new peptides, neural cartography (the mapping of transmitters and neuroactive peptides in the CNS), searching for toxins with specific effects on conduction or transmission, cloning and characterizing receptors for drugs as well as endogenous neuroactive agents, and identifying trophic factors involved in synaptogenesis and neuronal regulation. It can also easily be predicted that within the next few years an intensive search will be undertaken to explain the function and integration of the approximately three dozen "classical" neurotransmitters, the neuroactive peptides, and the unclassifiable items such as adenosine in eliciting behavioral changes. Clearly, neuropharmacologic agents will be invaluable probes in this search.

# 2 | Cellular Foundations of Neuropharmacology

As we begin to consider the particular problems that underlie the analysis of drug actions in the central nervous system, it may be asked, "Just what is so special about nervous tissue?" Nerve cells have two special properties that distinguish them from all other cells in the body. First, they can conduct bioelectric signals for long distances without any loss of signal strength. Second, they possess specific intercellular connections with other nerve cells and with innervated tissues such as muscles and glands. These connections determine the types of information a neuron can receive and the range of responses it can yield in return.

## CYTOLOGY OF THE NERVE CELL

We do not need the high resolution of the electron microscope to identify the characteristic structural features of the nerve cell. The classic studies of Cajal (Santiago Ramón y Cajal to his friends) demonstrated that nerve cells are heterogeneous in both size and shape. An essential structural feature of the nervous system is that each specific region of the brain and each part of each nerve cell often have several synonymous names. So, for example, we find that the body of the nerve cell is also called the soma and the perikaryon—literally, the part that surrounds the nucleus. A fundamental scheme classifies nerve cells by the number of cytoplasmic processes they possess. In the simplest case, the perikaryon has one process, called an axon; the best examples of this cell type are the sensory neurons whose perikarya occur in groups in the sensory or dorsal root ganglia. In this case, the axon conducts the signal—which was generated by

| 9

the sensory receptor in the skin or other viscera—centrally through the dorsal root into the spinal cord or cranial nerve nuclei. At the next step of complexity we find neurons possessing two processes: the bipolar nerve cells. The sensory receptor nerve cells of the retina, the olfactory mucosa, and the auditory nerve are of this form, as is a class of small nerve cells of the brain known as granule cells. All other nerve cells tend to fall into the class known as multipolar nerve cells. These cells possess only one axon or efferent-conducting process which may be short or long, branched or straight, and which may possess a recurrent or collateral branch that feeds back onto the same type of nerve cell from which the axon arises. Their main differences relate to the extent and size of the receptive field of the neuron, termed the dendrites or dendritic tree. In silver-stained preparations for the light microscope, the branches of the dendrites look like trees in wintertime, although the branches may be long and smooth, short and complex, or bearing short spines like a cactus. It is on these dendritic branches as well as on the cell body where the termination of axons from other neurons makes the specialized interneuronal communication point known as the synapse.

*The Synapse*

The characteristic specialized contact zone that has been presumptively identified as the site of functional interneuronal communication is the synapse. It contains special organelles. As the axon approaches the site of its termination, it exhibits structural features not found more proximally. Most striking is the occurrence of dilated regions of the axon (varicosities) within which are clustered large numbers of microvesicles (synaptic vesicles). These synaptic vesicles tend to be spherical in shape, with diameters varying between 400 and 1200 Å. Depending upon the type of fixation used, the shape and staining properties of the vesicles can be related to their neurotransmitter content. The nerve endings also exhibit mitochondria, but do not exhibit microtubules unless the varicosity is a "pre-terminal" region of an axon as it extends towards its terminal target. One or more of these varicosities may form a specialized contact with one or more dendritic branches before the ultimate termination. Such endings are known as *en passant* terminals. In this sense, the term "nerve terminal" or "nerve ending" connotes a functional transmitting site rather than the end of the axon.

Electron micrographs of synaptic regions in the central nervous system reveal a specialized contact zone between the axonal nerve ending and the postsynaptic structure (Fig. 2-1). This specialized contact zone is composed of presumed proteinaceous material lining the intracellular portions of the pre- and postsynaptic membranes and filling the synaptic cleft between the apposed cell surfaces. Such types of specialized contacts are a general form of the specialized cell contacts seen between many types of cells derived from the embryonic ectoderm, of which the nerve cell is but one. However, the specialized contact between neurons is polarized; that is, the presynaptic terminal intracellular material is composed of interrupted presynaptic dense projections measuring about 500–700 Å in diameter and separated from each other by distances of 300–400 Å. This material may be present only to bind specific presynaptic nerve endings permanently to specific postsynaptic cell sites. Alternatively, the specialized contact zone could assist in the efficiency of transmission and could constitute one potential method for modulating the efficacy of synaptic transmission. All aspects of the release and reuptake of transmitter function quite well, however, in the peripheral nervous system with no apparent specializations. In some neurons, especially these single-process small granule cell types, the "dendrite" may also be structurally specialized to store and release transmitter.

*Glia*

A second element in the maintenance of the neuron's integrity depends on a type of cell known as neuroglia. There are two main types of neuroglia. The first is called the fibrous astrocyte, a descriptive term based on its starlike shape when viewed in the light microscope and on the fibrous nature of its cytoplasmic organelles, which can be seen with both light and electron microscopy. The

FIGURE 2-1. High-power view of two nerve terminals contacting a small dentritic spine. At this magnification the synaptic vesicles can be seen clearly, as can the zones of specialized contact (Sy). Astrocyte processes containing glycogen (A) can be seen. Note that the larger nerve terminal makes a specialized contact on the small terminal (axo-axonic) as well as on the dendrite (axo-dentritic) × 12000.

astrocyte is found mainly in regions of axons and dendrites; they tend to surround and closely contact the adventitial surface of blood vessels. Functions such as insulation (between conducting surfaces) and organization (to surround and separate functional units of nerve endings and dendrites) have been empirically attributed to the astrocyte, mainly on the basis of its structural characteristics.

The second type of neuroglia is known as the oligodendrocyte. It is called the satellite cell when it occurs close to nerve cell bodies, and Schwann cell when it occurs in the peripheral nervous system. The cytoplasm of the oligodendrocyte is characterized by rough endoplasmic reticulum, but its most prominent characteristic is the enclosure of concentric layers of its own surface membrane around the axon. These concentric layers come together so closely that the oligodendrocyte cytoplasm is completely squeezed out and the original internal surfaces of the membrane become fused, presenting the ringlike appearance of the myelin sheath in cross section. Along the course of an axon, which may be many centimeters, many oligodendrocytes are required to constitute its myelin sheath. At the boundary between adjacent portions of the axon covered by separate oligodendrocytes, there is an uncovered axonal portion known as the node of Ranvier.

Many central axons and certain elements of the peripheral autonomic nervous system do not possess myelin sheaths. Even these axons, however, are not bare or exposed directly to the extracellular fluid, rather they are enclosed within single invaginations of the oligodendrocyte surface mambrane. Because of this close relationship between the conducting portions of the nerve cell, its axon, and the oligodendrocyte, it is easy to see the origin of the proposition that the oligodendrocyte may contribute to the nurture of the nerve cell. While this idea may be correct, evidence is meager. Clearly, the glia cannot support the axon when it has been severed from the cell body, for example, by trauma or by experimental lesions. This incapacity is fortuitous, since one of the primitive methods of defining nerve cell circuits within the brain is the staining of degenerating axons following brain lesions.

## Brain Permeability Barriers

While the unique cytological characteristics of neurons and glia are sufficient to establish the complex intercellular relationships of the brain, there is yet another histophysiologic concept to consider. Numerous chemical substances pass from the bloodstream into the brain at rates that are far slower than for entry into all other organs in the body. There are similar slow rates of transport between the cerebrospinal fluid and the brain, although there is no good standard in other organs against which to compare this latter movement.

These permeability barriers appear to be the end result of numerous contributing factors that present diffusional obstacles to chemicals on the basis of molecular size, charge, solubility, and specific carrier systems. The difficulty has not been in establishing the existence of these barriers, but in determining their mechanisms. When the relatively small protein (mol wt = 43,000) horseradish peroxidase is injected intravenously into mice, its location within the tissue can be demonstrated histochemically with the electron microscope. As opposed to the easy transvascular movement of this substance across muscle capillaries, in the brain the peroxidase molecule is unable to penetrate the continuous layer of vascular endothelial cells. The endothelial cells of brain capillaries differ from those of other tissues in that the intercellular zones of membrane apposition are much more highly developed in the brain and are virtually continuous along all surfaces of these cells. Furthermore, cerebral vascular endothelial cells lack pinocytotic vesicles, considered to be the transvascular carrier systems of both large and small molecules in other tissues.

Since the enzyme marker can neither go through nor between the endothelial cells, an operationally defined barrier exists. Whether or not the same barrier is also applicable to highly charged lipophobic small molecules cannot be determined from these observations. As neuropharmacologists, what concerns us more are the factors that retard the entrance of these smaller molecules, such as norepinephrine and serotonin, their amino-acid precursors, or drugs that affect the metabolism of these and other neurotransmitters. Charged molecules can diffuse widely through the extracellular spaces of the brain when permitted entry via the cerebrospinal fluid.

Astrocytes are currently thought to elicit expression in cerebral capillary endothelial cells of the proteins that constitute the blood-brain barrier. Recent research suggests that a model blood-brain barrier system may be attainable under culture conditions. So long as central astrocytes are viable, brain fragments transplanted to vascular beds, such as the anterior chamber of the eye, that would normally lack a blood-brain barrier, nevertheless retain a functional barrier when revascularized. This suggests that the properties of the barrier reside not in the endothelial cells themselves, but in some sort of functional response to central astrocytes.

Substances that find it difficult to get into the brain also find it exceedingly difficult to leave. Thus, when monoamines are increased in concentration by the blocking of their catabolism (see Chapter 9), high levels of amine persist until the inhibiting agents are metabolized or excreted. One such route is the "acid transport" system by which the choroid plexus and/or brain parenchymal cells actively secrete acid catabolites. This step can be blocked by the drug probenecid, resulting in increased brain and CSF catabolites of the amines.

The choroid plexus may also be an interface between the peripheral vascular system and the immune response system, where antigens for which immuno-surveillance is required can be recognized and immune responses can be mounted. Lymphocytes may normally "wander" through the brain in search of immune targets, although how they can slip through the endothelial cell barriers without reducing their normal barrier functions remains unclear.

Since the precise nature of these barriers still can not be formulated, students would be wise to avoid the "great wall of China" concept and lean toward the possibility of a series of variously placed, progressively selective filtration sites that discriminate substances on the basis of several molecular characteristics. With lipid-soluble weak electrolytes—a characteristic of most centrally acting drugs—transport occurs by a process of passive diffusion. Thus, a drug will penetrate the endothelial cell only in the undissociated form and at a rate consonant with its lipid solubility and its pKa.

Specialized sets of neurons known as the circumventricular organs exist within discrete sites along the linings of the cerebroventricles, but are functionally on the blood side of the blood-brain barrier. Considered to be "windows" through which the normally excluded central milieu can monitor the components of the blood stream, these neurons can communicate directly with neurons well within the enclosure of the blood-brain barrier.

## BIOELECTRIC PROPERTIES OF THE NERVE CELL

Given these structural details, we can now turn to the second striking feature of nerve cells, namely, their bioelectric property. However, even for this introductory presentation, we must understand certain

FIGURE 2-2. At the top is shown a hypothetical neuron ($N_1$) receiving a single excitatory pathway (E) and a single inhibitory pathway (I). A stimulating electrode (S) has been placed on the nerve cell's axon; microelectrode 1 is extracellular to nerve cell 1, while microelectrode 2 is in the cell body, and microelectrode 3 is in its nerve terminal. Microelectrode 4 is recording from within postsynaptic cell 2. The potentials and current, recorded by each of these electrodes, are being compared through a "black box" of electronics with a distant extracellular grounded electrode and displayed on an oscilloscope screen. When the cell is resting and the electrode is on the outside of the cell, no potential difference is observed (1). In the resting state, electrode 2 records a steady potential difference between inside and outside of approximately minus 50 millivolts (2). While recording from electrode 2 and stimulating the inhibitory pathway, the membrane potential is hyperpolarized during the inhibitory postsynaptic potential (2 + I). When recording from electrode 2 and stimulating the excitatory pathway, a subthreshold stimulus ($S_T$) produces an excitatory postsynaptic potential indicated by a brief depolarization of the resting membrane potential (2 + E). When the excitatory effects are sufficient to reach threshold (T), an

basic concepts of the physical phenomena of electricity in order to have a working knowledge of the bioelectric characteristics of living cells.

The initial concept to grasp is that of a difference in potential existing within a charged field, as occurs when charged particles are separated and prevented from randomly redistributing themselves. When a potential difference exists, the amount of charge per unit of time that will flow between the two sites (i.e., current flow) depends upon the resistance separating them. If the resistance tends to zero, no net current will flow since no potential difference can exist in the absence of a measurable resistance. If the resistance is extremely high, only a minimal current will flow and that will be proportional to the electromotive force or potential difference between the two sites. The relationship between voltage, current, and resistance is Ohm's law: $V = I \cdot R$.

When we come to the measurement of the electrical properties of living cells, these basic physical laws apply, but with one exception. The pioneer electrobiologists, who did their work before the discovery and definition of the electron, developed a convention for

---

action potential is generated which reverses the inside negativity to inside positivity (2 + E). On the lower scale, potentials recorded by electrodes 3 and 4 are compared on the same time-base following axonal stimulation of nerve cell 1, which is assumed to be excitatory. The point of stimulus is seen as an electrical artifact at point S. The action potential generated at the nerve terminal occurs after a finite lag period due to the conduction time (c) of the axon between the stimulating electrode and the nerve terminal. The action potential in the nerve ending does not directly influence post-synaptic cell 2 until after the transmitter has been liberated and can react with nerve cell 2's membrane, causing the excitatory postsynaptic potential indicated by the dotted line. The time between the beginning of the action potential recorded by microelectrode 3 and the excitatory postsynaptic potential recorded by electrode 4 (A) is the time required for excitation secretion coupling in the nerve terminal and the liberation of sufficient transmitter to produce effects on nerve cell 2. Electrode 5 is a patch clamp electrode attached to neuron 2; it indicates the effects of transmitters acting through receptors located elsewhere on the neuron's surface, mediating channel opening (o) and closing (c) events through intracellular second messengers.

the flow of charges based not on the electron but on the flow of positive charges. Therefore, since in biological systems the flow of charges is not carried by electrons but by ions, the direction of flow is expressed in terms of movement of positive charges. To analyze the electrical potentials of a living system, we use small electrodes (a microprobe for detecting current flow or potential), electronic amplifiers for increasing the size of the current or potential, and oscilloscopes or polygraphs for displaying the potentials observed against a time base.

*Membrane Potentials*

If we take two electrodes and place them on the outside of a living cell or tissue, we will find little, if any, difference in potential. However, if we injure a cell so as to break its membrane or insert one ultrafine electrode across the membrane, we will find a potential difference such that the inside of the cell is 50 or more millivolts negative with respect to the extracellular electrode (Fig. 2-2). This transmembrane potential difference is found in almost all types of living cells in which it has been sought; such a membrane is said to be electrically polarized. By passing negative ions into the cell through the microelectrode (or extracting cations), the inside can be made more negative (hyperpolarized). If positive current is applied to the inside of the cell, the transmembrane potential difference is decreased, and the potential is said to be depolarized. The potential difference across the membrane of most living cells can be accounted for by the relative distribution of the intracellular and extracellular ions.

The extracellular fluid is particularly rich in sodium and relatively low in potassium. Inside the cell, the cytoplasm is relatively high in potassium content and very low in sodium. While the membrane of the cell permits potassium ions ($K^+$) to flow back and forth with relative freedom, it resists the movement of the sodium ions ($Na^+$) from the extracellular fluid to the inside of the cell. Since the potassium ions can cross the membrane, they tend to flow along the concentration gradient—which is highest inside the cell. Potassium diffusion out of the cell leaves a relative negative charge behind owing to the negative charges of the macromolecular proteins. As the negative charge inside the cell begins to build up, the further diffusion of potassium from inside to outside is retarded. Eventually an equilibrium point will be reached that is proportional to certain physical constants and to the relative concentrations of intracellular and extracellular potassium and chloride ions. These concepts of ionic diffusion potentials across semipermeable membranes apply generally, not only to nerve and muscle, but to blood, glandular, and other cells large enough to have their transmembrane potential measured.

*Membrane Ion Pumps*

When the nerve cell or muscle fiber can be impaled by electrodes to record transmembrane potential, the relation between the membrane potential and external potassium concentration can be directly tested by exchanging the extracellular fluid for artificial solutions of varying potassium concentration. When this experiment is performed on muscle cells, we find that the membrane potential bears a linear relationship to the external potassium concentration at normal to high potassium concentrations but that it deviates from this linear relationship when the external potassium concentration is less than normal. To account for this discrepancy we must now reexamine an earlier statement. While the pasma membranes of nerve and muscle cells and other types of polarized cells are relatively impermeable to the flow of sodium ions along the high concentration gradient from extracellular to intracellular, they are not completely impermeable. With radioisotope experiments it can be established that a certain amount of sodium "leaks" into the resting cell from outside. The amount of measurable sodium entry into the cell occurs at a rate sufficient to double the intracellular sodium concentration in approximately one hour if there were not some opposing process to maintain the relatively low intracellular sodium concentration. The process that continuously maintains the low intracellular sodium concentration is known as active sodium transport, or colloquially as the "sodium pump." This pump mechanism ejects sodium from the inside of the cell against the high concentration and electrical gradients forcing it in. However, the "pump" does not handle sodium exclusively but requires the presence of extracellular potassium. Thus, when a sodium ion is ejected from the cell, a potassium ion is incorporated into the cell.

When the external potassium concentration is near normal, the transmembrane potential, which is based mainly on potassium concentration differences, behaves as if there were actually more extracellular potassium than really exists. This is because the sodium–potassium exchange mechanism elevates the amount of potassium coming into the cell. Remember that potassium permeability is relatively high and that potassium will tend to diffuse out of the cell because of its concentration gradient but to diffuse into the cell because of charge attraction. Therefore, two factors operate to drive potassium into the cell in the presence of relatively low external potassium concentration: (1) the electrical gradient across the membrane and (2) the sodium-potassium pump mechanism. The latter system could be considered "electrogenic" since at low external $K^+$ concentrations it modifies the electrical status of the muscle membrane. Other metabolic pumps operate simply to exchange cationic species across the membrane and are "nonelectrogenic." The relative "electrogenicity" of a pump may depend on the ratio of the exchange cations (i.e., 1:1 or 2:2 or 3:2). The pump is immediately dependent upon metabolic energy and can be blocked by several metabolic poisons such as dinitrophenol and the rapid-acting cardiac glycoside, ouabain.

## The Uniqueness of Nerve

All that we have said regarding the transmembrane ionic distributions applies equally as well to the red blood cell or glia as to the nerve membrane. Thus, the possession of a transmembrane potential difference is not sufficient to account for the bioelectric properties of the nerve cell. The essential difference between the red blood cell and the nerve cell can be brought out by applying depolarizing currents across the membrane. When the red blood cell membrane is depolarized, the difference in potential across the cell passively follows the imposed polarization. However, when a nerve cell membrane, such as the giant axon of an invertebrate, is depolarized from a resting value of approximately $-70$ millivolts to approximately $-10$ to $-15$ millivolts, an explosive self-limiting process occurs by which the transmembrane potential is reduced not merely to zero but overshoots zero, so that the inside of the membrane now becomes positive with respect to the outside. This overshoot may extend for 10 to 30 millivolts in the positive direction. Because of this explosive response to an electrical depolarization, the nerve membrane is said to be electrically excitable, and the resultant voltage polarity shift is the action potential.

*Analysis of Action Potentials*

In an elegant series of pioneering experiments that are now classical, Hodgkin, Huxley, and Katz were able to analyze the various ionic steps responsible for the action potential. When the cell begins to depolarize in response to stimulation, the current flow across the membrane is carried by potassium. As the membrane becomes more depolarized, the resistance to Na decreases (i.e., Na conductance increases) and more Na enters the cell along its electrical and concentration gradients. As Na enters, the membrane becomes more and more depolarized, which further increases the conductance to Na and thus depolarizes the membrane more and faster. Such conductance changes are termed voltage-dependent. This self-perpetuating process continues, driven by the flow of Na ions moving toward their equilibrium distribution, which should be proportional to the original extracellular and intracellular concentrations of Na.

However, the peak of the action potential does not attain the equilibrium potential predicted on the basis of transmembrane Na concentrations because of a second phase of events. The voltage-dependent increase in $Na^+$ conductance and the consequent depolarization also activates a voltage-dependent $K^+$ conductance, and K flow then also increases along its concentration gradient from inside to outside the cell. This process restricts the height of the reversal potential, since it tends to maintain the inside negativity of the cell and also begins to reduce the membrane conductance to Na, thus making the action potential a self-limiting phenomenon. In most nerve axons, the action potential lasts for approximately 0.2 to 0.5 milliseconds (ms), depend on the type of fiber and the temperature in which it is measured.

Once the axon has been sufficiently depolarized to reach threshold for an action potential, the wave of activity travels at a rate proportional to the diameter of the axons (through which the bioelectric currents will flow). In large axons, the rate is further accelerated by the insulation provided by myelin sheaths, restricting the flow of transmembrane currents to the opening at the nodes of Ranvier. Therefore, instead of the action potential propagating from minutely contiguous sites of the membrane, the action potential in the myelinated axon leaps from node to node. This saltatory conduction is consequently much more rapid.

The threshold level for an all-or-none action potential is also inversely proportional to the diameter of the axon: Large myelinated axons respond to low values of imposed stimulating current, whereas fine and unmyelinated axons require much greater depolarizing currents. Local anesthetics appear to act by blocking activation of the sodium conductance preventing depolarization.

Once the threshold has been reached, a complete action potential will be developed unless it occurs too soon after a preceding action potential, during the so-called refractory phase. This phase varies for different types of excitable nerve and muscle cells and appears to be related to the activation process increasing sodium conductance, a phenomenon that has a finite cycling period; that is, the membrane cannot be reactivated before a finite interval of time has occurred. Potassium conductance increases with the action potential and lasts slightly longer than the activation of sodium conductance. This results in a prolonged phase of after-hyperpolarization due to the continued redistribution of potassium from inside to outside the membrane. If the axonal membrane is artificially maintained at a transmembrane potential equal to the $K^+$ equilibrium potential, no after-hyperpolarization can be seen.

*Ion Channels*

The experiments of Hodgkin and Huxley defined the kinetics of cation movement during nerve membrane excitation without constraint on the mechanisms accounting for the movement of ions through the membrane. The discovery that cation movement can be selectively blocked by drugs, and that $Na^+$ permeability (blocked by tetrodotoxin) can be separated from $K^+$ permeability (blocked by tetraethylammonium [TEA]), made more detailed analysis of the ion movement mechanisms feasible. Membrane physiologists now agree that there are several ion-specific pathways that form separate and independent "channels" for passive movement of $Na^+$, $K^+$, $Ca^{2+}$, and $Cl^-$. According to Hille, the channels are pores that open and close in an all-or-nothing fashion on time scales of 0.1 to 10 ms to provide aqueous channels through the plasma membrane that ions can traverse. In his view, the channels can be conceived as protein macromolecules within the fluid lipid plane of the membrane; these channel macromolecules can exist in several interconvertible conformations, one of which permits ion movement while the others do not. The conformational shifts from one form to another are sensitive to the bioelectric fields operating on the membrane; by facilitating or retarding the conformational shifts, the ion channels are "gated." In this concept, $Ca^{2+}$ acts as the membrane surface to alter permeability only by virtue of the effect its charge has on the electric fields of otherwise fixed (mainly negative) organic charges. The altered fields in turn can gate the channels because a part of the channel protein is able to sense the field and thus to modulate the conformational shifts that open or close the gate. When ions flow across the membrane, the ionic current changes membrane potential and other membrane properties.

From a variety of experimental methods, including methods that can sample single ion channels in cultured neurons and other excitable cells, a large number of specific ion channels have been described. In current terminology, one recognizes (1) "non-gated" passive ion channels, previously referred to as "leakage channels," that are continuously open; (2) voltage-gated (i.e., voltage sensitive) channels whose opening and closing are affected by the membrane potential inside of the cell; (3) chemically gated channels whose openings and closings are affected by receptors on the external plasma membrane, such as those affected by drugs and other transmitters; and (4) ion-gated channels, whose openings and closings are affected by shifts in intracellular ion concentrations. Ion-gated channels are often also sensitive to membrane potential and to external regulatory receptors, and chemically gated channels are often also voltage sensitive. These various modes of interaction provide an extremely rich spectrum of responses, thus greatly complicating what were once simple rules of excitability and ion conductance regulation. Additional forms of more complex ion flow regulation provide the means by which neurons communicate to their target cells through junctional transmission.

## Junctional Transmission

While these ionic mechanisms appear to account adequately for the phenomena occurring in the propagation of an action potential down an axon, they do not per se explain what happens when the action potential reaches the nerve ending. At the nerve ending the membrane of the axon is separated from the membrane of the postjunctional nerve cell, muscle, or gland by an intercellular space of 50–200 Å (Fig. 2-1). When an electrode can be placed in both the terminal axon and the postsynaptic cell, depolarization of the nerve terminal does not result in a direct instantaneous shift in the transmembrane potential of the postsynaptic element, except in those cases in which the connected cells are electronically coupled. With this exception, the junctional site seldom exhibits direct electrical excitability like the axon.

## Postsynaptic Potentials

With the advent of microelectrode techniques for recording the transmembrane potential of nerve cells in vivo, it was possible to determine the effects of stimulation of nerve pathways that had previously been shown to cause either excitation or inhibition of synaptic transmission. From just such studies Eccles and his colleagues observed that subthreshold excitatory stimuli would produce postsynaptic potentials with time durations of 2 to 20 ms. The excitatory postsynaptic potentials could algebraically accumulate both with the excitatory and inhibitory postsynaptic potentials. Most importantly, the duration of these postsynaptic potentials was longer than could be accounted for on the basis of electrical activity in the preterminal axon or on the electrotonic conductive properties of the postsynaptic membrane (Fig. 2-2). This latter observation, combined with the fact that synaptic sites are not directly electrically excitable, provides the conclusive evidence that central synaptic transmission must be chemical: The prolonged time course is compatible with a rapidly released chemical transmitter whose time course of action is terminated by local enzymes, diffusion, and reuptake by the nerve ending.

By such experiments it was possible to work out the basic ionic mechanisms for inhibitory and excitatory postsynaptic potentials. When an ideal excitatory pathway is stimulated, the presynaptic element liberates an excitatory transmitter that activates an ionic conductance of the postsynaptic membrane. This response leads to an increase in one or more transmembrane ionic conductances, depolarizing the membrane toward the sodium equilibrium potential; in the resting state, as has already been discussed, the membrane resides near the potassium equilibrium potential. If the depolarization reaches the threshold for activating adjacent voltage-dependent conductances, an all-or-none action potential (spike) will be triggered. For many neurons the axon hillock has the lowest spike threshold. If the resultant depolarization is insufficient to reach threshold, the cell can still discharge if additional excitatory postsynaptic potentials summate to threshold.

The postsynaptic potential resulting from the stimulation of an ideal inhibitory pathway to the postsynaptic cell has been explained in terms of the fact that inhibitory transmitter selectively activates channels for $Cl^-$ or $K^+$ resulting in a diffusion of ions and a hyperpolarization of the membrane. This counterbalances the excitatory postsynaptic potentials.

Because the sites of synaptic or junctional transmission are electrically inexcitable, the postsynaptic membrane potential can be maintained at various levels by applying current through intracellular electrodes and changing the intracellular concentrations of various ions. By such maneuvers, it is possible to poise the membrane at or near the so-called equilibrium potentials for each of the ionic species and to determine the ionic species whose equilibrium potential corresponds to the conductance change caused by the synaptic transmitter. This is the most molecular test for the identification of actions of a synaptic transmitter substance. (However, certain objections can be raised to this test in terms of those nerve endings making junctional contacts on distal portions of the dendritic tree. Here, the postsynaptic potentials may be incompletely transmitted to the cell body where the recording electrode is placed.)

On re-reading the above section, note the insidious use of the term "ideal." It is generally considered that classically acting neurotransmitters produce their effects on receptor-coupled ion conductances which are voltage independent, that is, the receptor will alter the coupled ion channel regardless of the membrane potential at the moment. Nevertheless, many nonclassical transmitters do seem to operate on receptors coupled to voltage-sensitive mechanisms. Transmitters whose receptors are associated with activation of cyclic nucleotide synthesis frequently produce these more complex forms of interaction. Similarly, many neuropeptides appear to affect certain of their target cells by modifying responses to other transmitters while not showing any direct shifts in membrane potential or conductance when tested for actions on their own. For example, the β-adrenergic actions of locus ceruleus neurons on their central targets produce excitability changes that depend upon which other afferent systems are activated synchronously. These β-adrenergic actions can enhance either excitatory afferents or inhibitory afferents, a general effect referred to as "enabling" or, more ambiguously, "modulatory". Some pharmacological actions of neuropeptides have been described as having the opposite effect, or "disenabling" (such as the effects of opioid peptides on the excitatory actions of sensory transmitters within the spinal cord (see Chapter 12). This story is more complex (surprised?) because neuropeptides coexist with amino acid and amine transmitters, and therefore their effects are more properly assessed as conceptually coordinating the responses of target cells to the array of transmitters that the pre-synaptic neuron can release, thereby "enabling", "disenabling", or affecting transmission in some other way not yet defined (see Iversen, Bloom).

However, two other aspects of ionic mechanisms bear some passing mention. First, despite our preoccupation with action potentials and their modification, Bullock has pointed out that the most numerous CNS neurons, the small single-process type of granule-like cell, may conduct its neuronal business within its restricted small spatial domain with no need ever to fire a spike. Second, those neurons that do fire spikes may sometimes do so unconventionally by using an influx of $Ca^{++}$ ions (a voltage-sensitive Ca conductance) rather than $Na^+$. This Ca spike may represent a mechanism to transmit activity from the cell body out to the dendritic system and may play a functional role in those neurons whose dendrites can also release transmitter—such as the catecholamine cell-body nuclei. Thus, the simplified ideal version of ionic mechanisms may be only one of many regulatory mechanisms between connected cells. In addition, astrocytes in long-term cell cultures can exhibit ionic responses that look very much like voltage-dependent K and Ca channels of neurons. Although, it may eventually be possible to evolve a set of experimental criteria to discriminate between classical transmitters acting to alter voltage-independent receptor mechanisms and "modulators" acting to modify the effects of the classical transmitters on their targets, this is not now the case. The student is advised to maintain an appreciative awareness of these potentially complex interaction systems without attributing true or false flags to which molecules transmit which signals. In the following section, we examine some of these less-classical synaptic events and their advantageous properties.

During the 1980s, it became fashionable to accept transmitter response data only when they were recorded from stable neurons in vitro. In addition to slices of mammalian brains, other preferred systems included "model" neurons (i.e., neuronally-derived cell lines, neuron-glia hybrid cells, and endocrine cells of normal or tumor origin previously exploited in lieu of real neurons). As a result, many experimental findings previously obtained with great difficulty from intact living brains were neglected in deference to the new "simpler" preparations. According to Llinas, in vitro electrophysiological assay systems (i.e., brain slices, cultured neurons, and patch-clamp methods of whole cell and single channel observation) provided the rigorous data needed to expand the principles of specialized mammalian receptor transduction mechanisms beyond the classical modes of excitation and inhibition, and to define precisely the ion conductances through which different transmitters act. Still beyond the pale, given the frenzy to work in vitro, is the reexamination of these transmitter-related effects in the intact nervous system, where their role in specific circuitry operations and interactions could be evaluated.

The transductive mechanisms now considered to be part of the normal repertoire of regulatory processes include a variety of transmitter-regulated (transmitter-dependent) and voltage-sensitive ionic conductances that were formerly regarded as "unusual" for the mammalian CNS despite their nearly simultaneous demonstration in invertebrate ganglia, mammalian autonomic ganglia, and selected central mammalian neurons. Most of these unusual transmitter-regulated conductance mechanisms relate to an unexpectedly large number of distinctive ionic conductances for $Ca^{++}$ and $K^+$, with more modest expansions in the channels for $Cl^-$ or $Na^+$ currents.

*Calcium channels.* Among the multiple voltage-sensitive $Ca^{++}$ conductances described in neurons, three are most consistent: The first is a transient low-threshold $Ca^{++}$ conductance (T). This $Ca^{++}$ conductance has a low threshold, first observed in neurons of the inferior olive, that is inactive at resting membrane potentials but is "deinactivated" by modest hyperpolarizations, providing a feature of oscillatory behavior. It is most frequently inhibited by $Cd^{++}$ or $Co^{++}$, and in some cases by Ni, Mg, or Mn as well, and can be activated by $Ba^{++}$. The second is a slowly inactivating, high-threshold $Ca^{++}$ conductance (L) seen mainly in nerve terminals. The third is a transient high-threshold Ca conductance (N) observed in the soma and dendrites of large neurons in neocortex, olfactory cortex, and hippocampal formation. The latter are blocked by $Mn^{++}$, $Co^{++}$, and $Cd^{++}$, and activated by $Ba^{++}$ and tetraethylammonium, and these responses may be inhibited functionally by endogenous purinergic receptors. Because the effects of adenosine and analogs on this conductance may be further blocked by pertussis toxin, it has been inferred that the purine receptors are linked to the conductance through G-protein regulatory mechanisms (see Chapter 5).

*Potassium channels.* At least three types of K channels have been described in central neurons: (1) the "A" or "A-like" fast transient K conductances inhibited by 4-aminopyridine, $Ba^{++}$, or $Co^{++}$; (2) the so-called "anomalous rectifying" K conductances (see below) of which the M current (closed by cholinergic muscarinic receptors) is one example of the class; (3) the Ca-activated K conductances, blocked by Co, Mn, Cd, and by some neurotransmitters (see Siggins and Gruol, 1986). Although most data on these $K^+$ channel effects are pharmacological, their properties can clearly regulate cell firing and response patterns in distinct manners. By closing the M current, muscarinic receptors transduce cholinergic signals into a more effective depolarization, once a partial depolarization brings this channel into play. Somatostatin can oppose this effect, forcing the M channel to open. The latter effect may be mediated intracellularly by second messengers derived from arachidonic acid metabolism (see Chapter 6). By blocking the Ca-activated K channel of central neurons, the transmitter receptors for β-adrenergic agonists, 5-HT, histamine, and corticotropin-releasing hormone enhance the ability of responsive neurons to follow long depolarizing pulses, thereby generating longer trains of spikes per afferent impulse.

Depending upon the specific cells in which they were recognized (even Ca-activated K channels exist in many glands and completely nonneural cell types) and the conditions and possible inhibitors that may have been evaluated, as many as 12 different K conductances have been proposed. For example, many K channels are linked to second messenger mediation (e.g., the channels activated by $GABA_B$ receptors and by D2 receptors on rat substantia nigra neurons). With patch clamp analyses of single K channels in locus ceruleus neurons acutely isolated from 1- to 7-day-old rats, opioids (at μ receptors), somatostatin, and $\alpha_2$ adrenergic agonists all seem to open a K channel that is not voltage dependent and seems to be directly regulated by receptor occupancy through a G protein but with no known intervening second messenger.

*Other ion-specific channels.* A "persistent" $Na^+$ conductance was first observed in cerebellar Purkinje neurons and later in hippocampal pyramidal neurons, as well as neurons throughout the neuraxis. This conductance provides a long-lasting but low amplitude depolarization that does not lead directly to neuronal firing but rather provides a bias from which the conventional fast Na channels can produce full spike initiation. Persistent Na channels are typically blocked by tetrodotoxin and activated by tetraethylammonium.

### Slow Postsynaptic Potentials

Most of the postsynaptic potentials described by Eccles and his colleagues were relatively short, usually 20 ms or less, and appeared to result from passive changes in ionic conductance. Post-synaptic potentials of slow onset and several seconds' duration have been described (Fig. 2-2), both of a hyperpolarizing nature and of a depolarizing nature. While such prolonged postsynaptic potentials could be the result of either a prolonged release of transmitter or a persistence of the transmitter at postsynaptic receptor sites, there is substantial support for the possibility that slow postsynaptic potentials could also be caused by other forms of synaptic communication. Many of these slower synaptic potentials are not accompanied by the expected increase in transmembrane ionic conductances, but are instead accompanied by increased transmembrane ionic impedance. The most simple explanations for membrane potential changes accompanied by increased membrane resistance are (1) that the effect is generated at a "presynaptic" site whereby tonically active excitatory or inhibitory synapses are inactivated by synapses on their terminals; or (2) that the action of the transmitter released by a slow synapse inactivates a normal finite resting conductance, such as that of sodium or potassium. Since most of the sites where slow synaptic potentials have been observed do not fulfill the anatomical prerequisite of axo-axonic presynaptic synapses, the second explanation may be more likely. A third explanation for such potentials has also been advanced, namely, that the transmitter activates an electrogenic pump mechanism, that is, a metabolically driven ionic "pump" that exchanges unequal numbers of similarly charged ions across the membrane. Studies on invertebrate neurons indicate that such electrogenic mechanisms should have several distinguishable properties: They should be virtually independent of the distribution of the ions to be pumped; they should not exhibit an equilibrium potential; they should be temperature dependent; and they should be sensitive to metabolic poisons and uncouplers of oxidative phosphorylation. Such data are extremely complex to analyze because several membrane properties also include temperature dependency and metabolic poison sensitivity. Thus, at the present time, a true electrogenic synapse in the mammalian central nervous system remains to be described. However, it also seems likely that transmitters such as the catecholamines can activate the synthesis of cyclic nucleotides, which in turn can activate intraneuronal protein kinases that can phosphorylate specific membrane proteins. The phosphorylation of a membrane protein could be expected to alter its ionic permeability, and perhaps such changes lie at the root of the membrane effects of several types of neurotransmitters.

## Conditional Actions of Transmitters

Frequently, transmitters produce novel actions unlike those of classically conceived transmitters. These unconventional actions suggest that broader definitions are useful for conceptualizing the range of regulatory signals involved in interneuronal communication and are helpful for examination of transmitter actions. For example, when the β-adrenergic effects of locus ceruleus stimulation are examined, target cell responses no longer adhere to standard concepts of inhibition. Rather, they appear to fit better the designation of "biasing" or "enabling." The latter term indicates that the enabling transmitter (in this example, norepinephrine) can enhance or amplify the effectiveness of other transmitter actions converging on the common target neurons during the time period of the enabling circuit's activity (see Chapter 7).

To reexplore the issue of time course on the more complex interactions, it may be useful to speak of "conditional" and "unconditional" actions. Unconditional actions refer to those which a given transmitter evokes by itself (i.e., in the absence of other transmitters acting on the common target cell). Conditional actions, occurring either pre- or postsynaptically, include but would not be limited to the type of enhancement that is subsumed by "enabling." In such a conditional interaction each transmitter would act at its own pre- or postsynaptic transmitter receptor, and would interact on that target cell when both transmitters occupy their receptors simultaneously.

Thus, it can be seen that there are abundant circuits, abundant transmitters and, for each of these, many classes of chemically coupled systems that can transduce the effects of active transmitter receptors. These receptors can operate either actively or passively, conditionally or unconditionally, over a wide range of time through nonspecific, dependent, or independent metabolic events. Clearly, neurons have a broad but finite and, as yet, incompletely characterized repertoire of molecular responses that messenger molecules (transmitters, hormones, and drugs) can elicit. The power of the chemical vocabulary of such components is their combinatorial capacity to act conditionally and coordinatively and to integrate the temporal and spatial domains within the nervous system.

*Transmitter Secretion*

We have already seen that the cellular machinery of the neuron suggests it functions as a secretory cell. The secretion of synaptic transmitters is the activity-locked expression of neuronal activity induced by the depolarization of the nerve terminal. Recently, it has been possible to separate the excitation–secretion coupling process of the presynaptic terminal into at least two distinct phases. This has been made possible through an analysis of the action of the puffer fish poison tetrodotoxin, which blocks the electrical excitation of the axon but does not block the release of transmitter substance from the depolarized nerve terminal. The best of these experiments have been performed in the giant synaptic junctions of the squid stellate ganglion, in which the nerve terminals are large enough to be impaled by recording and stimulating microelectrodes, and with recording from the postsynaptic and presynaptic neurons. In this case, when tetrodotoxin blocks conduction of action potentials down the axon, electrical depolarization of the presynaptic terminal still results in the appearance of an excitatory postsynaptic potential in the ganglion neuron. Since tetrodotoxin selectively blocks the voltage-dependent $Na^+$ conductance, the excitation secretion must be coupled more closely to other ions. Present evidence strongly favors the view that a voltage-sensitive $Ca^{2+}$ conductance is required for transmitter secretion. In review, we see that the spike-generating and conducting events rest on voltage-dependent ion conductance changes, while synaptic events rest on voltage-independent or voltage-sensitive conductances.

Biochemical, ultrastructural, and physiological experiments have led to the concept that transmitter molecules are stored within vesicles in the nerve terminal and that the Ca-dependent excitation–secretion coupling within the depolarized nerve terminal requires the transient exchange of vesicular contents into the synaptic cleft. It is unclear whether the vesicle simply undergoes a rapid fusion with the presynaptic specialized membrane to allow the transmitter stored in the vesicle to diffuse out, or whether the process of exocytotic release simultaneously requires the insertion of the vesicle membrane into the synaptic plasma membrane, reappearing later by the reverse process, namely, endocytosis. Information on the lipid and protein components of the two types of membranes once suggested that long-term fusion–endocytosis cycles were unlikely, but more recent data are compatible with either fusion release or contact release. In noradrenergic vesicles, for example, the transmitter is stored in very high concentrations in ternary complexes involving ATP, Ca, and possibly additional lipids or lipoproteins. Unfortunately, neurochemically homogeneous vesicles from central synapses have never been completely purified, and therefore all such analyses remain somewhat open to interpretation. For other molecules under active consideration as neurotransmitters, storage within brain synaptic vesicles has been extremely difficult to document chemically. The difficulties arise from the fact that homogenization of the brain to prepare synaptosomes disrupts both structural and functional integrity, and under these conditions the failure to demonstrate that amino-acid transmitters are stored in vesicles is rationalized as uncontrollable leakage. With electron microscopy and autoradiography, however, sites accumulating transmitters for which there is a high-affinity, energy-dependent uptake process can be demonstrated. Under these conditions, authentic "synaptic terminals" are identified, but glial processes are also labeled. The vesicle story is further discussed in Chapter 8.

In some cases, release of the transmitter can be modulated "presynaptically" by the neuron's own transmitter (autoreceptors) or by the effects of transmitters released by other neurons in the vicinity of the terminal or the cell body. Autoreceptors are conceived to be receptors that are generally distributed over the surface of a neuron and are sensitive to the transmitter secreted by that neuron. In the case of the central dopamine-secreting neurons, such receptors have been related to the release of the transmitter and to its synthesis. Such effects seem to be achieved through different receptor mechanisms than those by which the same transmitter molecule acts postsynaptically.

## ANALYSIS OF MEMBRANE ACTIONS OF DRUGS AND TRANSMITTERS IN VITRO

The development of methods for the nearly complete functional maintenance of central neurons in vitro for several hours, such as the tissue slice preparations, and for several days to weeks in single-cell or in explant culture systems has led to a proliferation of additional electrophysiological methods to examine transmitter and drug action. In slice preparations, neuronal targets can be readily localized by inspection, and intracellular electrodes can be inserted into suitably large neurons under visual control, while sources of afferent circuitry within the slice may be activated by additional stimulating electrodes. Transmitters and drugs can then be applied to the whole slice by superfusion within oxygenated buffered salt solutions, or more locally by micropressure pulse or iontophoretic application methods. In many cases, excellent intracellular recordings can be obtained for long periods of time because there are no annoying respiratory, cardiac, or other movements to dislodge tht electrode.

When long-term intracellular recordings can be obtained, two additional sources of information on transmitter actions can be analyzed. In *voltage clamp* analysis, the experimenter inserts one or two electrodes into the cell and by injecting current holds the membrane potential of the neuron at a constant value. The cell is usually poised at a membrane potential more negative than resting in order to prevent spontaneous spikes. Transmitter action is monitored by the amount of current required to keep the membrane potential constant, and thus measures transmembrane current flow directly. However, since the membrane potential stays constant, any of the nonlinear properties of that neuron's response that could occur when sufficient depolarization has occurred will be prevented.

The clamp can also be quickly changed to a new level of membrane potential, and the neuron's responses to this shift provides the basis for a pharmacological dissection (e.g., with ion channel blockers or ion substitutions) of the degree to which the effects of a transmitter can be explained as ion dependent or voltage dependent. Many of the actions ascribed to neuropeptides and some of those ascribed to monoamines fit the concept of voltage dependent, since they are modest effects at best at resting membrane potential levels, but they emerge as more substantive effects when the responding neuron is depolarized or hyperpolarized by other convergent transmitters.

Another of the newer methods, termed *noise analysis*, also examines ion channel activity more directly than the standard *in vivo* methods. This method assumes that ion channels are either open or closed and that they switch instantaneously, and do so independently, between the two conditions. Using intracellular electrodes, the fluctuations in membrane potential (or, if voltage clamping is used, the fluctuations in membrane current flow) are analyzed statistically to infer the conductance of individual types of channels and the mean time they are open in the absence or presence of the transmitter to be analyzed.

When the neurons considered to be the appropriate targets of a specific transmitter can be maintained in long-term tissue culture, the method of *patch clamp analysis* can be applied, as the current superstar of membrane action analysis methods. This method offers the ability to study the behavior of single-ion channels and to do so under conditions of almost unbelievable precision. Special "fire-polished" microelectrodes are placed on the neuron's surface, and a slight vacuum applied to the pipette to attain a very tight junction with the exposed surface of the neuronal membrane, thus requiring near-nude neurons for best application. The resulting cell electrode junction will have such a high electrical resistance (gigohms!) that the patch of enclosed membrane within the microelectrode's tip will be essentially isolated from the rest of the cell. Current flowing within that patch can then be analyzed independently of the responses of the rest of the neuron. With state-of-the-art, low-noise amplifiers, current flow through individual channels can be monitored and transmitter actions evaluated in terms of open time, amplitudes (number of channels opened), and closing times.

In addition, with clever micromanipulations, the patch clamps can be done in three configurations. In the "cell attached" mode, the pipette is sealed to the intact cell and the measurements made with no further physical disruption. However, further application of slight vacuum allows the patch of enclosed membrane to be removed from the cell, but with enclosed ion channels still viable and responsive. In the "inside-out" patch, the previously intracellular surface will be on the exterior of the sealed membrane patch, and the ion channel can be examined for regulation by simulations of changes in intracellular ions or, for example, catalysts of protein phosphorylations. It is also possible to demonstrate that, with clever handling and with further negative pressure before pulling the membrane patch off the cell, an "outside-out" patch can be obtained. Here the original patch is ruptured, the perimeter remains attached, and then the surrounding external membrane segments reseal once they are excised from the cell surface. By placing the outside surface into solutions with differing doses of transmitter, drug, or ion channel toxin, it is possible to analyze very discrete, single-channel pharmacology.

### An Approach to Neuropharmacological Analysis

You can now see that the business of analyzing bioelectrical potentials can be very complicated, even when restricted to the changes in single neurons or to small portions of contiguous neurons. But if we restrict our examination of centrally active drugs to analyses of effects on single cells, we can ask rather precise questions. For example, does drug X act on resting membrane potential or resistance, on an electrogenic pump, or on the sodium- or potassium-activation phase of the action potential? Or does it act by blocking or modulating the effects of junctional transmission between two specific groups of cells?

Unfortunately we have not had these precise electrophysiological tools for very long. Earlier neuropharmacologists were thus required to examine effects of drugs on populations of nerve cells. This was usually done in one of two ways. Large macroelectrodes were employed to measure the potential difference between one brain region and another. These electroencephalograms reflect mainly the moment-to-moment algebraic and spatial summations of slow synaptic potentials, and almost none of their electrical activity is due to actual action potentials generated by individual neurons (unit discharges). A second type of analysis was based on evoked changes occurring when a gross sensory stimulation (such as a flash of light or a quick sound) was delivered. Changes in recordings from cortical or subcortical sites along the sensory pathway were then sought during the action of a drug. While we can criticize the technical and interpretative shortcomings of such methods of central drug analysis, these methods were able to reflect the population response of a group of neurons to a drug, something that single unit analysis can do only after many single recordings are collated. The macroelectrode methods are now receiving increased attention again since, as noninvasive methods, they can be used to examine drug actions clinically.

APPROACHES

If, as modern-day neuropharmacologists, we are chiefly concerned with uncovering the mechanisms of action of drugs in the brain, there are several avenues along which we can organize our attack: We could choose to examine the way in which drugs influence the perception of sensory signals by higher integrative centers of the brain. This is compatible with a single-neuron and ionic conductance type of analysis, directed, say, at how drugs affect inhibitory postsynaptic potentials. Drugs that cause convulsions, such as strychnine, have been analyzed in this respect, but all types of inhibitory postsynaptic potential are not affected by strychnine.

A second basic approach would be to use both macroelectrodes and microelectrodes to compare the drug response of single units and populations of units in the same brain region. This approach is clearly limited, however, unless we understand the intimate functional relations between the multiple types of cells found even within one region of the brain.

A third approach is also possible. We could choose to separate the effects of drugs between those affecting generation of the action potential and its propagation and those acting on junctional transmission. For this type of analysis, we must identify the chemical synaptic transmitter for the junctions to be studied. Many of the interpretative problems already alluded to can be attacked through this approach. Thus, as you might expect, there is likely to be more than one type of excitatory and inhibitory transmitter substance, and a convulsant drug may affect the response to one type of inhibitory transmitter without affecting another. Moreover, a drug may have specific regional effects in the brain if it affects a unique synaptic transmitter there. In fact, by using this approach it may be possible to find drug effects not directly reflected in electrical activity at all but related more to the catabolic or anabolic systems maintaining the required functional levels of transmitter. We shall conclude this chapter by considering the techniques for identifying the synaptic transmitter for particular synaptic connections. The chapters that follow are organized to present in detail our current understanding of putative central neurotransmitter substances.

## IDENTIFICATION OF SYNAPTIC TRANSMITTERS

How then, do we identify the substance released by nerve endings? The entire concept of chemical junctional transmission arose from the classical experiments of Otto Loewi, who demonstrated chemical transmission by transferring the ventricular fluid of a stimulated frog heart onto a nonstimulated frog heart, thereby showing that the effects of the nerve stimulus on the first heart were reproduced by the chemical activity of the solution flowing onto the second heart. Since the phenomenon of chemical transmission originated from studies of peripheral autonomic organs, these peripheral junctions have become convenient model systems for central neuropharmacological analysis.

Certain interdependent criteria have been developed to identify junctional transmitters. By common-sense analysis, one would suspect that the most important criterion would be that a substance suspected of being a junctional transmitter must be demonstrated to be released from the prejunctional nerve endings when the nerve fibers are selectively stimulated. This criterion was relatively easily satisfied for isolated autonomic organs in which only one or at most two nerve trunks enter the tissue and the whole system can be isolated in an organ bath. In the central nervous system, however, satisfaction of this criterion presumes: (1) that the proper nerve trunk or set of nerve axons can be selectively stimulated and (2) that release of the transmitter can be detected in the amounts released by single nerve endings after one action potential. This last subcriterion is necessary since we wish to restrict our analysis to the first set of activated nerve endings and not examine the substances released by the secondary and tertiary interneurons in the chain, some of which might reside quite close to the primary endings. The biggest problem with this criterion in the brain, however, is the lack of a method for detecting release that does not in itself destroy the functional and structural integrity of the region of the brain being analyzed. Such techniques are internally perfused cannulae or surface suction cups are chemically at the same level of resolution as the evoked potential and the cortical electroencephalogram. Each of these methods records the resultant activity of thousands if not millions of nerve endings and synaptic potentials. Release has also been studied in brain slices or homogenate subfractions incubated in "physiological buffer solutions" in vitro. These techniques can demonstrate the effects of depolarizing drugs or electric fields to simulate events in the living brain.

*Localization*

Because it is difficult, if not impossible, to identify the substance released from single nerve endings by selective stimulation, the next-best evidence might be to prove that a suspected synaptic transmitter resides in the presynaptic terminal of our selected nerve pathway. Normally, we would expect the enzymes for synthesizing and catabolizing this substance to also be in the vicinity of this nerve ending, if not actually part of the nerve-ending cellular machinery. In the case of neurons secreting peptides or simple amino-acid transmitters, however, these metabolic requirements may need further consideration. To document the presence of neurotransmitter, several types of specific cytochemical methods for both light microscopy and electron microscopy have been developed. More commonly employed is the biochemical population approach, which analyzes the regional concentrations of suspected synaptic transmitter substances. However, presence per se indicates neither releasability nor neuroeffectiveness (e.g., acetylcholine in the nerve-free placenta or serotonin in the enterochromaffin cell). Although it has generally been conceived that a neuron makes only one transmitter and secretes that same substance everywhere synaptic release occurs, neuropeptide exceptions to this rule have become common.

*Synaptic Mimicry: Drug Injections*

A third criterion arising from the peripheral autonomic nervous system analysis is that the suspected exogenous substance mimics the action of the transmitter released by nerve stimulation. In most pharmacological studies of the nervous system, drugs are administered intravascularly or onto one of the external or internal surfaces of the brain. The substances could also be directly injected into a given region of the brain, although the resultant structural damage would have to be controlled and the target verified histologically. The analysis of the effects of drugs given by each of these various gross routes of administration is quite complex.

We know that diffusional barriers selectively retard the entrance from the bloodstream of many types of molecules into the brain. These barriers have been demonstrated for most of the suspected central synaptic agents. In addition, we suspect that extracellular catabolic enzymes could destroy the transmitter as it diffuses to the postulated site of action. A further complicating aspect of these gross methods of administration is that the interval of time from the administration of the agent to the recording of the response is usually quite long (several seconds to several minutes) in comparison with the millisecond intervals required for junctional transmission. The delay in response further reduces the likelihood of detecting the primary site of action on one of a chain of neurons.

*Microelectrophoresis*

The student will now realize how important it is to have methods of drug administration equal in sophistication to those with which the electrical phenomena are detected. The most practical micromethod of drug administration yet devised is based upon the principle of electrophoresis. Micropipettes are constructed in which one or several barrels contain an ionized solution of the chemical substance under investigation. The substance is applied by appropriately directing the current flow. The microelectrophoretic technique, when applied with controls to rule out the effects of pH, electrical current, and diffusion of the drug to neighboring neurons, has been able to overcome the major limitations of classical neuropharmacological techniques. Frequently, a multiple-barreled electrode is constructed from which one records the spontaneous extracellular discharges of single neurons while other attached pipettes are utilized to apply drugs. One can also construct an intracellular microelectrode glued to an extracellular drug-containing multielectrode, so that the transmembrane effects of these suspected transmitter agents can be compared with the effects of nerve pathway stimulation. The intracellular electrode can also be used to poise the relative polarization of the membrane and let us detect whether the applied suspected transmitter and that released by nerve stimulation cause the membrane to approach identical ionic equilibrium potentials.

Considerable experimentation with this technique has made possible certain generalizations regarding the actions of each putative neurotransmitter that has been studied. These substances are reviewed in detail in each of the chapters that follow. However, it should be borne in mind that certain substances have more or less invariable actions; for example, gamma-aminobutyrate and glycine always act to inhibit, while glutamate and aspartate always excite. Insofar as we know, these actions arise from increased membrane conductances to Na, K, Ca, or Cl in every case. Other substances have many kinds of effects, depending upon the nature of the cell whose receptors are being tested. Thus, acetylcholine frequently excites but can also inhibit, and the receptors for either response can be nicotinic or muscarinic. Similarly, dopamine, norepinephrine, and serotonin almost always inhibit, but they have a few excitatory actions that are probably not completely artifactual.

### Pharmacology of Synaptic Effects

The fourth criterion for identification of a synaptic transmitter requires identical pharmacological effects of drugs potentiating or blocking postsynaptic responses to both the neurally released and administered samples. Because the pharmacological effects are often not identical (most "classical" blocking agents are extrapolated to brain from effects on peripheral autonomic organs), this fourth criterion is often satisfied indirectly with a series of circumstantial pieces of data. Recently, with the advent of drugs that block the synthesis of specific transmitter agents, the pharmacology for certain families of transmitters has been improved.

The electrophysiological analysis of drug and transmitter actions in the central nervous system was traditionally accomplished in terms of single cell activity in vivo. Four types of physiological responses served as the major indices to compare exogenously applied transmitter candidates and drugs with the effects of endogenous transmitters: (1) spontaneous activity, (2) orthodromic synaptically evoked activity, (3) antidromic activity, and (4) relative responses to independently acting excitatory or inhibitory transmitter released from another experimental source, such as another barrel of a multibarrel pipette. These techniques have been most successful when applied to large neurons, whose selected afferent pathways can be stimulated and the transmembrane effects specifically analyzed. However, when the unit recording techniques are applied to the mammalian brain, visualization and selection of the neuron under investigation are almost impossible. Although we can generally select a relatively specific brain region in which to insert the microelectrode assembly, we must utilize electrophysiological criteria for cell identification. We must also depend upon geometrical attributes of the nerve cell to encounter its electrical activity as the electrode is navigated by blind mechanical means through the brain. Our ability to encounter cells in the brain depends partly on the size and type of the electrode assembly we use, partly on the size and spontaneous activity of the cell we are approaching, and partly on the surgical or chemical means by which we have prepared the animal (viz., presence or absence of anesthesia, homeostatic levels of blood pressure, and tissue oxygen and carbon dioxide). Even with very fine microelectrodes, the analysis does not take place in a completely undisturbed system, since many connections must be broken by the physical maneuvering of the electrode. The leakage of cytoplasmic constituents, including potential transmitter agents and metabolic enzymes, can only be considered as part of the background artifact of the system. In the past few years, additional electrophysiological methods pertinent to transmitter action have been developed that can be applied to neuronal systems analyzed in vitro to provide additional insight into ionic channel regulation.

## THE STEPS OF SYNAPTIC TRANSMISSION

Let us now conclude this chapter by briefly examining the mechanisms of presumed synaptic transmission for the mammalian central nervous system. Each step in such transmission constitutes one of the potential sites of central drug action (Fig. 2-3). A stimulus ac-

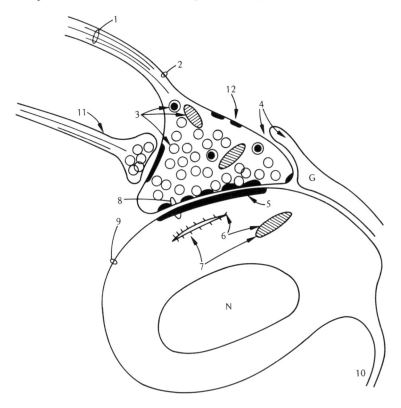

FIGURE 2-3. Twelve steps in the synaptic transmission process are indicated in this idealized synaptic connection. Step 1 is transport down the axon. Step 2 is the electrically excitable membrane of the axon. Step 3 involves the organelles and enzymes present in the nerve terminal for synthesizing, storing, and releasing the transmitter, as well as for the process of active reuptake. Step 4 includes the enzymes present in the extracellular space and within the glia for catabolizing excess transmitter released from nerve

tivates an all-or-none action potential in a spiking axon by depolar-izing its transmembrane potential above the threshold level. The action potential propagates unattenuated to the nerve terminal where ion fluxes activate a mobilization process leading to transmitter se-cretion and "transmission" to the postsynaptic cell. From companion biochemical experiments (to be described in the next chapters), the transmitter substance is believed to be stored within the microves-icles or synaptic vesicles seen in nerve endings by electron micros-copy. In certain types of nerve junctions, miniature postsynaptic potentials can be seen in the absence of conducted presynaptic action potentials. These miniature potentials have a quantal effect on the postsynaptic membrane in that occasional potentials are statistical multiples of the smallest measurable potentials. The biophysical quanta have been related to the synaptic vesicles, although the proof for this relationship is still circumstantial.

When the transmitter is released from its storage site by the pre-synaptic action potential, the effects on the postsynaptic cells cause either excitatory or inhibitory postsynaptic potentials, depending upon the nature of the postsynaptic cell's receptor for the particular transmitter agent. If sufficient excitatory postsynaptic potentials

---

terminals. Step 5 is the postsynaptic receptor that triggers the response of the postsynaptic cell to the transmitter. Step 6 shows the organelles within the postsynaptic cells which respond to the receptor trigger. Step 7 is the interaction between genetic expression of the postsynaptic nerve cell and its influences on the cytoplasmic organelles that respond to transmitter action. Step 8 includes the possible "plastic" steps modifiable by events at the specialized synaptic contact zone. Step 9 includes the electrical portion of the nerve cell membrane which, in response to the various transmitters, is able to integrate the postsynaptic potentials and produce an action po-tential. Step 10 is the continuation of the information transmission by which the postsynaptic cell sends an action potential down its axon. Step 11, release of transmitter, is subjected to modification by a presynaptic (axoaxonic) synapse; in some cases an analogous control can be achieved between den-dritic elements. Step 12, release of the transmitter from a nerve terminal or secreting dendritic site, may be further subject to modulation through autoreceptors that respond to the transmitter which the same secreting structure has released.

summate temporally from various inputs onto the cell, the postsynaptic cell will integrate these potentials and give off its own all-or-nothing action potential, which is then transmitted to each of its own axon terminals, and the process continues.

In trying to solve the problem of interneuronal chemical communication, it may be useful, nevertheless, to maintain an open mind with regard to three dimensions by which neuronal circuits can be characterized: (1) the spatial domain (those areas of the brain or peripheral receptive fields that feed onto a given cell and those areas into which that cell sends its efferent signals); (2) the temporal domain (the time spans over which the spatial signals are active); and (3) the functional domain (the mechanism by which the secreted transmitter substance operates on the receptive cell). When the receptive cell is closely coupled in time, space, and function to the secreting cell, almost everyone would agree that "real" synaptic actions have occurred. When the effects are long lasting and widely distributed, however, many would prefer to call this action something else, even though the molecular agonist is stored in and released presynaptically from neurons onto the nerve cells they contact.

## Selected References

Bloom, F. E. (1984). The functional significance of neurotransmitter diversity. *Am. J. Physiol. 246*, C184–C194.

Bloom, F. E. (1988) Neurotransmitters: Past, present and future directions. *FASEB Journal 2*, 32–41.

Bloom, F. E. (1990). Neurohumoral transmission and the central nervous system. In *The Pharmacological Basis of Therapeutics*, 8th ed. (A. G. Gilman, L. Goodman, and A. Gilman, eds.), 244–268, Pergamon Press, New York.

Bullock, T. H. (1980). Spikeless neurones: Where do we go from here? *Soc. Exp. Biol. Seminar Series 6*, 269–284.

Eccles, J. C. (1964). *The Physiology of Synapses*. Academic Press, New York.

Fox, A. P., M. C. Nowycky, and R. A. Tsien (1987) Kinetic and pharmacological properties distinguishing three types of calcium currents in chick sensory neurones. *J. Physiol. 394*, 149–172.

Gross, R. A., R. L. MacDonald, and T. Ryan-Jastrow (1989) 2-Chloroadenosine reduces the N Ca current of cultured mouse sensory neurons in a pertussis toxin-sensitive manner. *J. Physiol. 411*, 585–595.

Hille, B. (1984). *Ionic Channels of Excitable Membranes*. Sinauer Associates, Inc. Publishers, Sunderland, MA, 426 pp.

Hodgkin, A. L. and A. F. Huxley (1952). Currents carried by sodium and potassium ions through the membrane of the giant axon of Loligo. *J. Physiol. 116*, 449.

Iversen, L. L. (1984). The Ferrier Lecture, 1983. Amino acids and peptides: Fast and slow chemical signals in the nervous system? *Proc. R. Soc. Lond. B221*, 245–260.

Katz, B. (1966). *Nerve, Muscle and Synapse*. McGraw-Hill, New York.

Kupferman, I. (1979). Modulatory actions of neurotransmitters. *Ann. Rev. Neurosci. 2*, 447–465.

Llinas, R. R. (1988) The intrinsic electrophysiological properties of mammalian neurons: Insights into central nervous system function. *Science 242*, 1654–1660.

Loewi, O. (1921). Über humorale Übertragbarkeit der Herznervenwirkung. *Pfluegers Arch. 189*, 239.

Miller, R. J. (1989) Multiple calcium channels and neuronal function. In *Molecules to Models Advances in Neurosciences* (K. L. Kelner and D. E. Koshland, eds.) American Association for the Advancement of Science, Washington, DC. pp. 1–17.

Miyake, M., M. J. Christie, and R. A. North (1989) Single potassium channels opened by opioids in rat locus ceruleus neurons. *Proc. Natl. Acad. Sci. (USA) 86*, 3419–3422.

Nicoll, R. A. (1988) The coupling of neurotransmitters to ion channels in the brain. *Science 241*, 545–553.

Schmitt, F. O. (1984). Molecular regulators of brain function: A new view. *Neuroscience 13*, 994–1004.

Schweitzer, P., S. Madamba, and G. R. Siggins (1990) Arachidonic acid metabolites as mediators of somatostatin-induced increase of neuronal M-current. *Nature 346*, 464–467.

Siggins, G. R. and D. L. Gruol (1986). Synaptic mechanisms in the vertebrate central nervous system. In *Handbook of Physiology*, *Intrinsic Regulatory Systems of the Brain* (F. E. Bloom, ed.), Vol. IV. The American Physiological Society, Bethesda, MD.

# 3 | Molecular Foundations of Neuropharmacology

Complete understanding of the basis for a drug's actions on the brain requires knowledge of all the molecules involved. A drug acts selectively when it elicits responses from discrete populations of cells that possess "drug-recognizing" macromolecules. Such recognition sites are known more colloquially as receptors. Drug receptors with important regulatory actions on the nervous system are generally on the external surface of neurons if they involve sites where neurotransmitters act. Some drugs can act on the nervous system because they resemble, at the molecular level, endogenous intercellular signals like those of a neurotransmitter. However, drugs may also act by regulating intracellular enzymes critical for normal transmitter synthesis or breakdown. Receptors recognize drugs for a variety of reasons that this book explores in subsequent chapters. Once having made that recognition, the activated receptor usually interacts with other molecules to alter membrane properties or intracellular metabolism. These cellular changes in turn regulate the interactions between cells in circuits. These circuit changes regulate the performance of functional systems (like the sensory, motor, or vegetative control systems) and eventually the behavior of the whole organism.

Thus, understanding the actions of drugs on the function of the brain, whether it be on single cells or behavior, is a multilevel, multifaceted process that begins with and builds upon the concept of molecular interactions. Even beginning students of drug action on the nervous system will probably accept this statement as a reasonable hypothetical principle. In practice, however, this principle is severely compromised because most molecules in a very complex organ like the brain are unknown. Furthermore, until the recent explosion of knowledge in molecular biology, there was little hope that the necessary details would be obtained.

When Watson and Crick deduced the three-dimensional, double-helical structure of DNA in 1953, the implications for the coding and replication of genetic information were recognized but could not be experimentally tested. Almost 25 years of effort were required before the new biological technology was launched. During this interval it became clear how to combine genes and gene fragments from multicelled organisms with those of viruses, fungi, and bacteria to produce new genetic instructions and novel gene products. At last, the concept of a *gene* and its cellular product attained concrete form. Almost immediately, neuroscientists, who are always ready to exploit new technologies, began to apply these methods to the most complex cellular system known—the brain.

The power of molecular biological methods is gained from several related but independent developments: (1) the ability to *clone* genetic information (i.e., to isolate a selected segment and accurately reproduce it in large amounts); (2) the ability to determine the nucleic acid sequence of the selected gene segment (i.e., to read the complete molecular structure of a gene); and (3) the ability to practice *genetic engineering* (i.e., to perturb and control gene expression and alter the structure of gene products by chemically modifying precise sites in the molecular structure of the genes). Within a decade the possibilities for applying this basic triad of powerful tools were dramatically revealed by two additional innovative technologies: the *polymerase chain reaction* (by which large amounts of specific nucleic acid sequences can be produced without their prior purification, cloning, or even a complete knowledge of their sequences) and the ability to create *transgenic animals* (i.e., transfer synthetic genes into embryonic cells to make new mice, pigs, and cows to the experimentalist's specifications).

All of these developments have contributed to a very rapid advance towards a truly molecular basis for the understanding of the nervous system and the way it can be altered by drug actions. In this chapter we explore these molecular foundations.

*Cellular Variation*

Before we can deal effectively with the critical details of molecules that regulate the function of the nervous system and mediate the responses to drugs that act there, we must begin by briefly considering how the cells of the brain differ from the other cells of the body, and what it is that allows for differences between types of cells.

Except for erythrocytes, all mammalian cells have a nucleus that separates the basic units of genetic information from the cytoplasm. The cytoplasm and its organelles allow the cell to generate energy that the cell uses to synthesize the structural and enzymatic molecules that give it and its enveloping plasma membrane the functional properties by which it contributes to the overall operation of the organism. Liver cells, kidney cells, skin cells, white blood cells, and cells of the nervous system all possess these basic similarities and these basic individual properties. In a single individual organism, all of these somatic cells (with only one exception), including the cells of the central and peripheral nervous system, possess entirely the same basic set of genetic information. The exception to this basic rule is the antibody-producing lymphocytes, and they have their own books.

The total set of potential genetic instructions of an individual, its *genotype*, is composed of basic instructional units—the *genes*—each having a specific location on a specific chromosome. Each type of specialized cell expresses a subset of genes that encode the special structural and enzymatic proteins that endow the cell with its size, shape, location, and other functional characteristics. This set of characteristic features that are expressed by a cell is termed its *phenotype*.

Classically the "phenotype" of the cell classes in the brain (i.e., neurons or glia) has been addressed through description of their physical features (e.g., location, size, shape, connections) and their transmitter-specific neurochemistry. Understanding the genetic basis for cell typing affords the opportunity to explain how neurons of the same shape and size can have different connections or transmitters, and what this diversity achieves. For now, we can assume that these cellular archetypes and the almost innumerable variants within each of those two large classes are the outward reflection of their corresponding specific expression of subsets of their genes. The next section provides a brief overview of this process, with additional complexities in the expanded coverage that follows. Neuropharmacology students recently exposed to molecular biology or biochemistry courses may find the next few sections "old hat." However, we include this material so that everyone reaching the end of this chapter will have the fundamentals necessary for a full appreciation of the material to follow (see Fig. 3-1).

1. The genetic information, stored in the form of long strands of deoxyribonucleic acid (DNA) chains, is selectively expressed. That is, each specialized cell attains its specialized functional and structural status by expressing a subset of all of its genetic instructions. To express selective segments of the genome, the DNA-encoded information is converted, or *transcribed*, into a second similar molecular form as strands of ribonucleic acid (RNA) under the control of special proteins and RNA synthesizing enzymes (polymerases) that perform the transcription steps. We will deal in slightly more detail with the actual molecular properties of DNA and RNA below.

2. The primary transcript form of the selected genetic information is then edited by several rapid steps and exported from the nucleus to the cytoplasm. The edited RNA transcript, or *messenger RNA* (mRNA), is then *translated* by special cytoplasmic organelles, also made of RNA and proteins, called *ribosomes*. The translation is a chemical language shift from the nucleic acid code of the RNA into the amino acid sequence of the protein that is to be expressed.

3. In some brain cells, such as the glia, that make their proteins largely for use within the cell, the ribosomes occur free within the cytoplasm. In neurons, and other dedicated secretory cells, the translated protein undergoes *post-translational processing*, in which the protein's structure may be modified to attain the folded, globular, or linear structural properties that allow it to become associated with the proper

FIGURE 3-1. A schematic overview of the basic steps and cellular compartments involved in determining the specific phenotype of a neuron (above) and in cloning the mRNAs that allow the neuron to translate its genetic information into specific proteins. An mRNA is converted to a single-stranded DNA that is further converted into a double-stranded segment that is then inserted into a plasmid. Bacteria are infected with individual plasmids, and individual, plasmid-infected bacteria are grown into colonies. Replicates of the culture plate are screened by nucleic acid or antibody probes to select clones of interest.

intracellular compartments (e.g., within the plasma membrane or within the cytoplasm) where it is intended to function.

4. In cells, like neurons, that transport large amounts of protein products within the cell's interior for purposes of secretion, more extensive post-translational processing occurs. In such cells, the ribosomes are physically associated with a special set of endoplasmic reticular membranes, giving the membranes a "rough" appearance, for which they are known as the "rough ER." Within the channels of this inside-the-cell network, the newly synthesized proteins are lead to a set of smooth endoplasmic reticular membranes, the *Golgi apparatus*, where they are packaged into secretory organelles for transport to the secretory, or releasing, segments of the cell.

All of these organelle systems of the cell, essential for the selective transcription, translation, and packaging or compartmentalization of the specific proteins by which a given class of cells attains its specific phenotype, were well known to classical cytologists long before the molecular mechanisms underlying these events were understandable. Although the details of these molecular revelations are well beyond the capacities of this book, an exploration of the basic features will help the interested reader begin to comprehend the special analytic advantages that arise from the methods of molecular biology.

FUNDAMENTAL MOLECULAR INTERACTIONS

The cornerstone discovery of molecular biology was the formulation by Watson and Crick in 1953 of the *double-stranded helix* model of DNA structure. The insightful model they developed provided a coherent integration of the regular x-ray crystallographic structure of partially purified DNA with the previously known quantitative chemical data on the relative frequency within DNA of its four nucleotide bases, thus explaining why the purine–pyrimidine pairs adenine (A)–thymidine (T) and guanine (G)–cytosine (C) occur in precisely equal frequency. The Watson-Crick molecular model for

DNA also accurately predicted the basic mechanism of DNA replication.

### Nucleic Acid Base Pairing Complementarity

In the Watson-Crick double helix, two right-handed helical poly-nucleotide chains coil around the same central axis, making a complete helical turn every 10 nucleotides (Fig. 3-2) In the interior of the helix, the purine and pyrimidine bases (A with T and G with C) are paired through hydrogen bonding of their complementary structures, placing the phosphate groups around the outside of the helix. The crucial structural feature that is the focal point for gene expression is the precise molecular complementarity between the primary sequences of nucleotide bases in one strand of the DNA helix with the antiparallel sequence of the second strand. The strand that encodes the genetic information is termed the sense strand. Wherever a particular base occurs in the sense strand, there will be

FIGURE 3-2. The arrangement of bases within the DNA double helix and the relationships between nucleic acid base pairs, RNA, and amino acids during the process of transcription and translation.

a complementary base, and only that base in the antisense strand, such that A always pairs with T, and vice versa, and G always pairs with C, and vice versa.

The base pair complementarity allows for duplication of the genetic information in dividing cells. This is accomplished by enzymes known as DNA polymerases that open the helix and replicate each single strand back into double strands according to the single strand's template. The double-stranded complementarity also provides a means to repair the DNA should it be damaged, since whichever single strand survives the damage can act as a template for the repair.

In a similar manner, the information-bearing, or sense strand of the helical DNA chain is copied into a complementary single-stranded RNA during the process of transcription. RNA is thus a single-stranded complementary copy of the DNA antisense strand (so that its sequence resembles closely that of the DNA sense strand; see Fig. 3-2). RNA differs chemically with the substitution of uridine for thymidine, and ribose phosphates for deoxyribose phosphates. The process of transcription is accomplished by enzymes known as RNA polymerases. The affinity of the base pairs along sequences of a single DNA strand for their complementary base pair sequences in DNA or RNA are so precise that small segments can be used as *probes* for the detection of homologous sequences between large domains of DNA and RNA because the molecular complementarity will allow the probe to bind to its complementary structure only when there is a long sequence of consistent match. The ability of a single-stranded nucleic acid to bind, or hybridize, to its complementary sequence is an essential component of many molecular biological techniques.

## The Genetic Code

To translate genetic information from sequences of RNA into linear sequences of amino acids in proteins requires a strict coding, in order that the 20 or so amino acids commonly found in proteins can be specified by various combinations of the four nucleotides. Through an ingenious series of important experiments, which space does not permit us to describe here, it was demonstrated that sets of three RNA bases (triplets) provide the code words that specify the order of amino acids to be incorporated into protein (Fig. 3-2), and that other triplet sequences mark the point at which synthesis would begin or end or be modified in other ways.

Often, mRNAs encode far more protein sequence than is represented in the final form of the processed gene product. One feature that was only detected through recent cellular biological insight was the *signal peptide:* a 15- to 30-amino acid sequence at the *N*-terminal end of the encoded gene product in which the amino acids are highly hydrophobic. The signal peptide is a near-constant feature of proteins intended for secretion, such as neuropeptides; its function seems to be to guide the nascent protein chain through the endoplasmic reticulum membrane for subsequent packaging by the Golgi membrane apparatus. (A corollary that might be anticipated is that proteins that are not intended for secretion would lack signal peptides and thus represent a means to predict from the structure of novel proteins whether they are or are not secretory products; regrettably, this corollary does not always hold.)

### DNA Segments for Genes Are Interrupted

Almost as essential to the progress in application of this base pairing complementarity and nucleic acid to protein translation was another totally unanticipated wrinkle in the molecular basis for gene regulation in eukaryotic cells that stemmed from even earlier observations on the adenoviruses. In the late 1970s, with the analysis of the genes encoding immunoglobulins and the hemoglobins, it was recognized that the basic organization of genes in eukaryotic cells (cells with nuclei, as in all multicellular organisms) did not follow the principles that had been uncovered from the study of prokaryotes (cells, like bacteria, that lack a separable genetic compartment). Instead, higher organisms (and some viruses) have their gene segments split up into coding regions that are expressed (*exons*) separated by intervening regions (*introns*) that are not found in the mRNA.

This interrupted DNA coding structure leads to two outcomes:

(1) the primary gene transcript, formally termed the heterogeneous nuclear RNA, or hnRNA, will contain extra RNA sequences, and the introns must be edited out before the mRNA can successfully direct protein synthesis by ribosomes (see Fig. 3-3). The editing process opens up the hnRNA, removes introns and resplices the cut ends; (2) in some cells, including neurons, the composition of the transcribed mRNA can also be edited by splicing out certain exon segments. The editing-splicing process provides a means by which a gene containing several exons can give rise to several different gene product proteins, in which certain protein domains may be shared and others will be unique. When gene products share similar nucleotide and protein sequences, we often speak of them as a "structural family."

This editing and splicing may seem to be an unnecessarily complicated route to follow for a process that is intended to translate important genes with great fidelity into equally important enzymatic and structural proteins. However, the reader should be cautioned that such biological complexity almost always implies important and

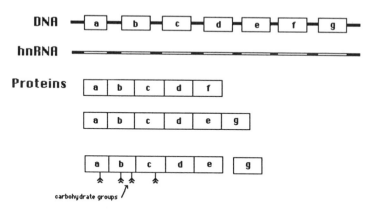

FIGURE 3-3. The relationship between DNA base sequences in introns and exons (a–g), the resulting primary RNA transcript, the subsequently edited forms of mRNA (two different forms of hypothetical editing and splicing are depicted), and the resulting proteins, which can then undergo posttranslational processing to yield small peptides, or to add carbohydrates or other chemical modifications to the molecule.

unanticipated regulatory control and enrichment. In the case of gene regulation and expression, the added complexities offer the means by which new life forms can evolve.

## Nucleic Acid Sequence Determinations

The final fundamental procedural development that accelerated discoveries made with molecular biological methods was the body of techniques to determine the sequence of DNA molecules, even those that are several thousand base pairs in length. The methods for doing this sequencing are clearly outside the province of this book. Two different approaches to sequence determination (that of Maxam and Gilbert, and that of Sanger), each based on some very clever chemistry, had profound enough importance to merit Nobel recognition. From these DNA sequences, it is possible to deduce the nucleotide sequences of the RNA, and thereby the amino-acid sequence of the protein product. The structures of the DNA and of the gene product can then be analyzed, often via computer, to compare their sequences with data banks of previously characterized proteins or nucleic acids. In addition to structural comparison of gene or RNA sequences, additional important clues to the functional features of the encoded molecule may be inferred from the domains of hydrophobic, hydrophilic, or other consensus structural sites for possible post-translational modification.

## Once-Over Quickly Cloning

When mRNAs are converted into DNA by the enzyme *reverse transcriptase*, the copied double-stranded DNA form, or *cDNA*, can be incorporated (inserted) into specific sites within an infectious vector, or plasmid. The sites for insertion are selected by identifying DNA sequences that can be "cut" by the actions of *restriction endonucleases*, enzymes from purified bacterial sources that cleave DNA sequences at specific palindromic repeated sequence sites. By using plasmids of known DNA sequence that can be tailored to include the proper restriction cleavage sites to allow for the DNA insertion, the same enzyme can then later be used to cleave out the insert. The restriction sites for insertion are typically chosen within plasmid genes that code for some discernible functional property (such as antibiotic resistance). Thus, interruption of its coding and expression (when insertion has been successful) leads to the loss of that functional property and results in a means to identify which plasmids have successful inserts. Each plasmid can generally only incorporate one cDNA insert, and with a great excess of host bacteria, each insert-bearing plasmid will infect only a single host (almost always *Escherichia coli*).

By growing these infected bacteria in such a way that each individual bacterium gives rise to a *colony* of identical bacteria bearing identical replicates of the plasmid and insert, the DNA has been *cloned*. The *cDNA* can then be recovered from the plasmid through another exposure to the restriction enzyme selected for the original opening of the plasmid insertion site. Thus, in a relatively few steps, one can start with a mixture of mRNAs in widely differing proportions from common to very rare, and purify them individually, as well as preparing virtually unlimited pure samples of the DNA insert.

### The Polymerase Chain Reaction (PCR)

In early 1988, the final touches were put onto a startling new technology for preparing large amounts of specific and rare nucleic acid sequences through amplification in vitro without the necessity of first purifying the desired product through cloning. The changes in molecular biological research wrought by this new technology were immediate and dramatic. At this writing, there are already more than 1,200 papers and 50 review articles on the innovative uses of PCR.

As originally conceived by scientists at the biotech company Cetus, the goal was to develop a quick diagnostic tool for the genetic disorder sickle cell hemoglobinopathy. Using previously selected restriction enzymes, human DNA was sliced into small sections, one of which contained the complete hemoglobin gene sequence.

When the DNA is heated to 95° C, the double-stranded DNA "melts" and the strands separate. Two small DNA sequences were synthesized (oligonucleotides) to be complementary to opposite strands of the hemoglobin gene separated by the part of the gene structure that was known to be altered in patients with the sickle cell mutation. These oligonucleotide "primers" will hybridize to their complementary sequences on the single-stranded DNA. In the presence of large amounts of a purified DNA polymerase and large amounts of all the deoxynucleotides, the primers will be extended to the end of the single strand. In the original experiments, this span covered only a distance of 20–30 bases; subsequent modifications now permit the amplification of nucleotide sequences that are several hundred bases long.

By then separating through heat denaturation the dual helical strands of the newly synthesized material, cooling the reaction mixture, and adding fresh DNA polymerase and nucleotides, the cycle of *denature*, *anneal*, and *extend* reactions, each lasting only a few seconds, can be rapidly repeated. So long as the polymerase and the nucleotide substrates remain in excess, the extended sequences of the first reaction each serve as templates for opposite strand synthesis in subsequent cycles, thereby providing a geometric rate of amplification. By identifying a DNA polymerase from a bacterial strain that survived in the heat of a Yellowstone geyser (*Thermus aquaticus*, or Taq for short), it was possible to develop a kit that would allow large amounts of polymerase to survive the heat denaturation step. Thus, with the Taq polymerase and large starting amounts of d-nucleotides, a series of rapid cycles allow for the exponential in vitro amplification of the desired gene segment.

If the sequences selected are known to be generally constant in the genome of the species to be studied, the same primers can be used to select, amplify, and then evaluate the same intervening gene segment from many individuals. If the amplified segment is simply evaluated for its length, it is possible to determine whether a given individual has had a major structural gene mutation, such as a deletion or insertion. However, many other clever applications of the technology have pushed its advantages even more broadly than ini-

# Applied Cloning

FIGURE 3-4. Applied cloning. Schematic overview of the major currently employed methods for applying molecular cloning methods to resolving the molecular structure of brain proteins. Brain mRNA, taken from whole brain or subfractions, is the starting material for a brain cDNA library that can be further selected for clones of interest by the several indicated strategic protocols. Alternatively (lower left) DNA can be prepared as a total genomic library, or (lower right) selected nucleic acid probes can be tailored to features of known proteins. Immunological methods are also critical in evaluating the gene product's location and possible functional properties.

tially imagined. By first using reverse transcriptase to make double-stranded copy DNA (cDNA), one can also apply PCR to mRNAs, and even make the assessment quantitative. By modifying the ends of the probes to be used, it is possible to incorporate special synthetic sequences that will later make it easier to clone or sequence the amplified segments, or to re-insert modified versions to assess the functional importance of a specific sequence domain. By using special nucleotides that will form complementary base pairs even if the sequences do not match precisely, it is possible to amplify homologous sequences from different but related genes (such as the transmembrane domains for the 7-transmembrane domain receptors like the noradrenergic, cholinergic, or serotonergic receptors).

This highly superficial survey should indicate the facility of cloning DNA segments (taken directly from genomic digests or from mRNA copies) and then sequencing the cloned segments and deducing the structure of their product. However, we have glossed over the one potentially sour note in this rhapsody of high-tech molecular music making: How do you identify which clone is carrying the insert that encodes the gene product you want to identify? Suppose you don't even know what it is you want to look for and clone? As it turns out, through more cleverness and a few good breaks from Mother Nature, biologists have found multiple methods to do these feats of molecular magic, although some of the screening methods have given new meaning to the term "a search for needles in haystacks" (Figs. 3–4).

## MOLECULAR STRATEGIES IN NEUROPHARMACOLOGY

The immediate applications of molecular biological strategies within neuropharmacology are shortcuts in molecular isolation and sequence determination—for instance, to uncover new peptides or to provide more complete understanding of enzymes, receptors, channels, or other integral proteins of the cell. A rather likely premise holds that the phenotype of a cell within the nervous system depends upon the structural, metabolic, and regulatory proteins by which it establishes its recognizable structural and functional properties. If this is valid, then complex, multifaceted neurons will probably rely upon hundreds, if not thousands, of special-purpose proteins, many of which may exist in rather limited amounts. Purifying such rare proteins by the methods that existed before molecular cloning, especially in the absence of a functional assay to guide the purification process, is an overwhelming task requiring exceptional patience, resources, and a very large supply of the proper starting tissue material. For some of the very rare hypothalamic hypophysiotrophic releasing factors (see Chapter 12), hundreds of thousands of hypothalami were required, as well as the development of unique purification schemes for each subsequent factor to be pursued.

Converting the quest for the structure of specific proteins into a molecular biological quest for the mRNA or gene segment that encodes this protein greatly facilitates the experimental analysis, simply because of the powers of cloning, complementarity, and rapid sequencing. Several methods have been developed that increase the chances of finding whatever the researcher is seeking (Fig. 3-4). These methods depend in part on the nature of the cDNA being pursued and how the investigator is able to probe either for the insert or for the translation of the fusion gene product in a cell system capable of processing the primary translation product into a structural form that will resemble its natural configuration and sometimes even its natural function.

## GENERAL STRATEGIES FOR CLONE SCREENING AND SELECTION

### Enrichment by Tissue Selection and Preparation

The basic starting point is to select the brain cells or regions that are presumed to express the molecule to be studied and then to enrich sources of mRNA to favor the detection of the one being pursued. Cell lines and even tumors that produce large amounts of a hormone (such as pheochromocytomas or VIP-omas) or bear large numbers of the desired receptors or channels (like electroplax or striated muscle) have proved to be excellent starting materials. Once the cell source is selected, the desired mRNAs can be further enriched (e.g., by sucrose gradient centrifugation or electrophoresis) provided that some characteristics of the mRNA being sought are known.

*Recognizing the Wanted Clone*

A general strategy for detecting desired colonies of cloned bacteria is known as *colony hybridization*. In this approach, the bacteria are grown on a special culture plate from which their colonies can be copied (transferred as a group by lightly pressing them to another supporting surface, called "replica plating," and thereby sampling and preserving the spatial identity of all the colonies on the plate.) The bacteria on the replicate supports are treated to expose their DNA and are screened with radioactive nucleic acid probes. Colonies that hybridize with the probe can then be identified by autoradiography. Alternatively, if the plasmid-carrying inserts were tailored to allow for expression of the protein encoded by the transferred genetic material, it might also be possible to identify the desired clones by immunological reactivity. When a reactive colony has been identified, its original bacterial colony is recovered from the original culture plate and the living bacteria are then grown in large amounts to provide the starting material for DNA sequence analysis.

*Building Your Own DNA*

If partial protein (or peptide) sequences are known, it is possible to make predictions of what the mRNA sequence should be (by back-translating the genetic code for amino acids) and including enough alternatives to overcome the ambiguous cases where a specific amino acid may be encoded by several variant triplets. From this predicted RNA structure, it is then possible to design and synthesize the hypothetical cDNA. This approach has been used, for example, to create hypothetical cDNAs for the hypophysiotrophic hormones whose amino-acid sequences had been accurately determined "the old-fashioned way," by earning it one amino acid at a time from highly purified brain extracts. The main reason to do this with a biologically active protein or peptide whose structure is already known would be to get at the complete structure of its prohormone, or to obtain its complete genomic structure and analyze its regulatory control and expression mechanisms. As will be seen in Chapter 12, when this is done, more often than not, the prohormone of the known peptide is found to encode more than one active product. However, because of the redundancy of triplet RNA codons for some amino acids (there are six different codes for leucine alone) it is generally difficult to acquire a functional full-length mRNA by predictive synthesis.

An alternative approach is to synthesize a shorter complementary single-stranded DNA (a so-called "oligodeoxynucleotide probe") and use it as a *probe* to screen libraries of clones. Such libraries may be prepared from mRNA extracts or from special digests of the whole genome. In the former case, the starting material would be brain, while in the latter case, in theory, any somatic cells could be used to prepare the library. With the availability of automated "gene machines" it is now possible to synthesize a proper probe or two overnight, and use them to screen an awaiting genomic or cDNA library and thereby determine the complete coding sequences for a partially purified protein within a few weeks.

On such a screening expedition, likely candidate colonies can be cross-screened by a second synthetic oligodeoxynucleotide probe, based upon another separate domain of the full protein. Clones positive for both probes would then have to contain the gene sequence that encodes the two sequences against which the probes were made as well as the sequence between them. This strategy has been used with many neuropeptide mRNAs (see Chapter 12).

## When You Haven't Got a Clue

It is also possible to penetrate the large treasure trove of cellular proteins that have not yet been identified by conventional strategies. Given the length of the mammalian genome, and the relatively short list of identified specific molecules in cells of all classes, we must conclude that there is an awful lot left to be identified, and few clues as to what it is we don't know about. The methods of molecular biology can help here too.

In nonneural tissues, for example, it has been possible to identify the unique proteins expressed in a male versus a female liver, or those that are unique to thymus-derived versus bone marrow-derived lymphocytes by exploiting the fact that a very high proportion of the proteins expressed in these pairs of tissues are, for the most part, very similar. Depending on how the pairs of tissues or cell types are defined and how similar or dissimilar they actually turn out to be, this method can be made highly sensitive and can reveal unique differences in cell-specific gene expression.

The discovery strategy can also be broadened to look for large sets of tissue-specific genes. For example, Sutcliffe, Milner, and Bloom have employed molecular cloning methods to ask what proteins are generally made by brain that are not found in other major tissues, and to determine the degree to which neurons differ in specific proteins underlying their phenotypes that at present are only defined empirically. In their general approach, a cDNA library was prepared from mRNAs extracted from whole rat brain, and the individual cDNAs were characterized for their ability to hybridize to mRNAs extracted from brain, liver, or kidney. Those expressed in brain, but not detectable in extracts of liver or kidney, were found to represent well over half of the total brain mRNA population (approximately 30,000 out of an estimated total of 50,000) suggesting that much of the genome contains information pertinent to the generation of neuronal function. Individual brain-specific clones are then analyzed further by determining their nucleotide sequence, and deducing the amino acid sequence of its encoded protein. Proteins that are unique to the data base of known sequences can then be identified further by raising antisera against synthetic peptides that mimic selected regions of the deduced protein structure. One such clone appears to resemble a possible precursor for neuropeptides.

Yet another strategic approach involves injecting mRNAs from enriched or prepared sources into frog oocytes where complex eukaryotic genes may be expressed more efficiently. Because the oocytes are relatively large, their expression of a novel functional protein can be assessed physiologically or biochemically to identify species of mRNA for isolation and cloning. By injecting groups of mRNAs and evaluating the oocytes for the response one seeks, it is possible through trial and error to identify the mRNA for a specific functional protein, like an ion channel or a cell surface receptor.

*An All-points Search*

Would-be molecular neuropharmacologists attending a seminar involving these approaches may find initial exposure to the jargon confusing without some orientation. (Orientation is an appropriate term, for such presentations are sprinkled with what may sound like references to compass points; see Fig. 3-4). When DNA is fractionated by restriction enzymes, and the resulting fragments are separated by gel electrophoresis, it is possible to transfer, or "blot," the resulting fragments, separated mainly on the basis of their lengths, from the acrylamide gel to a nitrocellulose or nylon support, and there to analyze them for the ability to hybridize with cDNA or RNA probes. This method is referred to as a "Southern" blot analysis, named for the scientist (Dr. E. M. Southern) who started the evolution of this method. Later, a similar approach was devised in which the starting material was RNA. Here, the separated RNAs were blotted for probing with radioactive, single-stranded cDNA probes. Because the starting material is, speaking in terms of nucleic acid, the opposite of the Southern, this RNA blot is referred to as a "Northern blot."

More recently, immunological methods have been used to probe protein extracts that were separated by acrylamide gel electrophoresis and then "blotted" (by an electrical transfer) for identification by peroxidase or radioisotope-labeled antibodies to specific protein antigens. The result is termed a "Western blot." If RNA or protein samples are simply dried directly onto nitrocellulose for probing analysis without first separating them for size, the resulting blots are termed "slot blots" or "dot blots." These blots are useful when screening a large number of clone extracts for insert or expressed products quickly. As of this writing, no method has yet earned the accolade of being an "Eastern blot."

Given the resourcefulness with which molecular biologic methods are being applied to all aspects of specialized cell biology, including the actions of drugs on the nervous system, one senses that we are about to experience a logarithmic increase in the number of specific molecules that will be fully characterized, and that will enable pharmacological engineers to shape drug molecules precisely to fit the pocket of receptors or enzymes for the ultimate in specificity. Any biological phenomenon in the brain that is mediated by proteins, which seems to exclude hardly any brain function, is therefore amenable to the ultimate in molecular analysis. The range of such specific molecules would then include (but is definitely not limited to) the enzymes needed for transmitter synthesis, storage, release and catabolism, the receptors and related macromolecules needed for response, and response mediation to broader-scale events such as establishing the shape and orientation of a cell by the proper anchoring of its microtubules and filaments to the plasma membrane and the repair and maintainence of synaptic connectivity.

## BEYOND THE CLONES

Although we may rightly marvel at the advances that have been achieved through the use of molecular biological techniques, all that we have in essence discussed so far in this chapter is a set of methods that provides a novel, powerful, and accurate way to identify, isolate, and characterize the amino acid sequences of a host of intracellular proteins and their possible subsequent metabolic products. While this is unquestionably a very major advance in the research armamentarium, it still does not really begin to deal with a wide range of other important questions that are also approachable through the molecular tools that recombinant methodologies provide.

For example, once a cDNA has been proven to represent the mRNA for a specific molecule, the deduced protein's sequence can be inspected to infer potential functional properties. Thus, the acetylcholine receptor molecule and the myelin proteolipid protein exhibit several stretches of 20–24 hydrophobic amino acids in a row, which are strong presumptive evidence of membrane-crossing domains and thus suggestive of plasma membrane constitutive proteins.

In any case, when the protein structure can be deduced, the entire molecule or selected fragments of it can be synthesized and used to raise antisera. These antisera can then be used to develop radioimmunoassays for the protein. The antisera can also be used for immunocytochemical analysis of the nervous system to determine which cell and which compartments of those cells exhibit the protein that has been identified. The synthetic fragments can be used to determine whether the protein's domains may be substrates for posttranslational modification, being processed by further proteolytic cleavage or by structural modification with glycosylation, phosphorylation, sulfation, or acylation. Subcellular fractions and ultrastructural cytochemistry may suggest organelle specialization or cell surface associations.

The products of cDNA cloning can also be taken back to the genome, to probe the regions around the location of the exons to search for their molecular mechanisms for control of expression. Once the location of the surrounding elements in the genome have been located, the cDNA probes can be used to determine the degree to which the mRNA or the underlying gene exons have been conserved across eukaryotic species and to determine the position on the chromosomes to which the gene can be mapped. The chromosomal location of many proteins has been determined in this or a similar manner. However, the human genome, and that of most mammals, is estimated to be on the order of $3 \times 10^9$ base pairs long, of which fewer than 1000 genes have been mapped, most of them being on the relatively small X chromosome. What this means is that there are vast expanses of the genome with no known markers of any kind. For students of genetic diseases of the nervous system, the situation is even worse, because much less than 1% of the genome is associated with known nervous system markers even though a significant fraction of the genome may be expressed selectively in the brain.

These considerations of length and complexity of neuronal gene expression suggest that efforts to link specific patterns of DNA polymorphism may be a critical future development. The genetic linkages are defined on the basis of Southern blot analysis of family members whose genomic DNA has been treated with various different restriction enzymes to provide *restriction fragment length polymorphisms*. Because there can be considerable individual variation in nucleotide sequences without disturbing the function of the encoded proteins, the degree to which the patterns of restriction endonuclease-digested fragments differ reflects this individual variation. The ability to link fragments of DNA with inheritance of genetic disorders and to specific markers within the digested fragments helps to establish approximate locations of genetic mutations, such as the localization of the gene for Huntington's disease to human chromosome 4.

Although new modifications on these basic strategies are reported continuously, and although there is a steady growth of molecular information on the elements of neuronal function, most of the details that follow in this book deal with those still relatively rare molecules (e.g., the major known neurotransmitters, their synthetic and catabolic enzymes, their receptors and response mediators), whose nature is already partly established. While this list may well be lengthened ever more rapidly by the shortcuts made possible by molecular biological methods, the student should recognize that identifying new molecules per se is merely a first step towards an important pharmacological end but is nowhere near the true strength of what molecular biology may have to offer our field.

We have already spoken of some important tools as though they were only to be used for molecular identification, and it would be somewhat misleading to let those impressions stand without a pedagogical challenge. The awareness of how to "tailor" purified mRNAs can be taken far beyond simply sticking them into a plasmid: More complex tailoring, leading to real "designer genes," can be used to prepare synthetic genes that carry with them the basis for being incorporated and being expressed by novel cellular hosts, bacterial or mammalian. Directly injecting mRNAs into frog oocytes and allowing them to be translated and incorporated into the oocyte's cellular machinery is useful for detecting specific mRNAs for specific functional proteins, but again there is more: The cell bearing a known receptor whose complete amino-acid sequence is known could be used as an ideal template for drug design, by combining x-ray crystallographic information on the gene product protein, amino-acid sequences, and functional responses in a responsive cell. Such methods have already been employed in part to derive potent enzyme inhibitors for membrane lipolytic enzymes. Furthermore, once that mRNA has been identified, synthetic versions of it that are lacking certain nucleotide segments can be evaluated to determine the functional consequences of tinkering around with the molecule in specifically designated sites. This strategy would be capable of indicating the active sites of a receptor, or its membrane anchoring, or its sites of interactions with the ion channels or enzymes that the receptor can regulate. Such mutagenesis can also be achieved by other treatments for the same objective.

The use of viable gene expression systems can go considerably beyond the frog oocyte, however. Effective use has already been made of cell lines, most of them derived from spontaneous, chemical or virus-induced tumors of the central or peripheral nervous systems, or from fused representatives of such originally tumorous cells. The ideal cell lines characteristically differ, depending upon the situations in which they will be used—such as an abundant receptor (to look for genes that transduce it when activated), or no receptors and abundant second messenger systems, so that a gene encoding a receptor can be screened for its natural ligand or for its mechanisms of transduction.

Even more promising in its implications for neuropharmacology is the microinjection of a segment of cloned DNA into the pronucleus of a single cell zygote (a fertilized ovum) to create a *transgenic mouse*. After injecting a large number of fertilized ova (a success rate of 10% is considered good), one transfers the eggs to the uterine cavity of a foster mother that has been pseudo-bred with a sterile male. When the pups are born, they are evaluated through skin fibroblast cultures for incorporation of the injected DNA, and, if possible, for expression of the gene product (e.g. overproduction of a circulating hormone). After puberty, their sperm can also be evaluated for integration of the foreign DNA sample into germ cells; these are best evaluated by their ability to transmit the integrated gene to the mouse's own progeny. If the integration of the foreign DNA is successful, and if the resultant gene structure (at the site of integration) does not itself produce mutational consequences that may be troublesome, the founder mice give rise to lines of mice bearing the transgene. By preparing gene constructs that induce the overproduction of growth hormone, it has been possible to use the technology to make not only supermice, but super pigs and super goats as well.

Transgenic mice are now being used for a variety of experimental purposes. They are used to express the products of a virus such as the hepatitis B or the human immunodeficiency virus, and they determine which, if any, of the virus gene products may be directly cytotoxic, immunogenic, or immunocytotoxic. Other partially tested strategies include removing a natural gene to determine the effects on tissue or organ function, as for example producing an artificial demyelination disorder by eliminating gene for myelin basic protein. The reverse application of transgenic technology was actually done first, namely, preparing a transgene for expression of myelin basic protein and using that to "cure" the gene mutation of the myelin-deficient mouse, which is ordinarily unable to make the protein.

Among the more experimental applications of transgenic technology is the preparation of a gene construct in which the regulatory domains of a known gene (say for a neuropeptide) are coupled with the expression of a novel "reporter" gene (such as an enzyme that is normally absent in the mouse); under these conditions, one can evaluate whole animal treatments (or whole cell treatments if cell lines are transfected instead of embryonic cells) that "turn on the reporter gene," thus providing inferential evidence of what controls (ie., elevated cyclic AMP) the activation of the natural gene. Finally, applications rumored to be in progress include the use of a retrovirus to carry a gene segment to be transfected into cells beyond the single cell embryo level; this is especially useful in systems where partial development can reveal the effects of the added gene. A third creative but not yet well-developed application involves the transfection of embryonic "stem" cells, undifferentiated blast-like cells taken from the blastocyst level of embryonic development. When these transfected stem cells are then returned to blastocyst embryos, they spread throughout the developing organism, and if the researcher is fortunate, the foreign gene will appear in the germ cell lines as well. Should gene markers ever be identified that predict the development of single gene-dependent neuropsychiatric diseases (such as Huntington's, familial Alzheimer's, or scrapie), it should be possible to prepare true animal models of the diseases and their treatment.

These examples are by no means exhausting the idea banks now being formulated, and if some of these ideas don't seem as old hat to you as you thought they might, perhaps it's time you paid a trip to your intellectual haberdashery and check out your skullcap for the reading material necessary to work in the gene library world.

## Selected References
### General Sources

Chirgwin, J. M. (1990). Molecular biology for nonmolecular biologists. *Diabetes CARE 13:* 188–198.

Erlich, H. A. (1989). *PCR Technology*, Stockton Press, New York.

Goodman, R. H. (1990). Regulation of neuropeptide gene expression. *Annu. Rev. Neurosci. 13:* 111–127.

Lewin, B. (1987) *Genes*. 3rd ed. Wiley & Sons, New York.

Milner, R. J. and J. G. Sutcliffe (1988). Molecular biological strategies applied to the nervous system. *Disc. Neurosci. 5(2):* 11–63.

Watson, J. D., J. Tooze, and D. T. Kurtz (1983). *Recombinant DNA. A Short Course.* W.H. Freeman and Co., New York.

Watson, J. D., N. H. Hopkins, J. W. Roberts, J. A. Steitz, and A. M. Weiner (1987). *Molecular Biology of the Gene.* 4th ed. Benjamin-Cummings, New York.

Weintraub, H. M. (1990). Antisense RNA and DNA. *Sci. Am.,* 40–46.

### Specific References

Cepko, C. (1988). Immortalization of neural cells via oncogene transduction. *Trends Neurosci. 11,* 6–9.

Cohen, S. A., A. Chang, S. Boyer, and R. Helling (1973). Construction of biologically functional bacterial plasmids in vitro. *Proc. Nat. Acad. Sci. U.S.A. 70,* 3240–3244.

Crick, F. H. C., L. Barnett, S. Brenner, and R. J. Watts-Tobin (1961). General nature of the genetic code for proteins. *Nature 192,* 1227–1232.

Gilbert, W. (1985). Genes-in-pieces revisited. *Science 228*, 823.

Gusella, J. F., R. E. Tanzi, M. A. Anderson, W. Hobbs, K. Gibbons, R. Raschtchian, T. C. Gilliam, M. R. Wallace, N. S. Wexler, and P. M. Conneally (1984). DNA markers for nervous system diseases. *Science 225*, 1320–1325.

Hanley, M. R. (1987). Analysis of receptor-coupled events in neuropeptide action using clonal cell lines. *Prog. Brain Res. 72*, 189–196.

Katsuki, M., M. Sato, M. Kimura, M. Yokoyama, K. Kobayashi, and T. Nomura. (1988). Conversion of normal behavior to shiverer by myelin basic protein antisense cDNA in transgenic mice. *Science 241*, 593–595.

Maxam, A. M. and W. Gilbert (1977). A new method of sequencing DNA. *Proc. Nat. Acad. Sci. U.S.A. 74*, 5463–5467.

Palmiter, R. D., R. R. Behringer, C. J. Quaife, F. Maxwell, I. H. Maxwell, and R. L. Brinster (1987). Cell lineage ablation in transgenic mice by cell specific expression of a toxin gene. *Cell 50*, 435–443.

Popko, B., C. Puckett, E. Lai, H. D. Shine, C. Readhead, N. Takahashi, S. W., 3d. Hunt, R. L. Sidman, and L. Hood (1987). Myelin deficient mice: Expression of myelin basic protein and generation of mice with varying levels of myelin. *Cell 48*, 713–21.

Rosenfeld, M. G., S. G. Amara, and R. M. Evans (1984). Alternative RNA processing: Determining neuronal phenotype. *Science 225*, 1315–1319.

Ruddle, F. H. (1981). A new era in mammalian gene mapping. Somatic cell genetics and recombinant DNA. *Nature 294*, 115–120.

Sanger, F. and A. R. Coulson (1975). A rapid method for determining sequences in DNA by primed synthesis with DNA polymerase. *J. Mol. Biol. 94*, 444–448.

Southern, E. M. (1975). Detection of specific sequences among DNA fragments separated by gel electrophoresis. *J. Mol. Biol. 98*, 503–517.

Sutcliffe, J. G., R. J. Milner, T. M. Shinnick, and F. E. Bloom (1983). Identifying the protein products of brain-specific genes with antibodies to chemically synthesized peptides. *Cell 33*, 671–682.

Sutcliffe, J. G., R. J. Milner, J. M. Gottesfeld, and W. Reynolds (1984). Control of neuronal gene expression. *Science 225*, 1308–1314.

Thomas, K. R. and M. R. Capecchi (1987). Site-directed mutagenesis by gene targetting in mouse embryo derived stem cells. *Cell 51*, 503–512.

Watson, J. D. and F. H. C. Crick (1953). Molecular structure of nucleic acids: A structure for deoxyribose nucleic acid. *Nature 171*, 737–738.

# 4 | Metabolism in the Central Nervous System

One way to approach the biochemistry of the brain is to go through the litany of the Embden-Meyerhof glycolytic pathway, the tricarboxylic acid cycle, the pentose phosphate shunt, and the biosynthetic and metabolic pathways of carbohydrates, lipids, nucleic acids, and proteins. All of these enzyme systems occur in the brain and have been studied in more or less detail, but qualitatively nothing of striking import distinguishes these enzyme activities in nervous tissue from their activity in extraneuronal tissue. For example, the synthesis of ATP from glycolysis and oxidative phosphorylation appears not to be fundamentally different in brain than in other tissues and does nothing to illuminate the brain as a specialized organ. In particular, if one recalls the diversity as well as the specificity of the effects of neurotropic agents, it is difficult to see the relevance of such a universal and basic mechanism as energy production in a discussion of neuropharmacology. Unless neuropharmacological agents had a peculiar affinity for nervous tissue, one would not expect to encounter such a specificity among these agents if they directly inhibited glycolysis or oxidative phosphorylation. More logically, the mechanism of action of these agents might be anticipated to lie in their ability ultimately to affect neurotransmission. This could take place primarily by affecting the synthesis, release, catabolism, storage, or reuptake of transmitters, by altering ion movements, or by altering receptor sensitivity or density.

To state the obvious, then, since the brain is an organ that processes information, it seems most profitable in discussing the biochemistry of the brain to look at enzyme systems and substrates that may contribute to this specialization. In other words, if one were asked to prove biochemically that a piece of tissue was from the brain, what would one measure? There are two types of compounds and enzyme systems that can be used to elucidate the biochemical uniqueness of the brain:

(A) *Compounds with demonstrated electrophysiological activity.*

(B) *Compounds that either occur only in the CNS or whose concentration in the brain is extraordinarily high compared with that of other tissues.* A concentration of $>3mM$ has been arbitrarily chosen as a cutoff point.

To a large extent the composite flow sheet of Fig. 4-1 covers these possibilities. The arrows are not intended to imply direct conversions but merely precursor relationships. For convenience, compounds in Group A are in capital letters; compounds in Group B are screened.

The figure properly begins with glucose because in brain, in contrast to other tissues, virtually everything except essential fatty acids and amino acids is derived from this substrate. For example, when labeled glucose is incubated with brain cortical slices, labeled aspartate and glutamate are synthesized within a few minutes after the addition of the glucose to the flasks. The same occurs in vivo as well as in brain perfusion experiments. The brain accounts for about 20% of the total oxygen consumption of the body; the energy associated with this oxygen consumption comes from the utilization of glucose.

The knowledge that glucose under normal conditions is the primary if not the sole substrate of the brain in vivo derives from two experimental findings. First, in measuring A-V differences in $O_2$ and $CO_2$ in the blood going through the brain, a respiratory quotient of 1 was obtained, indicating that the oxidation of carbohydrates rather than amino acids or fatty acids is the primary source of energy. Further, when the A-V differences of glucose, glutamate, lactate, and pyruvate were determined, the only compound removed in large amounts from the arterial blood was glucose, and the only product that was released in large quantities was $CO_2$. The second line of evidence implicating glucose derives from experiments on the hypoglycemia induced either by hepatectomy or by the administration

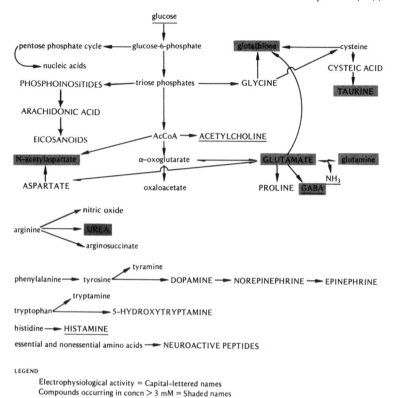

FIGURE 4-1. Various interrelationships among compounds of neurochemical interest.

of insulin. In these experiments the fall in blood glucose correlated with a cerebral dysfunction that ranged from mild behavioral impairment to coma. The CNS effect can be completely reversed by the administration of glucose, maltose, or mannose: maltose is hydrolyzed to glucose; mannose is phosphorylated and converted to fructose-6-phosphate. The CNS effect is not reversed by lactate, pyruvate, or glutamate (perhaps because these agents do not penetrate the blood–brain barrier at a fast enough rate). In insulin coma, with its concomitant low cerebral metabolic rate, there is enough glucose and glycogen to last about ninety minutes; then other cerebral metabolites are utilized. This calculation correlates with the observation that in insulin coma irreversible damage occurs after 90 minutes despite the subsequent administration of glucose. This irreversibility may be due to the fact that vital amino acids and lipids are utilized in an attempt to maintain cerebral metabolism.

Although a diversion, it is worthwhile in discussing glucose metabolism to mention the imaginative 2-deoxyglucose technique developed by Sokoloff and co-workers to correlate functional brain activity and energy metabolism. By injecting labeled 2-deoxyglucose, whose metabolism essentially stops at the 2-deoxyglucose-6-phosphate level, and ultimately measuring radioactivity in brain sections by autoradiography, these researchers made possible the pictorial representation of relative rates of glucose utilization in all brain areas and the mapping of functional neural pathways under pharmacological and pathological conditions on the basis of the evoked metabolic response. Recently, this metabolic encephalographic technique has been developed for in vivo human use by employing the derivative [18] fluorodeoxyglucose and scanning with positron-emission tomography.

The first step in glucose metabolism involves phosphorylation by ATP to form glucose-6-phosphate. Over 90% of this phosphate ester is metabolized through the well-known Embden-Meyerhof glycolytic pathway and less than 10% is oxidized via the pentose phosphate cycle. This latter system, sometimes referred to as the hexose monophosphate shunt, does not lead directly to ATP synthesis, as is the case with glycolysis or oxidative phosphorylation. Instead, it appears to function primarily in providing reduced nicotinamide adenine dinucleotide phosphate (NADPH), vital in lipid biosynthesis, and the pentose phosphates that are required in the de novo synthesis of nucleotides.

The Embden-Meyerhof pathway leads to triose phosphates, which are involved in the synthesis of lipids. The high concentration of lipids is a unique feature of the brain since about 50% of the dry weight of the brain is lipid compared with 6–20% in other organs of the body. In further contrast to other tissues, cholesterol occurs almost exclusively in the free form, with only a minute amount esterified; the concentration of triglycerides and free fatty acids is minimal compared to other organs, and, whereas other organs contain glucocerebroside, the brain contains only galactocerebroside.

In addition to cholesterol, brain lipids include glycerides and sphingolipids of very complex composition. The composition of some of these compounds is shown in Table 4-1. Protein-lipid complexes are also found in nervous tissue and are referred to as proteolipids or lipoproteins, depending on the physical characteristics of the molecule. Phosphatidopeptides have also been reported in the brain. Although the chemistry of brain lipids is fairly well known and currently much is being learned of the synthesis and catabolism of lipids, the function of these compounds is still unclear. What is clear is that most lipids serve as structural components, either in myelin or in membranes of the various cellular organelles, and exhibit a slow turnover. However, a metabolic function for phosphoinositides has received considerable attention ("the P. I. effect") as a modulatory mechanism, as has arachidonic acid and the eicosanoids; these metabolites are discussed in Chapter 6. Another recent development in lipid metabolism, deriving from the imaginative investigations of Hirata and Axelrod, indicates that methylation of membrane-bound phospholipids is initiated by a variety of agents acting on the receptors of cells. This transduction of receptor-mediated signals is also discussed in Chapter 6. With respect to glycerophospholipids, there are three key phospholipases whose hydrolytic activity leads to compounds that are involved in synaptic transmission: *Phospholipase $A_2$* hydrolyzes the linkage designated as $R_1$ in Table 4-1. The fatty acid at this position is generally arachidonic acid, the precursor of prostaglandins, thromboxanes, and leukotrienes (see Chapter 6). *Phospholipase D* splits the bond between O and X and can yield choline in the case of phosphatidylcholine, which may then be acetylated to ACh. When the phospholipid is phosphatidyl inositide, *Phospholipase C* activity yields two neuroactive metabolites, diacylglycerol and inositol trisphosphate, also to be discussed in Chapter 6.

Although the function of the complex lipids is unknown, their implication in certain genetic types of mental retardation known as

TABLE 4-1. Lipid Structures

| Basic structure | $R_1$ | $R_2$ | X | Compound |
|---|---|---|---|---|
| Glycerophosphate | Fatty acid | Fatty acid | $CH_2CH_2\overset{+}{N}H_2$ | Phosphatidylethanolamine |
| | Fatty acid | Fatty acid | $CH_2CH(\overset{+}{N}H_3)$-COOH | Phosphatidyl serine |
| | Fatty acid | Fatty acid | $CH_2CH_2\overset{+}{N}(CH_3)_3$ | Phosphatidylcholine |
| | Fatty acid | Fatty acid | | Phosphatidylinositol (di- and triphosphoinositides have phosphate on position 4 and 5) Cardiolipin (diphosphatidyl glycerol) |
| | $OPO_3H$ | H | | |

| Basic Structure | Addition | Compound |
|---|---|---|
| $CH_3(CH_2)_{12}CH = CH(OH)CH(NH_2)CH_2OH$ Sphingosine | Fatty acid | Ceramide |
| | Fatty acid, phosphorylcholine | Sphingomyelin |
| | Galactose | Psychosine |
| | Galactose, fatty acid | Cerebroside |
| | Galactose, fatty acid, sulfate | Sulfatide |
| | Glucose, galactose, fatty acid, N-Acetylneuraminic acid, N-Acetylgalactosamine | Ganglioside |

N-Acetylneuraminic acid (sialic acid)

the cerebral lipidoses is well documented. Thus, for example, in Tay-Sachs disease there is an accumulation of gangliosides, in Gaucher's disease there is a rise in the cerebroside content of the brain, and in Niemann-Pick disease there is an accumulation of both sphingomyelin and gangliosides. It is also known that in demyelinating diseases the cerebroside and sphingomyelin content of the brain declines and that there is a formation of cholesterol esters.

Gangliosides are of particular interest in that they bind black-widow spider venom as well as cholera, tetanus, and botulinum toxins; recently a cholinergic terminal antigen, referred to as chol-1, has been identified as a ganglioside. In addition, these glycolipids have repeatedly been shown to induce neurite extension in a variety of neuronal cultures. Finally, antibodies to gangliosides when injected intracerebrally produce a variety of CNS effects that are relatively selective. Thus, with this range of effects, among the complex lipids the gangliosides deserve particular attention.

Continuing with the scheme in Figure 4-1, the offshoot giving rise to ACh and glycine, will be dealt with in subsequent chapters.

Glutamate is the next compound of neuropharmacological interest listed in Figure 4-1. Besides its obvious utility in the brain as an energy source in coupled phosphorylation and as an amino acid for protein synthesis, glutamate has five other functions. It serves as

1. a "detoxifying" substrate trapping $NH_3$ to form glutamine;
2. the precursor of γ-aminobutyric acid (GABA);
3. the precursor of proline;
4. one of the amino acids in glutathione;
5. a "universal" excitatory amino acid.

The possible neurotransmitter roles of glutamate and GABA will be discussed in Chapter 7. Also to be discussed in that chapter is the "GABA shunt," a sequence of reactions unique to the brain, in which glutamate functions catalytically to produce succinate from α-oxoglutarate without invoking α-oxoglutarate dehydrogenase.

It is well established that glutamate exists in the brain in at least two pools: a small one thought to be glial and a larger one that is neuronal. It is not known with any certainty how the pools relate to the various activities of this amino acid, but it has been suggested that glutamate is first converted to glutamine in the small pool, is transported to the large pool, and then is released as either glutamate or GABA. (Because of these pools, and since glutamate and the other amino acid transmitters all derive from glucose, it would be wise to use labeled glucose as the precursor for these amino acids rather than employing the labeled amino acid in experiments involving the release of these agents.)

The relationship between ammonia levels in the brain and convulsions has been demonstrated in a variety of experimental procedures. Although the cerebral origin of endogenous ammonia production is still unclear, the role of glutamate and glutamine synthetase in ammonia disposal is well established. Thus the infusion of ammonium salts into dogs results in an increased level of cerebral glutamine. Glutamine levels are presumably regulated by diffusion of the compound into the general circulation to the kidney where glutaminase would remove ammonia. The ammonia would be eliminated either as a cation or via the urea cycle. Under normal conditions glutamine in glial cells appears to serve as a storehouse for neuronal glutamate and may regulate the level of this amino acid and, consequently, of GABA. The observation that glutaminase is an allosteric enzyme that is activated by phosphate, ammonia, and nucleoside triphosphates and is inhibited by glutamate suggests that the conversion of glutamine to glutamate is under fine metabolic control.

Glutathione, a tripeptide consisting of glutamic acid, cysteine, and glycine, has been known for over forty years, but its function still remains elusive. It does serve as the coenzyme for formaldehyde dehydrogenase, glyoxylase, and for the isomerization of maleylacetoacetate to fumarylacetoacetate, but these reactions are not considered important enough to explain its high concentration in brain. Rather, speculation on the role of the tripeptide has always revolved around its oxidation and reduction. Its primary function may be to destroy free radicals and to maintain a proper ratio of sulfhydryl and disulfide groups in proteins or other cerebral constituents. Alternatively, according to Meister, it may function as the substrate for γ-glutamyl transpeptidase in the γ-glutamyl cycle that operates in amino acid transport. The oxidized or disulfide form of glutathione is rapidly reduced by a specific NADPH-dependent glutathione reductase in brain; the reaction is essentially irreversible.

The worldly student should also be aware of a final neuropharmacological implication of glutamate in the Chinese-restaurant syndrome. Some individuals experience painful reactions after eating Chinese food. The syndrome has been traced to the large amount of monosodium glutamate used in some recipes.

The transamination of glutamate with oxaloacetate leads to aspartate. Although in some invertebrates this amino acid serves as an organic anion reservoir, in mammalian tissue its role appears to be metabolic. Like glutamate, aspartate has central excitatory activity on iontophoretic application, can serve as a readily available energy source, and can also trap ammonia to form asparagine. Aspartic acid is a requisite in de novo nucleotide synthesis and in the arginosuccinic acid synthetase reaction in brain.

In the presence of acetyl CoA and a membrane-bound enzyme from brain or spinal cord, aspartate forms $N$-acetylaspartate. This compound is of interest in that (1) next to glutamic acid it is the amino acid or derivative in highest concentration in the brain; (2) it appears to have a primarily neuronal localization; and (3) the hydrolysis of $N$-acetylaspartate is catalyzed by a relatively specific enzyme designated acylase II that resides primarily in glial tissue. Although in weanling animals the acetyl group can contribute to lipid biosynthesis in the brain, in adults the compound is believed to be somewhat inert metabolically.

The fact that endogenous $N$-acetylaspartate has been shown to be localized in cell cytoplasm, that it has an apparently long turnover time, and that as a dicarboxylic acid it contributes approximately 11 mEq of anion/kg of brain, raises the possibility that acetylaspartate functions solely as an anion to help defray the so-called "anion deficit" that exists. Another possible function relates to the suggestion that $N$-acetylaspartyl peptides may be involved in behavioral changes. Specifically, $N$-acetylaspartyl glutamate, which when applied iontophoretically excites the pyriform cortex, has been implicated as the neurotransmitter in the lateral olfactory tract.

Arising from the metabolism of the essential amino acid methionine are cysteic acid and taurine. This pair is reminiscent electrophysiologically of the glutamate-GABA duo in that the first member of the pair is excitatory and the second is inhibitory.

A rather puzzling situation exists with respect to urea in the brain.

Arginosuccinate synthetase, the arginosuccinate-splitting enzyme, and arginase have been found in the brain. However, attempts to find carbamyl phosphate synthetase and ornithine transcarbamylase have been negative. It now appears that via the recently discovered enzyme, nitric oxide synthase, arginine produces both nitric oxide and citrulline. Nitric oxide is an unusual second messenger whose major function to date is to raise cGMP levels.

It is interesting to look at the three essential aromatic amino acids—phenylalanine, tryptophan, and histidine—as a group since (1) they all are associated with congenital errors of metabolism that produce mental retardation; and (2) they all give rise to neuroactive amines. In the case of tyrosine (derived from phenylalanine in the liver or from the diet) and tryptophan, the metabolic pathways are strikingly similar since decarboxylation produces pressor agents (tyramine, tryptamine), whereas oxidation prior to decarboxylation yields neurotransmitters (dopamine, norepinephrine, epinephrine, and serotonin). With histidine, decarboxylation also gives rise to a vasoactive substance (histamine). Two histidine peptides, homocarnosine (γ-aminobutyrylhistidine) and homoanserine (γ-aminobutyryl-1-methylhistidine), are present only in brain. Carnosine (β-alanylhistidine), a major constituent of muscle, is found in high concentrations in the olfactory bulb and disappears after deafferentation. Also found in the olfactory bulb are carnosine synthetase, carnosinase, and a specific olfactory marker protein. The function of carnosine and of the marker protein is obscure at present.

In this chapter on the biochemistry of the central nervous system, no attempt has been made to discuss the two dozen or more genetic abnormalities that are associated with mental retardation; those that are noted are mentioned only because they were associated with compounds that were discussed for other reasons. Aberrant amino acid, carbohydrate, and lipid metabolism may all produce mental deficiencies. Rather than illuminating a specific reaction that is vital to normal mental development, these genetic blocks dramatically point out the necessity of totally integrated metabolism. Table 4-2 lists some genetic abnormalities that are associated with cerebral impairment.

No discussion of nucleic acids and proteins has been presented in

TABLE 4-2. Hereditary Diseases Associated With Cerebral Impairment

| Disorder | Defect |
|---|---|
| (A) AMINO ACID METABOLISM | |
| Arginosuccinic aciduria | Arginosuccinase |
| Citrullinemia | Arginosuccinic acid synthetase |
| Cystathionuria | Cystathionine-cleaving enzyme |
| Hartnup disease | Tryptophan transport |
| Histidinemia | Histidase |
| Homocystinuria | Cystathionine synthetase |
| Hydroxyprolinemia | Hydroxyproline oxidase |
| Hyperammonemia | Ornithine transcarbamylase |
| Hyperprolinemia | Proline oxidase |
| Maple syrup urine disease | Valine, leucine, and isoleucine decarboxylation |
| Phenylketonuria | Phenylalanine hydroxylase |
| (B) LIPID METABOLISM | |
| Abetalipoproteinemia (acanthocytosis) | β-lipoproteins |
| Cerebrotendonous xanthomatosis | Cholesterol |
| Gaucher's disease | Cerebrosides |
| Juvenile amaurotic idiocy | Gangliosides (?) |
| Krabbe's globoid dystrophy | Cerebrosides |
| Kuf's disease | Gangliosides (?) |
| Metachromatic leukodystrophy | Sulfatides |
| Niemann-Pick disease | Gangliosides and sphingomyelins |
| Refsum's disease | 3, 7, 11, 15-Tetramethylhexa-decanoic acid |
| Tay-Sachs disease | Gangliosides |
| (C) CARBOHYDRATE METABOLISM | |
| Galactosemia | Galactose-1-phosphate uridyl transferase |

*continued*

TABLE 4-2. *continued*

| Disorder | Defect |
|---|---|
| Glycogen storage disease (Type 2) | α-Glucosidase |
| Hurler's disease | Chondroitin sulfuric acid β, gangliosides |
| Unverricht's myoclonus epilepsy | Polysaccharides (?) |
| Lafora's disease | Polyglucosan |
| (D) MISCELLANEOUS | |
| Cretinism | Thyroid hormone |
| Hallevorden-Spaatz disease | Iron deposition in basal ganglia |
| Intermittent acute porphyria | δ-Aminolevulinic acid |
| Subacute necrotizing encephalomyelopathy (Leigh's disease) | Thiamin triphosphate |
| Lesch-Nyhan syndrome | Hypoxanthine-guanine Phosphoribosyl transferase |
| Methylmalonic acidemia | Methylmalonyl CoA mutase |
| Wilson's disease | Ceruloplasmin |

this chapter since the synthetic and catabolic pathways of these macromolecules in the brain do not appear to be basically different enough from those in other tissues so that they do not fit into the scheme as shown in Figure 4-1. This omission is, of course, not meant to imply that either nucleic acids or proteins of the brain are identical with their extraneural counterparts. Several soluble proteins have been isolated which immunologically represent brain-specific proteins. The two most prominently studied proteins are the S-100 and the 14-3-2, the former with a glial localization (function unknown); the latter, with an isozyme that is found in neurons only, has been shown to be enolase.

This chapter attempts to explain the functional uniqueness of the brain in terms of biochemistry. To this end, although we have answered the question posed at the beginning of this chapter, (what biochemical substrates or reactions distinguish the brain from other tissue?), major items remain to be discussed. These are the neurotransmitters and the enzymes, receptors, and other proteins involved in their function.

The fundamental specialization of the brain, as is true of other organs, is morphological with its basis in genetic transcription. Given the current intense activity in recombinant DNA techniques, it is perhaps not too farfetched to imagine gene replacement therapy not only as a cure of the myriad genetic deficiency diseases such as the cerebral lipidoses, but even as the ultimate therapy for diseases such as convulsive disorders, which are now merely controlled by drugs.

### SELECTED REFERENCES

Garthwaite, J. (1991). Glutamate, nitric oxide, and cell-cell signaling in the nervous system. *TINS 14*, 60.

Hirata, F. and J. Axelrod (1980). Phospholipid methylation and biological signal transmission. *Science 209*, 1082.

Ledeen, R. W., R. K. Yu, M. W. Rappaport, and K. Suzuki (1984). Ganglioside Structure, Function, and Biomedical Potential, AEMB Vol. 174. Plenum, New York.

McIlwain, H. and H. S. Bachelard (1985). *Biochemistry and the Central Nervous System*. Churchill, London.

Margolis, F. (1980). Carnosine: An olfactory neuropeptide. In *The Role of Peptides in Nuronal Function* (J. L. Barker and T. G. Smith, Jr., eds.), p. 546. Marcel Dekker, New York.

Meister, A. and M. E. Anderson (1983). Glutathione. *Ann. Rev. Biochem. 52*, 711.

Nadler, J. V. and J. R. Cooper (1972). Metabolism of the aspartyl moiety of *N*-acetyl-1-aspartic acid in the rat brain. *J. Neurochem. 19*, 2091.

Siegel, G. J., B. W. Agranoff, R. W. Albers, and P. Molinoff (1989). Basic Neurochemistry, 4th ed. Raven Press, N.Y.

Sokoloff, L. (1984). Localization of functional activity in the central nervous system by metabolic probes. In IUPHAR *Proceeding*, London, 9.

Stanbury, J. B., J. B.Wyngaarden, and D. S. Fredrickson (1983). *The Metabolic Basis of Inherited Disease*. McGraw-Hill, New York.

# 5 | Receptors

The concept that most drugs, hormones, and neurotransmitters produce their biological effects by interacting with receptor substances in cells was introduced by Langley in 1905. It was based on his observations of the extraordinary potency and specificity with which some drugs mimicked a biological response (agonists) while others prevented it (antagonists). Later, Hill, Gaddum, and Clark independently described the quantitative characteristics of competitive antagonism between agonists and antagonists in combining with specific receptors in intact preparations. This receptor concept has been substantiated in the past several years by the actual isolation of macromolecular substances that fit all the criteria of being receptors. To date, although they have not all been cloned, receptors have been identified for all the proven neurotransmitters as well as for histamine, opioid peptides, neurotensin, VIP, bradykinin, CCK, somatostatin, Substance P, insulin, angiotensin II, gonadotropin, glucagon, prolactin, and TSH. In addition, as noted in Table 5-1, multiple receptors have been shown to exist for all the biogenic amines, ACh, GABA, histamine, opiates, and the amino acid transmitters. According to a literature survey, multiple receptors appear to metastasize at an uncontrollable rate, but this should be viewed skeptically until a physiological response to the ligand has been shown or a specific gene has been cloned and expressed. Some of the receptor subtypes have only been identified by binding techniques (see below) that can lead to erroneous conclusions. All the receptors for neurotransmitters and peptide hormones that have been studied, regardless of whether they have been isolated, are localized on the surface of the cell; among other receptors, only those for steroid and thyroid hormones are apparently intracellular.

In earlier days, after the discovery that the action of physostigmine (eserine) resulted from its anticholinesterase activity, it was assumed that most drugs probably acted by inhibiting an enzyme. However, it now appears that with few exceptions the mechanism of action of

TABLE 5-1. Classification of Neuronal Receptors

| Subtype | Characteristics |
|---------|-----------------|

**ADRENERGIC**

$\alpha_1$

Postsynaptic: contracts smooth muscle, localized in heart, vas deferens and brain: phenylephrine is moderately selective agonist; prazosin is selective antagonist. Linked to hydrolysis of phosphatidylinositide.

$\alpha_2$

This receptor is now at least two, variously referred to as $\alpha_{2A}$ and $\alpha_{2B}$, $R_i$ and $R_s$ or $\alpha_2$-C10 and $\alpha_2$-C4. Guanfacine and UK14304, selective $\alpha_{2A}$ agonists, improve memory in aged monkeys without producing sedation or hypotension. In contrast, clonidine and BHT920 produce hypotension and sedation with a greater selectivity for the $\alpha_{2B}$ subtype. Both subtypes are blocked by idazoxan with equal high affinity while rauwolscine has a higher affinity for $\alpha_{2B}$.

$\beta_1$

Activates adenylyl cyclase. Produces cardiac stimulation and lipolysis in fat cells. Dobutamine is selective agonist; metoprolol is selective antagonist.

$\beta_2$

Activates adenylyl cyclase. Relaxes bronchial smooth muscles. Terbutaline and albuterol are selective agonists. IPS339 is selective antagonist.

**DOPAMINERGIC**

$D_1$

Stimulates adenylyl cyclase: SKF38393 and dihydroxidine are selective agonists; SCH23390 is an antagonist: present in retina and pyramidal cells of olfactory tubercle.

$D_2$

Inhibits adenylyl cyclase: quinperole and PHN0434 are agonists. (-)Sulpiride, domperidone, and eticlopride are selective antagonists; when localized on terminals and cell

*continued*

TABLE 5-1. *continued*

| Subtype | Characteristics |
| --- | --- |

bodies of nigrostriatal and mesolimbic dopamine, neurons are classified as autoreceptors. Recently a $D_2$ subtype has been cloned.

SEROTINERGIC

5-HT$_{1A}$

Preferentially localized in raphe nuclei and hippocampus; opens $K^+$ channels. Buspirone and 8-OH-DPAT are selective agonists and spiperone is an antagonist.

5-HT$_{1B}$

In high concentrations in globus pallidus and substantia nigra. High affinity for RU24969.

5-HT$_{1C}$

In choroid plexus, increased $Cl^-$ conductance, high affinity for LSD and methysergide. Recently cloned and sequenced.

5-HT$_{1D}$

High density in basal ganglia, high affinity for 5-methoxytryptamine as agonist and metergoline as antagonist.

5-HT$_2$

Highest level in cortex. Spiperone is selective antagonist. Depolarizes facial motor neurones and cortical pyramidal neurons. Coupled to phosphoinositide hydrolysis. High degree of homology with 5-HT$_{1C}$.

5-HT$_3$

May be a mixture of three subtypes, high density in peripheral nervous system and recently found in CNS. High affinity for zacopride as antagonist. Ligand-gated channel.

5-HT$_{1P}$

Found in gut, different susceptibility to pharmacological agents than other 5-HT subtypes.

*continued*

TABLE 5-1. *continued*

| Subtype | Characteristics |
|---|---|

**CHOLINERGIC**

**MUSCARINIC**

Currently five subtypes designated $M_1$–$M_5$ have been cloned. All are linked to G proteins and inhibited by quinuclidinyl benzilate (QNB). Pirenzepine is selective antagonist for $M_1$ sites and $M^cN$-A-343 is a moderately selective agonist. The $M_2$ receptor appears to be predominantly presynaptic. $M_1$, $M_3$ and $M_5$ activate phosphatidylinositide hydrolysis, $M_2$ and $M_4$ inhibit adenylyl cyclase. AF-DX 116 is a selective antagonist for the cardiac $M_2$ subtype.

**NICOTINIC**

Four subtypes recently described, based on pharmacology, cloning, and monoclonal antibody procedures. Neuromuscular blocking drugs, α-bungarotoxin and venom from *Naja naja siamensis* are specific antagonists at the neuromuscular junction. At autonomic ganglia, α-bungarotoxin binds but does not block transmission.

**OPIATE**

**MU (μ)**

Morphine, opiate alkaloids, B-endorphin, and enkephalins are agonists. Cyclic somatostatin and analogs are antagonists.

**DELTA (δ)**

Receptor for enkephalins, KI-176 is antagonist.

**KAPPA (κ)**

Dynorphin and U50488 are preferential agonists, norbinaltorphimine is selective antagonist.

**SIGMA (σ)**

May not be legitimate opiate receptor since PCP and haloperidol as well as N-allylnormetazocine are agonists and naloxone does not reverse agonist activity. An epsilon

*continued*

TABLE 5-1. *continued*

| Subtype | Characteristics |
| --- | --- |

(ε) receptor, activated by β-endorphin is found in vas deferens but not yet in brain.

GABAERGIC

GABA$_A$

Activated by muscinol, inhibited by bicuculline. Localized in hippocampus, striatum, and spinal cord. Increases chloride conductance. Two subtypes have been cloned with Type I in cerebellum. CL 218872 and β-CCM are selective agonists.

GABA$_B$

Primarily presynaptic localization. Baclofen is selective agonist. Phaclofen is an antagonist. May affect Ca and K channels through G protein.

Excitatory amino acids (glutamate and aspartate)

N-methyl-D-aspartate (NMDA)

This compound is the distinguishing agonist. This receptor is activated only at high frequency stimulation in hippocampal pyramidal cells. D-AP5 is selective antagonist. Localized in forebrain. Implicated in long-term potentiation, convulsive disorders, synaptic plasticity, and learning.

AMPA

This compound and quisqualate are selective agonists. Antagonist is CNQX. Activated by glutamate but not aspartate. Major source of EPSPs in the CNS. In high concentration in forebrain. Implicated in convulsive disorders.

KAINIC

This compound is the selective agonist. In high concentration in limbic system. No specific antagonist available but CNQX will inhibit. Physiological function of this receptor as defined by binding studies is still unclear.

Two new receptors have recently been identified. These are

*continued*

TABLE 5-1. *continued*

| Subtype | Characteristics |
|---------|-----------------|
| | L-AP4, which excites presynaptic glutamate autoreceptors, and APCD that is G-protein linked and coupled to phosphatidyl inositide hydrolysis. |
| HISTAMINERGIC | An increase in gastric acid secretion can result from attempting to unravel the electrophysiological effect of either stimulating or blocking the three identified histamine receptors, $H_1$, $H_2$ and $H_3$ in the CNS. The $H_1$ receptor is blocked by antihistamines, e.g., pyrilamine. Tiodimine or cimetidine will block $H_2$ receptors, and the $H_3$ receptor, an autoreceptor, is selectively antagonized by thioperamide. All receptors are linked to G proteins, but second messenger systems are controversial. |

SOURCE: References and personal communications: G. K. Aghajanian, A. Arnsten, S. K. Fisher, D. W. Gallager, J. Kebabian, H. Loh, J. V. Nadler, and E. J. Simon.

neuroactive drugs usually stems from their effect on specific receptors. Predictably, the current search for receptors is among the most intensively investigated areas in the neurosciences. This interest is not purely academic. The recent identification of adrenergic, dopaminergic, muscarinic, serotinergic, and histaminergic receptor subtypes has led to the synthesis of highly selective drugs that are considerably more specific than their prototypes which were developed after general screening for activity. And with advances in gene cloning and expression, more and more receptor subtypes are being identified, each presumably having its own function. What this indicates is that future drugs can be designed to fit a single receptor subtype, thus precluding what are now called the "side effects" of a nonspecific drug.

## DEFINITION

In this rapidly developing field, considerable confusion has arisen as to what functional characteristics are required of an isolated, ligand-binding molecule to qualify as a receptor. This confusion, a semantic problem, developed after the successful isolation of macromolecules that exhibit selective binding properties (see below), which made it mandatory to determine whether this material comprised both the binding element and the element that initiated a biological response, or merely the former. Some investigators use the term "receptor" only when both the binding and signal generation occur; they use the term "acceptor" if no biological response has been demonstrated. Others are content to ignore the bifunctional aspect and use "receptor" without specifications. In this chapter, we will define a *receptor* as the binding or recognition component and refer to the element involved in the biological response as the *effector*, without specifying whether the receptor and effector reside in the same or separate units. The criteria for receptors will be dealt with shortly; the biological response that is generated by the effector obviously has a wider range of complexity, from a simple one-step coupling to an unknown number of steps (Fig. 5-1).

## ASSAYS

Basically, there are two ways to study the interaction of neurotransmitters, hormones, or drugs with cells. The first procedure (and until recently the only one) is to determine the biological response of an intact isolated organ, such as the guinea pig ileum, to applied agonists or antagonists. The disadvantage of this procedure is that one is obviously enmeshed in a cascade of events beginning with transport, distribution, and metabolism of the agent before it even interacts with a receptor, ranging through an unknown multiplicity of steps before the final biological response of the tissue is measured. Thus, although studies with agonists may be interpretable, it is not difficult to envision problems when antagonists are employed, since these compounds may be competing at a different level than receptor

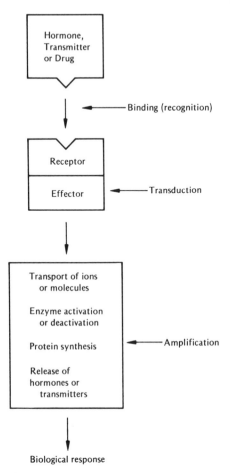

FIGURE 5-1. Schematic model of ligand-receptor interaction.

binding. Despite the not unusual problem of a nonlinear relationship between receptor occupancy and biological response, this approach has yielded a considerable amount of information.

The second approach to studying receptors is by measuring ligand binding to a homogenate or slice preparation. This technique became feasible with the development of ligands of a high specific radioactivity and a high affinity for the receptor. Here the direct method is to incubate labeled agonist or antagonist with the receptor preparation and then separate the receptor-ligand complex from free ligand by centrifugation, filtration, or precipitation. The indirect technique is to use equilibrium dialysis where the receptor-ligand complex is determined by subtracting the ligand concentration in the bath from that in the dialysis sac.

Recently, a third, electrophysiological approach to identifying receptors has emerged. Intracellular stimulation and recording via microelectrodes inserted into a brain slice or neurons in culture, combined with the application of receptor agonists and antagonists, can functionally identify receptor subtypes.

Though not always appreciated, the advantage of using isolated tissues is that both the efficacy and the functional activity of an agonist is assessed, in contrast to binding procedures using broken cell preparations where only affinity or a biochemical sequella of binding can be appraised. Ideally, both techniques should be used, but, alas, this is rarely done. It should be noted in passing that efficacy and affinity are independent. To date it appears that the drugs that exhibit a high affinity but low efficacy have a more efficient coupling to the effector than the reverse situation; therefore, these are the most potent and selective agents. For detailed discussion of the above, the review by Kenakin is recommended.

IDENTIFICATION

In the midst of an intensive drive to isolate and characterize receptors, some zealous investigators have lost sight of basic tenets that must be satisfied before it is certain that a receptor has indeed been isolated. Thus, on occasion, enzymes, transport proteins, and merely extraneous lipoproteins or proteolipids that exhibit binding properties have been mistakenly identified as receptors. Authentic receptors should have the following properties:

1. *Saturability.* The great majority of receptors are on the surface of a cell. Since there are a finite number of receptors per cell, it follows that a dose-response curve for the binding

of a ligand should reveal saturability. In general, specific receptor binding is characterized by a high affinity and low capacity, whereas nonspecific binding usually exhibits high capacity and low-affinity binding that is virtually nonsaturable.

2. *Specificity*. This is one of the most difficult and important criteria to fulfill because of the enormous mass of nonspecific binding sites compared to receptor sites in tissue. For this reason, in binding assays it is necessary to explore the displacement of the labeled ligand with a series of agonists and antagonists that represent both the same and different chemical structures and pharmacological properties as the binding ligand. One should also be aware of the avidity with which inert surfaces bind ligands. For example, Substance P binds tenaciously to glass, and insulin can bind to talcum powder in the nanomolar range. With agents that exist as optical isomers, it is of obvious importance to show that the binding of the ligand is stereospecific. Even here problems arise. With opiates it is the levorotatory enantiomorph that exerts the dominant pharmacological effect. Snyder, for example, has found glass fiber filters that selectively bind the levorotatory isomer. Specificity obviously means that one should find receptors only in cells known to respond to the particular transmitter or hormone under examination. Further, it is a truism that a correlation should be evident between the binding affinity of a series of ligands and the biological response produced by this series. This correlation, the *sine qua non* for receptor identification, is unfortunately a criterion that is not often investigated.

3. *Reversibility*. Since transmitters, hormones, and most drugs act in a reversible manner, it follows that the binding of these agents to receptors should be reversible. It is also to be expected that the ligand of a reversible receptor should be not only dissociable but recoverable in its natural (i.e., nonmetabolized) form. This last dictum distinguishes receptor-agonist interactions but not receptor-antagonist binding from enzyme-substrate reactions.

4. *Restoration of function on reconstitution.* Following the isolation and identification of the components of the receptor system, to put them back together again is the goal of all receptorologists. Although a difficult task, this has been accomplished with the nicotinic ACh receptor and the peripheral β-adrenergic receptor.

5. *Molecular neurobiology.* The ultimate identification is to isolate the gene for a receptor, express it, and demonstrate the exact similarity of the cloned receptor to the natural one.

Finally, it is important to recognize that the quantitative and spatial measurement of receptors utilizing autoradiography is also a key problem. Where labeled ligands are employed to map receptors in brain via light microscopy, a mismatch is often encountered. Reasons offered for this problem are (1) except for autoreceptors, neurotransmitters and receptors are located in different neurons; (2) in addition to the synapse, receptors and transmitters are found throughout the neuron and in glial cells; (3) ligands may label only a subunit of a receptor or only one state of the receptor; (4) autoradiography is subject to quenching. With immunohistochemical peptide mapping, a possible problem is the recognition by the antibody of a prohormone or, alternatively, a fragment of a peptide hormone in addition to the well-recognized problem of crossreactivity of the antibody with a physiologically different peptide.

## KINETICS AND THEORIES OF DRUG ACTION

From the law of mass action, the binding of a ligand (L) to its receptor (R) leads to the equation

$$L + R \underset{k_2}{\overset{k_1}{\rightleftharpoons}} LR$$

$$\text{thus } K_D = \frac{k_2}{k_1} = \frac{[L][R]}{[LR]}$$

where $k_1$ = association rate constant
$k_2$ = dissociation rate constant

[L] = concentration of free ligand
[R] = concentration of free receptors
[LR] = concentration of occupied binding sites
$K_d$ = dissociation equilibrium constant

Since the total number of receptors = $[R_t] = [R] + [LR]$

$$[R] = [R_t] - [LR]$$

therefore $K_d = \dfrac{[L]([R_t] - [LR])}{[LR]}$

and $[LR] = \dfrac{[L][R_t]}{[L] + K_d}$

Since the fraction of receptors occupied (r) = $\dfrac{bound}{total} = \dfrac{[LR]}{[R_t]}$

therefore $r = \dfrac{[L]}{[L] + K_d}$

If experiments are performed in which the receptor concentration is kept constant and the ligand concentration is varied, then a plot of r versus [L] will produce a rectangular hyperbole, the usual Langmuir adsorption isotherm. Here r approaches the saturation value equal to the number of binding sites per molecule of ligand. If r is plotted against log [L], a sigmoid curve will result; log [L] at half saturation will give log $K_d$ on the horizontal axis (Fig. 5-2).

This equation can be rearranged as follows:

$$K_d r + r[L] = [L]$$

$$\frac{r}{[L]} = \frac{-r}{K_d} + \frac{I}{K_d}$$

Now if $\dfrac{r}{[L]}$ is plotted against r, a straight line will result (assuming only one set of binding sites) with two intercepts, the one on the x axis giving the number of binding sites per molecule and the y intercept yielding $I/K_d$. This type of plot is the Scatchard plot (more correctly, Rosenthal plot) widely used in studying receptor-ligand

FIGURE 5-2. Ligand–receptor interactions plotted in two ways where [L] is the concentration of ligand (drug, hormone, or neurotransmitter) and r is the biological response, proportional to the moles ligand bound per mole of protein. The number of binding sites per molecule of protein is designated by n.

interactions (Fig. 5-3). Among the pitfalls that are encountered in a Scatchard analysis is the problem that the system is not in true equilibrium.

Another useful representation that can be derived from the general equation is the Hill plot (Fig. 5-4).

If $\log \dfrac{E}{E_{max} - E}$ is plotted versus $\log [L]$ when E is the effect produced and $E_{max}$ is the maximum effect, then the slope, indicative of the nature of the binding, gives a Hill coefficient of unity in cases where $E/E_{max}$ is proportional to the fraction of total number of sites occupied (r). In many situations, the slope turns out to be a non-integer number different from unity. This finding indicates that cooperativity may be involved in the binding of the ligand to the receptor. Cooperativity is the phenomenon where by the ligand binding at one site influences, either positively or negatively, the binding of the ligand at sites on other subunits of the oligomeric protein. This idea, originally suggested in 1965 by Monod, Wyman, and Changeux to explain allosteric enzyme properties, currently offers the most attractive hypothesis for studying reactions of receptors with hormones, transmitters, or drugs. We will utilize this

FIGURE 5-3. Scatchard plots of the binding of a ligand to a receptor. In (a) only one binding affinity occurs, but in (b) both a high- and low-affinity binding sites are suggested.

hypothesis later in an attempt to explain drug action, including the problem of efficacy (intrinsic activity), spare receptors, and desensitization.

Another useful analysis when competitive inhibitors of the receptor binding ligand are studied is the equation derived by Cheng and Prusoff in their kinetic analysis of enzyme inhibitors:

$$K_i = \frac{I_{50}}{1 + (L)/K_d}$$

FIGURE 5-4. Hill plots for receptor-ligand binding: (a) noncooperative binding; (b) idealized plot of cooperative binding with four sites; (c) a typical Hill plot of multiple binding sites but less than four. (Modified after Van Holde, *Physical Biochemistry*, Englewood Cliffs, N.J.: Prentice-Hall, Inc., 1971, p. 63) where $K_i$ is the equilibrium dissociation constant of the competitive inhibitor, and $I_{50}$ is the concentration of the inhibitor producing 50% inhibition at the concentration of the labeled ligand that is used in the study.

Clark produced the first model of drug-receptor action, known as the occupation theory, in which the response of a drug was held to be directly proportional to the fraction of receptors that were occupied by the drug. Here, as mentioned earlier, one should find the usual Langmuir absorption isotherm. But instead of the expected rectangular hyperbole when drug concentration was plotted against the drug bound, in most cases a sigmoid curve resulted. A second problem with the occupancy theory is that in many instances only a small fraction of the total receptors available are occupied, and yet a maximum response is obtained. These additional receptors, which may represent as much as 95–99% of the total, are referred to as spare receptors. The occupancy theory is further complicated when the activity of a series of related agents is explored and the biological response varies from maximum to zero, even though the agents all occupy the receptor. In other words, these agents could be full agonists, partial agonists that gave less than a maximal response, and antagonists whose occupancy produced no response. This phenomenon is referred to as efficacy or intrinsic activity of a drug and is obviously not directly related to the binding affinity of the drug. A fourth characteristic of drug-receptor interaction that is sometimes observed is desensitization, which is defined as the lack or decline of a response in a previously activated receptor.

These problems—the sigmoidal dose-response curve, some anomalous effects with antagonists that spare receptors might account for, efficacy, and desensitization—can all be comfortably fitted into a two-state model of a receptor analogous to the allosteric model of Monod, Wyman, and Changeux, proposed independently by Changeux and by Karlin in 1967.

According to the two-state model, receptors exist in an active (R) and an inactive (T) state, and each is capable of combining with the drug (A):

$$A + R \underset{K_{AR}}{\rightleftharpoons} AR$$
$$\updownarrow \quad K_{AT} \quad \updownarrow$$
$$A + T \underset{}{\rightleftharpoons} AT$$

Here an agonist prefers the R (active configuration of the receptor), and the efficacy (i.e., intrinsic action) of the drug will be determined by the ratio of its affinity for the two states. In contrast, competitive antagonists prefer the T form of the receptor and will shift the equilibrium to AT. The sigmoid relationship between the fraction of receptors activated and the drug concentration (i.e., cooperativity) can be explained by this model with its equilibrium between R and T, if one designates T as a subunit of R that binds A and thereby influences the further binding of A to R. Cooperativity can also explain anomalous effects of antagonists whenever the effect of an antagonist persists even in the presence of a high concentration of agonist. Here it could be postulated that by tightly binding to one conformational state of the receptor, the antagonist inhibits the binding of the agonist. One might even use this two-state model to account for desensitization where T would be a receptor that has been desensitized perhaps by a local change in the ionic environment. The ionic environment, in fact, may be one of the factors that dictate the two conformational states of a receptor. Other possibilities include polymerization (clustering) of the subunits, depolymerization, or phosphorylation. It should be emphasized that this model is conjectural, subject to modifications as the need arises.

When one considers the finite number of receptors per cell and the fact that virtually all receptors are found on the plasma membrane, it is not surprising that progress in this area has been slow and laborious. It has been calculated that, assuming one binding site and an average molecular weight of 200,000 for a receptor, complete purification of a receptor protein would require about a 25,000-fold enrichment. The extraordinary density of ACh receptors in electric tissue has made this preparation so popular a choice that considerable information is now available on this cholinergic receptor. Two snake neurotoxins, *Naja siamensis*, and α-bungarotoxin, which specifically bind nicotinic cholinergic receptors, have been the key agents that have helped in isolating this receptor.

Also to be considered is the relationship between receptors and effectors as they interact in the fluid mosaic membrane. As envisaged by Singer and Nicolson, membranes are composed of a fluid lipid bilayer that contains globular protein. Some of these proteins extend through the membrane, and others are partially embedded in or on the surface. The hydrophilic ends of the protein protrude from the membrane, while the hydrophobic ends are localized in the lipid bilayer. Some of the proteins are immobilized, but others, floating in an oily sea of lipids, are capable of free movement. In this concept of membrane fluidity, the receptor protein would be on the surface of the membrane and the effector within the membrane. Although the ratio of receptors to effectors may in some cases be unity (thus explaining instances in which the occupancy theory is satisfied), it may also be greater than one. Consequently, in a situation where multiple hormones activate a response (e.g., there is only one form of adenylyl cyclase in a fat cell, but it may be activated by epinephrine, glucagon, ACTH, or histamine), it would be concluded that an excess of receptors over effectors is present. This model would also explain spare receptors and is exemplified by the fact that only 3% of insulin receptors need to be occupied in order to catalyze glucose oxidation in adipocytes. With the possibility of easy lateral movement of effector in the membrane, it is also understandable why one receptor may activate several types of effector. Membrane fluidity will account for the observation that hormones can influence the state of aggregation of the receptor, thus giving rise to either positive or negative cooperativity as determined in kinetic studies of binding. Although direct evidence of the interaction and migration of receptors and effectors is difficult to obtain (but see the review article by Poo), current information is easily accommodated by the fluid mosaic membrane model.

A recently (1988) emerging view of the structure and activity of neurotransmitter receptors, as reviewed by Strange, is that they can be divided into two classes, fast and slow. Class I (fast) receptors are directly linked to an ion channel and mediate millisecond responses when activated by a transmitter. Structurally, this ligand-gated ion channel family appears to contain four hydropathic membrane-spanning segments. Examples of Class I receptors are the nicotinic ACh receptor, the $GABA_A$ receptor and the glycine receptor. (The glutamate and $5HT_3$ receptors probably will be shown to belong to this class as they are also subject to regulation by phosphorylation.) In contrast, Class II (slow) receptors mediate slower responses that are generally modulatory, either dampening or enhancing the signal that acts on Class I receptors. Class II receptors are coupled to G proteins (discussed below), which in turn may be directly coupled to ion channels or linked to second messenger systems. Structurally, all known Class II receptors contain seven hydrophobic transmembrane domains that are linked by hydrophilic groups. Examples of Class II receptors are adrenergic (all subtypes), muscarinic cholinergic ($M_1$ and $M_2$), dopaminergic ($D_1$ and $D_2$), serotonergic ($5HT_{1A}$, $5HT_2$), and opiate ($\delta$ and $\mu$). It is likely that most neuropeptide receptors are also of the slow, Class II type. It is also likely that presynaptic receptors which, when activated, alter the amount of transmitter released are of the Class II group. The structure of Class II receptors as exemplified by the $\beta_2$-adrenergic receptor is illustrated in Fig. 5-5.

It was noted above that Class II receptors are linked to G proteins. These transducing proteins are a family of guanine nucleotide binding proteins with a heterotrimer structure consisting of $\alpha$, $\beta$ and $\gamma$ subunits. These regulatory proteins are activated by the exchange of GTP for GDP. At last count, nine different G proteins had been identified on the basis of possessing different $\alpha$ subunits. These proteins can be roughly classified into four groups: $G_s$ stimulates the adenylyl cyclase second messenger system; $G_i$ inhibits this system; $G_t$, designating transducin, mediates rhodopsin activation of cyclic GMP phosphodiesterase; and $G_0$ comprises a largely undefined group of G proteins, one of which may be coupled to the phosphoinositide second messenger system. (Second messenger systems are dealt with in Chapter 6). An observation that has helped assign G proteins a role in signal transduction is that bacterial toxins catalyze the NAD-dependent ADP ribosylation of the $\alpha$ subunit of

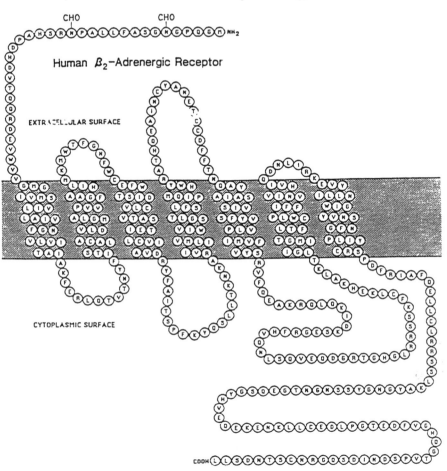

FIGURE 5-5. Topographical representation of the primary sequence of the human β₂-adrenergic receptor. The receptor protein is illustrated as possessing seven hydrophobic regions each capable of spanning the plasma membrane, thus creating extracellular as well as intracellular loops as well as an extracellular amino terminus and a cytoplasmic carboxyl terminal region. (From Lefkowitz et al., 1989)

many of the G proteins and inhibit their activity. Cholera toxin ribosylates $G_s$ and $G_t$, whereas $G_i$ and $G_0$ are substrates for pertussis toxin. Some G proteins (unclassified) are resistant to both toxins.

Currently, the molecular mechanism involving G proteins in signal transmission is conceived as follows: The ternary complex following the binding of a ligand to a receptor and association with a G protein containing GDP promotes the dissociation of GDP and the rapid association of GTP which is present in the microenvironment. The binding of GTP to the $\alpha$ subunit of the G protein causes a dissociation of the $\beta\gamma$ subunits and also releases the receptor from the complex, allowing it to recycle and activate further G proteins. The GTP-$\alpha$ subunit can now interact with the appropriate effector to produce the biological response. Signal transduction is terminated by the hydrolysis of GTP, which is catalyzed by the GTPase activity of the $\alpha$ subunit, a reassociation of the $\alpha$ subunit with the B$\gamma$, and the return of the G protein-GDP complex. The binding and dissociation of $Mg^{++}$ with these complexes is thought to be a determining factor in the kinetics of this cycle. It has not been determined whether each of the multitude of G proteins acts on a specific receptor or whether they all interact with families of receptors, and whether specificity is conferred by kinetics or by discrete intracellular localizations. Effectors that are coupled to G proteins currently include adenyl and guanylcyclase, phospholipase C, phospholipase $A_2$, phosphodiesterase and both $K^+$ and $Ca^{2+}$ channels.

Continued administration of agonists can cause many receptors to desensitize and to down-regulate. Desensitization, occurring on a time scale of minutes, is reflected by a decreased response of the cell and is often related to receptor phosphorylation. Down-regulation of receptors is observed on a time scale of hours after prolonged agonist exposure when receptors are internalized and degraded.

Many neuroactive agents act on receptors that are coupled to the adenylyl cyclase system (see Fig. 5-6). The components of this complex are the receptor, the catalytic portion of adenylyl cyclase that converts ATP to cAMP, and two G proteins referred to as $N_s$ and $N_i$ that are coupled to the catalytic unit of the enzyme. When the receptor is stimulated (e.g., a $\beta_2$-adrenergic receptor), the coupling protein is $N_s$. Conversely, when the receptor is inhibited (e.g., an $\alpha_2$-adrenergic receptor), $N_i$ is the coupling protein. Examples of adrenergic receptors whose activity is linked to the adenylate cyclase

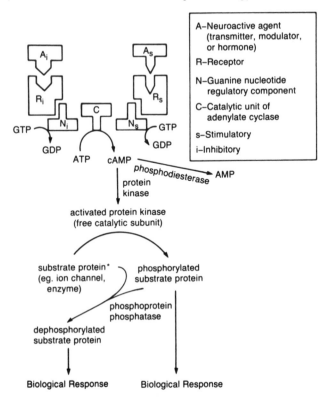

FIGURE 5-6. Components of a receptor-activated, cyclic nucleotide-linked system. (After Lefkowitz et al., 1984)

complex are the receptors $\alpha_2$, $\beta_1$, and $\beta_2$ (but not $\alpha_1$, which may be coupled to phosphatidyl inositide hydrolysis).

Because of space limitations, this chapter has not covered such topics as the factors regulating synthesis and degradation of receptors, complex kinetics, isolation techniques, or the chemical composition of these macromolecules. Students who are interested in these subjects may consult a number of recent books and reviews listed in the selected references.

SELECTED REFERENCES

Ariens, E. J. and A. J. Beld (1977). The receptor concept in evolution. *Biochem. Pharmacol. 26*, 913.

Bonner, T. I. (1989). The molecular basis of muscarinic receptor diversity. *Trends Neurosci. 12*, 148.

Changeux, J. P., J. Thiery, Y. Tung, and C. Kittel (1976). On the cooperativity of biological membranes. *Proc. Nat. Acad. Sci. U.S.A. 57*, 335.

Cheng, Y.-C. and W. H. Prusoff (1973). Relationship between the inhibition constant ($K_i$) and the concentration of inhibitor which causes 50 percent inhibition ($I_{50}$) of an enzymatic reaction. *Biochem. Pharmacol. 22*, 3099.

Clark, A. J. (1937). General pharmacology. In *Heffter's Handbuch d-exp. Pharmacol. Erg. band 4*. Springer, Berlin.

Freissmuth M., P. J. Casey, and A. G. Gilman (1989). G proteins control diverse pathways of transmembrane signaling. *FASEB J. 3*, 2125.

Goyal, R. K. (1989). Muscarinic receptor subtypes. *N. Engl. J. Med. 321*, 1022.

Kahn, C. R. (1976). Membrane receptors for hormones and neurotransmitters. *J. Cell Biol. 70*, 261.

Karlin, A. (1967). On the application of a plausible model of allosteric proteins to the receptor for acetylcholine. *J. Theor. Biol. 16*, 306.

Kenakin, T. P. (1984). The classification of drugs and drug receptors in isolated tissues. *Pharmacol. Rev. 36*, 165.

Kito, S., T. Segawa, K. Kuriyama, H. I. Yamamura, and R. W. Olsen, eds. (1984). *Neurotransmitter Receptors*. Plenum Press, New York.

Laduron, P. M. (1984). Criteria for receptor sites in binding studies. *Biochem. Pharmacol. 33*, 833.

Lefkowitz, R. J., M. G. Caron, and G. L. Stiles (1984). Mechanisms of membrane-receptor regulation. *N. Engl. J. Med. 310*, 1570.

Lefkowitz, R. J., B. K. Kobilka, and M. G. Caron (1989). The new biology of drug receptors. *Biochem. Pharmacol. 38*, 2941.

Neer, E. J. and D. E. Clapham (1988). Roles of G protein subunits in transmembrane signalling. *Nature 333*, 129.

Peroutka, S. J. (1990). 5-hydroxytryptamine receptor subtypes. *Pharmacol. Toxicol. 67*, 373.

Poo, M. (1985). Mobility and localization of proteins in excitable membranes. *Ann. Rev. Neurosci. 8*, 369.

Rakic, P., P. S. Goldman-Rakic, and D. Gallager (1988). Quantitative autoradiography of major neurotransmitters in monkey striate and extrastriate cortex. *J. Neurosci. 8*, 3670.

Ross, E. M. and A. G. Gilman (1980). Biochemical properties of hormone-sensitive adenylate cyclase. *Ann. Rev. Biochem.* *49*, 533.

Singer, S. J. and G. L. Nicolson (1972). The fluid mosaic model of the structure of cell membranes. *Science 175*, 720.

Strader, C. D., I. S. Sigal, and R. F. Dixon (1989). Structural basis of B-adrenergic receptor function. *FASEB J. 3*, 1825.

Strange, P. G. (1988). The structure and mechanism of neurotransmitter receptors. *Biochem J. 249*, 309.

Strange, P. G. (1991). Interesting times for dopamine receptors. *Trends Neurosci. 14*: 43.

Tallarida, R. J. (1988). Pharmacologic methods for identification of receptors. *Life Sci. 43*, 2169.

# 6 | Modulation of Synaptic Transmission

Contrary to what one might assume, the more we learn about intercellular communication in the nervous system, the more complicated the situation appears. Up to about the mid-1970s, synaptologists smugly focused on a straight point-to-point transmission where a presynaptically released transmitter impinged on a postsynaptic cell. Gradually, situations emerged where previously identified neurotransmitters were observed as not acting in this fashion but rather "modulating" transmission. These departures from the previous norm and the continuing discovery of peptides and small molecules such as adenosine, which exhibited neuroactivity but which did not appear to be transmitters in the classical sense, supported the broader view of modulation of synaptic transmission. In retrospect, it is a concept that should have been apparent early on, since it imparts to neural circuitry an extraordinary degree of flexibility that is necessary in considering mechanisms to account for behavioral changes. It should also be noted that modulation is not a neurophysiological property that is seen only in higher forms: Birds do it, bees do it, even educated fleas do it.

## DEFINITIONS

Primarily via the activation of a receptor, synaptic transmission may be modulated either presynaptically or postsynaptically. With presynaptic modulation, regardless of the mechanism, the ultimate effect is a change in the amount of transmitter that is released. With postsynaptic modulation, the ultimate effect is a change in the firing pattern of the postsynaptic neuron or in the activity of a postsynaptic tissue (e.g., blood vessel, gland, muscle).

Because some confusion has arisen on the correct nomenclature of pre- and postsynaptic receptors, an explanation is in order. It should be recognized that what may be classified as a presynaptic receptor on the terminal of neuron B may be a postsynaptic receptor of neuron A, which is making an axoaxonic contact with neuron B (see Fig. 2-3). Thus, depending on which neuron you are investigating, the receptor will be denoted as either pre- or postsynaptic.

Procedures that have been employed to fix activity at the presynaptic receptor level in a terminal are (1) to use synaptosomes; (2) the addition of tetrodotoxin to the preparation to block action potentials in neighboring interneurons; (3) to use neurons from the peripheral nervous system in cell culture where no postsynaptic cells exist; or (4) where feasible, either chemical destruction of terminals or lesioning of the neuron and demonstration by ligand binding the loss of the receptor. To complete the nomenclature on presynaptic receptors, an *autoreceptor* is located on the terminal or somatic-dendritic area of a neuron that is activated by the transmitter(s) released from that neuron. A *heteroreceptor* is a presynaptic receptor that is activated by a modulating agent that originates from a different neuron or cell. As we shall now detail, there exists an extraordinary number of possibilities that are available to alter the point-to-point synaptic transmission that was mentioned above. Let us count the ways.

Presynaptic modulation can be affected by

1. Receptor activation of a presynaptic neuron causing
   a. A change in the firing frequency in the presynaptic neuron: This is probably the most common type of modulation, particularly in the CNS, where it can be assumed that the firing rate of virtually every neuron is governed by inputs on dendrites, soma, or axons. The firing rate determines the frequency of impulse conduction, thus the invasion of action potentials into terminals or varicosities and consequently the amount of transmitter that is liberated.
   b. A change in the transport or reuptake of a transmitter or precursor, or in the synthesis, storage, release, or catab-

olism of a transmitter. All of these possibilities will result in a change in the concentration of a transmitter at the terminal. In practice, it has been shown that presynaptic activation of biogenic amine neurons promotes the phosphorylation of both tyrosine and tryphophan hydroxylase, which increases the synthesis of norepinephrine, dopamine, and serotonin. Curiously, phosphorylation of the pyruvate dehydrogenase complex causes a decrease in enzyme activity and in theory would decrease the levels of ACh and the amino acid transmitters. To date, however, modulation of this enzyme activity by presynaptic receptor activation has not been observed.

   c. An effect on ion conductances at the terminal: The three ions and their respective channels that one might focus on would be $K^+$, $Ca^{2+}$, or $Cl^-$. Endogenous neuroactive agents or drugs could alter transmitter release by opening or blocking the channels or changing the kinetics of channel open time via the possible mediation of protein phosphorylation or other second messengers.

2. A direct effect of neuropharmacological agents on some element of the release process. This could be an effect of the modulating agent on vesicular apposition to a terminal, fusion, or fission if an exocytotic mechanism is operating, or, in a nonexocytotic release process, an effect possibly on $Na^+$, $K^+$-ATPase.

3. A drug-induced direct effect without the mediation of second messenger systems (see below) on ionic conductance. Like the presynaptic changes described above, $Ca^{2+}$, $Na^+$, $K^+$, or $Cl^-$ channels could be directly altered in their kinetics by the administration of a drug.

Postsynaptic modulation can be affected by:

1. A long-term change in the number of receptors: This is a situation that is not observed under normal physiological conditions. It is, however, commonly noted pharmacologically where the administration of a receptor agonist for a

period of time will result in the down-regulation of the receptor, and, conversely, treatment with a receptor antagonist produces an increase in receptor density.

2. A change in the affinity of a ligand for a receptor. The now classical example is the salivary nerve of the cat where both ACh and VIP are colocalized. When VIP is released on electrical stimulation, it increases the affinity of ACh for the muscarinic receptor on the salivary gland up to 10,000-fold, with a consequent increase in salivation.

3. An effect on ionic conductances. As discussed in 1-a above, this is frequency modulation. This is a postsynaptic effect on the first neuron in a relay, but it would be classified as a presynaptic effect on the second neuron.

References to all the neurons and all the modulating agents that have been investigated are given in the reviews by Starke et al. and Chesselet, and in books by Vizi and Levitan and Kaczmarek. These reviews can be summarized by stating that virtually every neuronal pathway is modulated and virtually every endogenous neuroactive agent has been shown in one preparation or another to be capable of affecting synaptic transmission. All this information is descriptive: The question of the second messenger systems that may be ultimately involved in regulating synaptic activity is addressed in the following section. Figure 6-1 depicts a major pathway for modulation of synaptic transmission. Rapidly accumulating evidence suggests that in most cases of receptor-activated inhibitory presynaptic modulation, the ultimate effect is to open K channels. This hyperolarizes terminals; less $Ca^{2+}$ enters; and as a consequence, less transmitter is released.

SECOND MESSENGERS

Currently, three major biochemical cascades have been described:

1. *Protein phosphorylation.* Following the identification of cyclic nucleotides by Sutherland and associates, and the implication that they act as a second messenger system preceded by an initial nerve impulse or hormonal signal, E. Krebs and colleagues demonstrated a

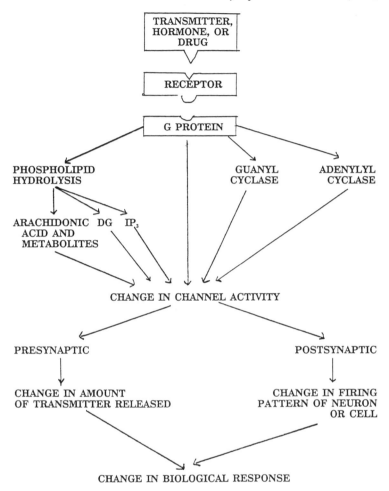

FIGURE 6-1. A major pathway for modulation of synaptic transmission. DG, diacylglycerol; IP₃, inositoltrisphosphate.

multistep sequence of events that linked cyclic AMP generation in muscle to regulation of carbohydrate metabolism. Since that time, the cyclic nucleotides have been shown to regulate an enormous diversity of processes ranging from axoplasmic transport to neuronal differentiation and including transmitter synthesis and release and the generation of postsynaptic potentials. All of these effects are attributable to the cAMP- or cGMP-activating protein kinases and thus protein phosphorylation. Second messenger activity, achieved via protein phosphorylation, can be mediated by cAMP- and cGMP-dependent protein kinases as well as by calcium-calmodulin-dependent protein kinase and calcium-phosphatidyl serine-dependent protein kinase. All protein kinases can themselves be autophosphorylated, a process that increases kinase activity. Although in most instances, biological activity results from kinase-activated phosphorylation of a substrate protein, in some cases it is phosphatase-activated de-phosphorylation of a phosphorylated protein that produces the biological response. Currently, four phosphoprotein phosphatases have been identified (protein phosphatase-2B is also referred to as calcineurin). Yet another level of regulation is suggested by the finding that protein phosphatase activity can be inhibited by other proteins, the most interesting of which is DARPP-32, found in $D_1$-dopaminoceptive neurons. DARPP-32, a dopamine and cAMP-regulated phosphoprotein, by acting as a protein phosphatase inhibitor when it is phosphorylated, can regulate effects of dopamine in dopaminoceptive cells. Phosphorylated DARPP-32 is inactivated by protein phosphatase-2B. It should be noted that in some instances, Ca acts as a second messenger without the participation of protein phosphorylation. The diversity of signals that are coupled to protein phosphorylation is depicted in Fig. 6-2. For a molecular illustration of receptor coupling, the reader is referred to Fig. 5-5.

Despite the vast number of systems in which protein phosphorylation is implicated, there are currently only about a dozen cases where direct evidence links this process to modulation of synaptic transmission, either pre- or postsynaptically. This information is presented in Table 6-1. It is not yet known if the proteins that make up the channels are phosphorylated, or if the phosphorylated proteins are morphologically associated with the channels. At any rate, with over 4 dozen proteins in brain that are known to be phosphorylated (Table 6-2), the story is far from complete. Questions that remain to be answered include (a) the regulation of the enormous number of steps in the cascade and the substrate specificity of the

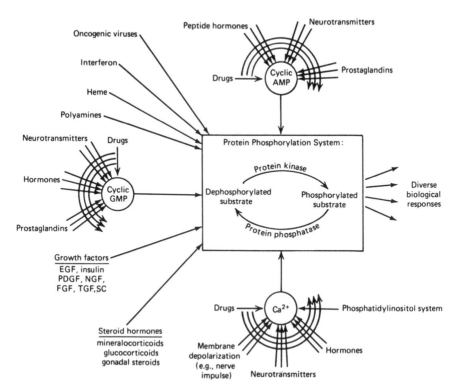

FIGURE 6-2. Schematic diagram of the role played by protein phosphorylation in mediating some of the biological effects of a variety of regulatory agents. Many of these agents regulate protein phosphorylation through altering intracellular levels of a second messenger, cAMP, cGMP, or $Ca^{2+}$. Other agents appear to regulate protein phosphorylation through mechanisms that do not involve these second messengers. Most drugs regulate protein phosphorylation by affecting the ability of first messengers to alter second-messenger levels (*curved arrows*). A small number of drugs (e.g., phosphodiesterase inhibitors, $Ca^{2+}$ channel blockers) regulate protein phosphorylation by directly altering second-messenger levels (*straight arrows*): (EGF) epidermal growth factor; (PDGF) platelet-derived growth factor; (NGF) nerve growth factor; (FGF) fibroblast growth factor; (TGF) transforming growth factor; (SC) somatomedin C. (From Nestler and Greengard, 1989)

TABLE 6-1. Modulation of Ionic Conductances Mediated by Protein Phosphorylation

| Genus | Cell | Experimental Finding |
|-------|------|---------------------|
| Aplysia | Bag cell neurons | Injection of cAMP-dependent protein kinase produces an after-discharge by decreasing conductance of $Ca^{2+}$-dependent $K^+$ channels and early ($I_A$) voltage-dependent $K^+$ channels. The injection of protein kinase C increases the height of action potentials via an increased conductance of $Ca^{2+}$ channels. |
| | Sensory neurons | Injection of cAMP-dependent protein kinase facilitates transmitter release via a decrease in conductance of serotonin-regulated $K^+$ channels |
| | Neuron R 15 | Injection of a protein kinase inhibitor blocks increased conductance of a serotonin-regulated anomalously-rectifying $K^+$ channel. |
| Helix | Unidentified neuron | Injection of cAMP-dependent protein kinase increases conductance of $Ca^+$-dependent rectifying $K^+$ channels. |
| | Unidentified neuron | Injection of protein kinase C mediates effect of cholecystokinin in shortening $Ca^{2+}$-dependent action potential via a decreased conductance of $Ca^{2+}$ channels. |

*continued*

TABLE 6-1. *continued*

| Genus | Cell | Experimental Finding |
|-------|------|---------------------|
| | Unidentified neuron | Injection of cAMP-dependent protein kinase increases conductance of voltage-dependent $Ca^+$ channels. |
| | Ventral neurons | Injection of cGMP-dependent protein kinase mediates effects of serotonin and cGMP in broadening the action potential, possibly through an increase in the conductance of $Ca^{2+}$ channels. |
| *Hermisenda* | Photoreceptor cells | Injection of cAMP-dependent protein kinase decreases the conductance of early ($I_A$) and late ($I_B$) voltage-dependent $K^+$ channels. |
| *Gallus* | Sensory neurons | A protein kinase C inhibitor reverses norepinephrine-induced inhibition of $Ca^{2+}$ channel conductance. |
| *Loligo* | Terminal digits of giant synapse | $Ca^{2+}$-calmodulin-dependent protein kinase injection facilitates transmitter release. |
| *Rattus* | Hippocampal pyramidal neurons | Injection of protein kinase C accounts for postsynaptic components of long-term potentiation. |

SOURCE: Modified from Hemmings et al., 1989.

TABLE 6-2. *continued*

Miscellaneous
    B-50
    Rhodopsin
    Myelin basic protein
    87 kDa protein
    100 kDa protein
    G-proteins

[a] Some of the proteins included are specific to neurons. The others are present in many cell types in addition to neurons and are included because among their multiple functions in the nervous system is the regulation of neuron-specific phenomena. Not included are the many phosphoproteins present in diverse tissues (including brain) that play a role in generalized cellular processes, such as intermediary metabolism, and that do not appear to play a role in neuron-specific phenomena.

[b] Several of the ion channels listed have been shown to be physiologically regulated by protein phosphorylation reactions, although it is not yet known whether such regulation is achieved directly through the phosphorylation of the ion channel or indirectly through the phosphorylation of a modulatory protein that is not a constituent of the ion channel molecule.

SOURCE: Hemmings et al., 1989.

this cyclic nucleotide is referable to the finding of a cGMP-dependent phosphodiesterase which regulates the level of cAMP.

2. *Phosphoinositide hydrolysis.* In 1953 Hokin and Hokin showed that the incorporation of inorganic phosphate (Pi) into phosphatidyl inositol (PI) and phosphatidic acid (PA) in pancreas slices was stimulated by ACh and ultimately resulted in the release of amylase. This receptor-activated hydrolysis of phosphoinositides is referred to as the phosphatidyl inositol effect. For nearly 30 years after the Hokin report, the literature on this effect was replete with the traditional scientific jargon "it is tempting to speculate that . . . ," with no one having solid evidence as to whether the phosphoinositides or the inositol phosphates were the message and, if so, exactly what was the medium for the exchange. That this situation has now dramatically improved is shown in Fig. 6-3.

The signals that initiate this transduction process in neuronal systms include ACh, norepinephrine, serotonin, histamine, glutamate bradykinins, Substance P, vasopressin, TRH, neurotensin, VIP, NGF, and angiotensin acting on brain, sympathetic ganglia, salivary glands, iris smooth muscle, adrenal cortex, and neuronal tumor cells. Specific receptors that have been implicated are muscarinic cholinergic receptors, $\alpha_1$-adrenergic receptors, the $H_1$-histaminergic receptor, Substance P and the $V_1$-vasopressin receptor. In each case, Ca appears to be the intracellular second messenger that activates phosphoinositide hydrolysis. Like the specific GTP binding proteins that link receptors to the adenylate cyclase system discussed earlier, evidence is accumulating to suggest that a specific GTP binding protein is also coupled to the phosphodiesterase that catalyzes the hydrolysis of phosphatidylinositol, 4,5-bisphosphate.

As noted in Fig. 6-3, the key participants in the transduction process are the receptor, the G protein, and a phosphodiesterase, a specific phospholipase C yielding two separate second messengers— the water-soluble $InsP_3$ and the lipid-soluble diacylglycerol. The former mobilizes calcium, (released in a wave form, i.e., oscillatory) which can act through calmodulin to phosphorylate specific proteins and the latter, by activating C-kinase, a calcium–phosphatidylserine-dependent family of protein kinases, also phosphorylates specific proteins. In addition, since diacylglycerol can activate guanylate cyclase to produce cGMP, an inference of a cGMP-dependent activity (protein kinase or otherwise), must be considered. With an assumed ambidexterity of neuronal cells, these two arms could function singly, cooperatively, or antagonistically, depending on the situation, thus providing subtle variations on the modulatory mechanism. In addition, as noted in Fig. 6-3, calcium may produce a physiological response directly without invoking an activation of calmodulin; so yet another control is indicated. On the subject of control, the activities of the various kinases, esterases, and phospholipases in the PI cycle would be expected to be vital control points. Free inositol in the brain must be derived from glycolysis since plasma inositol cannot pass the blood–brain barrier to any significant degree. Glycolysis, therefore, would be another regulatory factor in the response mechanism.

Finally, although the origin of the mobilized calcium is now clear

(5,8,11,14-eicosatetraenoic acid), derived on demand by either a G-protein-regulated phospholipase $A_2$ or diglyceride lipase activation (Fig. 6-4) yields a bewildering array of bioactive metabolites as shown in Fig. 6-5. The three major groups are prostaglandins, thromboxanes, and leukotrienes.

FIGURE 6-4. Pathways for the generation and metabolism of arachidonic acid. Arachidonate can arise directly from phospholipids through the action of phospholipase $A_2$ or prior action of phospholipase C, followed by the action of diglyceride lipase. Alternatively, the diglyceride may be phosphorylated to phosphatidic acid by action of diglyceride kinase, and arachidonate then can be released through the action of phospholipase $A_2$. The released arachidonate may then be metabolized by lipoxygenase, cyclooxygenase or epoxygenase enzymes to form leukotrienes (LTs), hydroxyeicosatetraenoic acids (HETEs), prostaglandins (PGs), thromboxanes (TXs), and epoxides. (From Axelrod et al. 1988)

Everybody knows that the eicosanoids, particularly the prostaglandin series, play an important modulatory role in nervous tissue but it is difficult to write a lucid account of specifically how and where they act. This situation is primarily due to the fact that they are not stored in tissue but are synthesized on demand, particularly in pathophysiological conditions; they act briefly (some with a half-life of seconds) and at extremely low concentrations ($10^{-10}$ M). Although indomethacin is a good inhibitor of cyclooxygenase, blocking the conversion of arachidonic acid to prostaglandins, there are no specific inhibitors available to block lipoxygenase and epoxygenase. Thus, although it had been postulated that the E series of prostaglandins modulates noradrenergic release, blocks the convulsant activity of pentylenetetrazol, strychnine, and picrotoxin (possibly by increasing the level of GABA in the brain) and increases the level of cAMP in cortical and hypothalamic slices, these effects were noted in vitro with the addition of substantial amounts of the prostaglandins. There was very little evidence in intact animals to support these neuronal findings, and since we all believe in *In Vivo Veritas*, the physiological relevance of the effect was in doubt.

Recently, however, direct evidence has implicated the eicosanoids as second messengers. The cascade begins with the binding of a neuroactive agent to its receptor. Then, according to findings from the Axelrod laboratory, the receptor is coupled to G-proteins which may either activate or inhibit phospholipase $A_2$, although this has not been conclusively established for all neural tissues. The activated enzyme promotes the release of arachidonic acid which will then act intracellularly as a second messenger. Arachidonic acid and its metabolites can also leave the cell to act extracellularly as first messengers on neighboring cells.

To continue this saga, the electrophysiological activity of the eicosanoids has been carefully elucidated in the laboratories of Schwartz and Siegelbaum. In several identified cells of the *Aplysia* abdominal ganglion, the mechanism of action of either histamine or the peptide FMRFamide, agents that cause presynaptic inhibition, is mediated by the lipoxygenase metabolite 12-HPETE. Further, in L-14, a follower cell, 8-HE$_p$ETE, a metabolite of 12-HPETE, appears to

squirrels to anticonvulsant activity, increasing cerebral blood flow, and interacting with the benzodiazepine receptor. At least two membrane-localized adenosine receptors have been identified with one stimulating and one inhibiting adenylate cyclase but it is questionable if this is a legitimate classification that explains all the activity of this purine.

Reflecting on the mechanisms available to nervous tissue to modulate synaptic transmission, one cannot fail to be overwhelmed by the almost infinite possibilities that provide the fine tuning for behavioral changes. The checks and balances in the United States Constitution pale into insignificance when compared to the myriad regulatory processes of the brain. To recycle an old saying, if the sun rises it must also set, if there is a heaven there must be a hell, and if a signal turns some physiological process on there must be a signal to turn it off. It may well turn out that the key player in this scenario is calcium. Since Ca is released as a wave, its concentration as well as its translocation at discrete sites might dictate the modulatory effect of the attachment of a ligand to its receptor. It may also be the key to nonsynaptic cellular effects that involve second messenger systems such as cell movement or proliferation, gene expression, and metabolism.

## SELECTED REFERENCES

Axelrod, J., R. M. Burch, and C. L. Jelsema (1988). Receptor-mediated activation of phospholipase $A_2$ via GTP-binding proteins: Arachidonic acid and its metabolites as second messengers. *Trends Neurosci.* *11*, 117.

Berridge, M. J. and R. F. Irvine (1984). Inositol triphosphate, a novel second messenger in cellular signal transduction. *Nature 312*, 315.

Berridge, M. J. and R. F. Irvine (1989). Inositol phosphates and cell signalling. *Nature 341*, 197.

Buttner, N., S. A. Siegelbaum, and A. Volterra (1989). Direct modulation of *Aplysia* S-$K^+$ channels by a 12-lipoxygenase metabolite of arachidonic acid. *Nature 342*, 553.

Chesselet, M.-F. (1984). Presynaptic regulation of neurotransmitter release in the brain. *Neurosci. 12*, 347.

Chuang, D. (1989). Neurotransmitter receptors and phosphoinositide turnover. *Ann. Rev. Pharmacol. Toxciol. 29*, 71.

Cooper, J. R. and E. M. Meyer (1984). Possible mechanisms involved in the release and modulation of release of neuroactive agents. *Neurochem. Int.* 6, 419.

Dennis, E. A., S. G. Rhee, M. M. Billah, and Y. A. Hannun (1991). Role of phospholipases in generating lipid second messengers in signal transduction. *FASEB J.* 5, 2068.

Halushka, P. V., D. E. Mais, P. R. Mayeux, and T. A. Morinelli (1989). Thomboxane, prostaglandin, and leukotriene receptors. *Ann. Rev. Pharmacol. Toxicol.* 29, 213.

Hemmings, H. C., Jr., A. C. Nairn, T. L. McGuiness, R. L. Huganir, and P. Greengard (1989). Role of protein phosphorylation in neuronal signal transduction. *FASEB J.* 3, 1583.

Hirasawa K. and Y. Nishizuka (1985). Phosphatidylinositol turnover in receptor mechanism and signal transduction. *Ann. Rev. Pharmacol. Toxicol.* 25, 147.

Hokin, L. E. (1985). Receptors and phosphoinositide-generated second messengers. *Ann. Rev. Biochem.* 54, 205.

Laduron P. M. (1985). Presynaptic heteroreceptors in regulation of neuronal transmission. *Biochem. Pharmacol.* 34, 467.

Levitan I. B. and L. K. Kaczmarek (1991). *The Neuron: Cell and Molecular Biology.* Oxford Univ. Press, New York.

Lundberg, J. M., B. Hedlund, and T. Bartfai (1982). Vasoactive intestinal polypeptide enhances muscarinic ligand binding in cat submandibular salivary gland. *Nature* 295, 147.

Needleman, P., J. Turk, B. A. Jakschik, A. R. Morrison, and J. B. Lefkowitch (1986). Arachidonic acid metabolism. *Ann. Rev. Biochem.* 55, 69.

Nestler, E. J. and P. Greengard (1989). *Protein phosphorylation and the regulation of neuronal function.* In *Basic Neurochemistry: Molecular, Cellular and Medical Aspects*, 4th ed. G. J. Siegel, et al. eds. Raven Press, New York.

Nicoll, R. A. (1988). The coupling of neurotransmitter receptors to ion channels in the brain. *Science* 241, 545.

Nishizuka Y. (1988). The molecular heterogeneity of protein kinase C and its implication for cellular regulation. *Nature* 334, 661.

Piomelli, D., E. Shapiro, R. Zipkin, J. H. Schwartz, and S. J. Feinmark (1989). Formation and action of 8-hydroxy-11,12-epoxy-5,9,14-icosatrienoic acid in *Aplysia*: A possible second messenger. *Proc. Nat. Acad. Sci. USA* 86, 1721.

Putney, J. W., Jr., H. Takemura, A. R. Hughes, D. A. Horstman, and D. Thastrup (1989). How do inositol phosphates regulate calcium signalling. *FASEB J.* 3, 1899.

porting the hypothesis that the major share of GABA found in the brain functions as an inhibitory transmitter. The knowledge that GABA probably functions as an inhibitory transmitter in the brain has spurred a prodigious research effort to implicate GABA in the etiology of a host of neurological and psychiatric disorders. Although the present evidence is not overwhelming, GABA has been implicated, both directly and indirectly, in the pathogenesis of Huntington's disease, Parkinsonism, epilepsy, schizophrenia, tardive dyskinesias, and senile dementia, as well as several other behavioral disorders.

*Distribution*

In mammals, GABA is found in high concentrations in the brain and spinal cord, but it is absent or present only in trace amounts in peripheral nerve tissue such as sciatic nerve, splenic nerve, sympathetic ganglia, or in any other peripheral tissue such as liver, spleen, or heart. These findings give some idea of the uniqueness of the occurrence of GABA in the mammalian central nervous system. Like the monoamines, GABA also appears to have a discrete distribution within the central nervous system. However, unlike the monoamines, the concentration of GABA found in the central nervous system is in the order of μmoles/gm rather than nmoles/gm. It is interesting that the brain also contains large amounts of glutamic acid (8–13 μmoles/gm), which is the main precursor of GABA and is itself a neurotransmitter candidate. In the rat, the corpora quadrigemina and the diencephalic regions contain the highest levels of GABA, while much lower concentrations are found in whole cerebral hemispheres, the pons, and medulla; white matter contains relatively low concentrations of GABA. It should be noted that endogenous levels of GABA increase rapidly postmortem: a 30–45% increase in GABA occurs within 2 minutes after death in the rat if the tissue is not instantly frozen in situ. The origin of this sudden increase is uncertain, although it is believed to result in part from a transient activation of glutamic acid decarboxylase (GAD).

Progressive increases in GABA levels and in glutamic acid decarboxylase activity appear to occur in various regions of the brain during development. The high levels of GABA found in the various regions of the brain of the Rhesus monkey appear to correlate well with the activity of glutamate decarboxylase, the enzyme responsible for the conversion of L-glutamate to GABA. This is not the case for the degradative enzyme GABA-transaminase, since the globus pallidus and the substantia nigra, which have the highest concentration of GABA, have a relatively low transaminase activity. Yet there does not appear to be a consistent inverse relationship between GABA concentration and transminase activity. Thus, some areas of the brain, such as the dentate nucleus and the inferior colliculus, which have relatively high concentrations of GABA, also have large amounts of transaminase activity.

Since GABA does not easily penetrate the blood-brain barrier, it is difficult if not impossible to increase the brain concentrations of GABA by peripheral administration, unless one alters the blood–brain barrier. Some investigators have tried to circumvent this problem by the administration of GABA-lactam (2-pyrrolidinone) to animals in the hope that this less polar and more lipid soluble compound would penetrate more easily into the brain and be hydrolyzed to yield GABA. Although the idea seems plausible, it does not succeed: the GABA-lactam that reaches the central nervous system is not hydrolyzed to any extent. A more recent successful attempt has been the development of progabide (see Fig. 7-6). This agent does penetrate the brain and is subsequently metabolized into GABA.

*Metabolism*

Three primary enzymes are involved in the metabolism of GABA before its entry into the Krebs cycle. The relative activity of enzymes involved in the degradation of GABA suggests that, as with monoamines, they play only a minor role in the termination of the action of any neurally released GABA.

Figure 7-1 outlines the metabolism of GABA and its relationship to the Krebs cycle and carbohydrate metabolism. As mentioned previously, GABA is formed by the α-decarboxylation of L-glutamic acid, a reaction catalyzed by glutamic acid decarboxylase, an enzyme

of brain GAD with coenzyme and a decrease in GAD activity without any alteration in the amount of enzyme protein. Feeding of pyridoxine to deficient animals rapidly restores brain GAD to normal. However it is produced, pyridoxine deficiency causes an increased susceptibility to seizures that can be almost immediately reversed by parenteral administration of pyridoxine. Since the observed effects are rapid, there appears to be a very rapid conversion of pyridoxine to pyridoxal phosphate in the CNS, association of this coenzyme with the apoenzyme of GAD, and normalization of the synthesis of GABA. A dramatic example is in infants with vitamin $B_6$ deficiency-induced seizures. Seizures can be abolished completely and quickly by an intramuscular injection of pyridoxine.

Although the properties of GAD have been actively studied for 30 years, little was known until recently about the molecular mechanisms responsible for regulation of its in vivo activity in the CNS. Studies directed at the mechanism involved in the postmortem increase in GABA levels have been partly responsible for disclosing some interesting properties of mammalian GAD, which may provide some clues to its in vivo regulation. Since GAD appears to be only partially saturated by its cofactor, pyridoxal-5'-phosphate in the intact brain, it is apparent that conditions that alter the degree of saturation of this enzyme in vivo will influence its activity. Although most recent data suggest that pyridoxal phosphate is tightly bound to GAD, glutamate and adenine nucleotides can promote dissociation and block association of this important cofactor, respectively. Thus, it is conceivable that alterations in the availability of one or both of these endogenous substances could influence GAD activity and GABA formation in vivo. The possibility that the association and dissociation of pyridoxal phosphate from GAD may be important for the in vivo regulation of GABA synthesis is supported by the observation that GAD is no more than about 35 percent saturated with pyridoxal phosphate in vivo, despite the fact that the levels of this cofactor in the brain appear to be sufficiently high to fully activate this enzyme. The degree of saturation of GAD with pyridoxal phosphate in vivo may be determined in part by a balance between the rate of dissociation of pyridoxal phosphate from the enzyme brought about by glutamate and the rate of association of the cofactor with the apoenzyme which is inhibited by nucleotides. This possibility is consistent with the observation that a postmortem activation of GAD occurs in brain only when postmortem changes in ATP are allowed to take place.

*GABA-Transaminase (GABA-T)*

GABA-T, unlike the decarboxylase, has a wide tissue distribution. Therefore, although GABA cannot be formed to any extent outside the central nervous system, exogenous GABA can be rapidly metabolized by both central and peripheral tissue. However, since endogenous GABA is present only in nanomolar amounts in cerebrospinal fluid, it is unlikely that a significant amount of endogenous GABA leaves the brain intact. The brain transaminase has a pH optimum of 8.2 and also requires pyridoxal phosphate. It appears that the coenzyme is more tightly bound to this enzyme than it is to GAD. The brain ratio of GABA-T/GAD activity is almost always greater than one. Sulfhydryl reagents tend to decrease GABA-T activity, suggesting that this enzyme requires the integrity of one or more sulfhydryl groups for optimal activity. The transamination of GABA catalyzed by GABA-T is a reversible reaction; so if a metabolic source of succinic semialdehyde were made available it would be theoretically possible to form GABA by the reversal of this reaction. However, as indicated below, this does not appear to be the case in vivo under normal or experimental conditions investigated so far.

Recent studies with more sophisticated cell fractionation techniques and electron microscopic monitoring of the fractions obtained have borne out the original claims that both GAD and GABA-T are particulate to some extent. GAD was found associated with the synaptosome fraction, whereas the GABA-T was largely associated with mitochondria. Further studies on the mitochondrial distribution of GABA-T have suggested that the mitochondria released from synaptosomes have less activity than the crude unpurified mitochondrial fraction, and it has been inferred that the mitochondria

The hydrazide-induced seizures were accompanied by substantial decreases in the levels of GABA and reductions in GAD activity in various areas of the brain studied. (This decrease in GABA produced by thiosemicarbazide is now believed to be due at least in part to a decrease in the rapid postmortem increase in GABA mentioned previously.) The direct demonstration of the reversal of the action of the convulsant hydrazides by GABA itself proved to be difficult, because of the lack of ability of GABA to pass the blood–brain barrier in adult mammalian organisms. However, a preferential inhibition of GABA-T could be achieved in vivo with carbonyl reagents such as hydroxylamine ($NH_2OH$) or amino-oxyacetic acid, which resulted in an increase in GABA levels (up to 500% of control) in the CNS. Although these agents caused a decrease in the susceptibility to the seizures induced by some agents (such as metrazole), they did not exert any protective effect against the hydrazide-induced convulsions, even though they prevented the depletion of GABA and in some cases even increased the GABA levels above the controls. In fact, administration of very high doses of only amino-oxyacetic acid, instead of producing the normally observed sedation, caused some seizure activity in spite of the extremely high brain levels of GABA.

An interesting finding with amino-oxyacetic acid is that administration of this compound to a strain of genetically spastic mice in a single dose of 5–15 mg/kg results in a marked improvement of their symptomatology for 12–24 hr. This improvement is associated with an increase in GABA levels, but the GABA level increases with a similar time course and to the same extent as in normal control mice. All studies to date indicate that the principal genetic defect in these mice is not in the operation of the GABA system. However, the drug-induced increase in GABA may serve to quell an excess of or imbalance in excitatory input in some unknown area of the CNS.

Hydrazinopropionic acid has been described as a potent inhibitor of GABA-T. It has been suggested that this compound inhibits GABA-T because of its close similarity to GABA with respect to structural configuration, molecular size, and molecular charge distribution. Its inhibitory action cannot be reversed by the addition of pyridoxal phosphate. Hydrazinopropionic acid is about 1,000 times more potent than aminooxyacetic acid in inhibiting mouse brain transaminase.

### Alternate Metabolic Pathways

In addition to undergoing transamination and subsequently entering the Krebs cycle, GABA can apparently undergo various other transformations in the central nervous system, forming a number of compounds whose importance, and in some cases natural occurrence, has not been conclusively established. Fig. 7-2 depicts a variety of derivatives for which GABA may serve as a precursor. Perhaps the simplest of these metabolic conversions is the reduction of succinic semialdehyde (a product of GABA transamination) to γ-hydroxybutyrate (GHB). The transformation of GABA to GHB has been demonstrated in rat brain both in vivo and in vitro. Recent studies have demonstrated that GHB administered in physiologically relevant concentrations can also be converted to GABA by transamination.

GHB aciduria, a rare inborn error in the metabolism of GABA, has been reported in children and appears to be the result of a deficiency of succinic semialdehyde dehydrogenase, the enzyme that oxidizes succinic semialdehyde to succinic acid (see Fig. 7-1). GHB levels are increased in urine, plasma, and cerebrospinal fluid, but it is unclear whether the main clinical symptoms of motor and mental retardation, muscular hypotonia, and ataxia are all related to the elevated levels of GHB.

### GABA Receptors

The term "GABA receptor" usually refers to a GABA recognition site on postsynaptic membranes which, when coupled with GABA or an appropriate agonist, causes a shift in membrane permeability to inorganic ions, primarily chloride. This change in chloride permeability results in hyperpolarization of the receptive neuron in the case of postsynaptic inhibition or depolarization in the case of pre-

most neurons, increasing chloride permeability decreases the depolarizing effects of an excitatory input, thereby depressing excitability.

In the mid-1970s, the history of the GABA (GABA$_A$) receptor became intertwined with the history of the benzodiazepine receptor. Although the anxiolytic properties of the benzodiazepines were discovered in the 1950s, the mechanism of action of benzodiazepines was not understood for many years thereafter. In the late 1970s, it became clear that there were specific binding sites in the brain for the benzodiazepines and they became known as the benzodiazepine receptors. Concrete evidence of a biochemical relationship between the GABA$_A$ and benzodiazepine receptors was found by Tallman and Gallagher. These workers clearly showed that GABA enhances the binding of benzodiazepines, but the structural details of this linkage would not be characterized for another decade.

In the late 1980s, a large research group led by Eric Barnard reported the sequencing and functional expression of the genes encoding two subunits of the GABA$_A$ receptor and showed that these two subunits could form a functional chloride channel. Two years later, a group led by Peter Seeberg identified an additional substituent of the receptor and was able to form benzodiazepine-sensitive chloride channels, thus proving that the GABA and benzodiazepine receptors are part of the same complex. Activation of the GABA$_A$ receptor by GABA agonists results in the opening of the chloride channel. The ensuing influx of chloride anions inhibits the firing of the neurons by causing hyperpolarization. Benzodiazepines increase the frequency of channel opening without appreciably altering the channel conductance or duration of opening. Barbiturates, in contrast, slightly decrease the opening frequency and prolong the duration of opening. The GABA$_A$ receptor can be functionally altered by a variety of compounds that bind to the receptor at several different sites, including the GABA site, the picrotoxin/barbiturate site, the benzodiazepine site, and the steroid site (see Fig. 7-3). The activation and modulation of chloride flux by GABA and benzodiazepines are achieved by dynamic alterations in protein configuration. Benzodiazepines and related ligands bind to a unique site on

FIGURE 7-3. Schematic illustration of the $GABA_A$ receptor complex and the sites of action of different agents on the receptor.

the $GABA_A$ receptor complex that does not overlap the sites for GABA or picrotoxin. Drugs that bind to the benzodiazepine site and enhance the electrophysiological effects of GABA are called benzodiazepine agonists; compounds that bind to the benzodiazepine site and decrease the effects of GABA are called inverse agonists. Subtle modifications of the chemical structures of the benzodiazepine agonists and inverse agonists have produced a small number of antagonists, the most important of which is RO15-1788 or flumazenil. This compound has very few, if any, pharmacological effects when administered alone; however, it readily reverses all the effects of benzodiazepine agonists and inverse agonists and has proved to be a very useful experimental tool.

It is now common textbook knowledge that the major inhibitory neurotransmitter receptor, the $GABA_A$ receptor, is a multi-subunit receptor-channel complex that can be allosterically modulated by the two important classes of drugs mentioned above—the benzodiazepines and the barbiturates. The primary structures of the

TABLE 7-1. Subdivision of GABA receptors

| Receptor class | Pharmacology | | | Channels | Second messengers |
| | Agonists | Antagonists | Modulators | | |
|---|---|---|---|---|---|
| GABA$_A$ | GABA Muscimol Isoguvacine | Bicuculline Picrotoxin | Benzodiazepines Barbiturates Steroids | Cl$^-$ | None |
| GABA$_B$ | GABA Baclofen | Phaclofen | None | K$^+$ Ca$^{2+}$ | Adenylate cyclase Phosphatidyl inositol turnover |

and is eliminated by reuptake blockers such as nipicotic acid. The purification of rat brain GABA transporter protein provided a reagent for the molecular cloning of a GABA transporter cDNA. A complimentary DNA clone encoding a transporter for GABA has recently been isolated from rat brain and its functional properties examined in *Xenopus* oocytes. This cloned and expressed GABA transporter was found to have a high affinity for GABA, to exhibit sodium and chloride dependence, and to have a pharmacology similar to that of neuronal GABA transporter. The expressed protein also shares antigenic determinants with the native rat brain GABA transporter.

### Coexistence with Classical and Nonclassical Transmitters

During the last several years, an increasing number of neurons containing coexisting messenger molecules have been described. GABA neurons are no exception. GABA has been shown to coexist with such classical transmitters as 5-HT, DA, ACh, glycine, and histamine, as well as with a number of peptides including CCK, NPY, VIP, Substance P and others (see Table 7-2). The actual function of such coexistent molecules, especially the peptides, is often very difficult to evaluate in the CNS, so that work on the functional implications of multiple signalling through a single synapse by coexistent transmitters has proceeded slowly. Clearly, the realization that GABA can coexist with a large number of other messenger molecules provides a new dimension to the complexity of this neuronal system and the way it can influence follower cells.

### PHARMACOLOGY OF GABAERGIC NEURONS

Drugs can influence GABAergic function by interaction at many different sites, both pre- and postsynaptic (Fig. 7-4). Drugs can influence presynaptic events and modify the amount of GABA that ultimately reaches and interacts with postsynaptic GABA receptors. In most cases, presynaptic drug effects do not involve an interaction with "GABA receptors." The most extensively studied presynaptic drug actions involved inhibitory effects exerted on enzymes involved

FIGURE 7-4. Schematic illustration of a GABAergic neuron indicating possible sites of drug action.

Site 1: *Enzymatic synthesis*: Glutamic acid decarboxylase (GAD-I) is inhibited by a number of various hydrazines. These agents appear to act primarily as pyridoxal antagonists and are therefore very nonspecific inhibitors. L-glutamate-γ-hydrazide and allylglycine are more selective inhibitors of GAD-I, but these agents are also not entirely specific in their effects.

Site 2: *Release*: GABA release appears to be calcium dependent. At present no selective inhibitors of GABA release have been found.

Site 3: *Intereaction with postsynaptic receptor*: Bicuculline and picrotoxin block the action of GABA at postsynaptic receptors. 3-Aminopropane sulfonic acid and the hallucinogenic isoxazole derivative, muscimol, appear to be effective GABA agonists at postsynaptic receptors and autoreceptors.

Site 3a: *Presynaptic autoreceptors*: Possible involvement in the control of GABA release.

Site 4: *Reuptake*: In the brain GABA appears to be actively taken up into presynaptic endings by a sodium-dependent mechanism. A number of

TABLE 7-2. Coexistence of GABA with classical transmitter and peptides in the mammalian CNS

| Substance | Brain region (species) |
|---|---|
| **Peptide** | |
| Somatostatin | Thalamus (cat) |
| | Cortex, hippocampus (rat, cat, monkey) |
| CCK | Cortex, hippocampal formation (cat, monkey, rat) |
| NPY | Cortex (cat, monkey) |
| Enkephalin | Retina (chicken) |
| | Ventral pallidum, hypothalamus (rat) |
| Opiod peptide | Basal ganglia (rat) |
| Galanin | Hypothalamus (rat) |
| Substance P | Hypothalamus (rat) |
| VIP | Hippocampal formation (rat) |
| **Classical transmitter** | |
| 5-HT | Nucleus raphe dorsalis (rat) |
| | Medullary raphe nuclei and adjacent areas (rat) |
| | Retina (rabbit) |
| DA | Arcuate nucleus (rat) |
| | Olfactory bulb (rat) |
| Histamine | Hypothalamus (rat) |
| ACh | Medial septum/diagonal band (rat) |
| Glycine | Cerebellum (rat) |

CCK, cholecystokinin; NPY, neuropeptide Y; VIP, vasoactive intestinal polypeptide; 5-HT, DA, dopamine; ACh, acetylcholine.

---

(Fig. 7-4 cont.)

compounds will inhibit this uptake mechanism, such as 4-methyl-GABA and 2-hydroxy-GABA, but these agents are not completely specific in their inhibitory effects.

Site 5: *Metabolism*: GABA is metabolized primarily by transamination by GABA-transaminase (GABA-T), which appears to be localized primarily in mitochondria. Amino-oxyacetic acid, gabaculline, and acetylenic GABA are effective inhibitors of GABA-T.

in GABA synthesis (GAD) and degradation (GABA-T) and the neuronal reuptake of GABA. The major exception is the interaction of drugs with GABAergic autoreceptors to modulate both the physiological activity of GABA neurons and the release and synthesis of GABA in a manner analogous to the role played by dopamine autoreceptors in the regulation of dopaminergic function.

A great deal of emphasis has been directed recently to the study of drug interactions with GABA receptors. Drugs interacting at the level of GABA receptors can be assigned into two general categories, GABA antagonists and GABA agonists.

Figure 7-3 depicts possible sites of drug interaction in a hypothetical GABAergic synapse. The structures of compounds that act at GABAergic synapses are depicted in Figs. 7-4 and 7-5. Picrotoxinin is the active component of picrotoxin.

*GABA Antagonists*

The action of GABA at the receptor-ionophore complex may be antagonized by GABA antagonists either directly by competition with GABA for its receptor or indirectly by modification of the receptor or by inhibition of the GABA-activated ionophore. The two classical GABA antagonists (Fig. 7-4), bicuculline and picrotoxin, appear to act by different means. Bicuculline acts as a direct competitive antagonist of GABA at the receptor level, while picrotoxin acts as a noncompetitive antagonist, presumably due to its ability to block GABA-activated ionophores. Although early studies raised some doubts concerning the usefulness of bicuculline as a selective GABA antagonist, these expressions of skepticism have been largely resolved and appear primarily related to the instability of bicuculline at 37°C and physiological pH. Under normal physiological conditions bicuculline is hydrolyzed to bicucine, a relatively inactive GABA antagonist with a short half-life of several minutes. The quaternary salts now used for most electrophysiological experiments (bicuculline methiodide and bicuculline methochloride) are

FIGURE 7-5. Structures of compounds that act at GABAergic synapses.

much more water soluble and stable over a broad pH range of 2–8. It should be noted, however, that these quaternary salts are not suitable for systemic administration because of their poor penetration into the CNS.

## GABA Agonists

Electrophysiological studies have demonstrated that there are a wide variety of compounds that are capable of directly activating bicuculline-sensitive GABA receptors. These agonists can be readily subdivided into two groups based upon their ability to penetrate the blood–brain barrier, dictating whether they will be active or inactive following systemic administration. Agents such as 3-aminopropane-sulfonic acid, β-guanidinoproprionic acid, 4-aminotetrolic acid, *trans*-4-aminocrotonic acid, and *trans*-3-aminocyclopentane-1-carboxylic acid are all effective direct-acting GABA agonists. However, entry of these agents into the brain following systemic administration is minimal. In addition, compounds such as *trans*-4-aminotetrolic acid and 4-aminocrotonic acid also inhibit GABA-T and GABA uptake; therefore, their action is not totally attributable to their direct agonist properties.

In contrast to this class of direct-acting GABA agonists, the second group listed below readily passes the blood–brain barrier and is active following systemic administration. Muscimol (3-hydroxy-5-aminomethylisoxazole) is the agent in this group which has been most extensively studied. Some other agents in this group include (5)-(-)-5-(1-aminoethyl)-3-isoxazole, THIP (a bicyclic muscimol analogue), SL-76002 [a(chloro-4-phenyl)fluro-5-hydroxy-2 benzilideneamino-4H butyramide], and kojic amine (2-aminomethyl-3-hydroxy-4H-pyran-4-one).

In addition to classification based on their ability to penetrate the blood–brain barrier, GABAergic substances may be further divided into those compounds which stimulate GABA receptors directly or those that indirectly cause an activation of GABA receptors by several different mechanisms. For example, agents such as muscimol, isoguvacine, and THIP are true GABA mimetic agents that interact directly with GABA receptors. Indirectly acting GABA mimetics act to facilitate GABAergic transmission by increasing the amount of endogenous GABA which reaches the receptor or by altering in some manner the coupling of the GABA receptor-mediated change in chloride permeability. Thus many drugs often classified as indirect GABA agonists act presynaptically to modify GABA release and metabolism rather than by interacting directly with GABA receptors. For this reason, drugs like gabaculine (a GABA-T inhibitor), nipecotic acid (a GABA uptake inhibitor), and baclofen (an agent which, in addition to many other actions, causes release of GABA from intracellular stores) are often classified incorrectly as GABA agonists. The benzodiazepines mentioned earlier also appear to potentiate the action of tonically released GABA at the receptor by displacement of an endogenous inhibitor of GABA receptor binding, allowing more endogenous GABA to reach and bind receptors. Thus, benzodiazepines are sometimes also classified as GABA agonists. A GABA-like action can also be elicited by agents which bypass GABA receptors and influence GABA ionophores. It has been suggested that pentobarbital acts at the level of the GABA ionophore, but it is unclear whether its CNS depressant effects are explainable by this action.

The structures of some of the more potent and widely used direct-acting GABA agonists are illustrated in Figs. 7-5 and 7-6. Included are muscimol, isoguvacine, THIP, and (+)-*trans*-3-aminocyclopentane carboxylic acid. Useful therapeutic effects have not yet been obtained by use of agents of this sort that have direct GABA mimetic effects (such as muscimol), that inhibit the active reuptake of GABA (such as nipecotic acid), or that alter the rate of synthesis or degradation of GABA (such as amino-oxyacetic acid and gabaculine). However, useful therapeutic effects are achieved with the anxiolytic benzodiazepines (such as Valium (diazepam) and Librium (chlordiazepoxide), which may exert their actions by facilitating GABAergic transmission.

If the anatomical distribution and functional properties of GABA$_A$ receptor subtypes and subunits become clearly defined, this knowledge may enable the development of therapeutically useful subtype-specific agonists which can be directed to modify GABA-ergic function in selective brain areas.

FIGURE 7-6. Structures of compounds that act at GABAergic synapses.

## Endogenous Inhibitors

The concept of endogenous inhibitors or modulators of GABA receptors arose from studies on the binding of radioactive GABA to rat brain membranes. These studies revealed that the apparent affinity of GABA binding and the number of apparent binding sites were greatly influenced by the methods used to prepare the membranes. The availability of these latent GABA binding sites appeared to require the removal of endogenous substances that inhibit GABA binding and are normally incorporated into synaptic membranes. A variety of such endogenous inhibitors appear to exist, and they have been collectively called GABARINS (GABA Receptor Inhibitors). It has been speculated that GABARINS may function to control the affinity and availability of certain GABA receptors, ultimately altering the properties of the GABA–receptor–ionophore complexes; GABARINS may possibly be involved in desensitization and supersensitivity phenomena. The interaction between GABA receptors and GABARINS could also provide another important site at which drugs could act to alter the functions of GABAergic synapses.

One of these endogenous modulators of the GABA$_A$ receptor, termed DBI (diazepam-binding modulator), has been purified to homogeneity from rat and human brain and its structure has been determined by recombinant DNA technology. Several lines of evidence suggest that DBI functions as the precursor of a family of allosteric modulatory peptides of the GABA$_A$ receptor, causing a negative modulation of the GABA-operated Cl ion fluxes (see Chapter 12). A similar endogenous peptide has been found in human brain and CSF; it is noteworthy that the content of human DBI immunoreactivity is elevated in the CSF of severely depressed patients.

*Neurotransmitter Role in Invertebrates*

A strong case can be made for a transmitter role for GABA at inhibitory nerve endings to the muscle or to stretch-receptor neurons in crustacea. The evidence can be summarized as follows:

1. Externally applied GABA duplicates the effects of inhibitory nerve stimulation at the crustacean neuromuscular junction as well as at other crustacean synapses.
2. Both exogenous GABA and the endogenous inhibitory transmitter substance, when in contact with the postsynaptic membrane or receptor site, cause this membrane to become more permeable to chloride ion. This increase in chloride permeability in both cases can be blocked by picrotoxin (an antagonist of the GABA-receptor Cl$^-$ channel) and bicuculline (an antagonist of the GABA recognition site).
3. GABA appears to be the most potent inhibitory compound extractable from the lobster nervous system.
4. Inhibitory axons and cell bodies in the lobster nervous system have a much higher content of GABA than excitatory axons or cell bodies, the GABA ratio found being on the

order of 100:1. The endogenous GABA content of the inhibitory axon is approximately 0.1 M.

5. The enzymes necessary for the formation and destruction of GABA are present in the inhibitory axon and cell body.

6. A specific GABA uptake mechanism, which could be involved in transmitter inactivation, analogous to the monoamine systems, has been described in the crayfish stretch receptor and the lobster nerve-muscle preparation. However, it is not known if the uptake is primarily into presynaptic nerve terminals.

7. It has also been demonstrated that GABA is released by the lobster nerve-muscle preparation during stimulation of the inhibitory axons. This release was shown to be frequency dependent. Moreover, stimulation of the excitatory nerve to the same muscle does not liberate GABA. Also, GABA release induced by stimulation of the inhibitory fibers can be blocked by lowering the $Ca^{2+}$ content of the medium, which also blocks neuromuscular transmission.

These observations fully satisfy the criteria for identification of GABA as an inhibitory transmitter in the crustacea. The physiological and pharmacological observations made in invertebrates have also provided useful models for developing appropriate tests for evaluating the role of GABA as a transmitter in the mammalian CNS.

### Neurotransmitter Role in the Mammalian Central Nervous System

The evidence from the mammalian central nervous system to support a role of GABA as an inhibitory transmitter is not as complete as that generated from the crustacean. With substances such as the amino acids, which may play a dual role (both in metabolism and as neurotransmitters), it is only to be expected that it will be more difficult to obtain conclusive evidence as to their role as neurotransmitters.

Neurophysiological and biochemical studies have indicated that the majority of GABA found in brain may serve a neurotransmitter function. In recent years enough evidence has accumulated to allow the conclusion that GABA functions as an inhibitory transmitter in the mammalian CNS. GABA is considered an inhibitory transmitter even though this substance can induce both a hyperpolarizing and depolarizing response. Both actions are thought to be a result of GABA receptor-mediated change in chloride conductance. The hyperpolarization of neurons produced by an increase in membrane permeability to chloride ions appears identical to the changes induced by glycine-like amino acids. The depolarization induced by GABA of primary afferent terminals is also thought to be associated with an increased permeability to chloride ions, but this action is not produced by glycine-like amino acids. The depolarizing response to GABA predominates in spinal cord cells while the GABA-induced hyperpolarization is typical of cerebral cortical cells. These effects establish possible relationships between GABA and postsynaptic (hyperpolarizing) inhibition and between GABA and presynaptic inhibition.

The elementary criteria for identification of a compound as a putative transmitter have already been mentioned. In short, the agent in question must be produced, stored, released, exert its appropriate action, and then be removed from its site of action. There is sufficient evidence for the production, storage, and pharmacological activity of GABA consistent with its suggested role as an inhibitory transmitter, but it has not yet been possible to demonstrate an association of GABA with specific inhibitory pathways in the cortex. Until recently there was also no evidence that GABA could be released from mammalian brain under physiological conditions. Several reports now claim to have demonstrated the spontaneous release of GABA from the surface of the brain. However, only one group of investigators has claimed that the amount of GABA released from the cortex is dependent upon the activity of the brain. This group has found that in cats showing an aroused EEG, either following cervical cord section or in awake animals receiving local anesthesia, small amounts of GABA will leak out of the cerebral cortex and can be recovered by a superfusion technique (cortical cup), provided the pia-arachnoid membrane has been punctured. Jasper and co-workers demonstrated that this release of GABA into cortical cups occurs about three times more rapidly from the brains of cats showing an EEG sleeplike pattern with marked spindle activity following midbrain section than in cats showing an EEG awake pattern. When a continuous waking state was maintained by periodic stimulation of the brain stem reticular formation, no measurable amount of GABA could be found in the perfusates. Iversen and co-workers have also demonstrated that GABA is released from the surface of the posterior lateral gyri of cats during periods of cortical inhibition produced by either stimulation of the ipsilateral geniculate or by direct stimulation of the cortex.

The vertebrate neurons most clearly identified by physiological, chemical, and immunochemical criteria as GABAergic are the cerebellar Purkinje cells. When GABA is applied iontophoretically to Deiters' neurons, it induces IPSP-like changes and therefore mimics the action of the inhibitory transmitter released from axon terminals of the Purkinje cells. GABA is also known to be concentrated in Purkinje cells, which exert a monosynaptic inhibitory effect on neurons of Deiters' nucleus. Obata and Takeda observed that stimulation of the cerebellum, which presumably activates the Purkinje cell axons, which have their terminals in cerebellar subcortical nuclei adjacent to the fourth ventricle, induces about a threefold increase in the amount of GABA released into the ventricular perfusate. However, the extremely high voltage employed, the relatively crude perfusion system, and the lack of critical identification of GABA make the significance of these otherwise interesting observations on release somewhat difficult to interpret, although they are consistent with the hypothesis that GABA is an inhibitory transmitter in this particular pathway.

In addition, other experiments have indicated that labeled GABA can be released from brain slices by electrical stimulation or by the addition of high levels of potassium to the incubation medium. However, one should bear in mind that all the above-mentioned release experiments are somewhat gross in nature and do not provide evidence of the neuronal system involved in the release of GABA. Indeed, these experiments do not even indicate that this release is in any way associated with an inhibitory synaptic event. In fact, at the present time no suitable test system in the CNS has been developed that will be as appropriate as the lobster nerve–muscle preparation. The student is advised against holding his or her intellectual breath until it has.

Most of the investigations analyzing the mechanism of GABA's depressive action on the central nervous system have been conducted on spinal cord motoneurons. Until quite recently, GABA had not shown much evidence of closely mimicking the inhibitory transmitter. In fact, some years ago Curtis and his associates discounted the hypothesis that GABA might be the main inhibitory transmitter in the mammalian central nervous system. They noted that the action of GABA iontophoresed onto spinal neurons differed significantly from that of the inhibitory transmitter; whereas natural postsynaptic inhibition was associated with membrane hyperpolarization, experiments with coaxial pipettes failed to detect any hyperpolarization of motoneurons during the administration of GABA. Since at that time there was no evidence that GABA had a hyperpolarizing action in other parts of the CNS, Curtis concluded that GABA could not be the main central inhibitory transmitter. Recently, other investigators have demonstrated that in the cortical neurons of cat GABA imitates the action of the cortical inhibitory transmitter, at least qualitatively; it usually raises the membrane potential and increases conductance of cortical neurons, just like the normal inhibitory synaptic mechanism. When the latter inhibitory effect is artificially reversed by the administration of chloride into the neuron, the action of GABA is also reversed in a similar way. Similar results have been obtained on neurons in Deiters' nucleus. Therefore, at least as far as the cortex and Deiters' nucleus are concerned, there appears to be much support for the hypothesis that GABA is an inhibitory transmitter.

There appears to be no pharmacologically sensitive mechanism for the rapid destruction of GABA similar to the cholinesterase mechanism for destruction of acetylcholine. Thus, amino-oxyacetic acid or hydroxylamine given intravenously or iontophoresed does not appear to prolong significantly the duration of action of iontophoretically applied GABA. The exception is Deiters' nucleus, where the hyperpolarization produced by GABA on the neurons in Deiters' nucleus and the IPSP are prolonged in both cases by hydroxylamine, an agent of dubious pharmacological specificity. No functional reuptake mechanism for GABA within a mammalian system has been conclusively demonstrated either. However, GABA is actively and efficiently taken up by brain slices and synaptosomes, and this implies that some uptake phenomena are functional in the intact brain for recycling GABA and terminating its action. This mechanism could also explain why it has been difficult to collect GABA released from neural tissue. Unfortunately, no drug has been discovered that will effectively block the uptake of GABA into nervous tissue without exerting a number of other unwanted pharmacological actions. Therefore, it is difficult to evaluate the functional significance of this uptake mechanism. The development of a selective inhibitor of GABA uptake might prove to be quite useful in the study of GABA systems in the CNS. Some progress in the development of more specific agents has been made recently and the cloning of the "GABA" transporter should aid in this pursuit.

Several other potentially useful approaches can be identified: (1) It would be helpful to have a specific inhibitor of GAD, which would readily gain access to the CNS so that GABA formation could be selectively blocked. At present, no really specific inhibitors for GAD have been developed that will inhibit this enzyme in vivo without also inhibiting GABA-T to some extent as well as a number of other $B_6$-dependent enzymes; (2) Another real advance would be the development of a histochemical method for the visualization of GABA or GABA-related enzymes at both the light and electron microscope level. The recently developed immunohistochemical method for GAD and for GABA is an important step in this direction. This methodology is already providing useful cytological formation in mapping out GABA-containing and GAD-containing systems in the CNS.

A number of different techniques have been used to glean knowledge concerning the neuronal pathways in the brain using GABA as a transmitter. These include the binding of specific GABA receptor agonists in different brain regions and the autoradiographic localization of labeled GABA taken up through the high-affinity

uptake process, the calcium-dependent, depolarization-induced release of GABA from specific brain regions, the measurement of
GABA concentration and GAD activity in different brain regions,
and the changes in these various parameters after surgical or chemical
lesions of afferent pathways. However, the most powerful technique
has been the immunohistochemical localization of GAD-like and
GABA-like activity in the brain by means of specific antibodies
directed against GAD and GABA. In the most recent approach,
antibodies have been raised in rabbits against GABA conjugated to
bovine serum albumin. This antisera has been used to map GABA-
like neurons in the brain. In general, the distributions of GABA-
like and GAD-like activity parallel each other and detailed maps of
GABA- and GAD-containing neurons in brain are being produced.
The GABA antisera appears to provide better resolution of GABA-
containing cell bodies, while the GAD antisera provides better resolution of GAD-containing terminal fields. GAD localization studies
have already given additional support to a role for GABA as an
inhibitory transmitter in certain cerebellar, cortical, and striatonigral
neurons by localizing GABA synthesis to specific nerve terminals.

Studies employing the above techniques have demonstrated that
in the central nervous system of mammals, GABA is found primarily
in inhibitory interneurons with short axons. For example, the majority of GAD-like and GABA-like activity found in the cerebral
cortex, hippocampus, and spinal cord is present in inhibitory interneurons. At the present time, only two long axonal projections from
one brain region to another that utilize GABA as a transmitter are
known. These are the two systems alluded to above: the Purkinje
cells of the cerebellum and their projections to vestibular and cerebellar nuclei and a system of neurons in the striatum with axons
projecting to the substantia nigra. As noted in Table 7-1, this latter
region of brain (substantia nigra) contains the highest known concentration of GABA. It seems likely that these two immunocytochemical approaches will continue to be employed successfully and
will ultimately permit a detailed anatomical description of the GABA
pathways throughout the CNS. Once the anatomy of the GABA-
containing neuronal systems in the mammalian CNS is more clearly

defined, it should be possible to learn a great deal more about the functional aspects of these systems.

In summary, numerous biochemical observations have been made about brain GABA systems over the years which are consistent with a neurotransmitter role for this substance in mammalian brain. Similar to other neurotransmitters or neurotransmitter candidates, GABA and its biosynthetic enzyme (GAD) have a discrete nonuniform distribution in the brain. The brain contains a high-affinity, sodium-dependent transport system, and storage of GABA can be demonstrated in selected synaptosomal populations. The release of endogenous or radioactively labeled exogenously accumulated GABA can be evoked by the appropriate experimental conditions. Most recently, the presence of GABA-containing neurons has been verified, and the anatomical distribution of GABAergic neurons mapped out by use of autoradiographic and immunocytochemical techniques. However, the most compelling evidence that GABA plays a neurotransmitter role in mammalian brain has been provided by intracellular recording studies demonstrating that GABA causes a hyperpolarization of neurons similar to that evoked by the naturally occurring transmitter substance.

## GLYCINE

### As an Inhibitory Transmitter

Structurally, glycine is the simplest amino acid and is found in all mammalian body fluids and tissue proteins in substantial amounts. Although glycine is not an essential amino acid, it is an essential intermediate in the metabolism of protein, peptides, one-carbon fragments, nucleic acids, porphyrins, and bile salts. It is also believed to play a role as a neurotransmitter in the CNS. Over the past 2 decades, numerous neurochemical studies have attempted to separate and distinguish between the general "metabolic" and "transmitter" functions of glycine within the CNS. These studies have confirmed glycine's role as a neurotransmitter in the spinal cord and have suggested that this amino acid may play a similar role in more rostral portions of the CNS and also in the retina. Thus, glycine appears to have a more circumscribed function in the central nervous system than GABA since the inhibitory role for this substance is restricted to the spinal cord, lower brainstem, and perhaps the retina. Glycine also appears to be an exclusively vertebrate transmitter, making it unique among the transmitter substances. However, within the last several years very little progress has been achieved in developing pharmacological tools that act selectively on glycine systems or in generating more information concerning glycine metabolism in neuronal tissue.

Our knowledge of the metabolism of glycine in nervous tissue is still somewhat rudimentary despite the fact that the process has been studied extensively in other tissues. For example, we still do not know whether biosynthesis is important for the maintenance of glycine levels in the spinal cord or whether the neurons depend upon the uptake and accumulation of preformed glycine. As indicated in Figure 7-7, glycine can be formed from serine by a reversible folate-dependent reaction catalyzed by the enzyme, serine *trans*-hydroxymethylase. Serine itself can also be formed in nerve tissue from glucose via the intermediates 3-phosphoglycerate and 3-phosphoserine. It is also conceivable that glycine might be formed from glyoxylate via a transaminase reaction with glutamate. Although not established definitively, it seems likely that serine serves as the major precursor of glycine in the CNS and that serine hydroxy-methyl transferase and D-glycerate dehydrogenase are the best candidates for the rate-limiting enzymes involved in the biosynthesis of glycine. Not only is our knowledge of the metabolism of glycine in nervous tissue minimal, but at the present time only scanty information is available on the factors regulating the concentration of glycine in the CNS. Glycine in the spinal cord is labeled only slowly from radioactive glucose via one of the glycolytic intermediates indicated in Figure 7-7. It is also possible to label glycine by administration of labeled glyoxylate, which is readily transaminated to glycine by nervous tissue.

Substantial evidence now exists to indicate that glycine may play a role as an inhibitory transmitter in the mammalian spinal cord. From the evidence available we will try to assess how well this

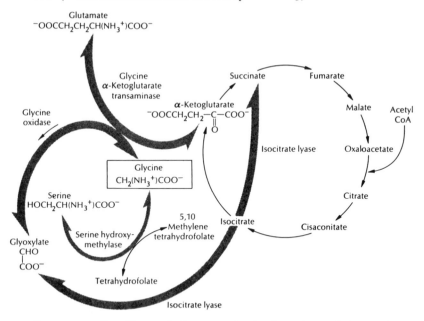

FIGURE 7-7. Possible metabolic routes for the formation and degradation of glycine by nervous tissue. (Modified after Roberts and Hammerschlag, in: *Basic Neurochemistry*, Little, Brown, Boston, 1972, p. 151)

compound fulfills the criteria necessary to categorize this substance as a central nervous system inhibitory transmitter. First, we can say that this amino acid is found in relatively high concentrations in the spinal cord compared with other amino acids. Table 7-3 illustrates the occurrence of glycine and other free amino acids in the spinal cord, and from these data it is apparent that glycine is more concentrated in the spinal gray matter than in the spinal white matter. The concentration found in the spinal gray matter is much higher than the level in whole brain or spinal roots. This high level of glycine in the ventral horn, together with the comparatively low content in ventral root fibers, initially suggested that glycine may be associated with the inhibitory interneurons, and subsequently this was shown to be the case. From iontophoretic studies the compounds in Table 7-3 can be divided into four main groups.

1. Excitatory   glutamate, aspartate
2. Inhibitory   GABA, glycine, alanine, cystathionine, and
                serine
3. Inactive    glutamine, leucine, threonine, and lysine
4. Untested    arginine and methyl histidine

Of the amino acids in group 2, cystathionine and serine appear to have a weaker and relatively sluggish action on spinal neurons compared with that of GABA and glycine. Therefore, in view of the distribution and the relative inhibitory potency of the compounds in this group, it was suggested by Aprison and Werman that GABA and glycine were the most likely candidates for spinal inhibitory transmitters. Glycine administered by iontophoretic techniques was consistently found to diminish the firing and excitability of both spinal motoneurons and interneurons. This is interesting in itself since glycine is quite ineffective as an inhibitor of cortical neurons. In addition, the hyperpolarization and the changes in membrane

TABLE 7-3. Amino acid concentration of cat spinal cord and roots
($\mu$moles/g)

| Amino acids | Spinal gray | Dorsal root | Ventral root |
|---|---|---|---|
| Alanine | 0.62 | 0.36 | 0.30 |
| Arginine | 0.14 | 0.07 | 0.06 |
| Aspartate | 2.14 | 0.79 | 1.13 |
| Cystathionine | 3.02 | 0.02 | 0.01 |
| GABA | 0.84 | Trace | Trace |
| Glutamate | 4.48 | 3.33 | 2.09 |
| Glutamine | 5.48 | 1.46 | 1.10 |
| Glycine | 4.47 | 0.28 | 0.32 |
| Leucine | 0.16 | 0.06 | 0.05 |
| Lysine | 0.16 | 0.07 | 0.05 |
| Serine | 0.41 | 0.32 | 0.23 |
| Threonine | 0.21 | 0.18 | 0.15 |

SOURCE: M. H. Aprison and R. Werman (1968), *Neurosciences Research* 1, 157, Academic Press, New York.

permeability produced by glycine seem to be quite similar to those produced by the spinal inhibitory transmitter. Alteration in $K^+$ or $Cl^-$ ion concentrations affect the inhibitory postsynapic potentials and the glycine-induced potentials in the same fashion. Strychnine, a compound that has been shown to reduce spinal postsynaptic inhibition, also blocks the effects of glycine on spinal motoneurons. It was originally reported that strychnine reversibly blocks the action of the natural inhibitory synaptic transmitter(s), as well as glycine and β-alanine, but does not have any effect on the hyperpolarizing action of GABA in cats anesthetized with pentobarbital. However, similar experiments on decerebrated, unanesthetized cats have indicated that the qualitative dichotomy between glycine and β-alanine and GABA originally reported does not usually hold. Instead, only a quantitative difference in the interaction of strychnine and the amino acids above is reported. It is of interest that except for experiments with strychnine, there has been little pharmacological manipulation of neurons that release glycine. In all these experiments, strychnine antagonized glycine more potently than GABA. However, GABA also inhibits these spinal neurons and is present endogenously, and in the course of distinguishing between the relative merits of GABA and glycine as inhibitory transmitter candidates in the spinal cord, it was of interest to see if a loss of function of inhibitory interneurons would be accompanied by a change in one or both of these compounds. Anoxia of the lumbosacral cord produced by clamping the thoracic aorta seems to destroy the interneurons preferentially, while leaving 80 percent or more of the motoneurons intact. Thus, the presynaptic cells responsible for inhibition (and other functions) are lost, and therefore the concentration of transmitter associated with those cells would be expected to be decreased. When the effect of anoxia on GABA and glycine content of the cat spinal cord was analyzed, glycine was the only potential inhibitory amino acid markedly decreased. Thus the distribution of glycine in the spinal cord of the cat appears to be related to the inhibitory interneurons. Some preliminary results with perfused toad spinal cord have indicated that glycine release appears to occur during stimulation of the dorsal roots. However, the release of glycine from interneurons in the cord has not yet been demonstrated. In summary, glycine thus satisfies many of the criteria sufficiently to warrant its consideration as a possible inhibitory transmitter in the cat spinal cord.

1. It occurs in the cat spinal cord associated with interneurons.
2. When administered iontophoretically, it hyperpolarizes motoneurons to the same equilibrium potential as postsynaptic inhibition.
3. The permeability changes of the postsynaptic membrane induced by glycine appear to be similar to those associated with postsynaptic inhibition.
4. Strychnine, a drug that blocks the action of glycine, also blocks postsynaptic inhibition.
5. Stimulation of dorsal roots causes release of glycine from perfused spinal cord.

The mechanisms by which the action of iontophoretically applied glycine or that of the putative spinal inhibitory transmitters are terminated are not known at this time. Recently, it has been demonstrated that there is an active and efficient sodium-dependent uptake mechanism for glycine in rat spinal cord and that labeled glycine taken up into slices can be released by electrical or potassium stimulation. However, whether or not this uptake mechanism is the physiological mechanism by which the action of administered or release glycine is terminated remains to be determined. Also, to date, very little appears to be known about the factors controlling the release of glycine from the spinal cord. Again, as with GABA, the efficient uptake process may explain why it is difficult to detect glycine release from the CNS. The main problems (as with GABA, glutamate, etc.) is that there is no distinct neuronal pathway that may be isolated and stimulated; thus, all the induced activity is very generalized, making the significance of any demonstrable release (metabolite or excess transmitter) very difficult to interpret.

In summary, probably the most critical missing piece of evidence to establish an even more complete identification of the inhibitory role of glycine in the spinal cord is the demonstration that glycine is the main substance contained in the terminals of the interneurons that synapse on the motoneurons and that it is glycine that is released from these terminals when direct inhibition is produced. Some partial support for the localization of glycine has been provided by autoradiographic localization of glycine uptake sites as visualized by electron microscopy. However, demonstration of discretely evoked release of glycine from spinal cord interneurons has been more difficult to obtain.

Recently, a new role has been proposed for glycine that is distinct from its established role as an inhibitory transmitter in lower brain stem areas and in spinal cord mediated by a strychnine-sensitive chloride conductance. Several groups have shown that nanomolar concentrations of glycine increase the frequency of NMDA-receptor channel opening in a strychnine-insensitive manner and have suggested a mechanism involving allosteric regulation of the NMDA-receptor complex through a distinct glycine-binding site (see pp. 000–000 and Fig. 8). This action can be mimicked with glycine agonists and blocked by glycine antagonists. This concept is supported by the existence of strychnine-insensitive glycine-binding sites which have an anatomical distribution identical to that of the NMDA receptor. When compared with the effects of benzodiazepines on the GABA receptor, the enhancement of NMDA responses observed with glycine is much greater. This suggests that the main effect of glycine is to prevent desensitization of the NMDA receptor during prolonged exposure to agonists. Glycine appears to accomplish this by an acceleration of the recovery of the receptor from its desensitized state rather than by blocking the onset of desensitization. It has been speculated that glycine facilitation of synaptic responses mediated by NMDA receptors may be a common regulatory mechanism for excitatory synapses, which raises the question of the processes that regulate extracellular glycine concentration in brain regions where NMDA receptors play a critical role in excitatory transmission. An important question is whether endogenous glycine antagonists (such as kynurenate) play a role in regulating neuronal function where NMDA receptors are involved.

## GLUTAMIC ACID

It has been recognized for many years that certain amino acids such as glutamate and aspartate occur in uniquely high concentrations in

## ANTAGONISTS

$$HO-\overset{\overset{O}{\|}}{\underset{\underset{OH}{|}}{P}}-CH_2CH_2CH_2\overset{\overset{}{\underset{\underset{NH_2}{|}}{CH}}}-\overset{\overset{O}{\|}}{C}-OH$$

AP5
(D-2-amino-5-phosphonopentanoic acid)

$$HO-\overset{\overset{O}{\|}}{\underset{\underset{OH}{|}}{P}}-CH_2CH_2CH_2CH_2\overset{\overset{}{\underset{\underset{NH_2}{|}}{CH}}}-\overset{\overset{O}{\|}}{C}-OH$$

AP7
(D-2-amino-7-phosphonoheptanoic acid)

$$H_2NCHCH_2CH_2\overset{\overset{O}{\|}}{\underset{\underset{COOH}{|}}{C}}NHCH_2SO_3H$$

γ-D-glutamylaminomethylsulphonic acid

## AGONISTS

Kainic acid

Ibotenic acid

Quisqualic acid

$$HO-\overset{\overset{O}{\|}}{C}CH_2\overset{\overset{COOH}{|}}{CH}NHCH_3$$

N-methyl-D-aspartate

FIGURE 7-8. Structures of several conformationally restricted analogs of glutamate and several antagonists.

the brain and that they can exert very powerful stimulatory effects on neuronal activity. Thus, if any amino acid is involved in regulation of nerve cell activity, as an excitatory transmitter or otherwise, it seems unnecessary to look beyond these two candidates.

The excitatory potency of glutamate was first demonstrated on crustacean muscle and later by direct topical application to mammalian brain. However, except for the invertebrate model where substantial evidence has accumulated to support a role for glutamate as an excitatory neuromuscular transmitter, its status as a neurotransmitter in mammalian brain was uncertain for many years. This is probably in part explainable by the fact that glutamate (and also aspartate) is a compound that is involved in intermediary metabolism in neural tissue. For example, glutamate plays an important function in the detoxification of ammonia in the brain, is an important building block in the synthesis of proteins and peptides including glutathione, and also plays a role as a precursor for the inhibitory neurotransmitter, GABA. Thus it has been extremely difficult to dissociate the role this amino acid plays in neuronal metabolism, and as a precursor for GABA, from its possible role as a transmitter substance. The transport of circulating glutamate to the brain normally plays only a very minor role in regulating the levels of brain glutamate. In fact, the influx of glutamate from the blood across the blood–brain barrier is much lower than the efflux of glutamate from the brain.

In view of the many different roles assigned to brain glutamate in addition to its role as a putative transmitter, it is not surprising that its synthesis and metabolism are compartmentalized in a very complex fashion. Compartmentalization studies have indicated that a number of immediate precursors for glutamate synthesis exist: (1) from 2-oxoglutarate and aspartate by aspartate aminotransferase; (2) from glutamine by phosphate-activated glutaminase; and (3) from 2-oxoglutarate by ornithine-aminotransferase. The relative contribution of glutamine or glucose to transmitter glutamate synthesis in the brain is still an open question. It may be that the transmitter pool of glutamate will utilize any glutamate available, independent of its source, and that the synthesis of glutamate itself is not, under normal conditions, a rate-limiting factor. In view of the numerous "metabolic" and precursor roles served by excitatory amino acids (including glutamate), the presence of these amino acids in brain is not restricted to a particular type of neuron as is acetylcholine and the catecholamines, norepinephrine, epinephrine, and dopamine. Thus, even though neuronal systems believed to utilize glutamate or aspartate as transmitter substances are being described in the

CNS, it seems quite unlikely that it will be possible to accurately map out these systems by simply following the presence of glutamate or aspartate or their synthesizing enzymes. Mapping will require the use of these techniques in conjunction with other less direct approaches.

Despite its ubiquitous occurrence in high levels throughout the CNS, the unequal regional distribution of glutamate in the spinal cord (higher in dorsal than corresponding ventral regions) is one of the main observations in support of the proposal that this common amino acid functions as an excitatory transmitter released from primary afferent nerve endings.

A unique approach to investigating the possible role of glutamate as a transmitter in mammalian CNS has been the employment of a virus that selectively destroys granule cells in the cerebellum. After viral infection had destroyed more than 95% of the granule cells, a marked decrease in cerebellar glutamate was observed, but no significant decrease in other amino acids, including aspartate, was detected. The high-affinity, sodium-dependent uptake of glutamate was also significantly reduced following destruction of the granule cells. The selective decline of glutamic acid levels and uptake does not prove that glutamic acid is a neurotransmitter in the granule cells, although it is consistent with this hypothesis, especially since the granule cell transmitter is known to be excitatory.

A recent technical advance that has aided in the elucidation of the excitatory effects of glutamate and related amino acids is the discovery of several conformationally restricted analogs of glutamic acid that exhibit marked potency and specificity in depolarizing central neurons. These agents include quisqualic acid (isolated from seeds), ibotenic acid (isolated from mushrooms), and kainic acid (isolated from seaweed). (See Fig. 7-8.) Of these agents, kainic acid has been the most extensively studied. Kainic acid is about fifty-fold more potent in depolarizing neurons in the mammalian CNS than glutamate and thus is one of the most potent of the amino acid neuroexcitants. Extensive studies with this substance have revealed that direct injection of kainic acid in discrete brain regions results in selective destruction of the neurons that have their cell bodies at or near the site of injection. Axons and nerve terminals appear to be more resistant to the destructive effects of kainic acid than the cell soma. Although it was originally believed that the selective neurotoxic effects of kainic acid were due simply to excessive excitation of all neuronal soma exposed to this agent, it is now clear that the mechanism of its neurotoxic action is more complex. The neurotoxic action appears to involve an interaction between specific receptors for kainic acid and certain types of presynaptic input. For example, studies in the striatum and hippocampus indicate that kainic acid toxicity depends on an intact glutaminergic innervation of the injected brain region.

Kainic acid is now being used extensively as a research tool in neurobiology to produce selective lesions in the brain of experimental animals and to explore the physiological pharmacology of excitatory transmission.

The status of glutamate and aspartate as neurotransmitters has suffered through many cycles of acceptability and nonacceptability in the past decade. Although the case for glutamate as a transmitter in the mammalian CNS is considerably weaker than that for acetylcholine, catecholamines, 5-HT, GABA, and glycine, its case has been fortified in the last several years. In the vertebrate CNS, iontophoretic application of both glutamate and aspartate to nerve cells does produce depolarization and an increase in firing rate. In this connection, as was mentioned above, both GABA and L-glutamate are released from the cerebral cortex of the cat at a rate that appears to be dependent on its state of CNS activation—more GABA and less L-glutamic acid being released under conditions associated with "sleeplike" EEG patterns, with the reverse situation occurring under arousal conditions. This differential release does not appear to result from alterations in cortical blood flow, since the release of other amino acids such as L-glutamine and L-aspartic acid does not vary similarly with different conditions. However, at this time it has not been demonstrated that the origin of these amino acids is in fact from neurons or, for that matter, even from brain cells. The possibility could not be ruled out that these amino acids were derived from blood or cerebrospinal fluid. Although these experiments can be taken as supportive evidence for a role of these agents as transmitters, they by no means establish this role.

In spite of the above evidence suggesting that glutamate may be an excitatory transmitter in the CNS, little was known until recently about the biosynthesis and release of the pool of releasable "transmitter glutamate." Utilizing the molecular layer of the dentate gyrus of the hippocampal formation to provide a definitive system in which the major input appears to be glutaminergic, Cotman and co-workers have addressed these questions. Glutamate was shown to be released by depolarization from slices of the dentate tyrus in a $Ca^{++}$-dependent manner, and lesions of the major input to the dentate gyrus originating from the entorhinal cortex diminished this release and the high-affinity uptake of glutamate. Glutamate biosynthesis in the releasable pools was rapidly regulated by the activity of glutaminase and by the uptake of glutamine. These properties are all consistent with the properties expected of a neurotransmitter, and the observations strengthened the premise that glutamate may be an important neurotransmitter in the molecular layer of the dentate gyrus. Furthermore, these studies demonstrate that the regulation of glutamate synthesis and release share many properties in common with other transmitters. For example, similar to acetylcholine synthesis, the synthesis of glutamate is regulated in part via the accumulation of its major precursor, glutamine, and newly synthesized glutamate, like acetylcholine, is preferentially released. In addition, the synthesis of glutamate is regulated by end-product inhibition. This is similar to the mechanism by which the rate-limiting enzyme in catecholamine synthesis, tyrosine hydroxylase, is regulated in catecholaminergic neurons by dopamine and norepinephrine. It is interesting that these similarities are demonstrable despite the involvement of glutamate in general brain metabolism.

The vesicle hypothesis describing the quantal release of acetylcholine at the neuromuscular junction was introduced in the mid-1950s, since then the concept of vesicular storage and release of acetylcholine has become firmly established and has been extended to a number of other synapses and neurotransmitters. However, there was no direct experimental evidence for the participation of synaptic vesicles in the storage and release of excitatory amino acid neurotransmitters until recently. The concept has received strong support from the studies of Jahn and Veda and co-workers on isolated synaptic vesicles from mammalian brain. These studies have shown that vesicles are capable of glutamate uptake and storage and that they have a specific carrier for L-glutamate.

These studies on the dentate gyrus as well as many others have demonstrated that lesion studies coupled with biochemical measures of alterations in high-affinity, sodium-dependent uptake of glutamate in brain synaptosomes provide a useful technique for mapping out glutaminergic neuronal systems in the brain, although this technique cannot be used to differentiate between glutamate and aspartate-containing neurons. Retrograde transport of D-aspartate after microinjection in terminal regions is another method that may be of value in tracing glutamate pathways. The success and specificity of this method is also dependent on the specificity of the uptake process and therefore is not capable of discriminating between glutamate and aspartate-containing neurons.

It is somewhat disturbing that glutamate, aspartate, and synthetic derivatives of these dicarboxylic acids result in almost universal activation of unit discharge; the endogenous excitants appear to be somewhat ubiquitous in the nervous system without the expected asymmetric distribution. It has also been reported that glutamate does not bring the cell membrane potential to the same level as the natural excitatory transmitter. In addition, both the D and the naturally occurring L isomers of excitatory amino acids are active, although in the case of glutamate the D isomer is often reported to be somewhat less active. These findings have led some investigators to suggest that the response to amino acids represents a nonspecific receptivity of the neuron to these agents and is therefore not necessarily indicative of a transmitter function.

However, based upon the current evidence, glutamate appears to have satisfied four of the main criteria for classification as an excitatory neurotransmitter in the mammalian CNS: (1) It is localized presynaptically in specific neurons where it is stored in and released from synaptic vesicles; (2) it is released by a calcium-dependent mechanism by physiologically relevant stimuli in amounts sufficient to elicit postsynaptic responses; (3) a mechanism (reuptake) exists that will rapidly terminate its transmitter action; and (4) it demonstrates pharmacological identity with the naturally occurring transmitter.

The most clearcut evidence that excitatory amino acids can act physiologically as excitatory neurotransmitters at a given synapse comes from experiments in which intracellular recordings of pre- and postsynaptic events can be made. In studies of this nature, the criterion of identical and parallel change induced by antagonists on synaptic events elicited by stimulation and those elicited by the action of the exogenously administered putative transmitter substance is of critical importance in identifying the excitatory amino transmitter involved. In many situations, however, such studies are not feasible and more indirect studies like those summarized above have been utilized.

It should be clearly stated that quite often at excitatory synapses the actual molecule acting at the postsynaptic receptor has not been definitively identified, even though pharmacological analysis indicates that the synaptic response is mediated by a particular excitatory amino acid receptor. Thus, a critical link in establishing a neurotransmitter role for an excitatory amino acid within a specific pathway is the demonstration and characterization of the excitatory amino acid receptor that mediates synaptic transmission at that synapse.

*Excitatory Amino Acid Receptors*

Our understanding of excitatory amino acid transmitters and their function and regulation has been greatly enhanced by studies directed at the identification, characterization, localization, and isolation of receptors for these amino acids. In fact, in the last decade, progress on the definition of receptor subtypes and the availability of more selective agonists and antagonists have produced a quantum leap in knowledge about excitatory amino acids at synaptic sites throughout the vertebrate CNS.

Until the mid-1980s, we were content with two major classes of excitatory amino acid (EAA) receptors—the NMDA (N-methyl-Dasparate) receptors and the non-NMDA receptors, the latter composed at that time of kainate and quisqualate receptors. With the development of more selective agonists and antagonists, however, the classes of EAA receptors have expanded to at least five different types (NMDA, kainate, AMPA, AP4, and ACPD) in the CNS, each displaying distinct physiological characteristics Three of these receptors have been defined by the depolarizing excitatory actions of select agonists (NMDA; kainate; and quisqualate, or alpha-amino-3-hydroxy-5-methyl-ioxyzole-4-propionic acid—also called AMPA) and the blockade of the effects of these agonists by selective antagonists. A fourth—the AP4 receptor (1-2-amino-4-phosphonobutyrate)—appears to represent an inhibitory autoreceptor. The fifth receptor, activated by trans-1-aminocyclopentane-1-3-dicarboxylic acid (ACPD) modifies inositol phosphate (IP) metabolism and has been called a metabotrophic receptor. A summary of representative agonists and antagonists for each of these excitatory amino acid receptor classes is given in Table 7-4.

Synaptic transmission in synapses using EAA does not appear to follow the simple model of fast-acting synaptic transmission mediated by a single receptor class. In fact, individual synapses that use EAA may not be restricted to distinct receptors but rather may have a combination of receptors and thereby exhibit different input/output properties and second messenger responses.

In recent years, a specific subtype of EAA receptors, the NMDA receptor, has become a major focus of attention because of evidence suggesting that it may be involved in a wide range of both neurophysiological and pathological processes as important and diverse as memory acquisition (see Chapter 13), developmental plasticity, epilepsy, and the neurotoxic effects of brain ischemia.

*NMDA Receptor-Ionophor Complex*

This receptor complex has been extensively characterized physiologically and pharmacologically and its anatomical distribution in the CNS has been traced. It is now clear that there are other functional subcomponents of the NMDA receptor in addition to the

TABLE 7-4. Classification of excitatory amino acid receptors in the mammalian CNS

| | NMDA | AMPA | Kainate | L-AP4 | Metabotropic |
|---|---|---|---|---|---|
| Other names | — | quisqualate | — | L-APB | ACPD |
| Selective agonists | NMDA, trans-2,3-PDA | AMPA, ATPA, 4-AHCP, 5-HPCA, 7-HPCA, Br-HIBO | — | L-AP4 | — |
| Other important agonists | *Recognition site:* Glu, Asp, quinolinate ibotenate *Glycine binding site:* Gly, D-Ser | Glu, kainate, L-ß-ODAP, 5-Br-willardine | Glu, kainate, domoate, 5-bromo-willardine | Glu, L-$0$-phosphoserine | Glu, quisqualate*, ibotenate*, trans-ACPD |
| Selective antagonists | D-AP5, CPP, CGS19755, CGP37849, D-CPPene | NBQX | — | — | — |
| Other antagonists | *Cbannel blockers:* Ketamine, PCP, SKF10047, MK801 *Glycine site:* HA966,7-chlorokynurenate, CNQX, DNQX, MNQX | CNQX, DNQX, NBQX | CNQZX/DNQX kynurenate, γ-DGG, GAMS | — | — |
| Effective pathways | $NA^+/CA^{2+}/K^+$ | $NA^+/K^+$ | presumed $Na^+/K^+$ (presynaptic?) | presynaptic inhibition? | $IP_3$/DAG |

*Selective in terms of $IP_3$/DG stimulation only. Glu, glutamate; Asp, aspartate; gly., glycine; Ser, serine; NMDA, N-methyl-D-aspartate; AMPA, α-amino-3-hydroxy-5-methyl-4-isoxazole propionic acid; L-APA, L-2-amino-4 phosphonobutanoic acid; ACPD, 1-amino-cyclopentane-1,3-dicarboxylic acid; PCP, phencyclidine; HA966, 3-amino-1-hydroxypyrrolidone-2. (Modified from Watkins et al, 1990)

transmitter recognition site, each with discrete ligand-binding domains. Thus, the NMDA receptor is analogous to the GABA-benzodiazepine receptor complex. At present, there appear to be at least five pharmacologically distinct sites through which compounds can alter the activity of this receptor (see Fig. 7-9). These sites include (1) a transmitter binding site that binds L-glutamate; (2) a regulatory site that binds glycine; (3) a site within the channel that binds phencyclidine and related compounds; (4) a voltage-dependent magnesium ($Mg^{2+}$) binding site; and (5) an inhibitory divalent cation site that binds zinc ($Zn^{2+}$). In addition, two distinct binding sites are also apparently associated with the transmitter recognition site, one that preferentially binds agonists and one that preferentially binds antagonists. It is of interest that quinolinic acid, a metabolite of tryptophan and thus a natural brain constituent, may be a specific antagonist for a particular subtype of NMDA receptor since it shows regional variation in potency. A number of glycine agonists and antagonists have already been identified for the glycine regulatory

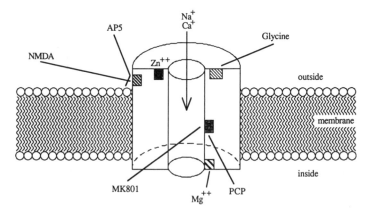

FIGURE 7-9. Schematic illustration of the NMDA receptor and the sites of action of different agents on the receptor. The NMDA receptor gates a cation channel that is permeable to $Ca^{2+}$ and $Na^+$ and is gated by $Mg^{2+}$ in a voltage-dependent fashion; $K^+$ is the counterion. The NMDA receptor channel is blocked by PCP and MK801 and the complex is regulated at two modulatory sites by glycine and $Zn^{2+}$; AP5 and CPP are competitive antagonists at the NMDA site.

site, even though the glycine binding component of the NMDA receptor was discovered only recently.

The glycine modulatory site has attracted a great deal of interest as a potential site for the action of new antiepileptic drugs or agents that might be useful in preventing ischemic brain damage. D-serine is a potent agonist at this site and (+)HA-966 is a selective antagonist. Glycine in submicromolar concentrations increases the frequency of the NMDA receptor channel opening in a strychnine-insensitive manner, and even though brain and CSF concentrations of glycine are in the millimolar range, glycine is effective in vivo, indicating that the glycine site is not saturated. Thus, conditions which alter the extracellular concentration of glycine or compete with its binding site can dramatically alter NMDA receptor-mediated responses. Attention has recently been directed to kynurenate, a tryptophan metabolite that has been shown to block the high-affinity glycine binding site. Kynurenate can be thought of as an endogenous neuroprotective agent which is released from glial cells following the transamination of L-kynurenine. Manipulation of endogenous kynurenate formation may provide further insight into the role it plays in modulating glycine's action on the NMDA receptor.

The function and distribution of the five classes of excitatory amino acid receptors are summarized in Table 7-5. The NMDA receptor is an essential component in the generation of long-term potentiation (LTP). LTP results in an increase in synaptic efficacy that has been proposed as an underlying mechanism involved in memory and learning (see Chapter 13).

In addition to the roles excitotoxic mechanisms may play in various chronic neurodegenerative disorders like Huntington's disease, two chronic neurological syndromes have been linked to dietary consumption of amino acid toxins of plant origin. Neurolathyrism, a spastic disorder occurring in East Africa and Southern Asia is associated with dietary consumption of the chick pea, *Lathyrus sativus*. β-N-oxalylamino-L-alanine (BOAA) has been identified as the responsible toxin in this plant. This amino acid acts as an agonist at AMPA receptors. Guam disease, also referred to as ALS/parkinsonism/dementia, is thought to be related to the consumption of

TABLE 7-5. Distribution and function of excitatory amino acid receptors in the mammalian CNS

| Receptor type | Distribution/Function |
| --- | --- |
| NMDA | Widely distributed in mammalian CNS (enriched in hippocampus, cerebral cortex). Demonstrated most easily by pharmacological antagonism under $MG^{2+}$-free or depolarizing conditions, or in binding experiments. Usually recognized as a slow component in repetitive activity generated primarily by non-NMDA receptors. Important in synaptic plasticity. |
| AMPA | Widespread in CNS; parallel distribution to NMDA receptors. Involved in the generation of fast component of EPSPs in many central excitatory pathways. |
| Kainate | Concentrated in a few specific areas of CNS, complementary to NMDA/AMPA distribution (e.g. stratum lucidum region of hippocampus). Difficult to distinguish from AMPA receptors pharmacologically, due to nonspecificity of kainate in electrophysiological experiments. However, present specificity (in absence of AMPA and NMDA receptors) on dorsal root C fibers. |
| L-AP4 | Inferred from the specific depressant effect of L-AP4 on certain excitatory pathways in brain and spinal cord in absence of antagonist effect on amino acid-induced responses. L-AP4 may act as an agonist at presynaptic glutamate autoreceptors (decreasing transmitter release). L-AP4 also mimics glutamate in hyperpolarizing ON bipolar cells in retina. |

*continued*

TABLE 7-5. *continued*

| Receptor type | Distribution/Function |
|---|---|
| ACPD (metabotropic) | Linked to $IP_3$ formation. Activated by glutamate, quisqualate, ibotenate and trans-1-aminocyclopentane-1,3-dicarboxylate (ACPD) but not by AMPA, NMDA, or kainate. Not antagonized by NMDA or non-NMDA antagonists but sensitive to pertussis toxin. May be involved in developmental plasticity. |

SOURCE: Modified from Watkins et al. (1990).

flour prepared from the seeds of the cycad *Cycas circinalis*, which contains the amino acid, β-N-methyl-amino-L-alanine (BMAA). Although BMAA is a neutral amino acid that is not directly excitatory or toxic in vitro, in the presence of bicarbonate it becomes excitotoxic and acts as an agonist at AMPA and NMDA receptors.

With the availability of more specific pharmacological agents, it should be possible to evaluate in more detail the involvement of excitatory amino acid pathways in normal brain function and in neuropathological conditions. The participation of NMDA receptors in long-term potentiation provides a strong link between these systems and the mechanisms of learning and memory. NMDA and other excitatory amino acid receptors also appear to play a role in cell damage caused by hypoglycemia, hypoxia, seizures, and other disturbances associated with excess excitatory amino acids.

SELECTED REFERENCES

*GABA*

Barbaccia, M.L., P. Guarneri, A. Berkovich, C. Wambebe, A. Guidotti, and E. Costa (1989). Studies on the endogenous modulator of $GABA_A$ receptors in human brain and CSF. In *Allosteric Modulation of Aminio Acid Receptors: Therapeutic Implications* (E.A. Barnard and E. Costa, eds.), pp. 125–138, Raven Press, NY.

Barnard, E.A., D.R. Burt, M.G. Darlison, N. Fujita, E.S. Levitan, P.R. Schofield, P.H. Seeburg, M.D. Squire, and F.A. Stephenson (1989).

Molecular biology of the GABA$_A$ receptor. In *Allosteric Modulation of Aminio Acid Receptors: Therapeutic Implications* (E.A. Barnard and E. Costa, eds.), pp. 19–30, Raven Press, NY.

Bowery, N. (1989). GABA$_B$ receptors and their significance in mammalian pharmacology. *Trends Pharmacol. Sci. 10*, 401–407.

Bowery, N.G., D.R. Hill, and R. Moratalla (1989). Neurochemistry and autoradiography of GABA$_B$ receptors in mammalian brain: Second-messenger system(s). In *Allosteric Modulation of Aminio Acid Receptors: Therapeutic Implications* (E.A. Barnard and E. Costa, eds.), pp. 159–172, Raven Press, NY.

Costa, E., H. Alho, M. Favaron, and H. Manev (1989). Pharmacological implications of the allosteric modulation of neurotransmitter amino acid receptors. In *Allosteric Modulation of Aminio Acid Receptors: Therapeutic Implications* (E.A. Barnard and E. Costa, eds.), pp. 3–19, Raven Press, NY.

Fahn, S. and L.J. Cote (1968). Regional distribution of γ-aminobutyric acid (GABA) in brain of the Rhesus monkey. *J. Neurochem. 15*, 209.

Gibson, K.M., L. Sweetman, W.L. Nyhan, G. Lenoir, and P. Divry (1984). Defective succinic semialdehyde dehydrogenase activity in 4-hydroxybutyric aciduria. *Eur. J. Pediatr. 1452*, 257–259.

Guastella, J., N. Nelson, H. Nelson, L. Czyzyk, S. Keynan, M.C. Miedel, N. Davidson, H.A. Lester, and B.I. Kanner (1990). Cloning and expression of a rat brain GABA transporter. *Science 249*:1303–1306.

Haefely, W.E. (1989). Pharmacology of the allosteric modulation of GABA$_A$ receptors by benzodiazepine receptor ligands. In *Allosteric Modulation of Aminio Acid Receptors: Therapeutic Implications* (E.A. Barnard and E. Costa, eds.), Raven Press, NY.

Jakobs, C., F. Hanefeld, M. Bojasch, E. Monch, D. Rating, and H. Siemes (1981). Urinary excretion of gammahydroxybutyric acid in a patient with neurological abnormalities. The possibility of a new inborn error of metabolism. *Clin. Chem. Acta 111*, 169–178.

Krogsgaard-Larsen, P., E. Falch, O.M. Larsson, and A. Schousboe (1987). GABA uptake inhibitors: Relevance to antiepileptic drug research. *Epilepsy Res. 1*, 77–93.

Krogsgaard-Larsen, P., A. Hedegaard, L. Nielsen, B. Nielsen, U. Madsen, L. Brehm, E. Falch, H. Hjeds, and J.J. Hansen (1989). Medicinal chemical and pharmacological focus on GABA and glutamic acid receptors in neurodegenerative disorders. In *Trends in Medicinal Chemistry '88* (H. van der Goot, G. Dományi, L. Pallos, and H. Timmerman, eds.), pp. 429–452, Elsevier Science Publishing, Amsterdam.

Mamelak, M. (1989). Gammahydroxybutyrate: An endogenous regulator of energy metabolism. *Neurosci. Biobehav. Rev. 13*, 187–198.

Möhler, H., P. Malherbe, J.M. Séquier, W. Bannwarth, P. Schoch, and J.G. Richards (1989). Location, structure, and sites of synthesis of the GABA$_A$ receptor in the central nervous system. In *Allosteric Modulation of Aminio Acid Receptors: Therapeutic Implications* (E.A. Barnard and E. Costa, eds.), pp. 31–45, Raven Press, NY.

Nicoll, R.A. and P. Dutar (1989). Physiological roles of GABA$_A$ and GABA$_B$ receptors in synaptic transmission in the hippocampus. In *Allosteric Modulation of Aminio Acid Receptors: Therapeutic Implications* (E.A. Barnard and E. Costa, eds.), pp. 195–205, Raven Press, NY.

Olsen, R.W. and A.J. Tobin (1990). Molecular biology of GABA$_A$ receptors. *FASEB J.* 4:1469–1480.

Price, G.W. and N.G. Bowery (1988). GABA$_A$ and GABA$_B$ receptor site distribution: An overview. *ISI Atlas of Sci.: Pharm.* 136–140.

Pritchett, D.B., H. Lüddens, and P.H. Seeburg Type I and Type II GABA$_A$-benzodiazepine receptors produced in transfected cells. *Science 245*, 1389–1392.

Schofield, P.R. (1989). The GABA$_A$ receptor: Molecular biology reveals a complex picture. *Trends Pharmacol. Sci. 10*, 476–477.

Sieghart, W. (1989). Multiplicity of GABA$_A$-benzodizepine receptors. *Trends Pharmacol. Sci. 10*, 407–411.

Ymer, S., P.R. Schofield, A. Draguhn, P. Werner, M. Koehler, and P.H. Seeburg (1989). GABA$_A$ receptor β subunit heterogeneity: Functional expression of cloned cDNAs. *EMBO J. 8*, 1665–1670.

*Glycine*

Becker, C.-M. (1990). Disorders of the inhibitory glycine receptor: The spastic mouse. *FASEB J. 4*, 2767–2774.

Betz, H. and C.-M. Becker (1988). The mammalian glycine receptor: Biology and structure of a neuronal chloride channel protein. *Neurochem. Int. 13*, 137–146.

Daly, E.C. and M.H. Aprison (1983). Glycine. In *Handbook of Neurochemistry*, Vol. 3 (A. Lajtha, ed.), p. 467. Plenum, New York.

Langosch, D., H. Betz, and C.-M. Becker. Molecular structure and developmental regulation of the inhibitory glycine receptor. In *Glycine Neurotransmission* (O. Ottersen and V. Storm-Mathisen, eds.). In press.

*Excitatory Amino Acid*

Cotman, C.W., A.C. Foster, and T. Lanthorn (1981). An overview of glutamate as a neurotransmitter. *Adv. Biochem. Psychopharmacol. 271*.

Cotman, C.W. and D.T. Monaghan (1987). Chemistry and anatomy of excitatory amino acid systems. In *Psychopharmacology: The Third Generation of Progress* (H.Y. Meltzer, ed.), pp. 197–210, Raven Press, NY.

Erik H., F. Wong, and J.A. Kemp (1991). Sites for antagonism on the N-methyl-D-aspartate receptor channel complex. *Annu. Rev. Pharmacol. Toxicol.* 31:401–425.

Headley, P.M. and S. Grillner (1990). Excitatory amino acids and synaptic transmission: The evidence for a physiological function. *Trends Pharmacol. Sci.* 11, 205–211.

Honoré, T. (1989). Excitatory amino acid receptor subtypes and specific antagonists. *Medicinal Res. Rev.* 9, 1–23.

Johnson, J.W. and Ascher, P. (1989). Modulation of the NMDA response by glycine. In *Allosteric Modulation of Aminio Acid Receptors: Therapeutic Implications* (E.A. Barnard and E. Costa, eds.), pp. 259–264, Raven Press, NY.

Marmo, E. (1988). L-Glutamic acid as a neurotransmitter in the CNS, *Med. Res. Rev.* 8, 441–458.

Maycox, P.R., J.W. Hell, and R. Jahn (1990). Amino acid neurotransmission: Spotlight on synaptic vesicles. *Trends Neurosci.* 13, 83–87.

Mayer, M.L. and R.J. Miller (1990). Excitatory amino acid receptors, second messengers and regulation of intracellular $Ca^{2+}$ in mammalian neurons. *Trends Pharmacol. Sci.* 11, 254–260.

Meldrum, B. (1985). Excitatory amino acids and anoxic/ischaemic brain damage. *Trends in Neurosci.* 9, 47.

Meldrum, B.S., A.G. Chapman, S. Patel, and J. Swan. (1989). In *The NMDA Receptor* (J.C. Watkins and G.L. Collingridge, eds.), pp. 207–216, Oxford University Press, New York.

Meldrum, B. and J. Garthwaite (1990). EAA pharmacology: Excitatory amino acid neurotoxicity and neurodegenerative disease. *Trends Pharmacol. Sci.* 11, 379–386.

Monaghan, D.T., R.J. Bridges, and C.W. Cotman (1989). The excitatory amino acid receptors: Their classes, pharmacology and distinct properties in the function of the central nervous system. *Annu. Rev. Pharmacol. Toxicol.* 29, 365–402.

Olney, J.W. (1989). Excitatory amino acids and neuropsychiatric disorders. *Biol. Psychiatry* 26, 505–525.

Olverman, H.J. and J.C. Watkins (1989). In *The NMDA Receptor* (J.C. Watkins and G.L. Collingridge, eds.), pp. 19–36, Oxford University Press, New York.

Pellicciari, R. et al. (1988). In *Frontiers in Excitatory Amino Acid Research* (E.A. Cavalheiro, J. Lehmann, and L. Turski, eds.), pp. 67–70, Alan R. Liss.

Schoepp, D., J. Bockaert and F. Sladeczek (1990). Pharmacological and functional characteristics of metabotropic excitatory amino acid receptors. *Trends Pharmacol Sci.*, *11*:508–515.

Watkins, J.C. (1989). The NMDA receptor concept: Origins and development. In *The NMDA Receptor* (J.C. Watkins and G.L. Collingridge, eds.), pp. 1–17, Oxford University Press, New York.

Watkins, J.C., P. Krogsgaard-Larsen, and T. Honoré (1990). Structure-activity relationships in the development of excitatory amino acid receptor agonists and competitive antagonists, *Trends Pharmacol. Sci.* *11*, 25–33.

Watkins, J.C., and H.J. Olverman (1988). In *Excitatory Amino Acids in Health and Disease* (D. Lodge, ed.), pp. 13–45, John Wiley & Sons, New York.

Young, A.B. and G.E. Fagg (1990). Excitatory amino acid receptors in the brain: Membrane binding and receptor autoradiographic approaches. *Trends Pharm. Sci.* *11*, 126–133.

# 8 | Acetylcholine

The neurophysiological activity of acetylcholine (ACh) has been known since the turn of the century and its neurotransmitter role since the mid-1920s. With this long history, it is not surprising when students assume that everything is known about the subject. Unfortunately, the lack of sophisticated methods for determining the presence of ACh in cholinergic tracts and terminals, which only recently has been partially overcome, has left this field far behind the biogenic amines. The structural formula of ACh is presented below:

$$(CH_3)_3N^+ - CH_2CH_2 - O - \overset{\overset{\displaystyle O}{\displaystyle \|}}{C} - CH_3$$

## Assay Procedures

ACh may be assayed by its effect on biological test systems or by physicochemical methods. Popular bioassay preparations include the frog rectus abdominis, the dorsal muscle of the leech, the guinea pig ileum, the blood pressure of the rat (or cat), and the heart of *Venus mercenaria*. In general, bioassays tend to be laborious, subject to interference by naturally occurring substances, and on occasion to behave in a mysterious fashion (e.g., the frog rectus abdominis is not as sensitive to ACh in the summer months as in the winter). Nevertheless, bioassays currently represent one of the most sensitive (0.01 pmol in the toad lung) and, under properly controlled conditions, the most specific procedures for determining ACh. It is probably fair to say that the neurochemically oriented investigator's natural fear and distrust of a bioassay have hampered progress in elucidating the biochemical and biophysical aspects of ACh. This statement is supported by a consideration of the plethora of information on norepinephrine. This neurotransmitter can also be bioassayed, but it was only after the development of sensitive fluorometric and radiometric procedures for determining components of the adrenergic nervous system that the information explosion occurred.

Until about 1965 physicochemical methods for determining ACh were so insensitive as to be virtually useless in measuring endogenous levels of ACh. Since then, however, papers have been published on enzymatic, fluorometric, gas chromatographic, chemiluminescent, and radioimmunoassay techniques that approach the sensitivity and specificity of the bioassays. Currently, the most popular assays are the GC-mass spectrometric procedure of Jenden and co-workers, the radiometric procedure of McCaman and Stetzler, the chemiluminescent assay of Israel and Lesbats, and the HPLC-electrochemical procedure of Potter and colleagues. Recently, Ricny and co-workers modified and combined several existing methods to develop a highly sensitive (0.2 pmols) determination of the transmitter.

SYNTHESIS

Acetylcholine is synthesized in a reaction catalyzed by choline acetyltransferase:

$$\text{Acetyl CoA} + \text{choline} \rightleftharpoons \text{ACh} + \text{CoA}$$

Before entering into a discussion of choline acetyltransferase, we should take note of Fig. 8-1, which depicts the possible sources of acetyl CoA and choline. In theory, the acetyl CoA for ACh synthesis may arise from glucose, through glycolysis and the pyruvate dehydrogenase system; from citrate, either by a reversal of the condensing enzyme (citrate synthetase) or by the citrate cleavage enzyme (citrate lyase); or from acetate through acetatethiokinase. In brain slices, homogenates, acetone powder extracts, and preparations of nerve-ending particles, glucose or citrate are the best sources for ACh synthesis, with acetate rarely showing any activity. In lobster axons, the electric organ of the *Torpedo*, corneal epithelium, and frog neuromuscular junction, acetate appears to be the preferred substrate. However, these systems are all in vitro and do not necessarily reflect the situation in vivo. Regardless of its source, acetyl CoA is primarily synthesized in mitochondria. Since, as detailed below, choline acetyltransferase appears to be in the synaptosomal cytoplasm, another still unsolved problem is how acetyl CoA is transported out of the mitochondria to participate in ACh synthesis. A probable carrier for acetyl CoA is citrate, which can diffuse into the cytosol and produce acetyl CoA via citrate lyase; a possible carrier is acetyl carnitine.

Evidence suggests that although phosphatidylethanolamine can be methylated to form phosphatidylcholine, free choline cannot be synthesized de novo in brain by successive methylations of ethanolamine. It is transported to the brain both free and in phospholipid form (possibly phosphatidylcholine) by the blood. Following the hydrolysis of ACh, about 35–50% of the liberated choline is transported back into the presynaptic terminal by a sodium-dependent, high-affinity active transport system, to be reutilized in ACh synthesis (see below). As outlined in Fig. 8-1, the remaining choline may be catabolized or become incorporated into phospholipids, which can again serve as a source of choline. It should be noted that le-

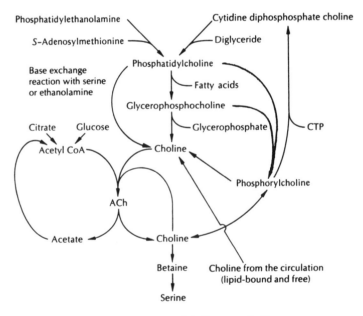

FIGURE 8-1. Acetylcholine metabolism.

sioning in the CNS or denervation in the superior cervical ganglion produces a decrease in choline content. A curious observation is that when brain cortical slices are incubated for 2 hours in a Krebs-Ringer medium, choline accumulates to a level about 10 times its original concentration. Similarly, a rapid postmortem increase in choline has been observed. The precise source of this choline is unknown; a probable candidate is phosphatidylcholine.

## CHOLINE TRANSPORT

Recent studies of choline transport have produced a number of significant findings:

1. Choline crosses cell membranes by two processes referred to as high-affinity and low-affinity transport. High-affinity transport with a $K_m$ for choline of $1-5$ $\mu$M is saturable, presumably carrier mediated, and dependent on sodium; it is also dependent on the membrane potential of the cell or organelle so that any agent (e.g., $K^+$) that depolarizes the cell will concurrently inhibit high-affinity transport. Low-affinity choline transport with a $K_m$ of $40-80$ $\mu$M appears to operate by a passive diffusion process, linearly dependent on the concentration of choline, and virtually nonsaturable.
2. In contrast to the other neurotransmitters, ACh is taken up only via low-affinity transport; it is only choline that exhibits high-affinity kinetics.
3. Current evidence suggests that the high-affinity transport of choline is specific for cholinergic terminals and is not present in aminergic nerve terminals. Furthermore, it is kinetically (but not physically) coupled to ACh synthesis. It has been calculated that about $50-85\%$ of the choline that is transported by the high-affinity process is utilized for ACh synthesis. Low-affinity transport, on the other hand, is found in cell bodies and in tissues such as the corneal epithelium, and it is thought to function in the synthesis of choline-containing phospholipids. On the other hand, tissues that do not synthesize ACh (e.g., fibroplasts, erythrocytes, pho-

toreceptor cells) exhibit high-affinity choline transport which is coupled to phospholipid synthesis.

4. Hemicholinium-3 is an extremely potent inhibitor of high-affinity transport ($K_m$ of $0.05-1$ $\mu$M) but a relatively weak ($K_m$ of $10-120$ $\mu$M) inhibitor of low-affinity transport.

5. There are three obvious mechanisms for regulating the level of ACh in cells: feedback inhibition by ACh on choline acetyltransferase, mass action, and the availability of acetyl CoA and/or choline. Of these three possibilities, the major regulatory factor seems to be high-affinity choline transport. This view derives from early observations that choline is rate limiting in the synthesis of ACh, coupled with findings in a number of laboratories. Using the septal-hippocampal pathway, a known cholinergic tract, Kuhar and his associates have shown that changes in impulse flow induced via electrical stimulation or pentylenetetrazol administration (both of which increase impulse flow) or via lesioning or the administration of pentobarbital (both of which decrease neuronal traffic) will alter high-affinity transport of choline into hippocampal synaptosomes. In their studies, procedures that activated impulse flow increased the $V_{max}$ of choline transport, while agents that stopped neuronal activity decreased $V_{max}$. In neither situation was the $K_m$ changed, a result to be expected since the concentration of choline outside the neuron ($5-10$ $\mu$M) normally exceeds the $K_m$ for transport ($1-5$ $\mu$M). Recent evidence, however, is accumulating to suggest that this relationship between impulse traffic and choline transport does not occur in all brain areas (e.g., in the striatum, where cholinergic interneurons abound). In addition, the endogenous concentration of ACh is also implicated in regulating the level of the transmitter in the brain. Thus, in several studies an increase in choline uptake following depolarization of a preparation has been attributed to the release of endogenous ACh on depolarization. Other studies, however, suggest that this increased choline uptake is not related to ACh release but rather to an increase in $Na^+$, $K^+$-ATPase activity.

## CHOLINE ACETYLTRANSFERASE

With respect to the cellular localization of choline acetyltransferase, (CAT), the highest activity is found in the interpeduncular nucleus, the caudate nucleus, retina, corneal opithelium, and central spinal roots (3000–4000 μg ACh synthesized/g/hr). In contrast, dorsal spinal roots contain only trace amounts of the enzyme, as does the cerebellum.

Intracellularly, after differential centrifugation in a sucrose medium, choline acetyltransferase is found in mammalian brain predominantly in the crude mitochondrial fraction. This fraction contains mitochondria, nerve ending particles (synaptosomes) with enclosed synaptic vesicles, and membrane fragments. When this fraction is subjected to sucrose density gradient centrifugation, the bulk of the choline acetyltransferase is found to be associated with nerve ending particles. When these synaptosomes are ruptured by hypo-osmotic shock, synaptosomal cytoplasm can be separated from synaptic vesicles. In a solution of low ionic strength, the choline acetyltransferase is adsorbed to membranes and to vesicles, but in the presence of salts at physiological concentration the enzyme is solubilized and remains in the cytoplasm. In vivo the enzyme is most likely present in the cytoplasm of the nerve ending particle. However, a particulate form of the enzyme has been found at nerve terminals. This CAT, which when solubilized has the same kinetic characteristics as the soluble form, occurs in a much lower concentration but with a higher specific activity. Since a kinetic coupling has been observed between uptake of choline and acetylation, it is conceivable that this membrane-bound CAT is the physiologically relevant form of the enzyme. Support for this contention derives from three experimental findings: (1) Homocholine cannot be acetylated with a purified soluble CAT but can form acetylhomocholine when a lysed synaptosomal preparation is used. (2) Choline mustard aziridinium ion, an inhibitor of choline transport as well as of CAT, is a much more potent inhibitor of membrane-bound CAT than the soluble form of the enzyme. (3) A monoclonal antibody raised against *Torpedo* terminal membranes inhibits CAT and ACh release.

A cell-free system of choline acetyltransferase was first described by Nachmansohn and Machado in 1943. Since that time, the enzyme from squid head ganglia, human placenta, *Drosophila melanogaster*, *Torpedo californica*, and brain has been purified and some of its characteristics have been defined.

When highly purified from rat brain, choline acetyltransferase has a molecular weight of 66–70 kiloDaltons: It has an apparent Michaelis constant (Km) for choline of $7.5 \times 10^{-4}$ M and for acetyl CoA of $1.0 \times 10^{-5}$ M. Currently there is a controversy about the extent of the reversibility of the reaction, with recent estimates giving an equilibrium constant of 13. The enzyme is activated by chloride and is inhibited by sulfhydryl reagents. A variety of studies on the substrate specificity of the enzyme indicates that various acyl derivatives both of CoA and of ethanolamine can be utilized by the enzyme. The major gap in our knowledge of choline acetyltransferase is that as yet we do not know of any useful (i.e., potent and specific) direct inhibitor of the enzyme. Styrylpyridine derivatives inhibit the enzyme but suffer from the fact that they are light sensitive, somewhat insoluble, and possess varying degrees of anticholinesterase activity. Hemicholinium (HC-3) inhibits the synthesis of ACh indirectly by preventing the transport of choline across cell membranes. Until recently, another problem with choline acetyltransferase is that it was difficult to raise specific antibodies to this enzyme. However, immunohistochemical procedures have now been sufficiently improved to permit confident interpretation of localization studies.

## ACETYLCHOLINESTERASE

Everybody agrees that ACh is hydrolyzed by cholinesterases, but nobody is sure just how many cholinesterases exist in the body. All cholinesterases will hydrolyze not only ACh but other esters. Conversely, hydrolytic enzymes such as arylesterases, trypsin, and chymotrypsin will not hydrolyze choline esters. The problem in deciding the number of cholinesterases that exist is that different species and organs sometimes exhibit maximal activity with different substrates. For our purposes we will divide the enzymes into two rigidly defined classes: acetylcholinesterase (also called "true" or specific cholinesterase) and butyrylcholinesterase (also called "pseudo" or nonspecific cholinesterase; the term "propionylcholinesterase" is sometimes used since in some tissues propionylcholine is hydrolyzed more rapidly than butyrylcholine). Although their molecular forms are similar, the two enzymes are distinct entities, encoded by specific genes. Current evidence suggests that in lower forms butyrylcholinesterase predominates, gradually giving way to acetylcholinesterase with evolution. When distinguishing between the two types of cholinesterases, at least two criteria should be used because of the aforementioned species or organ variation.

The first criterion is the optimum substrate. Acetylcholinesterase hydrolyzes ACh faster than butyrylcholine, propionylcholine, or tributyrin; the reverse is true with butyrylcholinesterase. In addition, acetyl-β-methyl choline (methachol) is only split by acetylcholinesterase. That this criterion for distinguishing between the two esterases is not inviolate and must be used along with other indices is illustrated by the fact that chicken brain acetylcholinesterase will hydrolyze acetyl-β-methyl choline but will also hydrolyze propionylcholine faster than ACh. Also the beehead enzyme will not hydrolyze either ACh or butyrylcholine but will split acetyl-β-methyl choline.

A second criterion for differentiating the cholinesterases is the substrate concentration versus activity relationship. Acetylcholinesterase is inhibited by high concentrations of ACh so that a bell-shaped substrate concentration curve results. This is observed also when butyrylcholine or propionylcholine is used. In contrast, butyrylcholinesterase is not inhibited by high substrate concentrations, so that the usual Michaelis-Menten type of substrate concentration curve is obtained. The reason for this difference is that in acetylcholinesterase there is at least a two-point attachment of substrate to enzyme, whereas with butyrylcholinesterase the substrate is attached at only one site.

The type of cholinesterase found in a tissue is often a reflection of the tissue. This fact is used as a discriminating index between cholinesterases. In general, neural tissue contains acetylcholinesterase, while nonneural tissue usually contains butyrylcholinesterase. However, this is a generalization, and some neural tissue (e.g., autonomic ganglia) contains both esterases, as do some extraneural organs (e.g., liver, lung). In the blood, erythrocytes contain only acetylcholinesterase, while plasma contains butyrylcholinesterase. But plasma has primary substrates varying from species to species. Because of its ubiquity, cholinesterase activity cannot be used as the sole indicator of a cholinergic system in the absence of additional supporting evidence. To generalize on this point, until neuron-specific transmitter-degradating enzymes are discovered, it is a neurochemical commandment that in order to delineate a neuronal tract, one must always assay an enzyme involved in the synthesis of a neurotransmitter and not one concerned with catabolism.

A final criterion that may be applied to differentiate between the esterases is their susceptibility to inhibitors. Thus the organophosphorus anticholinesterases such as diisopropyl phosphorofluoridate (DFP) are more potent inhibitors of butyrylcholinesterase whereas WIN8077 (Ambinonium) is about 2,000 times better an inhibitor of acetylcholinesterase. The compound BW284C51 (1,5- bis-(4-allyldimethylammoniumphenyl) penta-3-one dibromide) is presumed to be a specific reversible inhibitor of acetylcholinesterase.

In discussing the various techniques that are used to classify the cholinesterases, we touched on some aspects of the molecular properties of the enzymes. Because very little work has been done on butyrylcholinesterase and because no physiological role for this enzyme (or enzymes) has been demonstrated, we will focus our attention on acetylcholinesterase. In sucrose homogenates of mammalian brain subjected to differential centrifugation, acetylcholinesterase is found both in the mitochondrial and microsomal fractions. The latter, consisting of endoplasmic reticulum and plasma cell membranes, exhibits a higher specific activity. This localization of the enzyme is supported by electron microscopic and histochemical studies that fix the activity at membranes of all kinds both in the CNS and the peripheral nervous system.

Both cholinesterases occur in several molecular forms that are classified as either globular or asymmetric. The globular forms $G_1$, $G_2$ and $G_4$ (Fig. 8-2) exist as monomers, dimers, and tetramers.

FIGURE 8-2. Schematic model of the molecular polymorphism of AChE and BChE. Open circles designate catalytic subunits. Disulphide bonds are indicated by S-S. Hydrophilic forms are G1, G2 and G4 forms. The asymmetric A12 forms have three hydrophilic G4 heads linked to a collagen tail via disulphide bonds. The G4 amphiphilic forms of brain are anchored into a phospholipid membrane through a 20-kDa anchor. The G2 amphiphilic forms of erythrocytes have a glycolipid anchor. In *Torpedo* AChE hydrophilic forms and amphiphilic G2 forms are produced by alternative splicing, so that the proteins are identical at 535 amino acids but are nonidentical at their *C*-termini [6].

SOURCE: From Chatonnet and Lockridge (1989).

Elongated forms that contain as many as 12 subunits and are attached to a collagen tail are classified as asymmetric. Regardless of the form, both cholinesterases occur in both a water-soluble and membrane-bound state.

With its turnover time of 150 microseconds, equivalent to hydrolyzing 5,000 molecules of ACh per molecule of enzyme per second, acetylcholinesterase ranks as one of the most efficient enzymes extant.

With respect to the topography of the enzyme, the twin-hatted diagram of the anionic and esteratic sites has been reproduced countless times and need not be presented again here. However, some discussion is in order since this was the first enzyme to be dissected at a molecular level. For this initiation into molecular biology we owe a debt of gratitude to Nachmansohn and his colleagues, particularly Wilson.

The active center of acetylcholinesterase has two main subsites. The first is an anionic site that attracts the positive charge in ACh; the second, about 5 Å distant, is an esteratic site that binds the carbonyl carbon atom of ACh. Current information suggests that the anionic site contains at lest one carboxyl group, possibly from glutamate, and the esteratic site involves a histidine residue adjacent to serine. The overall reaction is written as follows:

$$E + ACh \longleftrightarrow E \cdot ACh \rightarrow E \cdot Acetyl \xrightarrow{H_2O} E + \text{acetic acid} + \text{choline}$$

Information on the architecture of the active center has been derived not only from kinetic studies using model compounds but from a group of inhibitors known as the anticholinesterases. (The pharmacology of these agents will be discussed in the last section of the chapter.) The anticholinesterases are classified as reversible and irreversible inhibitors of the enzyme. Like ACh, both types of inhibitor acylate the enzyme at the esteratic site. However, in contrast to ACh or to a reversible inhibitor such as physostigmine, the irreversible inhibitors, which are organophosphorus compounds, irreversibly phosphorylate the esteratic site. This phosphorylation has been shown to occur on the hydroxyl group of serine when DFP was incubated with purified acetylcholinesterase. Although the organophosphorus agents (referred to as nerve gases although they are actually oils) are classed as irreversible anticholinesterases, there is a slow detachment of the compounds from the enzyme. Wilson observed that hydroxylamine speeded up this dissociation and regenerated active enzyme. He then set about designing a nucleophilic agent with a spatial structure that would fit the active center of acetylcholinesterase, and he did in fact produce a compound that is very active in displacing the inhibitor. This is 2-pyridine aldoxime methiodide (PAM), which has been used with moderate success in treating poisoning from organophosphorus compounds used as insecticides. PAM, with its quaternary ammonium group, does not penetrate the blood–brain barrier well enough to overcome central actions of the anticholinesterase. For this reason, atropine is usually used as an antidote along with PAM. It will be recalled that atropine blocks the effect of ACh at neuroeffector sites and has nothing to do with acetylcholinesterase. Currently, the oxime of choice in dephosphorylating organophosphorus-inactivated cholinesterase is HI-6 (1 [2-(hydroxyimino) methyl pyridinium]-2-(4-carboxyamidopyridinium) dimethyl ether dichloride).

Although the hydrolysis of Substance P by purified serum cholinesterase has been described, evidence now suggests that this activity may be due to contamination by dipeptidyl peptidase. A recent review of the cholinesterases by Taylor is recommended.

UPTAKE, SYNTHESIS, AND RELEASE OF ACh
*Superior Cervical Ganglion, Brain, and Skeletal Muscle*

To date the only major and thorough studies of ACh turnover in nervous tissue were done originally by MacIntosh, Birks, and colleagues, and more recently by Collier using the superior cervical ganglion of the cat. By using one ganglion to assay the resting level of ACh and by perfusing the contralateral organ, these investigators have determined the amount of transmitter synthesized and released under a variety of experimental conditions including electrical stimulation, the addition of an anticholinesterase to the perfusion fluid, and perfusion media of varying ionic composition. Their results may be summarized as follows:

1. During stimulation, ACh turns over at a rate of 8–10% of its resting content every minute (i.e., about 24–30 ng/min).

At rest, the turnover rate is about 0.5 ng/min. Since there is no change in the ACh content of the ganglion during stimulation at physiological frequencies, it is evident that electrical stimulation not only releases the transmitter but also stimulates its synthesis.

2. Choline is the rate-limiting factor in the synthesis of ACh.

3. In the perfused ganglion, $Na^+$ is necessary for optimum synthesis and storage, and $Ca^{2+}$ is necessary for the release of the neurotransmitter.

4. Newly synthesized ACh appears to be more readily released on nerve stimulation than depot or stored ACh.

5. About half of the choline produced by cholinesterase activity is reutilized to make new ACh.

6. At least three separate stores of ACh in the ganglion are inferred from these studies: "surplus" ACh, considered to be intracellular, which accumulates only in an eserine-treated ganglion and which is not released by nerve stimulation but is released by $K^+$ depolarization; "depot" ACh, which is released by nerve impulses and accounts for about 85% of the original store; and "stationary" ACh, which constitutes the remaining 15% that is nonreleasable.

7. Choline analogs such as triethylcholine, homocholine, and pyrrolcholine are released by nerve stimulation only after they are acetylated in the ganglia.

8. Increasing the choline supply in the plasma during perfusion of the ganglion only transiently increases the amount of ACh that is releasable with electrical stimulation, despite an accumulation of the transmitter in the ganglion.

9. The compound AH5183 (Vesamicol), shown by the Parsons' lab to inhibit ACh transport into synaptic vesicles, ultimately blocks release of ACh from the stimulated ganglia. This finding supports the contention that there is vesicular release of the transmitter in the periphery.

As stated above, this work on the superior cervical ganglion represents the most complete information on the turnover of ACh in the nervous system. Using a constant infusion of labeled phosphoryl choline into the rat tail vein, Costa and co-workers have developed a procedure for determining the turnover rate of ACh in whole brain, various brain areas, and in specific nuclei. These studies have shown that the turnover of ACh is not uniform throughout the brain. With respect to regulation of ACh turnover in cholinergic terminals of skeletal muscle, Vaca and Pilar, using chick iris, have elaborated on the work of Potter with the rat phrenic nerve-diaphragm preparation. With the iris and the diaphragm preparation, the same relationship of high-affinity choline uptake, ACh synthesis, and regulation by endogenous ACh has been demonstrated as previously described with CNS and autonomic nervous system preparations.

Microdialysis is a relatively new technique that is now being used to determine ACh regulation in freely moving rats. The procedure is to stereotaxically implant a cannula covered with a dialysis membrane that is perfused with a physiological solution. The dialysate is led into an HPLC system for determining ACh. This technique offers considerable promise for measuring basal and evoked ACh release under various experimental conditions.

*Brain Slices, Nerve-Ending Particles (Synaptosomes), and Synaptic Vesicles*

In 1939 Mann, Tennenbaum, and Quastel demonstrated the synthesis and release of ACh in cerebral cortical slices. In the succeeding fifty-two years these observations have been repeatedly confirmed but only moderately extended. The major finding of interest in all these studies is that in the usual incubation medium the level of ACh in the slices reaches a limit and cannot be raised. In a high $K^+$ medium the total ACh is increased substantially because much of its leaks into the medium from the slices. The experiments again suggest that the intracellular concentration of the neurotransmitter may play a role in regulating its rate of synthesis, in addition to the high-affinity uptake system for choline. This concept of a feedback mechanism is supported by the findings that the administration of drugs such as morphine, oxotremorine, or anticholinesterases at the most only succeed in a doubling of the original level of ACh in the brain. Regardless of the dose of the drug, no higher level can be obtained.

Much of the current neurochemical work on the release of ACh from the brain involves the use of nerve ending particles (synaptosomes). This preparation, independently developed by DeRobertis and by Whittaker, is derived from sucrose density gradient centrifugation of a crude mitochondrial fraction of brain. Although synaptosomes represent presynaptic terminals with enclosed vesicles and mitochondria, some postsynaptic fragments are often attached to them. A disadvantage of the preparation is its heterogeneity; the usual synaptosome fraction is a mixture of cholinergic, noradrenergic, serotonergic, and other terminals. In addition, as judged by electron microscopy and enzyme markers, the purity is around 60%; the contaminants may include glial cells, ribosomes, and membrane fragments that may be axonal, mitochondrial, or perikaryal. On the other hand, the advantage of these preparations is that they can be isolated easily and that synaptic vesicles can be collected by hypoosmotically shocking the synaptosomes. With respect to the disposition of ACh in synaptosomes, roughly half of the transmitter is found in vesicles and the other half in synaptosomal cytoplasm. The cytosolic localization could be artifactual, resulting from the preparation methods.

Following the discovery of these presynaptically localized vesicles that contained ACh, the conclusion was almost unavoidable that these organelles are the source of the quantal release of transmitter as described in the neurophysiological experiments of Katz and his collaborators. Thus, the obvious interpretation has been that as the nerve is depolarized, vesicles in apposition to the terminal fuse with the presynaptic membrane, and ACh is released into the synaptic cleft to interact with receptors on the postsynaptic cell to change ion permeability. Synapsin I, a phosphoprotein that is localized in vesicles, may mediate the translocation of vesicles to the plasma membrane. The subsequent sequence of events is not clearly pictured, but in some fashion presynaptic membrane is pinocytotically recaptured, vesicles are resynthesized, and simultaneously or subsequently repleted with ACh; the neuron is then ready for the next quantal release of transmitter.

Although the exocytotic release of hormones is well established, the release of neurotransmitters from the CNS via this mechanism as opposed to a cytosolic release and a gated mechanism has been questioned by several investigators (see reviews by Cooper and Meyer, Dunant, MacIntosh, and Silinsky). Clearly, neither purely morphological nor neurochemical experimentation has unequivocally answered this question.

Utilizing the *Torpedo* electric organ, Dunant has carried out cryofixation, electrophysiological, and biochemical studies on a millisecond time scale. His conclusions are (1) Although the *Torpedo* preparation differs cytologically from the neuromuscular junction, electrophysiologically the quantal release of ACh is identical in both preparations; (2) in the *Torpedo* electroplaque, it is cytoplasmic ACh that is released rather than vesicular ACh; (3) doing stimulation and cryofixation on a 1-ms time scale, there is no change in the vesicle profiles, but a dramatic appearance of presynaptic intramembrane particles. Dunant reconciles these observations by suggesting that cytosolic ACh is released through some gating mechanism in the presynaptic terminal that confers a quantal release. Support for this interpretation comes from Israel and his colleagues, who have isolated a protein from *Torpedo* presynaptic membranes that is referred to as a mediatophore. When this protein (incidentally also found in mammalian nervous tissue) is incorporated into ACh-loaded proteoliposomes, the addition of calcium and the calcium ionophore A23187 to the medium triggers the release of the transmitter. It is still not yet known whether this release is quantal. Unquestionably, the data from the Dunant and Israel labs are correct; whether their interpretation is correct remains to be seen.

## CHOLINERGIC PATHWAYS

The identification of cholinergic synapses in the peripheral nervous system has been relatively easy, and we have known for a long time now that ACh is the transmitter at autonomic ganglia, at parasympathetic postganglionic synapses, and at the neuromuscular junction. In the CNS, however, until the past few years, technical difficulties have limited our knowledge of cholinergic tracts to the motoneuron collaterals to Renshaw cells in the spinal cord. With respect to the aforementioned technical difficulties, the traditional approach has been to lesion a suspected tract and then assay for ACh, choline acetyltransferase, or high-affinity choline uptake at the presumed terminal area. Problems with lesioning include the difficulty in making discrete, well-defined lesions and in interrupting fibers of passage. This latter problem is illustrated by the discovery that a habenula-interpeduncular nucleus projection which, based on lesioning of the habenula, was always quoted as a cholinergic pathway is not: it turned out that what was lesioned were cholinergic fibers which passed through the habenula. Thus, although the interpeduncular nucleus has the highest choline uptake and choline acetyltransferase activity of any area in the brain, the origin of this innervation remains largely unknown. A quantum leap in technology for tracing tracts in the CNS has occurred in the past few years. Through the use of histochemical techniques (originally developed by Koelle and co-workers) that stain for regenerated acetylcholinesterase after DFP treatment (Butcher, Fibiger), autoradiography with muscarinic receptor antagonists (Rotter, Kuhar), and immunohistochemical procedures with antibodies to choline acetyltransferase (McGeer, Salvaterra, Cuello, Wainer), a clear picture of cholinergic tracts in the CNS is now emerging. The well-documented tracts are depicted in Fig. 8-3. There is additional information that in the striatum and the nucleus accumbens septi, only cholinergic interneurons are found. Also, intrinsic cholinergic neurons recently have been reported to exist in the cerebral cortex, colocalized with VIP (vasoactive intestinal polypeptide) and often in close proximity to blood vessels.

With respect to other neurotransmitter functions of ACh, there are a few bits of information that suggest that ACh may participate in circuits involved with pain reception. Thus, the findings that nettles (*Urtica urens*) contain ACh and histamine, that high concentrations of ACh injected into the brachial artery of humans have been shown to result in intense pain, and that ACh applied to a blister produced a brief but severe pain, all indicate a relationship between ACh and pain. That ACh may act as a sensory transmitter in thermal receptors, taste fiber endings, and chemoreceptors has also been suggested, based on the excitatory activity of the compound on these sensory nerve endings.

*Cellular Effects*

A variety of actions of ACh that may be viewed as cellular effects rather than neurotransmitter activity have been described. These include ciliary movement in the gill plates of Mytilis edulis, ciliary motility of mammalian respiratory and esophageal tracts, a hyperpolarizing effect on atrial muscle, limb regeneration in salamanders, protein production in the silk gland of spiders, the induction of sporulation in the fungus *Trichoderma*, protoplasmic streaming in slime molds, and photic control of circadian rhythms and seasonal reproductive cycles.

There is also a variety of tissues and organisms, such as human placenta, *Lactobacillus plantarum*, *Trypanosoma rhodesience*, and the fungus *Claviceps purpurea* in which ACh is found but where nothing is known of its action. One of the most interesting situations is the corneal epithelium, which contains the highest concentrations of ACh of any tissue in the body and yet contains neither nicotinic nor muscarinic receptors. Some evidence suggests that ACh may be involved in sodium transport in this tissue.

All the activities of ACh and its localization in nonnervous tissue which we have noted above suggest that this agent may be a hormone as well as a neurotransmitter. It is worthwhile for the student to keep in mind that all known neurotransmitters may possess this dual function. These two activities have already been shown to occur with the biogenic amines. Even when a neurotransmitter is found in nervous tissue, its action may satisfy the criteria for defining a hormone or a modulator rather than the currently strict criteria for a "classical" neurotransmitter.

## CHOLINERGIC RECEPTORS

As noted in Chapter 5, cholinergic receptors fall into two classes, muscarinic (Table 8-1) and nicotinic. At last count, five muscarinic receptors ($M_1–M_5$) had been cloned. All of them exhibit a slow response time (100–250 ms), are coupled to G proteins, and either act directly on ion channels or are linked to a variety of second messenger systems. When activated, the final effect can be to open

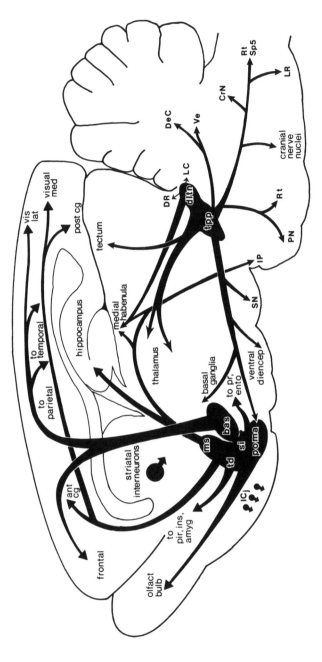

FIGURE 8-3.

or close K channels, Ca channels or Cl channels, depending on the cell type. With this array of channel activity, therefore, stimulation of muscarinic receptors will lead to either depolarization or hyperpolarization.

The pharmacological antagonists that have been used to define three of the muscarinic subtypes are pirenzepine, which has a high affinity for $M_1$; AFDX-116 with a high affinity for $M_2$; and 4-DAMP, which exhibits the highest affinity for $M_3$. The two classical muscarinic antagonists, atropine and QNB, do not distinguish the subtypes but block all equally well. What is needed are selective

---

FIGURE 8-3. Schematic representation of the major cholinergic systems in the mammalian brain. As illustrated, central cholinergic neurons exhibit two basic organizational schemata: (a) local circuit cells (i.e., those that morphologically are arrayed wholly within the neural structure in which they are found) exemplified by the interneurons of the caudate-putamen nucleus, nucleus accumbens, olfactory tubercle, and *Islands of Calleja complex (ICj)* and (b) projection neurons (i.e., those that connect two or more different regions). Of the cholinergic projection neurons that interconnect central structures, two major subconstellations have been identified: (a) the basal forebrain cholinergic complex composed of ChAT-positive neurons in the *medial septal nucleus (ms)*, *diagonal band nuclei (td)*, *substantia innominata (si)*, *magnocellular preoptic field (poma)*, and *nucleus basalis (bas)* and projecting to the entire nonstriatal telencephalon and (b) the pontomesencephalotegmental cholinergic complex composed of ChAT-immunoreactive cells in the *pendunculopontine (tpp)* and *laterodorsal (dltn) tegmental nuclei* and projecting ascendingly to the thalamus and other diencephalic loci and descendingly to the pontine and medullary *reticular formations (Rt)*, *deep cerebellar (DeC)* and *vestibular (Ve) nuclei*, and cranial nerve nuclei. Not shown are the somatic and parasympathetic cholinergic neurons of cranial nerves III-VII and IX-XII and the cholinergic α- and γ-motor and autonomic neurons of the spinal cord. Additional abbreviations: amyg, amygdada; ant cg, anterior cingulate cortex; CrN, dorsal cranial nerve nuclei; diencep, diencephalon; DR, dorsal raphe nucleus; ento, entorhinal cortex; frontal, frontal cortex; IP, interpeduncular nucleus; ins, insular cortex; LC, locus ceruleus; LR, lateral reticular nucleus; olfact, olfactory; pir, piriform cortex; PN, pontine nuclei; pr, perirhinal cortex; parietal, parietal cortex; post cg, posterior cingulate cortex; SN, substantia nigra; Sp5, spinal nucleus of cranial nerve five; (from Butcher & Woolf (1986) and Woolf & Butcher (1989).

## TABLE 8-1. Muscarinic receptors

| Subtype | $M_1$ | $M_2$ | $M_3$ | — | — |
|---|---|---|---|---|---|
| Previous names | $M_{1\alpha}$ | $M_{2\alpha}$, cardiac $M_2$ | $M_{2\beta}$, glandular $M_2$ | $M_2$ | — |
| Selective agonists | McN-A-343 | — | — | — | — |
| Selective antagonists[a] | pirenzepine (+)-telenzepine | methoctramine, AF-DX116, gallamine (not competitive), himbacine | hexahydro-siladifenidol, p-fluorohexahydro-siladifenidol | — | — |
| Effector pathways | $IP_3$/DG | cAMP↓ $K^+$ channel↑ | $IP_3$/DG | cAMP↓ | $IP_3$/DG |
| Gene | m1 | m2 | m3 | m4 | m5 |
| Amino acids | 460 (human) | 466 (human) | 590 (human) | 479 (human) | 532 (human) |

[a] No antagonist has a potency on one receptor that is more than tenfold greater than its potency on the other receptor subtypes. All receptors have $K_d$ values for (-)-N-methylscopolamine and (-)-3-quinuclidinylbenzilate of less than 1 nM.

SOURCE: Modified from *Trends Pharmacol. Sci.* supplement (1990).

muscarinic agonists that will define the various subtypes. More importantly, it would be a major advance if we knew whether each subtype subserved a specific function since, if this were the case, it would lead to the development of specific drugs.

Until relatively recently the identification of nicotinic cholinergic receptors in the CNS was an enigma. Using labeled α-bungarotoxin, nicotine, mecamylamine, or dihydro-β-erythroidine, each investigation yielded mystifying results in which the antagonist could not be easily displaced by ACh or by unlabeled ganglionic or neuromuscular antagonists but on occasion was displaced by muscarinic agonists and antagonists. A major problem has been the low density of nicotinic compared to muscarinic receptors in the brain.

Conversely, much is known about the properties of the nicotinic cholinergic receptor of *Torpedo* and *Electrophorus* electric organs. This reflects the abundance of the receptor in this tissue and the availability of two snake toxins, α-bungarotoxin and *naja naja siamensis*, that specifically bind to the receptor and have facilitated its isolation and purification. In the past four years, however, research with monoclonal antibodies and cDNAs has yielded considerable information about the mammalian nicotinic receptors (Fig. 8-4). At least four different receptors have been identified and can be tentatively differentiated by CNS, ganglionic, and muscle types as well as pre- and postsynaptic localizations in the CNS. Cholinergic nicotinic receptors from muscle or from electric organ contain 4 different subunits (alpha, beta, gamma and delta) with a stoichiometry of 2 alpha subunits and each of the other 3. In contrast, neuronal nicotinic receptors contain as of 1991) only 2 kinds of subunits (alpha and beta) with the alpha occurring in at least three different forms and the beta in two. When one considers the variety of combinations of these alpha and beta subunits that are theoretically possible, there appears to be a surfeit of nicotinic receptors in the brain. Whether future electrophysiological studies can assign a specific function to each of them is an open question.

As noted above, the nicotinic ACh receptor from electric organs is a pentameric integral membrane protein composed of four glycosylated polypeptide chains designated alpha, beta, gamma, and

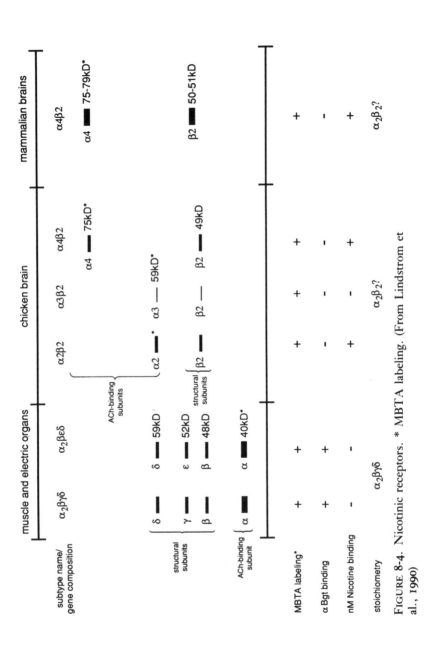

FIGURE 8-4. Nicotinic receptors. * MBTA labeling. (From Lindstrom et al., 1990)

delta, with a stoichiometry of 2 alpha subunits to 1 each of the other 3. All subunits traverse the membrane and, when viewed face on, resemble a five-petal rosette with a central pit. ACh binds to the alpha subunits and produces a conformational change in the channel that selectively allows cations rather than anions with a diameter of about 0.65 nm to pass through. The molecular weight of the receptor complex is about 255,000. Desensitization of the receptor increases when it is phosphorylated by cAMP protein kinase, protein kinase C, or tyrosine kinase.

An unexpected windfall resulting from the isolation of the nicotinic cholinergic receptor has been the demonstration that when this lipoprotein as isolated from *Electrophorus* is injected into rabbits, all the signs of myasthenia gravis appear. This finding, coupled with autoradiographic studies of muscle biopsies of myasthenics using labeled α-bungarotoxin as a tag where a marked deficiency of receptors is observed, has led to a better understanding of the disease at a molecular level. It is now clear that myasthenia gravis is an autoimmune disease in which a circulating antibody appears to be involved in an increased rate of degradation and damage, as well as antagonism of the ACh receptor. Since antibodies produced from *Electrophorus* or *Torpedo* ACh receptor result in myasthenic signs in rabbits, guinea pigs, and monkeys, this work also carries the implication that the ACh receptor is a phylogenetically conserved protein which can exhibit immunological cross-reactivity. For a complete account of the physicochemical properties of the ACh receptor and the kinetics of channel gating, the review by Aldrich et al. is recommended.

ACh in Disease States

Aside from myasthenia gravis and another autoimmune disease, the Lambert-Eaton myasthenic syndrome (a presynaptic problem involving diminished release of ACh), the role of ACh in nervous system dysfunction is unclear. Certainly a strong case can be made for familial dysautonomia, an autosomal recessive condition affecting Ashkenazi Jews that is in fact diagnosed by a supersensitivity of the iris to methacholine. Less clear are convulsive disorders where, experimentally, seizures can be induced by either applying ACh top-ically to the exposed cortex or by the administration of DFP, but where cholinergic drugs clinically have no therapeutic value. Huntington's chorea, involving a degeneration of Golgi Type-2 interneurons in the striatum, is reported to be partially ameliorated by physostigmine. The administration of physostigmine to patients with tardive dyskinesia has produced mixed results.

In Alzheimer's disease, characterized behaviorally by a severe impairment in cognitive function and neuropathologically by the appearance of neuritic plaques and neurofibrillary tangles, a cholinergic dysfunction has been implicated. This is based on the findings that (1) the administration of centrally acting muscarinic blocking agents to normal individuals induces a loss of recent memory; (2) in the cerebral cortex and hippocampus of patients with Alzheimer's disease there is a dramatic reduction of ACh, choline acetyltransferase, and high-affinity choline uptake; (3) in Alzheimer patients there is a severe reduction of neurons in the nucleus basalis of Meynert, the primary cholinergic input to the cortex; and (4) in some but not all studies, a decrease in muscarinic and nicotinic receptors has been noted. It should also be noted, however, that patients with Alzheimer's disease have decreased levels of somatostatin, neuropeptide Y, and NMDA receptors as well as reduced numbers of locus ceruleus neurons, and that a decrease in neuronal content in the nucleus basalis of Meynert has been observed in some patients with Down syndrome (trisomy 21) and with Parkinson's disease. Thus, the marriage of Alzheimer's disease to a cholinergic dysfunction may involve some extramarital relationships. Little success has been achieved to date by treating patients with choline, lecithin, physostigmine, or the muscarinic agonist arecoline. Until the genetic aspects can be sorted out, future therapy will perhaps require the development of a specific $M_2^-$ muscarinic antagonist, $M_1$ muscarinic or nicotinic agonist, or the transplantation of fetal cholinergic tissue to the brain with the hope that appropriate synaptic contacts or trophic factors can be restored.

Sites of drugs that affect the synthesis, release, and neurotransmitter activity of ACh are shown in Fig. 8-5. Structures of drugs that affect the cholinergic nervous system are illustrated in Fig. 8-6.

Figure 8-5. Sites of drug action at cholinergic synapses.

Site 1: ACh synthesis can be blocked by styryl pyridine derivatives such as NVP.

Site 2: ACh transport into vesicles is blocked by vesamicol (AH5183).

Site 3: Release is promoted by β-bungarotoxin, black widow spider venom, and $La^{3+}$. Release is blocked by botulinum toxin, cytochalasin B, collagenase pretreatment, and $Mg^{2+}$.

Site 4: Postsynaptic receptors are activated by cholinometic drugs and anticholinesterases. Nicotinic receptors, at least in the peripheral nervous system, are blocked by rabies virus, curare, hexamethonium, or dihydro-β-erythroidine; n-methylcarbamylcholine and dimethylphenyl piperazinium are nicotinic agonists. Muscarinic receptors are blocked by atropine, pirenzepine, and quinuclidinyl benzilate.

Site 5: Presynaptic muscarinic receptors may be blocked by AFDX-116 (an $M_2$ antagonist), atropine or quinuclidinyl benzilate. Muscarinic agonists (e.g., oxotremorine) will inhibit the evoked release of ACH by acting on these receptors.

Site 6: Acetylcholinesterase is inhibited reversibly by physostigmine (eserine) or irreversibly by DFP, or soman.

Site 7: Choline uptake competitive blockers include hemicholinium-3, troxypyrrolium tosylate, or AF64A (noncompetitive).

FIGURE 8-6. Structures of some drugs that affect the cholinergic nervous system.

## SELECTED REFERENCES

Aldrich, R.W., V.E. Dionne, E. Hawrot, and C.F. Stevens (1985). Ion transport through ligand-gated channels. In *Physiology of Membrane Disorders* (T.E. Andreoli, J.F. Hoffman, D.D. Farestil, and S.G. Schultz, eds.). Plenum Press, New York.

Benishin, C.G. and P.T. Carroll (1983). Multiple forms of choline-O-acetyltransferase in mouse and rat brain: Solubilization and characterization. *J. Neurochem. 41*, 1016.

Bonner, T.I. (1989) The molecular basis of muscarinic receptor diversity. *Trends Neurosci. 12*, 148.

Butcher, L.L. and N.J. Woolf (1986). Central cholinergic systems: Synopsis of anatomy and overview of physiology and pathology. In *The Biological Substrates of Alzheimer's Disease* (A.B. Scheibel and A.F. Wechsler, eds.). pp. 73–86. Academic Press, New York.

Chatonnet, A. and O. Lockridge (1989). Comparison of butyrylcholinesterase and acetylcholinesterase. *Biochem. J. 260*, 625.

Claudio, T. (1989). Molecular genetics of acetylcholine receptor-channels. In *Frontiers of Molecular Biology* (D. Glover and D. Hanes, eds.). IRL Press, London.

Cooper, J.R. and E.M. Meyer (1984). Possible mechanisms involved in the release and modulation of release of neuroactive agents. *Neurochem. Int.* 6, 419.

Cuello, A.C. and M.V. Sofroniew (1984). The anatomy of the CNS cholinergic neurons. *Trends Neurosci.* 7, 74.

Deneris, E.S., J. Boulter, J. Connoly, E. Wada, K. Wada, D. Goldman, L.W. Swanson, J. Patrick, and S. Heinenmann (1989). Genes encoding neuronal nicotinic acetylcholine receptors. *Clin. Chem.* 35, 731.

Dunant, Y (1986). On the mechanism of acetylcholine release. *Prog. Neurobiol.* 26, 55.

Eder-Colli, L., S. Amato, and Y. Froment (1986). Ampiphilic and hydrophilic forms of choline-o-acetyltransferase in cholinergic nerve endings of the Torpedo. *Neuroscience* 19, 275.

Eder-Colli, L., P.A. Briand, M. Pellegrini, and Y. Dunant (1989). A monoclonal antibody raised against plasma membrane of cholinergic nerve terminals of the Torpedo inhibits choline acetyltransferase activity and acetylcholine release. *J. Neurochem.* 53, 1419.

Fibiger, H.C. (1982). Organization and some projections of cholinergic neurons in the mammalian forebrain. *Brain Res. Rev.* 4, 327.

Goyal, R.K. (1989) Muscarinic receptor subtypes. *N. Engl. J. Med.* 321, 1022.

Israel, M. and B. Lesbats (1981). Chemiluminescent determination of acetylcholine and continuous detection of its release from torpedo electric organ synapses and synaptosomes. *Neurochem. Int.* 3, 81.

Israel, M., N. Morel, B. Lesbats, S. Birman, and R. Manaranche (1986). Purification of a presynaptic membrane protein which mediates a calcium-dependent translocation of acetylcholine. *Proc. Natl. Acad. Sci. (USA)* 83, 9226.

Jenden, D.J., M. Roch, and R.A. Booth (1973). Simultaneous measurement of endogenous and deuterium-labeled tracer variants of choline and acetylcholine in subpicomole quantities by gas chromatography/mass spectrometry. *Anal. Biochem.* 55, 438.

Kaufman R, G.A. Rogers, C. Fehlmann, and S.M. Parsons (1989). Fractional vesamicol receptor occupancy and acetylcholine active transport in synaptic vesicles. *Mol. Pharmacol.* 36, 452.

Kawashima, K., H. Ishikawa, and M. Mochizuki (1980). Radioimmunoassay for acetylcholine in the rat brain. *J. Pharmacol. Methods* 3, 115.

Kuhar, M.J. (1981). Autoradiographic localization of drug and neurotransmitter receptors in brain. *Trends Neurosci.* *4*, 10.

Lindstrom, J., R. Schoepfer, W.G. Conroy, and P. Whiting (1990). Structural and functional heterogeneity of nicotinic receptors. In *The Biology of Nicotine Dependence, Ciba Foundation Symposium 152*. London, England.

McCaman, R.E. and J. Stetzler (1977). Radiochemical assay for ACh: Modifications for sub-picomole measurements. *J. Neurochem.* *28*, 669.

McGeer, P.L., E.G. McGeer, and J.H. Peng (1984). Choline acetyltransferase: Purification and immunohistochemical localization. *Life Sci.* *34*, 2319.

MacIntosh, F.C. and B. Collier (1976). Neurochemistry of cholinergic nerve terminals. *Handbook of Experimental Pharmacology. Neuromuscular Junction* (V.P. Whittaker, ed.), Vol. 42, p. 991. Springer-Verlag, New York.

Marshall, I.G. and S.M. Parsons (1987). The vesicular acetylcholine transport system. *Trends Neurosci.* *10*, 174.

Massoulie, J. and S. Bon (1982). The molecular forms of cholinesterase and acetylcholinesterase in vertebrates. *Ann. Rev. Neurosci.* *5*, 57.

Mykita S. and B. Collier (1989). Acetylcholine synthesis by a sympathetic ganglion in the presence of 2-(4-phenylpiperidino) cyclohexanol (AH5183) and picrylsulfonic acid. *J. Neurochem.* *52*, 1686.

Nathanson, N.M. (1987). Molecular properties of the muscarinic acetylcholine receptor. *Ann. Rev. Neurosci.* *10*, 195.

Olsen, J.S. and A.H. Neufeld (1979). The rabbit cornea lacks cholinergic receptors. *Invest. Opthalmol.* *18*, 1216.

Potter, L.T. (1970). Synthesis, storage and release of [$^{14}$C]acetylcholine in isolated rat diaphragm muscles. *J. Physiol.* *206*, 145.

Potter, P.E., M. Hadjiconstantinou, J.L. Meek, and N.H. Neff (1984). Measurement of acetylcholine turnover rate in brain: An adjunct to a simple HPLC method for choline and acetylcholine. *J. Neurochem.* *43*, 288.

Ricny J., J. Coupek, and S. Tucek. (1989). Determination of acetylcholine and choline by flow-injection with immobilized enzymes and fluorometric or luminometric detection. *Anal. Biochem.* *176*, 221.

Rotter, A., N.J. Birdsall, A.S.V. Burgen, P.M. Field, E.C. Hulme, and G. Raisman (1979). Muscarinic receptors in the central neurons system of the rat. *Brain Res. Rev.* *1*, 141.

Rotundo, R.L. (1984). Purification and properties of the membrane bound form of acetylcholinesterase from chicken brain. *J. Biol. Chem.* *259*, 13186.

Salvaterra, P.M. and J.E. Vaughn (1989). Regulation of choline acetyltransferase. *Int. Rev. Neurobiol.* *31*, 81.

Sastry, B.V.R. and C. Sadarangivivad (1979). Cholinergic systems in nonnervous tissue. *Pharmacol. Rev.* 30, 65.

Schimerlik, M.L. (1989). Structure and regulation of muscarinic receptors. *Ann. Rev. Physiol.* *51*, 217.

Silinsky, E.M. (1985) The biophysical pharmacology of calcium-dependent acetylcholine secretion. *Pharmacol. Rev.* 37, 81.

Simon, R., S. Atweh, and M.J. Kuhar (1976). Sodium-dependent high affinity choline uptake: A regulatory step in the synthesis of acetylcholine. *J. Neurochem.* *26*, 909.

Steinbach, S. and C. Ifune (1989). How many kinds of nicotinic acetylcholine receptors are there? *Trends. Neurosci.* *12*, 3.

Taylor, P. (1991). The cholinesterases. *J. Biol. Chem.* *261*, 4025.

Tucek, S. (1984) Problems in the organization and control of acetylcholine synthesis in brain neurons. *Prog. Biophys. Mol. Biol.* *44*, 1.

Vaca, K. and G. Pilar (1979). Mechanisms controlling choline transport and acetylcholine synthesis in motor nerve terminals during electrical stimulation. *J. Gen. Physiol.* *73*, 605.

Wainer, B.H., A.I. Levey, E.J. Mutson, and M.-M. Mesulam (1984). Cholinergic systems in mammalian brain identified with antibodies against choline acetyltransferase. *Neurochem. Int.* *6*, 163.

Woolf, N.J., and L.L. Butcher (1989). Cholinergic systems: Synopsis of anatomy and overview of physiology and pathology. In *The Biological Substrates of Alzheimer's Disease* (A.B. Scheibel, and A.F. Wechsler, eds.). pp. 73–86. Academic Press, New York.

# 9 | Norepinephrine and Epinephrine

Norepinephrine and epinephrine belong to a class of compounds known as catecholamines. The term "catecholamine" refers generically to all organic compounds that contain a catechol nucleus (a benzene ring with two adjacent hydroxyl substituents) and an amine group (Fig. 9-1). In practice, the term usually means dihydroxyphenylethyl amine (dopamine, DA) and its metabolic products, norepinephrine (NE) and epinephrine (E). Major advances in the understanding of the biochemistry, physiology, and pharmacology of norepinephrine and related compounds have come mainly through the development of sensitive assay techniques and of methods for visualizing catecholamines and their metabolic enzymes or receptors in vivo and in vitro.

Bioassay procedures used to be one of the most sensitive methods for the estimation of epinephrine and norepinephrine in tissue extracts or biological fluids. However, the more recently developed radioenzymatic assays and high-performance liquid chromatographic techniques, coupled with electrochemical detection and mass fragmentographic methods are more sensitive and specific and have virtually displaced all other assay methods.

In 1946, it was demonstrated by Ulf von Euler in Sweden and shortly thereafter by Holtz in Germany that mammalian peripheral sympathetic adrenergic nerves use norepinephrine as a transmitter instead of epinephrine (which is the sympathetic transmitter in the frog). These findings laid the foundation for a new era of research in the field of catecholamines. At that time it was not technically possible to study the content of transmitter in terminal parts of the adrenergic fiber. Despite this, Euler predicted that norepinephrine was in fact highly concentrated in the nerve terminal region from which it was released to act as a neurotransmitter. This prediction was conclusively documented some 10 years later with the devel-

FIGURE 9-1. Catechol and catecholamine structure.

opment of techniques for visualizing catecholamines in freeze-dried tissue sections that helped define the anatomy of the adrenergic neuron.

## MORPHOLOGY OF ADRENERGIC NEURON

The morphology of the peripheral noradrenergic neuron became clear following the development by Falck and Hillarp of the fluorescent histochemical method for the visualization of catecholamines. Catecholamines in freeze-dried tissue sections are converted to highly fluorescent derivatives after exposure to dry formaldehyde vapor at 60–80° C. Under the fluorescent microscope all parts of the adrenergic neuron can be visualized (cell bodies, dendrites, axons, and nerve terminals) but the highest concentration of NE and strongest fluorescence is found in the nerve terminal varicosities. A diffuse innervation pattern is characteristic of the sympathetic nervous system and noradrenergic nerves. A single neuron can give rise to nerve terminal branches with lengths on the order of 10–20 cm, possessing several thousand nerve terminal varicosities (Fig. 9-2). The localization of catecholamines and their precursors within morphologically recognizable microscopic structures has been a great advantage to investigators interested in studying and understanding adrenergic mechanisms. The fluorescent histochemical method has also been used in conjunction with electron microscopy quite suc-

FIGURE 9-2. Schematic drawing of a noradrenergic neuron in the peripheral autonomic nervous system. Examples of innervated structures are illustrated. (Modified after Dahlstrom, 1986)

cessfully in the peripheral nervous system, where it is possible to correlate morphological changes (fluorescent intensity, content of granular vesicles) and catecholamine content. The lack of a suitable histochemical technique for the visualization of acetylcholine has been a serious handicap for those interested in cholinergic mechanisms.

Shortly after norepinephrine was established as the neurotransmitter substance of adrenergic nerves in the peripheral nervous system, Holtz identified NE as a normal constituent of mammalian brain. For some years, however, it was thought that the presence of norepinephrine in mammalian brain only reflected vasomotor innervation to the cerebral blood vessels. In 1954 Vogt demonstrated that norepinephrine was not uniformly distributed in the CNS and that this nonuniform distribution did not in any way coincide with the density of blood vessels found in a given brain region. This regional localization of norepinephrine within mammalian brain suggested that norepinephrine might subserve some specialized function, perhaps as a central neurotransmitter. The relative distribution of norepinephrine is quite similar in most mammalian species. The highest concentration is usually found in the hypothalamus and other areas of central sympathetic representation. More norepinephrine is generally found in gray matter than in white matter.

Dopamine is also present in the mammalian CNS and its distribution differs markedly from that of norepinephrine, an early indication that dopamine functions as more than a precursor of norepinephrine in the CNS. In fact, it represents more than 50% of the total catecholamine content of the central nervous system of most mammals. The highest levels of dopamine are found in the neostriatum, nucleus accumbens, and tuberculum olfactorium. The abundance of dopamine in the basal ganglia stimulated intensive research on the functional aspects of this compound, and there is now a wealth of evidence that it plays an important role in extrapyramidal motor function (see Chapter 10). Dopamine is also present in the carotid body and superior cervical ganglion, where it may play a role other than as a precursor of norepinephrine. The superior cervical ganglion appears to have at least three distinct populations of neurons: cholinergic neurons, noradrenergic neurons and small intensely fluorescent (SIF) cells. The SIF cells are believed to be the small interneurons that contain dopamine. The actual functional significance of these cells is unclear although it has been suggested that dopamine released from them is responsible for hyperpolarization of the ganglion.

Epinephrine concentration in the mammalian CNS is relatively low, approximately 5–17% (by bioassay) of the norepinephrine content. Many investigators have suggested that these original estimates are subject to error and in the past have discounted the importance of epinephrine in mammalian brain. However, its presence has now been documented by more sophisticated analytical techniques such as gas chromatography-mass spectrometry and liquid chromatography coupled with electrochemical detection, and has been confirmed by immunohistochemical techniques (see below).

The detailed topographical survey of brain catecholamines at different levels of organization within the central nervous system has provided a framework for organizing and conducting logical experiments concerning the possible functions of these amines. The anatomy, biochemistry and pharmacology of CNS norepinephrine and epinephrine systems are discussed in detail at the end of this chapter.

## LIFE CYCLE OF THE CATECHOLAMINES

### Biosynthesis

Catecholamines are formed in brain, chromaffin cells, sympathetic nerves, and sympathetic ganglia from their amino acid precursor tyrosine by a sequence of enzymatic steps first postulated by Blaschko in 1939 and finally confirmed by Nagatsu and co-workers in 1964 when they demonstrated that an enzyme (tyrosine hydroxylase) is involved in the conversion of L-tyrosine to 3,4-dihydroxyphenylalanine (DOPA). This amino acid precursor, tyrosine, is normally present in the circulation in a concentration of about $5–8 \times 10^{-5}$ M. It is taken up from the bloodstream and concentrated within the brain and presumably also in other sympathetically innervated tissue by an active transport mechanism. Once inside the peripheral neuron, tyrosine undergoes a series of chemical transformations resulting

FIGURE 9-3 Primary and alternative pathways in the formation of catecholamine: (1) tyrosine hydroxylase; (2) aromatic amino-acid decarboxylase; (3) dopamine-β-hydroxylase; (4) phenylethanolamine-*N*-methyl transferase; (5) nonspecific *N*-methyl transferase in lung and folate-dependent *N*-methyl transferase in brain; (6) catechol-forming enzyme (*Figure continues*).

in the ultimate formation of norepinephrine—or in the brain—norepinephrine, dopamine, or epinephrine, depending upon the availability of phenylethanolamine-*N*-methyl transferase and dopamine-β-hydroxylase. This biosynthetic pathway for the formation of catecholamines is illustrated in Fig. 9-3. The conversion of tyrosine to norepinephrine and epinephrine was first demonstrated in the adrenal medulla. The availability of radioactive precursors of high specific activity and chromatographic separation techniques has allowed the confirmation of the above-mentioned pathway to norepinephrine in sympathetic nerves, ganglia, heart, arterial and venous tissue, and brain. In mammals, tyrosine can be derived from dietary phenylalanine by a hydroxylase (phenylalanine hydroxylase) found primarily in liver. Both phenylalanine and tyrosine are normal con-

FIGURE 9-3. *Continued.*

stituents of the mammalian brain, present in a free form in a concentration of about $5 \times 10^{-5}$ M. However, norepinephrine biosynthesis is usually considered to begin with tyrosine, which represents a branch point for many important biosynthetic processes in animal tissues (Fig. 9-4). It should be emphasized that the percentage of tyrosine utilized for catecholamine biosynthesis as opposed to other biochemical pathways is very minimal (<2%).

## Tyrosine Hydroxylase

The first enzyme in the biosynthetic pathway, tyrosine hydroxylase, was the last enzyme in this series of reactions to be identified. It

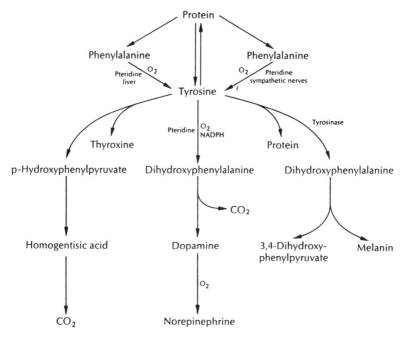

FIGURE 9-4. Metabolism of tyrosine.

was demonstrated by Udenfriend and his colleagues in 1964, and its properties have been reviewed repeatedly. It is present in the adrenal medulla, in brain, and in all sympathetically innervated tissue studied to date. This enzyme appears to be a unique constituent of catecholamine-containing neurons and chromaffin cells; it completely disappears from renal, salivary gland, vas deferens, and cardiac tissue upon chronic sympathetic denervation. The enzyme is stereospecific, requires molecular $O_2$, $Fe^{2+}$, and a tetrahydropteridine cofactor, and shows a fairly high degree of substrate specificity. Thus, this enzyme, in contrast to tyrosinase, oxidizes only the naturally occurring amino acid, L-tyrosine, and to a smaller extent L-phenylalanine. D-tyrosine, tyramine, or L-tryptophan will not serve as substrates for the enzyme. The human gene for tyrosine hydroxylase has been cloned. The single gene encodes multiple mRNAs that are heterogeneous at the 5' end of the coding region. The functional significance of the different messages remains to be determined.

The $K_m$ for the enzymatic conversion of tyrosine to DOPA by purified adrenal tyrosine hydroxylase is about $2 \times 10^{-5}$M, and in a preparation of brain synaptosomes about $0.4 \times 10^{-5}$M. Tyrosine hydroxylation appears to be the rate-limiting step in the biosynthesis of norepinephrine in the peripheral nervous system and is likely to be the rate-limiting step in the formation of norepinephrine and dopamine in the brain as well. In most sympathetically innervated tissues including the brain, the activity of DOPA decarboxylase and that of dopamine-β-oxidase have a magnitude 100–1000 times that of tyrosine hydroxylase. This lower activity of tyrosine hydroxylase may be due either to the presence of less enzyme or to a lower turnover number of the enzyme. Since this enzyme has been demonstrated to be the rate-limiting step in catecholamine biosynthesis, it is logical that pharmacological intervention at this step would cause a reduction of norepinephrine biosynthesis. Many earlier attempts to produce chemical sympathectomy by blockade of the last two steps in the synthesis of norepinephrine have proved largely unsuccessful. On the other hand, studies with inhibitors of tyrosine hydroxylase have proved to be much more successful producing a marked reduction in endogenous norepinephrine and dopamine in brain and norepinephrine in heart, spleen, and other sympathetically innervated tissues. Effective inhibitors of this enzymatic step can be categorized into four main groups: (1) amino-acid analogues, (2) catechol derivatives, (3) tropolones, and (4) selective iron chelators. Some effective amino acid analogues include α-methyl-p-tyrosine and its ester, α-methyl-3-iodotyrosine, 3-iodotyrosine, and α-methyl-5-hydroxytryptophan. In general, α-methyl-amino acids are more potent than the unmethylated analogues, and a marked increase in activity in the case of the tyrosine analogues can also be produced by substituting a halogen at the 3 position of the benzene ring. Most of the agents in this category act as competitive inhibitors of the substrate tyrosine. In this respect α-methyl-5-hydroxytryptophan appears to be unique, since it does not appear to compete with substrate or pteridine cofactor. Its actual mechanism remains unknown at the present time. The potent halogenated tyrosine analogues such as 3-iodotyrosine are about 100 times as active as α-methyl-p-tyrosine in vitro, but they are substantially less active in vivo. This is probably due to the very rapid deiodination of these compounds to tyrosine or tyrosine analogues which occurs in vivo. α-Methyl-p-tyrosine and its methyl ester have been the inhibitors most widely used to demonstrate the effects of exercise, stress, and various drugs on the turnover of catecholamines and also to lower norepinephrine formation in patients with pheochromocytoma and malignant hypertension.

*Dihydropteridine Reductase*

Although not directly involved in catecholamine biosynthesis, dihydropteridine reductase is intimately linked to the tyrosine hydroxylase step. This enzyme catalyzes the reduction of the quinonoid dihydropterin that has been oxidized during the hydroxylation of tyrosine to DOPA. Since reduced pteridines are essential for tyrosine hydroxylation, alterations in the activity of dihydropteridine reductase would effectively influence the activity of tyrosine hydroxylase. Thus, this might be a potential site for drug intervention in catecholamine biosynthesis. Dihydropteridines with amine substitution in positions 2 and 4 are effective inhibitors of this enzyme, while folic acid antagonists such as aminopterin and methotrexate are relatively ineffective. The distribution of dihydropteridine reductase is quite widespread, the highest activity being found in the liver, brain, and adrenal gland. The distribution of this enzyme activity in the brain does not appear to parallel the catecholamine or serotonin content of brain tissue, suggesting that reduced pterins most likely participate in other reactions besides the hydroxylation of tyrosine and tryptophan.

*Dihydroxyphenylalanine Decarboxylase*

The second enzyme involved in catecholamine biosynthesis is DOPA-decarboxylase, which was actually the first catecholamine synthetic enzyme to be discovered. Although originally believed to remove carboxyl groups only from L-DOPA, a study of purified enzyme preparations and specific inhibitors has subsequently demonstrated that this DOPA-decarboxylase acts on all naturally occurring aromatic L-amino acids, including histidine, tyrosine, tryptophan, and phenylalanine as well as both DOPA and 5-hydroxytryptophan. Therefore, this enzyme is more appropriately referred to as "L-aromatic amino acid decarboxylase." There is no appreciable binding of this enzyme to particles within the cell, since when tissues are disrupted and the resultant homogenates centrifuged at high speeds, the decarboxylase activity remains associated largely with the supernatant fraction. The exception to this is in the brain, where some of the decarboxylase activity is associated with synaptosomes. However, since synaptosomes are in essence pinched-off nerve endings, they would be expected to retain entrapped cytoplasm as well as other intracellular organelles. The DOPA-decarboxylase found in synaptosomal preparations is thought to be present in the entrapped cytoplasm. DOPA-decarboxylase is, relative to other enzymes in the biosynthetic pathway for norepinephrine formation, very active and requires pyridoxal phosphate (vitamin $B_6$) as a cofactor. The apparent $K_m$ value for this enzyme is $4 \times 10^{-4}$ M. The high activity of this enzyme may explain why it has been difficult to detect endogenous DOPA in sympathetically innervated tissue and brain. It is rather ubiquitous in nature, occurring in the cytoplasm of most tissue including the liver, stomach, brain, and kidney in high levels, suggesting that its function in metabolism is not limited solely to catecholamine biosynthesis. Although decarboxylase activity can be reduced by production of vitamin $B_6$ deficiency in animals, this does not usually result in a significant reduction of tissue catecholamines although it appears to interfere with the rate of repletion of adrenal catecholamines after insulin depletion. In addition, potent decarboxylase inhibitors also have very little effect on endogenous levels of norepinephrine in tissue. However, these inhibitors have been useful as pharmacological tools (e.g., DOPA accumulation following admininstration of a decarboxylase inhibitor as an in vivo index of tyrosine hydroxylation).

*Dopamine-β-Hydroxylase*

Although it has been known for many years that the brain, sympathetically innervated tissue, sympathetic ganglia, and adrenal medulla could transform dopamine into norepinephrine, it was not until 1960 that the enzyme responsible for this conversion was isolated from the adrenal medulla. This enzyme, called dopamine-β-hydroxylase, is, like tyrosine hydroxylase, a mixed-function oxidase. It requires molecular oxygen and utilizes ascorbic acid as a cofactor. The $K_m$ of this enzyme for its substrate dopamine is about $5 \times 10^{-3}$M. Dicarboxylic acids such as fumaric acid are not absolute requirements, but they stimulate the reaction. Dopamine-β-hydroxylase is a $Cu^{2+}$-containing protein, with about two moles of cupric ion/mole of enzyme. It appears to be associated with the particulate fraction from the heart, brain, sympathetic nerve, and adrenal medulla, and it is believed that this enzyme is localized primarily in the membrane of the amine storage granules. This enzyme usually disappears after chronic sympathetic denervation and therefore is believed to be present largely only in adrenergic neurons or adrenal chromaffin tissue. Dopamine-β-hydroxylase does not show a high degree of substrate specificity and acts in vitro on a variety of substrates besides dopamine, oxidizing almost any phenylethylamine to its corresponding phenylethanolamine (i.e., tyramine → octopamine, α-methyldopamine → α-methylnorepinephrine). A number of the resultant structurally analogous metabolites can replace norepinephrine at the noradrenergic nerve endings and function as "false neurotransmitters."

Dopamine-β-hydroxylase can be inhibited by a variety of compounds. The most effective are compounds which chelate copper: D-cysteine and L-cysteine, glutathione, mercaptoethanol, and coenzyme A. The inhibition can be reversed by addition of *N*-ethylmaleimide, which reacts with the sulfhydryl groups and interferes with the chelating properties of these substances. Copper chelating agents such as diethyldithiocarbamate and FLA-63 [bis-(l-methyl-4-homopiperazinyl-thiocarbonyl)-disulfide] have proved to be effective inhibitors both in vivo and in vitro. Thus, it has been possible to treat animals with disulfuram or FLA-63 and produce a reduction in brain norepinephrine and an elevation of brain dopamine.

Since dopamine-β-hydroxylase obtained from the bovine adrenal medulla can be prepared in a relatively pure form, it has been possible to produce a specific antibody to the enzyme. This antibody inactivates bovine dopamine-β-hydroxylase but does not appear to cross-react with either DOPA-decarboxylase or tyrosine hydroxylase. However, cross-reactivity between dopamine-β-hydroxylase from human, guinea pig, and dog with the antibody against the bovine enzyme was observed and indicates that the enzymes from these various sources are probably structurally related. By coupling immunochemical techniques with fluorescence and electron microscopy, this antibody has already proved useful in localization of this enzyme in intact tissue. Dopamine β-hydroxylase has recently been cloned. Further studies on the molecular structure and expression of the enzyme should yield interesting information.

### Phenylethanolamine-N-Methyl Transferase

In the adrenal medulla norepinephrine is N-methylated by the enzyme phenylethanolamine-N-methyl transferase to form epinephrine. This enzyme is largely restricted to the adrenal medulla, although low levels of activity have been reported in heart and mammalian brain (see Chapter 10). Like the decarboxylase, this enzyme also appears in the supernatant of homogenates. Demonstration of activity requires the presence of the methyl donor S-adenosyl methionine. The adrenal medullary enzyme shows poor substrate specificity and will transfer methyl groups to the nitrogen atom on a variety of β-hydroxylated amines. However, this adrenal enzyme is distinct from the nonspecific N-methyl transferase of rabbit lung, which, in addition to N-methylating phenylethanolamine derivatives, will also react with many normally occurring indoleamines and such diverse structures as phenylisopropylamine, aromatic amines, and phenanthrenes. Interest in the biosynthetic pathway for catecholamines has also led to the cloning of phenylethanolamine-N-methyl-transferase.

*Synthesis Regulation*

It has been known for a long time that the degree of sympathetic activity does not influence the endogenous levels of tissue norepinephrine; and it has been speculated that there must be some homeostatic mechanism whereby the level of transmitter is maintained at a relatively constant level in the sympathetic nerve endings despite the additional losses assumed to occur during enhanced sympathetic activity.

More than 20 years ago, Euler hypothesized on the basis of experiments carried out in the adrenal medulla that during periods of increased functional activity, the sympathetic neuron must also increase the synthesis of its transmitter substance, norepinephrine, to meet the increased demands placed upon the neuron. If the sympathetic neuron had the ability to increase transmitter synthesis, this would enable the neuron to maintain a constant steady-state level of transmitter despite substantial changes in transmitter utilization. Some years later, experiments carried out by several laboratories on different sympathetically innervated tissues directly demonstrated that this was, in fact, the case. Electrical stimulation of sympathetic nerves both in vivo or in vitro resulted in an increased formation of norepinephrine in the tissues innervated by these nerves. Further studies demonstrated that the observed acceleration of norepinephrine biosynthesis produced by enhanced sympathetic activity was due to an increase in the activity of the rate-limiting enzyme involved in catecholamine biosynthesis, tyrosine hydroxylase. Emphasis then shifted toward attempting to determine the mechanism by which an alteration in impulse flow within the sympathetic neuron could result in a change in the activity of this potential regulatory enzyme.

It was appreciated at an early stage that the observed enhancement of tyrosine hydroxylase activity that accompanied an increase in sympathetic activity was not the result of new enzyme synthesis but rather was related to an increase in the activity of existing enzyme molecules. The classical in vitro studies by Udenfriend and coworkers, demonstrating that catecholamines could act as feedback inhibitors of tyrosine hydroxylase, provided a reasonable theoretical mechanism by which impulse activity might regulate tyrosine hydroxylase. Since tyrosine hydroxylase is inhibited by catechols and catecholamines, presumably because of their ability to antagonize competitively the binding of the pteridine cofactor to the apoenzyme, it was proposed that free intraneuronal norepinephrine may control its own synthesis by negative feedback inhibition of tyrosine hydroxylase. This concept was supported by many pharmacological studies, including the observation that an increase in the endogenous norepinephrine content of peripheral sympathetically innervated tissue or of brain catecholamine content, which is produced by treatment with monoamine oxidase inhibitors (MAOI), results in a marked reduction of catecholamine biosynthesis. In addition, the increase in synthesis observed in vitro during neuronal depolarization is dependent upon the presence of $Ca^{2+}$ and appears inextricably coupled to catecholamine release. This latter observation suggested that the release-induced depletion of transmitter might be a prerequisite for the observed acceleration of catecholamine synthesis.

In the late 1960s the following conceptual model emerged. During periods of increased impulse flow when more transmitter is released and metabolized, a strategic regulatory pool of norepinephrine normally accessible to tyrosine hydroxylase is depleted, end-product inhibition is removed, and tyrosine hydroxylase activity is increased. Likewise, during periods of quiescence when transmitter utilization is decreased, norepinephrine accumulates and tyrosine hydroxylase activity is decreased. Over the past decade, much indirect evidence has amassed to suggest that the release of tyrosine hydroxylase from feedback inhibition is a mechanism that is operative in the sympathetic neuron and in central catecholamine neurons for increasing neurotransmitter synthesis in response to enhanced impulse flow.

In more recent years, it has been apparent that even in peripheral noradrenergic neurons the regulation of tyrosine hydroxylase is a much more complex process and that in addition to feedback regulation other processes intimately linked to neuronal activity control norepinephrine synthesis. The concept that the frequency of neuronal depolarization might in some way influence the physical properties of tyrosine hydroxylase is one of the more exciting possibilities that have emerged.

A significant advancement in our comprehension of the way in which short-term changes in impulse flow may regulate transmitter synthesis was provided by several experiments. It was demonstrated that electrical stimulation of both central and peripheral catecholamine neurons results in an apparent allosteric activation of tyrosine hydroxylase which persists following the termination of the stimulation period. This poststimulation increase in the activity of tyrosine hydroxylase is maximal after about 10 minutes of continuous stimulation and persists for a measurable period of time after the stimulation period ends. Kinetic studies demonstrated that this activation of tyrosine hydroxylase observed following depolarization is mediated in part by an increased affinity of the enzyme for pteridine cofactor and a decreased affinity for the natural endproduct inhibitors, norepinephrine and dopamine. The increased affinity for pterin cofactor (whose concentration in tissue is thought to be subsaturating) and the decreased affinity of the enzyme for catecholamine may be important physiologically for the regulation of transmitter synthesis in response to increased impulse flow. These studies provided the first direct experimental evidence that some short-term mechanism in addition to depletion of endogenous catecholamine is operative in altering tyrosine hydroxylase activity during increased neuronal activity. The precise molecular mechanism(s) responsible for the impulse-induced alterations in the physical properties of tyrosine hydroxylase remains elusive, although it has been speculated that calcium and/or cAMP may be intimately involved. Numerous in vitro studies have demonstrated that tyrosine hydroxylase can be activated by phosphorylation, providing credence for the speculation that phosphorylation is a process by which catecholamine neurons may regulate tyrosine hydroxylase activity in response to altered neuronal activity. Although C-kinase, cAMP-dependent protein kinase, and calcium–calmodulin-dependent kinase all phosphorylate tyrosine hydroxylase producing a kinetic activation of the enzyme, the question of which of these mechanisms is operative physiologically is still unresolved. The most recent studies favor the involvement of a $Ca^{++}$-calmodulin-dependent phosphorylation in the impulse-dependent activation process (Fig. 9-5).

FIGURE 9-5. Model illustrating mechanisms for regulation of transmitter synthesis in noradrenergic neurons.

In addition to the mechanisms for immediate adaptation to increased transmitter utilization discussed above, a second mechanism comes into play after prolonged increases in the activity of adrenergic neurons. This latter mechanism in contrast is reflected by an increase in the activity of tyrosine hydroxylase measured in vitro under saturating concentrations of substrate and cofactor. For a while, it was unclear whether this increase in activity observed in vitro was due to the disappearance of an inhibitor, the appearance of an activator, or an actual increase in the number of active enzyme sites. In recent years, however, much evidence has accumulated which indicates that there is a measurable increase in the formation of new enzyme molecules. This, prolonged neuronal activity is thought to result in an induction of tyrosine hydroxylase. This process of transsynaptic induction does not appear to be specific for tyrosine hydroxylase, since an increase in the formation of dopamine-β-hydroxylase is also observed. No significant increase in the formation of DOPA-decarboxylase has been reported. It has been proposed by Joh and co-workers, based on recent studies employing gene technology, that the major enzymes involved in catecholamine biosynthesis—tyrosine hydroxylase, dopamine-β-hydroxylase, and phenylethanolamine-N-methyltransferase—may derive from a common gene and thus may be coregulated (i.e., coinduced by various treatments). However, whether the story of shared molecular sequences across this big family of amine synthetic enzymes will hold when the sequences of these enzymes are fully in hand remains to be determined.

Even though tyrosine hydroxylase has been demonstrated to be rate limiting under most circumstances, this reaction may not remain rate limiting under all physiological or pharmacological conditions. Since there is a sequence of reactions, any one of these steps could assume a rate-limiting role depending upon the given pathological or pharmacologically induced situations. Thus, reserpine can transform the dopamine-β-hydroxylase step into the rate-limiting step presumably by blocking access of the substrate dopamine to the site of its conversion to norepinephrine.

Although it is well known that alterations in brain tryptophan can influence serotonin biosynthesis, the failure of tyrosine administration to increase levels of norepinephrine in sympathetically innervated tissue or catecholamine levels in brain has led most investigators to assume that tyrosine hydroxylase in catecholamine-containing neurons is normally saturated with its amino-acid substrate tyrosine in vivo and therefore its activity not readily influenced by alterations in the availability of tyrosine. A number of studies by Wurtman, Fernstrom, and their co-workers have demonstrated, however, that under conditions which are believed to cause an increase in impulse flow in peripheral sympathetic or central noradrenergic or dopaminergic neurons, that tyrosine hydroxylation and release (evaluated by measuring the accumulation of catecholamine metabolites) can be enhanced by systemic administration of tyrosine.

*Alternative Biosynthetic Pathways*

The question has often been raised as to whether the sequence of enzymatic reactions described in detail above is in fact obligatory.

Many attempts have been made to find alternative pathways in vivo and to determine whether they are functionally important. Thus, if labeled tyramine is administered to animals, both labeled norepinephrine and normetanephrine can be isolated in the urine. It has been very difficult to detect the conversion of tyramine to norepinephrine in sympathetically innervated tissue. However, the conversion of tyramine to dopamine has been demonstrated in liver microsomes. Therefore, it is possible that this conversion of tyramine to norepinephrine observed in vivo is a reflection of a metabolic reaction taking place in the liver rather than in the sympathetic neuron.

*Storage*

A great conceptual advance made in the study of catecholamines more than 25 years ago was the recognition that in almost all tissues a large percentage of the norepinephrine present is located within highly specialized subcellular particles (colloquially referred to as "granules") in sympathetic nerve endings, and chromaffin cells. Much of the norepinephrine in the central nervous system is also presumably located within similar particles. These granules contain adenosine triphosphate (ATP) in a molar ratio of catecholamine to ATP of about 4 : 1. Because of this perhaps fortuitous ratio, it is generally supposed that the anionic phosphate groups of ATP form a salt link with norepinephrine, which exists as a cation at physiological pH, and thereby serve as a means to bind the amines within the vesicles. Some such complex of the amines with ATP, with ATP associated with protein, or directly with protein is probably since the intravesicular concentration of amines, at least in the adrenal chromaffin granules and probably also in the splenic nerve granules (0.3 to 1.1 M), would be hypertonic if present in free solution and might be expected to lead to osmotic lysis of the vesicles.

The catecholamine storage vesicles in adrenal chromaffin and splenic nerve appear to have a number of general properties:

1. They possess an outer limiting membrane.
2. With appropriate fixation they possess an electron dense core when viewed in the electron microscope.

3. They contain the enzyme dopamine-β-hydroxylase.
4. They have a high concentration of catecholamine and ATP in a 4 : 1 ratio in adrenal and 6–8 : 1 in splenic nerve.
5. Chromaffin and splenic nerve granules contain a characteristic soluble protein (chromogranin) also suggested to be involved in the storage process.

The various types of vesicles found in neural tissue or chromaffin cells are summarized in Figure 9-6, which indicates their approximate size and distribution. A number of possible functions that have been proposed for the catecholamine storage vesicles are summarized below:

1. They bind and store norepinephrine, thereby retarding its diffusion out of the neuron, and protect it from being destroyed by monoamine oxidase (MAO), which is considered to be intraneuronal.

Neuronal and neuroendocrine vesicles in mammals

Peripheral and central = ? ACh, Peptides

Pineal, vas, iris, ganglion = NE

Ganglion, adrenal medulla, brain

Neurosecretory granules

Chromaffin granules

1000 Å

FIGURE 9-6. Size and electron microscopic appearance of the various types of synaptic vesicles, large granular vesicles, chromaffin granules, and neurosecretory granules found in various portions of the central and peripheral nervous system.

2. They serve as a depot of transmitter that may be released upon the appropriate physiological stimulus.
3. They oxidize dopamine to norepinephrine.
4. They take up dopamine from the cytoplasm, protecting it from oxidation by monoamine oxidase.

It is generally believed that the vesicles are formed in the neuronal cell body and subsequently transported to the nerve terminal region. This assumption is based upon a number of findings:

1. Only a minimal amount of protein biosynthesis occurs in axons or nerve terminals.
2. Following the depletion of norepinephrine by reserpine, the amines first reappear within the perinuclear cytoplasm of the cell body.
3. When the axon of a sympathetic nerve is constricted, structures (mainly large granular vesicles containing norepinephrine) tend to accumulate at the proximal border.

Neuropeptides are also found in the adrenal medulla, and it has been demonstrated that enkephalins are stored in chromaffin vesicles. Just as it has been demonstrated that catecholamine synthesis increases during stimulation of chromaffin cells, enkephalin activity also increases with stimulation. The function of the released enkephalin, however, is still unclear.

### Release

Much of the current knowledge regarding the release of catecholamines derives from the study of both adrenal medullary tissue and adrenergically innervated peripheral organs. Here it can be directly demonstrated that norepinephrine is released from the nerve terminals during periods of nerve stimulation and that adrenergic fibers can sustain this output of transmitter during prolonged periods of stimulation if synthesis and reuptake of the transmitter are not impaired. In the periphery it is possible to isolate the innervated end-organs, to collect a perfusate from the vascular system during nerve stimulation, and to analyze this for the presence and quantity of a given putative transmitter. However, we really know little about the mechanism by which axonal nerve impulses arriving at the terminal cause the release of norepinephrine (excitation-secretion coupling). Our best appreciation of the events comes from the possibly analogous release of catecholamines from the adrenal medulla, which has been extensively studied. For a comprehensive review of this area the reader is referred to Winkler, 1988.

The mechanism of catecholamine release by the adrenal medulla is thought to take place as follows: with activity in the preganglionic fibers, acetylcholine is released and thought to combine with the plasma membrane of the chromaffin cells. This produces a change in membrane protein conformation altering the permeability of this membrane to $Ca^{2+}$ and other ions, which then move inward. The influx of $Ca^{+2}$ is believed to be the main stimulus responsible for the mobilization of the catecholamines and for their secretion. The current view is that the catecholamines are released from the chromaffin cell by a process of exocytosis, along with chromogranin, ATP, and a little dopamine-β-hydroxylase. Whether or not these cellular phenomena are applicable to the sympathetic nerve endings in general remains to be determined.

Teleologically, it appears rather unlikely that transmitter release from sympathetic nerve terminals does occur exclusively by a process of exocytosis. Exocytosis requires that the entire content of the granular vesicle be released (i.e., catecholamine, ATP, and soluble protein). Since the nerve terminal region, as far as we know now, cannot sustain any sort of protein biosynthesis, high rates of axonal flow from the nerve cell body would be required to replenish the protein lost during the process of exocytosis. Alternatively, one might propose a "protein reuptake" mechanism in order to recapture that protein released during the process of synaptic transmission. In peripheral nerve, release of norepinephrine has been shown to be frequency dependent within a physiological range of frequency. This release of norepinephrine, similar to the release of ACh, is $Ca^{2+}$-dependent. Some evidence has also been presented which indicates that newly synthesized norepinephrine may be released preferentially. This preferential release is additional evidence to support the contention that norepinephrine exists in more than one pool within the sympathetic neuron.

It has been a great deal more difficult to demonstrate release of a putative transmitter from a given type of nerve ending in the central nervous system. Thus it is impossible to perfuse specific localized brain areas through their vascular system. In addition, it is also difficult but not necessarily impossible to stimulate selectively a well-defined neuronal pathway within the brain. (See below.) However, with the independent development of the push-pull cannula, microdialysis techniques, and electrochemical detectors, it has become possible to collect catecholamines from certain deep nuclear masses of the CNS or to measure release directly by in vivo voltammetry. In addition, many less-sophisticated techniques such as cortical cups, ventricular perfusions, brain slices, and isolated spinal cords have been used to demonstrate release of putative transmitters, including norepinephrine and dopamine from CNS tissue. All of these physiological techniques for studying release have some disadvantages and limitations, and many are somewhat gross and indirect. Nevertheless, they do represent increasing sophistication in research on release occurring in the CNS.

### Regulation of Release

Much evidence is accumulating to suggest that endogenous humoral factors may regulate release by a direct local action on catecholamine nerve terminals. Not only can the local synaptic concentration of catecholamines modulate their own release by interacting with pre-synaptic autoreceptors but also prostaglandins, vasoactive amines, polypeptides such as angiotensin II, and acetylcholine have all been implicated in regulation of catecholamine release.

The most convincing evidence, however, has been generated in support of a role for presynaptic receptors in the modulation of impulse-induced catecholamine release in both central and peripheral catecholamine neurons. In most catecholamine-containing systems tested, administration of catecholamine agonists appears to attenuate stimulus-induced release while administration of catecholamine receptor blockers augments release. These pharmacological studies have established the concept that presynaptic receptors modulate release by responding to the concentration of catecholamine in the synapse (high concentrations inhibiting release and low concentrations augmenting release). Most recently presynaptic autoreceptors have also been implicated in the regulation of dopamine synthesis. (See *Autoreceptors*, below.)

Several presynaptic receptors are involved in the inhibition of transmitter release from adrenergic nerves. These include $\alpha_2$-adrenergic autoreceptors as well as muscarinic, opiate, and dopamine receptors. Other presynaptic receptors are linked to facilitation rather than inhibition of norepinephrine release. These receptor subtypes include $\beta_2$-adrenergic adrenoceptors and nicotinic and angiotensin II receptors. The precise mechanism by which autoreceptors influence neurotransmitter release from adrenergic neurons is unclear, although it has been suggested that the activation of $\alpha_2$-adrenoceptors may inhibit norepinephrine release by several mechanisms including (a) an attenuation of the rate of $Ca^{2+}$ entry through inhibition of voltage-sensitive $Ca^{2+}$ channels; (b) a blockade of the spread of the action potential along the terminal varicosity; (c) an opening of potassium channels leading to hyperpolarization of the neuron terminals; (d) an inhibition of adenylate cyclase resulting in a decrease of intracellular cAMP and $Ca^{2+}$ concentration.

Presynaptic $\beta$-adrenergic receptors are also present in some sympathetic tissues. These presynaptic receptors are usually believed to be of the $\beta_2$ subtype. The $\beta_2$-adrenoceptor-mediated facilitation of norepinephrine release may be due to stimulation of adenylate cyclase leading to an increase in cAMP and a subsequent increase in intracellular $Ca^{2+}$ concentrations. Alternatively, it has been suggested that the facilitation may be due to a trans-synaptic signal involving a local renin-angiotensin response. This hypothesis posits that $\beta$-adrenoceptor agonists activate postsynaptic $\beta_2$-adrenoceptors in the vascular wall. This activation results in the synthesis of angiotensin II, which diffuses across the synaptic cleft to activate presynaptic angiotensin II receptors that facilitate norepinephrine release.

The presence of presynaptic facilitatory and inhibitory adrenergic receptors on the same nerve terminals may provide for a fine-tuning control of stimulus-evoked release of norepinephrine. Since the affinity of epinephrine for $\beta_2$-adrenoceptors is much greater than that of norepinephrine, this subset of adrenoceptors is more likely to be activated by endogenous epinephrine than norepinephrine. Thus, low synaptic concentrations of epinephrine could activate presynaptic $\beta_2$-adrenoceptors preferentially, leading to an increase in norepinephrine release. At higher concentrations of epinephrine or norepinephrine, activation of $\alpha_2$-adrenoceptors would predominate and norepinephrine release would be diminished rather than enhanced.

Prostaglandins of the E series are also potent inhibitors of neurally induced release of norepinephrine in a great number of tissues, and their action appears to be dissociated from any interaction with presynaptic receptors. These substances are released from sympathetically innervated tissues, and most evidence indicates that inhibition of local prostaglandin production is associated with an increase in the release of norepinephrine and subsequent effector responses induced by neuronal activity. The control of norepinephrine release by this prostaglandin-mediated feedback mechanism appears to operate through restriction of calcium availability for the norepinephrine release process and seems to be most efficient within the physiological frequency range of nerve impulses.

*Metabolism*

The metabolism of exogenously administered or endogenous catecholamines differs markedly from that of acetylcholine in that the speed of degradation of the amines is considerably slower than that of the ACh-ACh-esterase system. The major mammalian enzymes of importance in the metabolic degradation of catecholamines are monoamine oxidase and catechol-$O$-methyltransferase (COMT) (Fig. 9-7). Monoamine oxidase is an enzyme which converts catecholamines to their corresponding aldehydes. This aldehyde intermediate is rapidly metabolized, usually by oxidation by the enzyme aldehyde dehydrogenase to the corresponding acid. In some circumstances, the aldehyde is reduced to the alcohol or glycol by aldehyde

FIGURE 9-7. Dopamine and norepinephrine metabolism. The following abbreviations are used: DOPA, dihydroxyphenylalanine; DA, dopamine; NE, norepinephrine; DOMA, 3,4-dihydroxymandelic acid; DOPAC, 3,4-dihydroxyphenylacetic acid; DOPEG, 3,4-dihyroxyphenylglycol; DOPET, 3,4-dihydroxyphenylethanol; MOPET, 3-methoxy-4-hydroxyphenylethanol; MHPG, 3-methoxy-4-hydroxy-phenylglycol; HVA, homovanillic acid; VMA, 3-methoxy-4-hydroxy-mandelic acid; NM, normetanephrine; MTA, 3-methoxytyramine; MAO, monoamine oxidase; COMT, catechol-O-methyl transferase; Dashed arrows indicate steps that have not been firmly established.

reductase. In the case of brain norepinephrine, reduction of the aldehyde metabolite appears to be the favored route of metabolism. Neither of these latter enzymes has been extensively studied in neuronal tissue. Monoamine oxidase is a particle-bound protein, localized largely in the outer membrane of mitochondria, although a partial microsomal localization cannot be excluded. There is also some evidence for a riboflavin-like material in monoamine oxidase isolated from liver mitochondria. Monoamine oxidase is usually considered to be an intraneuronal enzyme, but it occurs in abundance extraneuronally. In fact, most experiments indicate that chronic denervation of a sympathetic end-organ leads only to a relatively small reduction in monoamine oxidase, suggesting that the greater proportion of this enzyme is, in fact, extraneuronal. However, it is the intraneuronal enzyme that seems to be important in catecholamine metabolism. Monoamine oxidase present in human and rat brain exists in at least two different forms, designated type A and type B based on substrate specificity and sensitivity to inhibition by selected inhibitors. Clorgyline is a specific inhibitor of the A-type enzyme, which has a substrate preference for norepinephrine and serotonin. Deprenyl is a selective inhibitor of the B-type enzyme, which has a substrate preference for $\beta$-phenylethylamine and benzylamine as substrates. Dopamine, tyramine, and tryptamine appear to be equally good substrates for both forms of the enzyme. The role and relative importance of these two types of MAO in physiological and pathological states is currently unknown, but this is an important area for further research. It has been speculated that under certain circumstances monoamine oxidase could serve to regulate norepinephrine biosynthesis by controlling the amount of substrate, dopamine, available to the enzyme dopamine-$\beta$-hydroxylase. Monoamine oxidase is not an exclusive catabolic enzyme for the catecholamines since it also oxidatively deaminates other biogenic amines such as 5-hydroxytryptamine, tryptamine, and tyramine. The intraneuronal localization of monoamine oxidase in mitochondria or other structures suggests that this would limit its action to amines that are present in a free (unbound) form in the axoplasm. Here, monoamine oxidase can act on amines that have been taken up by the axon before they are granule bound, or it can even act on amines that are released from the granules before they pass out through the axonal membrane. Interestingly, the latter possibility seems of minor physiological importance, since monoamine oxidase inhibition does not potentiate the effects of peripheral sympathetic nerve stimulation.

The second enzyme of importance in the catabolism of catecholamines is catechol-$O$-methyl transferase discovered by Axelrod in 1957. This enzyme is a relatively nonspecific enzyme that catalyzes the transfer of methyl groups from $S$-adenosyl methionine to the $m$-hydroxyl group of catecholamines and various other catechol compounds. Catechol-$O$-methyl transferase is found in the cytoplasm of most animal tissue, being particularly abundant in kidney and liver. A substantial amount of this enzyme is also found in the central nervous system and in various sympathetically innervated organs. The precise cellular localization of catechol-$O$-methyl transferase has not been determined, although it has been suggested (with little foundation) that it functions extraneuronally. The purified enzyme requires $S$-adenosyl methionine and $Mg^{2+}$ ions for activity. As with monoamine oxidase, inhibition of catechol-$O$-methyl transferase activity does not markedly potentiate the effects of sympathetic nerve stimulation, although in some tissue it tends to prolong the duration of the response to stimulation. Therefore, neither monoamine oxidase nor catechol-$O$-methyl transferase would seem to be the primary mechanism for terminating the action of norepinephrine liberated at sympathetic nerve terminals. It may be, however, that these enzymes play a more important role in terminating transmitter action and regulating catecholamine function in the central nervous system.

*Uptake*

When sympathetic postganglionic nerves are stimulated at frequencies low enough to be comparable to those encountered physiologically, very little intact norepinephrine overflows into the circulation, suggesting that local inactivation is very efficient. This local inactivation is not significantly blocked when catechol-$O$-methyl transferase or monoamine oxidase or both are inhibited, and it is believed to involve mainly reuptake of the transmitter by sympathetic neurons.

Much attention has been focused on the role of tissue uptake mechanisms in the physiological inactivation of catecholamines. But only in recent years has this concept received direct experimental support, although a number of earlier findings had suggested that catecholamines might be inactivated by some sort of nonmetabolic process. For example, more than 40 years ago Burn suggested the possibility that exogenous norepinephrine might be taken up in storage sites in peripheral tissue. About 30 years ago it was demonstrated that an increase in the catecholamine content of cat and dog heart occurred after administration of norepinephrine and epinephrine in vivo. However, in view of the very high doses (mg) employed in these experiments, the significance of these findings remained questionable. It was really not until labeled catecholamines with high specific activity became available that similar experiments using doses of norepinephrine comparable to those likely to be encountered under physiological circumstances could be performed. Uptake studies of this nature carried out in vivo have indicated that approximately 40–60% of a relatively small intravenous dose of norepinephrine is metabolized enzymatically be catechol-$O$-methyl transferase and monoamine oxidase, while the remainder is inactivated by uptake into various tissues. This uptake appears to be extremely rapid, and in most cases the magnitude of the uptake is related to the density of sympathetic innervation and the proportion of cardiac output received by the tissue in question. Thus, after administration of $^3$H-norepinephrine in vivo, the greatest uptake and binding occur in tissues such as spleen and heart. The brain is also capable of taking up norepinephrine but, since the uptake from the circulation is prevented by the blood–brain barrier, efficient uptake can only be observed when brain slices, minces, or brain synaptosomes are exposed to norepinephrine, or when the labeled amines are administered intraventricularly or intracisternally.

A large amount of data now suggests that the major site of this uptake (and subsequently binding) is actually in sympathetic nerves. This evidence can be summarized as follows:

1. In most cases norepinephrine uptake correlates directly with the density of sympathetic innervation (or the endogenous

content of norepinephrine) providing that sufficient allowance is made for differences in regional blood flow to various tissues.

2. In tissues without a normal sympathetic nerve supply, the ability to take up exogenous catecholamines is severely impaired. This can be demonstrated by surgical sympathectomy, chemical sympathectomy, or immunosympathectomy.

3. Labeled norepinephrine taken up by heart, spleen, artery, vein, or other tissues can be subsequently released by sympathetic nerve stimulation.

4. Autoradiographic studies at the electron microscope level have directly localized labeled catecholamines within the neuronal elements of the tissue.

5. Fluorescence microscopy has also provided equally direct evidence for the localization of norepinephrine uptake to sympathetic nerves.

A number of studies demonstrate that the uptake of catecholamines is active as it proceeds against a concentration gradient. For example, slices or minces of heart, spleen, and brain can concentrate norepinephrine to levels 5–8 times those in the incubation medium. In intact tissues even greater concentration ratios between tissue and medium may be obtained. In isolated rat heart perfused with Krebs solution containing 10 ng/ml of norepinephrine, Iversen finds concentrations of labeled norepinephrine rise 30–40 times above that present in the perfusion medium. If we assume that norepinephrine uptake occurs almost exclusively into cardiac sympathetic neurons, the uptake process clearly has an exceptionally high affinity for norepinephrine. In fact, the actual concentration ratios between exogenous norepinephrine accumulated within the sympathetic neurons and that present in the medium could approach 10,000 : 1.

This uptake process is a saturable membrane transport process dependent upon temperature and requiring energy. The stereochemically preferred substrate is L-norepinephrine; furthermore, norepinephrine is taken up more efficiently than its $N$-substituted derivatives. The uptake process is sodium dependent and can be blocked by inhibition of $Na^+$, $K^+$-activated ATPase. In fact, most evidence suggests that catecholamine uptake is mediated by some sort of active membrane transport mechanism located in the presynaptic terminal membrane of postganglionic sympathetic neurons.

A complimentary DNA clone encoding a human norepinephrine transporter has recently been isolated. The isolated cDNA sequence predicts a protein of 617 amino acids with 12–13 highly hydrophobic regions compatible with membrane-spanning domains. Expression of the cDNA clone in transfected HeLa cells indicates that the norepinephrine transport activity is sodium dependent and sensitive to norepinephrine transport inhibitors. Striking sequence homology is notable between the norepinephrine transporter and the rat and human GABA transporters, suggesting a new transporter gene family. The availability of cDNAs encoding transporter proteins may facilitate the development of sensitive screening techniques to aid in the development of new and selective agents which target specific neurotransmitter transporters. Also the availability of human cDNA encoding the norepinephrine transporter offers the opportunity to determine whether alterations in transporter genes could have important etiological implications for major depressive or affective disorders.

### Adrenergic Receptors

When catecholamines are released from either noradrenergic nerve terminals or the adrenal medulla, they are recognized by and bind to specific receptor molecules on the plasma membrane of the neuroeffector cells that transduce catecholamine interactions with the cell into a physiological response. Depending upon the nature of the receptor, this interaction sets off a cascade of membrane and intracellular events that cause the cell to carry out its specialized function. Classically, peripheral adrenergic receptors have been divided into two distinct classes called $\alpha$ and $\beta$ receptors. The development of synthetic compounds active at adrenergic receptors has allowed further differentiation of adrenergic receptors into $\alpha_1$, $\alpha_2$ and $\beta_1$ and $\beta_2$ subtypes (Fig. 9-8). Genes for these subtypes of adrenergic re-

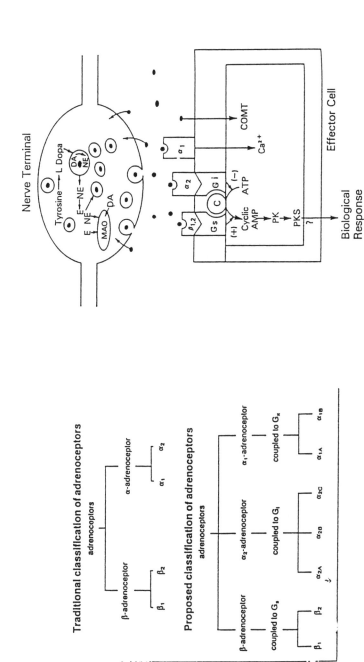

FIGURE 9-8. Classification and coupling of adrenoceptors. See text for details. Abbreviations: $G_i$, inhibitory G protein; $G_s$, stimulatory G protein; PK, protein kinase; PKS, protein kinase substrate; $\beta_1$, $\beta_2$, $\alpha_1$, $\alpha_2$: adrenergic receptor subtypes.

| 251

ceptors have been cloned; this has shown that these receptors are members of a larger family of hormone receptors that mediate their activity through an interaction with one of a series of guanine nucleotide-binding regulatory proteins (G-proteins). In addition to traditional classification based on their pharmacological profile, adrenergic receptors can be divided into three major classes by their differential coupling to G-proteins (see Fig. 9-8). The $\beta$-adrenergic receptors activate $G_s$ to stimulate adenyl cyclase. The $\alpha_2$-adrenergic receptors decrease adenyl cyclase activity through coupling to $G_i$. The $\alpha_1$-adrenergic receptor stimulates phospholipase C action through a still ill-defined $G_x$. As schematically illustrated in Fig. 9-8, $\beta$-adrenoceptor signals are transmitted through the effector cell membrane via the adenylate cyclase system. The occupation of the $\beta$-adrenoceptor by the catecholamines stimulates the adenylate cyclase to generate cyclic adenosine-3'5'-monophosphate (cAMP) by a series of intramembrane events (see Chap. 5). Initially, the receptor interacts with a guanosine triphosphate (GTP)-dependent protein, $G_s$. The GTP-dependent $G_s$ is linked to a catalytic unit (C) that generates cAMP upon activation by $G_s$; the catalytic unit then converts AMP to cAMP. The latter compound triggers a series of intracellular events involving protein kinases. The protein kinases activate further unknown biochemical changes to generate the final biological response to the transmitter.

The order of potency for stimulation of $\beta_1$-adrenergic receptors by catecholamines is isoproterenol > epinephrine = norepinephrine. For the $\beta_2$-adrenoceptor the order of potency is isoproterenol > epinephrine > norepinephrine. Adrenergic blocking agents such as propranolol and alprenolol prevent the activation of the $\beta$ receptors. The interaction of adrenergic agents with their receptors is saturable, stereospecific, and reversible. Prolonged exposure of $\beta$-adrenoceptors to endogenous or exogenous agonists often reduces the responsiveness of these receptors (desensitization). Desensitization can also be caused by uncoupling of $\beta$-receptors from the adenylate cyclase and by a decrease in the number of receptors (down regulation). Depriving the $\beta$-adrenoceptors of catecholamine (by chemical or surgical denervation) increases the responsiveness of these receptors.

The $\alpha_1$-adrenoceptor appears to be associated with calcium mobilization (Fig. 9-8), possibly via stimulation of phospholipase C. The $\alpha_1$ receptor is distinguished from the $\alpha_2$ adrenoceptor by its ability to be inhibited by the selective $\alpha_1$-blocking agent, prazosin. The $\alpha_2$-adrenergic receptor is negatively linked to the adenylate cyclase complex via an inhibitory G protein ($G_i$). Like $G_s$, $G_i$ is activated by guanosine triphosphate, but in this case it inhibits the generation of cyclic AMP by the catalytic unit (C).

In the peripheral sympathetic nervous system, the $\alpha_2$ receptor is mainly localized on presynaptic nerve terminals, where it functions to modulate norepinephrine release. Stimulation of this receptor by catecholamines inhibits impulse-dependent release of transmitter; blockade of this receptor facilitates release.

*Dynamics of Adrenergic Receptors*

Adrenergic receptors do not seem to be static entities but change in number and affinity in response to altered synaptic activity. In both brain and the peripheral sympathetic nervous system, destruction of adrenergic neurons is associated with functional supersensitivity of postsynaptic sites. Conversely, increasing synaptic norepinephrine by administering uptake blockers (tricyclic antidepressants) or inhibitors of MAO leads to functional subsensitivity. These changes appear to be a compensatory response to altered levels of synaptic transmitter. The number of $\alpha_1$ and $\alpha_2$ receptors also increases after noradrenergic neurons in the brain and/or sympathetically innervated tissue have been destroyed by administration of 6-hydroxydopamine. It is interesting that after lesions in norepinephrine-containing neurons are made in the cerebral cortex, the number of $\beta_1$ receptors increases markedly, but no change occurs in the number of $\beta_2$ receptors. This may be because $\beta_2$ receptors have a low affinity for norepinephrine, and the concentration of epinephrine in the cerebral cortex is relatively low. Likewise, the chronic administration of tricyclic antidepressants leads to a selective decrease in the density of $\beta_1$-adrenergic receptors in the cerebral cortex. This finding implies that the $\beta_1$-adrenergic receptors in the cortex are functionally innervated by adrenergic neurons.

## Desensitization

The waning of a stimulated response in the face of continuous agonist exposure has been termed desensitization. Desensitization has been demonstrated in many hormone- and neurotransmitter-receptor systems, including those that activate different G proteins and effector systems. Desensitization of the cAMP response elicited by β-adrenergic agonists is a useful model system for studying this phenomenon. Desensitization has been viewed historically as two separate processes: heterologous and homologous desensitization. Heterologous desensitization occurs when exposure of cells to a desensitizing agent leads to diminished responsiveness to a number of different stimuli. In contrast, homologous desensitization is much more specific and involves only the loss of responsiveness to the specific desensitizing agent. A number of molecular mechanisms operating at the receptor level have been implicated in the process of desensitization. The heterologous pattern of desensitization is thought to be mediated by phosphorylation of receptors coupled to $G_s$ by cAMP-dependent protein kinase (PKA), whereas the homologous pattern of desensitization is thought to involve phosphorylation of receptors by a novel, cAMP-independent kinase, such as β adrenergic receptor kinase or βARK. Recent studies on the β-adrenergic receptor have suggested that the principal mechanisms underlying rapid, agonist-induced desensitization of β-adrenergic receptor function in intact mammalian cells are a combination of these two processes and involve phosphorylation of the receptor by both types of kinases. Phosphorylation of the receptor is thought to lead to uncoupling of the β adrenergic receptor from the stimulatory G protein ($G_s$). It is not yet clear exactly how phosphorylation leads to uncoupling of β adrenergic receptor from $G_s$; for example, phosphorylation of one specific residue may directly impair interaction of the receptor with $G_s$, whereas phosphorylation of another residue may allow cytosolic factors such as β-arrestin to bind to the phorphorylated β adrenergic

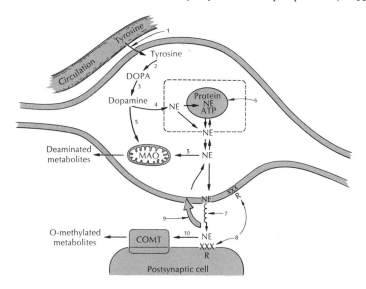

FIGURE 9-9. Schematic model of noradrenergic neuron.

receptor and decrease or prevent the coupling of the β adrenergic receptor with $G_s$, leading to desensitization.

## PHARMACOLOGY OF NORADRENERGIC NEURONS

In this section we will focus on the pharmacology of peripheral noradrenergic neurons and discuss possible sites of drug involvement in the life cycle of the catecholamines. Figure 9-9 depicts a schematic model of a noradrenergic nerve varicosity.

*Site 1—Precursor transport.* As noted earlier there appears to be an active uptake or transport of tyrosine as well as other aromatic amino acids into the central nervous system. In addition it is also probable that tyrosine is actively taken up by adrenergic neurons both in the periphery and in the CNS. At present, we have no pharmacologic agent that specifically antagonizes the uptake of tyrosine into the brain or into the catecholamine-containing neuron. However, it is known that various aromatic amino acids will compete with each other for transport into the CNS. This competition might become important under a pathological situation in which blood aromatic amino acids are elevated. Thus, in phenylketonuria, when plasma levels of phenylalanine are elevated to about $10^{-3}$ M, it might be expected that tyrosine and tryptophan uptake into the brain might be diminished.

*Site 2—Tyrosine hydroxylase.* The conversion of tyrosine to DOPA is the rate-limiting step in this biosynthetic pathway and thus is the step most susceptible to pharmacological manipulation. The various classes of tyrosine hydroxylase inhibitors were considered earlier in this chapter. An effective inhibitor of tryosine hydroxylase both in vivo and in vitro, α-methyl-ρ-tyrosine is one of the few tyrosine hydroxylase inhibitors which has been employed clinically and found to be effective in the treatment of inoperable pheochromocytomas; it is of little or no value in the treatment of essential hypertension.

*Sites 3 and 4—DOPA-decarboxylase and dopamine-β-hydroxylase.* Potent inhibitors of DOPA-decarboxylase and dopamine-β-hydroxylase do exist, but they are generally not effective in vivo in reducing tissue concentrations of catecholamines.

Due to the nonspecificity of these two enzymes (see above) as well as the relatively nonspecific vesicular storage sites, certain drugs or even amines or amine precursors in foodstuff can be synthesized to phenylethylamine derivatives with a catechol or a β-hydroxyl group and taken up and stored in the storage vesicles. These compounds can subsequently be released by sympathetic nerves, in part replacing some of the norepinephrine normally released by sympathetic impulses. Since these "false neurotransmitters" are usually less potent in their action, replacement of some of the endogenous, releasable pool of norepinephrine with these agents results in a diminished sympathetic response. Thus, a drug such as α-methyl-dihydroxphenylalanine, which is converted in the sympathetic neuron to α-methyl-norepinephrine, replaces a portion of the endogenous norepinephrine and itself can be subsequently released as a "false transmitter." The false transmitter theory also has been used to explain the hypotensive action of various monoamine oxidase inhibitors. Tyramine, an endogenous metabolite that is normally disposed of by monoamine oxidase in the liver and other tissues, is no longer rapidly deaminated in the presence of monoamine oxidase inhibitors and thus can be converted to the β-hydroxylated derivative, octopamine, which then accumulates in sympathetic neurons. Upon activation of these nerves, octopamine is released and acts as a false neurotransmitter, producing a resultant decrease in sympathetic tone (observed with monoamine oxidase inhibitors). "False neurotransmitters" can also be formed in the brain, but at the present time the action of these agents is unclear.

*Site 5—Metabolic degradation by monoamine oxidase.* The monoamine oxidase inhibitors belong to quite a heterogeneous group of drugs that have in common the ability to block the oxidative deamination of various biogenic amines. These agents all produce marked increases in tissue amine concentrations. These compounds are in most cases employed clinically for the treatment of depression. However, some of these agents are used for the treatment of hypertension and angina pectoris. In the case of monoamine oxidase inhibitors, it should be immediately pointed out that while these drugs inhibit monoamine oxidase, there is no firmly established correlation between monoamine oxidase inhibition and therapeutic effect. In fact, it is generally well appreciated that monoamine oxidase inhibitors inhibit not only enzymes involved in oxidative deamination of monoamines but also many other enzymes unrelated to monoamine oxidase such as succinic dehydrogenase, dopamine β-hydroxylase, 5-hydroxy-tryptophan decarboxylase, choline dehydrogenase, and diamine oxidase.

*Site 6—Storage.* A number of drugs, mostly notable the Rauwolfia alkaloids, interfere with the storage of monoamines by blocking the uptake of amine into the storage granules or by disrupting the binding of the amines. Thus drugs interfering with the storage mechanism will cause amines to be released intraneuronally. Amines released intraneuronally appear to be preferentially metabolized by monoamine oxidase.

*Site 7—Release.* The release of catecholamines is dependent upon $Ca^{2+}$ ions. Thus, in an in vitro system it is possible to block release by lowering the $Ca^{2+}$ concentration of the medium. Although drugs such as bretylium act to inhibit the release of norepinephrine in the peripheral nervous system, this drug does not easily penetrate the brain and therefore has little or no effect on central monoaminergic neurons.

*Site 8—Interaction with receptors.* In the peripheral nervous system, α- and β-adrenergic blocking agents are effective. These agents block both the effects of sympathetic nerve stimulation and the action of exogenously administered norepinephrine. Some of these agents also have central activity. Evidence has indicated that presynaptic-α-receptors, termed $\alpha_2$-receptors, are involved in the regulation of norepinephrine release. A blockade of these receptors facilitates release, while stimulation leads to an inhibition of release. Presynaptic β-receptors have also been identified in certain tissues. In contrast to $\alpha_2$-receptors, activation of these presynaptic β-receptors facilitates rather than attenuates norepinephrine release.

*Site 9—Reuptake.* Drugs such as cocaine, desipramine, amitryptyline, and other related tricyclic antidepressants are effective inhibitors of norepinephrine uptake both at peripheral and central sites. Pharmacological intervention at these sites makes more norepinephrine available to interact with postsynaptic receptors and thus tends to potentiate adrenergic transmission.

*Site 10—Catechol-O-methyl transferase.* Catechol-O-methyl transferase can be inhibited by pyrogallol or various tropolone derivatives. Inhibition of this enzyme in most sympathetically innervated tissue such as heart does not significantly potentiate the effects of nerve stimulation. In vascular tissue, however, inhibition of this enzyme does lead to a significant prolongation of the response to nerve stimulation. It appears possible that in this tissue catechol-O-methyl transferase may play some role in terminating transmitter action.

## CNS CATECHOLAMINE NEURONS

The cellular organization of the brain and spinal cord has been studied for many decades by classical histological and silver impregnation techniques. With the development in the last decade of completely different histological techniques based on the presence of a given type of transmitter substance or on specific synthetic enzymes involved in the formation of a given transmitter, it became possible to map chemically defined neuronal systems in the CNS of many species. With the formaldehyde fluorescence histochemical method of Falck and Hillarp, it has bèen possible to delineate norepinephrine- dopamine- and 5-hydroxytryptamine-containing systems in mammalian brain. By the time such techniques had been employed for several years, it became clear that the distribution of these chemically defined neuronal systems did not necessarily correspond to that of systems described earlier with the classical techniques.

It was really not until the mid-1960s that the histochemical fluorescent technique was applied to brain tissue and the anatomy of the monoamine-containing neuronal systems was described. By a variety of pharmacological and chemical methods, it has subsequently been possible to discriminate between norepinephrine, epinephrine, and dopamine-containing neurons and to describe in detail the distribution of these catecholamine-containing neurons in the mammalian CNS. Several recent and thorough surveys of these systems are available.

Figure 9-10 provides a schematic model of a central monoamine-containing neuron as observed by fluorescence and electron microscopy. The cell bodies contain relatively low concentrations of amine (about $10-100$ μg/gm), while the terminal varicosities contain a very high concentration (about $1000-3000$ μg/gm). The axons, on the other hand, consist of highly branched, largely unmyelinated fibers which have such a low concentration of amine that they are barely visible in untreated adult animals. With the electron microscope, depending on the type of fixation, it is possible to observe the presence of small granular vesicles that are thought to represent the subcellular storage sites containing the catecholamines. These granular vesicles are concentrated in the terminal varicosities of the central noradrenergic neuron just as they are observed in the peripheral sympathetic neuron.

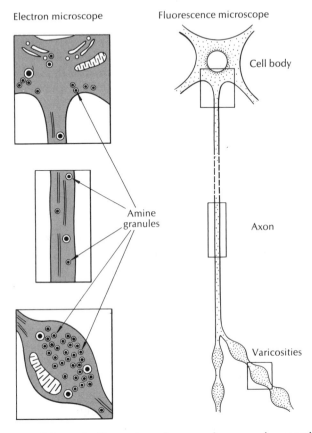

Schematic diagram of Monoamine Neuron

Electron microscope

Fluorescence microscope

Cell body

Amine granules

Axon

Varicosities

FIGURE 9-10. Schematic illustration of a central monoamine-containing neuron. The right side depicts the general appearance and intraneuronal distribution of monoamines based upon fluorescence microscopy. The cell bodies contain a relatively low concentration of catecholamine (about 10–100 µg/gm) while the terminal varicosities contain a very high concentration 1000–3000 µg/gm). The preterminal axons contain very low concentration of amine. At the electron microscopic level (left side), dense core granules can be observed in the cell bodies and axons but appear to be highly concentrated in the terminal varicosities. (Illustration adapted after K. Fuxe and T. Hökfelt, *Triangle 30*: 73, 1971)

## SYSTEMS OF CATECHOLAMINE PATHWAYS IN THE CNS

Detailed analysis of catecholamine pathways in the CNS has been greatly accelerated by recent improvements in the application of fluorescence histochemistry, such as the use of glyoxylic acid as the fluorogen, and by the application of numerous auxiliary mapping methods, such as anterograde and retrograde markers, immunocytochemical localization of catecholamine-synthesizing enzymes, and direct methods for observing noradrenergic terminals with the electron microscope. Extensive progress in the functional analysis of these systems has also been made possible by evaluation with microelectrodes of the effects produced by selective electrical stimulation of the catecholamine (especially norepinephrine) cell-body groups. From such studies it is clear that the systems can be characterized in simple terms only by ignoring large amounts of detailed cytological and functional data and that the earlier catecholamine wiring diagrams are no longer tenable. Furthermore, anatomic details for monoamine systems in rodents seem to bear only rudimentary homologies to their detailed selective anatomic configurations in human and nonhuman primates.

### Noradrenergic Systems

There are two major clusterings of norepinephrine cell bodies from which axonal systems arise to innervate targets throughout the entire neuraxis:

#### LOCUS CERULEUS

This compact cell group within the caudal pontine central grey is named for the pigment the cells bear in humans and in some higher primates; in the rat the nucleus contains about 1,500 neurons on each side of the brain (Fig. 9-11). In humans, the locus ceruleus is composed of about 12,000 large neurons on each side of the brain. The axons of these neurons form extensive collateral branches that project widely along well-defined tracts. At the electron microscope level, terminals of these axons exhibit—under appropriate fixation methods—the same type of small granular vesicles seen in the peripheral sympathetic nerves (Fig. 9-2).

Fibers from the locus ceruleus form five major noradrenergic tracts (Fig. 9-12): the central tegmental tract (or dorsal bundle described by Ungerstedt), a central gray dorsal longitudinal facsiculus tract, and a ventral tegmental-medial forebrain bundle tract. These tracts remain largely ipsilateral, although there is a crossing over in some species of up to 25% of the fibers. These three ascending tracts then follow other major vascular and fascicular routes to innervate all cortices, specific thalamic and hypothalamic nuclei, and the olfactory bulb. Another major fascicle ascends in the superior cerebellar peduncle to innervate the cerebellar cortex. The fifth major tract is

FIGURE 9-11 Formaldehyde-induced fluorescence of the rat nucleus locus ceruleus. In this frontal section through the principal portion of the nucleus, intensely fluorescent neurons can be seen clustered closely together. Within the neurons, the cell nucleus, which is not fluorescent after this treatment, appears dark except for the nucleolus. (Bloom, unpublished) (× 650)

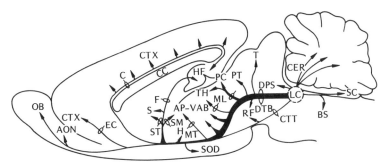

FIGURE 9-12. Diagram of the projections of the locus ceruleus viewed in the sagittal plane. See text for description. Abbreviations: AON, anterior olfactory nucleus; AP–VAB, ansa peduncularis-ventral amygdaloid bundle system; BS, brainstem nuclei; C, cingulum; CC, corpus callosum; CER, cerebellum; CTT, central tegmental tract; CTX, cerebral neocortex; DPS, dorsal periventricular system; DTB, dorsal catecholamine bundle; EC, external capsule; F, fornix; H, hypothalamus; HF, hippocampal formation; LC, locus ceruleus; ML, medial lemniscus; MT, mammillothalamic tract; OB, olfactory bulb; PC, posterior commissure; PT, pretectal area; RF, reticular formation; S, septal area; SC, spinal cord; SM, stria medullaris; SOD, supraoptic decussations; ST, stria terminalis; T, tectum; TH, thalamus. (Diagram compiled by R. Y. Moore, from the observations of Lindvall and Björklund, 1974b; Jones and Moore, 1977)

that which descends into the mesencephalon and spinal cord, where the fibers course in the ventral–lateral column. At their terminals the locus ceruleus fibers form a plexiform network in which the incoming fibers gain access to a cortical region by passing through the major myelinated tracts, turning vertically toward the outer cortical surface, and then forming characteristic T-shaped branches that run parallel to the surface in the molecular layer; this pattern is seen in the cerebellar, hippocampal, and cerebral cortices.

Virtually all of the noradrenergic pathways that have been studied physiologically so far are efferent pathways of the locus ceruleus neurons; in cerebellum, hippocampus, and cerebral cortex, the major effect of activating this pathway is to produce an inhibition of spontaneous discharge. This effect has been associated with the slow type of synaptic transaction in which the hyperpolarizing response of the target cell is accompanied by increased membrane resistance. The mechanism of this action has been experimentally related to the second messenger scheme in which the noradrenergic receptor elicits its characteristic action on the target cells by activating the synthesis of cyclic AMP in or on the postsynaptic membrane. Pharmacologically and cytochemically, target cells responding to norepinephrine or the locus coeruleus projection in these cortical areas exhibit β-adrenergic receptors.

## THE LATERAL TEGMENTAL NORADRENERGIC NEURONS

A large number of noradrenergic neurons lie outside of the locus ceruleus where they are more loosely scattered throughout the lateral ventral tegmental fields. In general, the fibers from these neurons intermingle with those arising from the locus ceruleus, with those from the more posterior tegmental levels contributing mainly descending fibers within the mesencephalon and spinal cord, and those from the more anterior tegmental levels contributing to the innervation of the forebrain and diencephalon. Because of the complex intermingling of the fibers from the various noradrenergic cell body sources, the physiological and pharmacological analysis of the effects of brain lesions becomes extremely difficult. The neurons of the lateral tegmental system may be the primary source of the noradrenergic fibers observed in the basal forebrain, such as amygdala and septum. No specific analysis of the physiology of these projections has yet been reported; therefore it remains to be established whether the β-receptive cAMP mechanism associated with the cortical projections of the locus ceruleus group also apply to the synapses of the lateral tegmental neurons.

## EPINEPHRINE NEURONS

In the sympathetic nervous system and the adrenal medulla, epinephrine shares with norepinephrine the role of final neurotransmitter; the proportion of this sharing being a species-dependent, hormonally modified arrangement. However, until recently, little evidence could be gathered to document the existence of epinephrine in the CNS because the chemical methods for analyzing epinephrine levels or for detecting activity attributable to the synthesizing enzyme, phenylethanolamine-N-methyl transferase were unable to provide unequivocal data. However, with the development of sensitive immunoassays for phenylethanolamine-N-methyl transferase, and their application in immunohistochemistry, and with the application of gas chromatography-mass fragmentography (GCMF) and high performance liquid chromatography (HPLC) with electrochemical detection to brain neurotransmitter measurements, the necessary data were rapidly acquired, and the existence of epinephrine-containing neurons in the CNS confirmed. By immunohistochemistry, epinephrine-containing neurons are defined as those that are positively stained (in serial sections) with antibodies to tyrosine hydroxylase, dopamine-β-hydroxylse, and with antibodies to phenylethanolamine-N-methyl transferase. These cells are found largely in two groups: one group—called C-1 by Hökfelt—is intermingled with noradrenergic cells of the lateral tegmental system; the other group—called C-2—is found in the regions in which the noradrenergic cells of the dorsal medulla are also found. The axons of these two epinephrine systems ascend to the hypothalamus with the central tegmental tract, then via the ventral periventricular system into the hypothalamus. A third group of cells (C3) in the midline (medial longitudinal fascicle) has also been described (Fig. 9-13). Within the mesencephalon, the epinephrine-containing fibers innervate the nuclei of visceral efferent and afferent systems, especially the dorsal motor nucleus of the vagus nerve. In addition, epinephrine fibers also innervate the locus ceruleus, the intermediolateral cell columns of the spinal cord, and the periventricular regions of the fourth ventricle. Except for tests of epinephrine on the locus ceruleus (where it inhibits firing), no other tests of the cellular physiology of this system have thus far been reported. Our understanding concerning the function of epinephrine-containing neurons in brain is still very limited, but based on the distribution of epinephrine in specific brain regions, attention has been directed to their possible role in neuroendocrine mechanisms and blood pressure control.

*Coexistence of Classical Transmitters and Peptides*

The findings of numerous peptides in the CNS has raised the question of the relationship of the neurons containing these substances

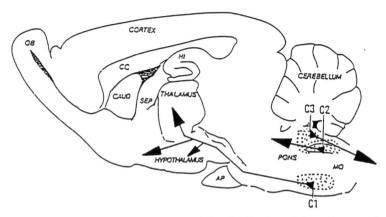

FIGURE 9-13. Schematic illustration of the distribution of the main central neuronal pathways containing epinephrine. The C1 group represents a rostral continuation of the noradrenergic cell group in the ventrolateral medulla oblongata. The dorsal C2 group of cells is mainly located in the dorsal vagal complex with the vast majority of cell bodies in the solitary tract nucleus. A C3 group of cells in the midline (medial longitudinal fascicle) has also been described. The ventral group of epinephrine-containing neurons gives rise to both ascending and descending pathways, innervating largely periventricular regions such as the periaqueductal central gray and various hypothalamic nuclei and the lateral sympathetic column in the spinal cord. (Data from Hökfelt, et al. 1984)

to neurons containing classical neurotransmitters. It was originally believed that the peptide–containing nerves represented separate identifiable systems. However, when studies in the peripheral nervous system clearly indicated the coexistence of peptides with the sympathetic and parasympathetic transmitters NE and ACh respectively, this initiated a series of systematic studies in the CNS to determine if classical neurotransmitter in the brain coexisted with one or more peptides. These studies revealed that coexistence of classical transmitter and peptides may represent a rule rather than an exception. The functional significance of the occurrence of a classical transmitter and a peptide in the same neuron and their possible release from the same nerve ending is still unclear in the CNS. However, some insight may be obtained from studies in the periphery where two distinct types of interactions have been noted.

In the salivary gland, the parasympathetic cholinergic neurons contain a VIP-like peptide while the sympathetic NE neurons contain a neuropeptide Y-like peptide. In this system, the peptides seem to augment the action of the classical transmitters. Thus, VIP induces vasodilation and enhances the secretory effects of ACh while neuropeptide Y causes vasoconstriction like NE. In contrast, in the vas deferens where the NE neurons innervating this tissue also contain neuropeptide Y, the peptide seems to inhibit the release of norepinephrine via a presynaptic action. There is also some indication of preferential storage and release of NE and neuropeptide Y, with release of the peptide occurring preferentially at higher frequencies.

The physiological significance of multiple messengers at the synapse in the CNS is still unclear, but an appreciation of coexistence phenomena may influence our view on interneuronal communication and in a larger perspective may be of importance in our efforts to treat or prevent various disease states or abnormalities of the nervous system.

*Catecholamine Metabolism*

Catecholamine metabolism was discussed earlier, and only a few aspects pertinent to central catecholamine metabolism will be covered here.

In the peripheral sympathetic nervous system, the aldehyde intermediate produced by the action of MAO on norepinephrine and normetanephrine can be oxidized to the corresponding acid or reduced to the corresponding glycol. Oxidation usually exceeds reduction and quantitatively vanilylmandelic acid (VMA) is the major metabolite of norepinephrine and is readily detectable in the urine. In fact, the urinary levels of VMA are routinely measured in clinical laboratories in order to provide an index of peripheral sympathetic nerve function as well as to diagnose the presence of catecholamine-secreting tumors such as pheochromocytomas and neuroblastomas. In the CNS, however, reduction of the intermediate aldehyde formed by the action of MAO on catecholamines or catecholamine metabolites predominates, and a major metabolite of norepinephrine found in brain is the glycol derivative, 3-methoxy-4-hydroxy-phenethylenetyleneglycol (MHPG). Very little, if any, VMA is found in brain.

In many species a large fraction of the MHPG formed in the brain is sulfate conjugated. However in primates, MHPG exists primarily in an unconjugated "free" form in the brain. Some normetanephrine is also found in the brain and spinal cord. Destruction of noradrenergic neurons in the brain or spinal cord causes a reduction in the endogenous levels of these metabolites although not as marked as the corresponding reduction in endogenous norepinephrine. Recently, it has been demonstrated that direct electrical stimulation of the locus ceruleus or severe stress produces an increase in the turnover of norepinephrine as well as an increase in the accumulation of the sulfate conjugate of MHPG in the rat cerebral cortex. These effects are completely abolished by ablation of the locus ceruleus or by transection of the dorsal pathway, which suggests that the accumulation of MHPG/sulfate in brain may reflect the functional activity of central noradrenergic neurons. Since MHPG-sulfate readily diffuses from the brain into the CSF or general circulation, estimates of its concentration in the CSF or in urine are thought to provide a possible reflection of activity of noradrenergic neurons in the brain. Even though MHPG is proportionately a minor metabolite or norepinephrine in the peripheral sympathetic nervous system, a fairly large portion of the MHPG in the urine still derives from the periphery. In the rodent it has been estimated that the brain provides a minor contribution (25–30%) to urinary MHPG, while in primates the brain contribution is quite large (60%). Thus, at least in the rodent, it is quite probable that relatively large changes in the formation of MHPG by the brain are necessary to produce detectable changes in urinary MHPG. For example, in the rat destruction of the majority of norepinephrine-containing neurons in the brain by treatment with 6-hydroxy-dopamine leads to only about a 25% decrease in urinary MHPG levels. Nevertheless, measurement of urinary changes in MHPG is still a reasonable strategy for obtaining some insight into possible alterations of brain norepinephrine metabolism in patients with psychiatric illnesses. Measurement of CSF levels of MHPG also provides another possible approach to assessing central adrenergic function in human subjects. More recent studies have suggested that plasma levels of MHPG might provide a reflection of central noradrenergic activity. In these studies, stimulation of the locus ceruleus in the rat was shown to result in a significant increase in the levels of plasma MHPG; and administration of drugs that are known to alter noradrenergic activity in rodents have predictably changed plasma levels and venous-arterial differences in MHPG in nonhuman primates. Although changes in either urinary, plasma, or CSF levels of MHPG and their relationship to central noradrenergic function have to be interpreted with considerable caution, these measurements do provide a starting point for clinical investigation.

## BIOCHEMICAL ORGANIZATION

In general, noradrenergic neurons in the central nervous system appear to behave in a fashion very similar to the postganglionic sympathetic noradrenergic neurons in the periphery and have the same presynaptic regulatory controls. Electrical stimulation of the noradrenergic neurons in the locus ceruleus causes both an activation of tyrosine hydroxylase and an increase in the turnover of norepinephrine as well as a frequency-dependent accumulation of MHPG-sulfate (a major metabolite of norepinephrine in the rat CNS) in the cortex. Interruption of impulse flow in these neurons decreases turnover of norepinephrine but has little or no effect on the steady-state level of transmitter. Similar effects are also obtained in the serotonin-containing neurons of the midbrain raphe (stimulation increases synthesis and turnover, and interruption of impulse flow slows turnover).

It is well known that acute severe stress increases the turnover of norepinephrine in the CNS, apparently as a result of increase in impulse flow in noradrenergic neurons. Recent experiments have confirmed this speculation. If impulse flow in noradrenergic neurons projecting to the cortex is acutely interrupted by destruction of the locus ceruleus, the increase in norepinephrine turnover and accumulation of MHPG-sulfate induced by stress is completely blocked. Also, microdialysis experiments have demonstrated stress-induced increases in norepinephrine release in hippocampus and frontal cortex.

FIGURE 9-14. schematic model of central noradrenergic neuron indicating possible sites of drug action.

Site 1: *Enzymatic synthesis:*

    a. Tyrosine hydroxylase reaction blocked by the competitive inhibitor, α-methyltyrosine.

    b. Dopamine-β-hydroxylase reaction blocked by a dithiocarbamate derivative, Fla-63 bis-(1-methyl-4-homopiperazinyl-thiocarbonyl)-disulfide.

Site 2: *Storage:* Reserpine and tetrabenazine interfere with the uptake—storage mechanism of the amine granules. The depletion of norepinephrine produced by reserpine is long-lasting and the storage granules are irreversibly damaged. Tetrabenazine also interferes with the uptake—storage mechanism of the granules, except the effects of this drug are of a shorter duration and do not appear to be irreversible.

Site 3: *Release:* Amphetamine appears to cause an increase in the net release of norepinephrine. Probably the primary mechanism by which amphetamine causes release is by its ability to block effectively the reuptake mechanism.

Site 4: *Receptor interaction:*

a. Presynaptic α$_2$-autoreceptors

b. Postsynaptic α-receptors

## PHARMACOLOGY OF CENTRAL CATECHOLAMINE-CONTAINING NEURONS

The psychotropic drugs (drugs that alter behavior, mood, and perception in humans and behavior in animals) can be divided into two main categories, the psychotherapeutic drugs and the psychotomimetic agents. Psychotherapeutic drugs can be further divided, on the basis of their activity in humans, into at least four general classes: antipsychotics, antianxiety drugs, antidepressants, and stimulants.

In recent years a great deal more information has become available concerning the anatomy, biochemistry, and functional organization of catecholamine systems. This has fostered knowledge concerning the mechanisms and sites of action of many psychotropic drugs. It is now appreciated that drugs can influence the output of monoamine systems by interacting at several distinct sites. For example, drugs

---

FIGURE 9-14. *Continued.*

Clonidine appears to be a very potent autoreceptor-stimulating drug. At higher doses clonidine will also stimulate postsynaptic receptors. Phenoxybenzamine and phenotolamine are effective α-receptor blocking agents. Recent experiments indicate that these drugs may also have some presynaptic alpha$_2$ receptor blocking action. However, yohimbine and piperoxane are more selective as α$_2$-receptor-blocking agents.

Site 5: *Reuptake:* Norepinephrine has its action terminated by being taken up into the presynaptic terminal. The tricyclic drug desipramine is an example of a potent inhibitor of this uptake mechanism.

Site 6: *Monoamine Oxidase (MAO):* Norepinephrine or dopamine present in a free state within the presynaptic terminal can be degraded by the enzyme MAO, which appears to be located in the outer membrane of mitochondria. Pargyline is an effective inhibitor of MAO.

Site 7: *Catchol-O-methyl transferase (COMT):* Norepinephrine can be inactivated by the enzyme COMT, which is believed to be localized outside the presynaptic neuron. Tropolone is an inhibitor of COMT. The normetanephrine (NM) formed by the action of COMT on NE can be further metabolized by MAO and aldehyde reductase to 3-methoxy-4-hydroxyphenylglycol (MHPG). The MHPG formed can be further metabolized to MHPG-sulfate by the action of a sulfotransferase found in the brain. Although MHPG-sulfate is the predominant form of this metabolite found in rodent brain, the free, unconjugated MHPG is the major form found in primate brain.

can act to influence the output of catecholamine systems by (1) acting presynaptically to alter the life cycle of the transmitter (i.e., synthesis, storage, and release, etc. [see Figs. 9-14 and 10-7]); (2) acting postsynaptically to mimic or block the action of the transmitter at the level of postsynaptic receptors; and (3) acting at the level of cell body autoreceptors to influence the physiological activity of catecholamine neurons. The activity of catecholamine neurons can also be influenced by postsynaptic receptors via negative neuronal feedback loops. In the latter two actions, drugs appear to exert their influence by interacting with catecholamine receptors. Figure 9-15 illustrates the various neuronal pathways and local mechanisms regulating synaptic homeostasis in central noradrenergic neurons. In general, catecholamine receptors can be subdivided into two broad categories: those which are localized directly on catecholamine neurons (often referred to as presynaptic receptors) and those on other cell types which are often termed simply postsynaptic receptors, since they are postsynaptic to the catecholamine neurons, the source of the endogenous ligand. When it became appreciated that catecholamine neurons, in addition to possessing receptors on the nerve terminals, appear to have receptors distributed over all parts of the neurons (i.e., soma, dendrites, and preterminal axons), the term presynaptic receptors really became inappropriate as a description for all these receptors. Carlsson, in 1975, suggested that "autoreceptor" was a more appropriate term to describe these receptors since the sensitivity of these catecholamine receptors to the neurons' own transmitter seemed more significant than their location relative to the synapse. The term autoreceptor achieved rapid acceptance and pharmacological research in the succeeding years resulted in the detection and description of autoreceptors on neurons in almost all chemically defined neuronal systems.

The presence of autoreceptors on some neurons may turn out to be only of pharmacological interest since they may never encounter effective concentrations of the appropriate endogenous agonist in vivo. Others, however, in addition to their pharmacological responsiveness, may play a very important physiological role in the main-

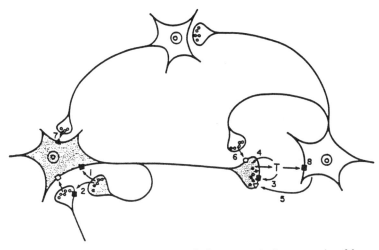

FIGURE 9-15. Neural pathways regulating synaptic homeostasis of locus ceruleus neurons. Influence of locus ceruleus neuron (shaded) on its target cells can be regulated both by modulation of transmitter release (1-7) and by amplification of signal provided by that release (8). This involves a large variety of cell surface receptors, including receptors that respond to NE itself ( ), as well as receptors responding to other chemical signals ($\bigcirc,\square,\blacktriangle,\triangle$). Principal pathways for regulating NE release: 1, direct action of recurrent collaterals onto soma; 2, indirect action of recurrent colaterals, mediated via influence on presynaptic afferents; 3, direct action of NE on presynaptic terminal; 4, alterations in rate of NE reuptake; 5, humoral signals generated by target; 6, neural signals providing short-loop negative feedback from target; and 7, neural signals providing long-loop negative feedback from target; 8, extent to which signal is amplified can be modulated by short-term modification of the sensitivity of the target, by long-term changes in number of receptors, and by other means. (Modified from Stricker and Zigmond, 1986)

tenance of presynaptic events. This certainly appears to be the case for catecholamine autoreceptors. (See Chapter 10)

The pharmacology of central and peripheral NE neurons is quite similar (Figs. 9-9 and 9-14). The main differences seem to be related primarily to drug delivery and the greater complexity of the neuronal pathways regulating synaptic homeostasis of the central NE systems (Fig. 9-15).

*Effect of Drugs on the Electrophysiological Activity of Noradrenergic Neurons*

In recent years a number of drugs have been found to influence the activity of the noradrenergic neurons in the locus ceruleus. Table 9-1 lists the drugs that have been studied and their influence on locus cell firing. Amphetamine inhibits locus cell firing, and it appears to do so by activating a neuronal feedback loop. The effects of amphetamine on locus firing are partially blocked by chlorpromazine. L-Amphetamine is equipotent with D-amphetamine in its inhibitory effects. Alpha-receptor agonists and antagonists also influence locus cell firing. This is due in part to the interaction of these adrenergic agents with autoreceptors on the NE cell bodies or dendrites in the locus. Alpha$_2$-agonists such as clonidine or guanfacine cause a suppression of locus cell firing and these inhibitory effects are reversed by $\alpha_2$-antagonists. Piperoxane, yohimbine and idazoxane, $\alpha_2$-antagonists, cause a marked increase in single cell activity. Morphine and morphine-like peptides such as enkephalins or endorphins have been shown to exert an inhibitory influence on locus cell firing. The inhibitory effects of morphine or enkephalin are reversed by the opiate antagonist naloxone but are uninfluenced by $\alpha_2$-antagonists. Methylxanthines such as isobutyl-methylxanthines (IBMX), which induce a quasi-opiate withdrawal syndrome, cause an increase in locus cell firing; this increase is antagonized by $\alpha_2$-agonists such as clonidine. LC cells in chronic morphine-treated rats dramatically increase locus cell firing during naloxone-induced withdrawal, and this increase in firing is suppressed by clonidine. These animal studies, viewed in conjunction with the clinical data demonstrating the effectiveness of treating opiate withdrawal with clonidine, have suggested that NE hyperactivity may be an important component of the opiate withdrawal syndrome in humans. These studies have thus provided new insight into the rational design of a new class of drugs ($\alpha_2$-agonists) to treat opiate withdrawal, although the role of the locus ceruleus in this treatment effect has not actually been established.

Numerous pharmacological studies, mostly conducted in rodents, have demonstrated that there is a good correlation between drug-

TABLE 9-1. Correlation between brain levels of MHPG and electrophysiological activity of noradrenergic neurons in the locus ceruleus

| Drug or experimental condition | Change in locus ceruleus unit activity | Change in brain MHPG |
|---|---|---|
| *Alpha₂-agonists*<br>Clonidine<br>Guanfacine | Decrease | Decrease |
| *Alpha₂-antagonists*<br>Yohimbine<br>Piperoxane<br>Idazoxane | Increase | Increase |
| *Tricyclic antidepressants*<br>Desipramine<br>Imipramine<br>Amitriptyline | Decrease | Decrease |
| *Amphetamine* | Decrease | Decrease, increase (dose dependent) |
| *Morphine* | Decrease | Increase |
| *Methylxanthines*<br>Isobutylmethylxanthine | Increase | Increase |
| *Naloxone* | No change | No change |
| *Naloxone-precipitated morphine withdrawal* | Increase | Increase |
| *Stress* | Increase | Increase |
| *Electrical stimulation LC* | Increase | Increase |
| *Transection of dorsal NE bundle* | Decrease | Decrease |

induced changes in the firing rate of locus ceruleus neurons monitored by extracellular single-unit recording and alterations in brain levels of MHPG. For example, drug-induced suppression of central noradrenergic activity produced by administration of clonidine or tricyclic antidepressants is accompanied by a reduction in MHPG. The $\alpha_2$-antagonists (e.g., idazoxane, piperoxane, or yohimbine) or experimental conditions (e.g., stress or naloxone-precipitated withdrawal), which cause an increase in noradrenergic activity, produce an increase in the brain levels of MHPG. The magnitude of the increase in MHPG produced by naloxone-precipitated morphine withdrawal exceeds that produced by administration of supramaximal doses of $\alpha_2$-antagonists such as piperoxane or yohimbine. The biochemical observation is consistent with electrophysiological studies indicating that the increase in locus ceruleus cell activity produced during naloxone-precipitated withdrawal exceeds that achieved by administration of $\alpha_2$-antagonists such as piperoxane and yohimbine. Since MHPG levels in brain measured under controlled experimental conditions provide an index of physiological activity in the locus ceruleus, measures of this metabolite in accessible body fluids may be useful for the assessment of changes in central NE function in intact animals or patients. Many clinical researchers are currently monitoring this metabolite in CSF, plasma, and urine in the hope that this measure will provide insight concerning alterations in central noradrenergic function.

*Physiological Functions of Central Noradrenergic Neurons*

Many functions have been proposed for the central norepinephrine neurons and their several sets of synaptic connections. Among the hypotheses that have the most supportive data are ideas concerning their role in affective psychoses (described below), in learning and memory, in reinforcement, in sleep–wake cycle regulation, and in the anxiety–nociception hypothesis. It has also been suggested that a major function of central noradrenergic neurons is not on neuronal activity and related behavioral phenomena at all, but rather a more general role in cerebral blood flow and metabolism. However, data available at present fit better into a more general proposal: The main function of the locus ceruleus (LC) and its projections is to determine the brain's global orientation concerning events in the external world and within the viscera. Such a hypothesis of central noradrenergic neuron function has been generated by observations of locus ceruleus unit discharge in untreated, awake, behaviorally responsive rats and monkeys. These studies reveal the locus ceruleus units to be highly responsive to a variety of nonnoxious sensory stimuli, and also reveals that the responsiveness of these units varies as a function of the animal's level of behavioral vigilance. Increased neuronal activity in the locus ceruleus is associated with unexpected sensory events in the subject's external environment, while decreased noradrenergic activity is associated with behaviors that mediate tonic vegetative behaviors. Such a global-orienting function can also incorporate other aspects of presumptive function expressed by earlier data, but none of those more discrete functions can be documented as necessary or sufficient explanations of locus ceruleus function.

*Pharmacology of Adrenergic Neurons*

Limited experiments have suggested that the pharmacology of central adrenergic neurons is similar to that of central noradrenergic neurons. Agents that block tyrosine hydroxylase, DOPA decarboxylase, and dopamine β-hydroxylase lead to a reduction of both norepinephrine and epinephrine in the brain. Depleting agents, such as reserpine, which cause release of norepinephrine and dopamine, also are effective in releasing epinephrine. MAO inhibitors cause an elevation of norepinephrine, dopamine, and epinephrine; but inhibitors of the A form of MAO are much more effective in elevation of epinephrine. In fact, most of the pharmacological data is consistent with the hypothesis that, at least in the rat hypothalamus, oxidative deamination is an important metabolic process by which epinephrine is degraded and that type A MAO is predominantly involved in this degradation.

Similar to observations made in central noradrenergic neurons, $\alpha_2$-agonists such as clonidine decrease epinephrine formation, and $\alpha_2$-antagonists increase epinephrine turnover. These data are also consistent with the possibility that $\alpha_2$-receptors are involved in the regulation of synthesis and release of epinephrine and perhaps also in the control of the functional activity of adrenergic neurons.

## CATECHOLAMINE THEORY OF AFFECTIVE DISORDER

The catecholamines play a fairly well-established role in the periphery with regard to stress and emotional behavior. By contrast, their suggested role in the central nervous system in affective disorders is still quite speculative, although evidence for some involvement of these agents is becoming increasingly compelling.

A catecholamine hypothesis of affective disorder states that, in general, behavioral depression may be related to a deficiency of catecholamine (usually norepinephrine) at functionally important central adrenergic receptors, while mania results from excess catecholamine. While substantial experimental work supports this proposal, it must be kept in mind that most of the experiments on which this hypothesis is based derive from "normal" animals. Second, from a nosological standpoint, depression itself is rather ill-defined. In fact, Giarman has suggested that "nosologically it might be fair to compare the depressive syndrome with the anemias. Certainly, no self-respecting hematologist would subscribe to a unitary biochemical explanation for all of the anemias."

The original impetus for formulation of the catecholamine hypothesis was the finding that various monoamine oxidase inhibitors, notably iproniazid, acted clinically as mood elevators or antidepressants. Shortly thereafter, it was found that this class of compounds also produced marked increases in brain amine levels. By the same token, reserpine, a potent tranquilizer that causes depletion of brain amines, sometimes produces a serious depressed state (clinically indistinguishable from endogenous depression) and even suicidal attempts in humans. Although both classes of drugs alter brain levels of catecholamines and serotonin quite equally, the fact that a precursor of catecholamine biosynthesis, notably DOPA, can reverse most of the reserpine-induced symptomology in animals has tended to bias many researchers in favor of the catecholamine theory. In general, many pharmacological studies appear to implicate the catecholamines as the amines involved in affective disorders. However, it must be realized that a great deal more work has been done on norepinephrine than on other transmitter candidates. In fact, by no means does the available evidence obtained for the involvement of norepinephrine rule out the participation of dopamine, 5-hydroxy-tryptamine epinephrine, or other putative transmitters in similar events.

The three general classes of drugs most commonly used to treat various depressive disorders are the monoamine oxidase inhibitors, the tricyclic antidepressants, and the psychomotor stimulants of which amphetamine was the prototype. All of these pharmacological agents appear to interact with catecholamines in a way that is consistent with the catecholamine hypothesis.

Even if one considers all the suggested modes of action of amphetamines—(1) partial agonist, mimicking action of norepinephrine at receptor; (2) inhibition of catecholamine reuptake; (3) inhibition of monoamine oxidase; (4) displacement of norepinephrine, releasing it onto receptors—these amphetamines appear to exert an action compatible with the hypothesis above, since the net result of all these actions is a temporary increase of norepinephrine at the receptor or a direct stimulatory action at the receptor. Upon administration of long-term or high doses of amphetamine, it is possible to produce an eventual depletion of brain norepinephrine, perhaps owing to a displacement of norepinephrine in the neuron and/or an inhibition of synthesis. Also, as indicated earlier, amphetamine causes an inhibition of neuronal activity in catecholamine neurons. This chronic depletion of transmitter or a prolonged inactivity of catecholamine neurons may relate to the clinical observation of amphetamine tolerance or to the well-known poststimulation depression or fatigue observed after chronic administration of this class of drugs.

Many of the tricyclic antidepressants influence catecholamine neurons by inhibiting the catecholamine reuptake system (see above). While these findings are of course also consistent with the catecholamine hypothesis, the tricyclics do not affect this system exclusively. Some of the tricyclic agents, notably imipramine, also potentiate peripheral and central effects of serotonin; they also have both central and peripheral anticholinergic actions.

The action of the monoamine oxidase inhibitors also supports the catecholamine hypothesis. All these agents inhibit an enzyme responsible for the metabolism of norepinephrine and various other amines (5-hydroxytryptamine, dopamine, tyramine, tryptamine). This inhibition results in a marked increase in the intraneuronal levels of norepinephrine. Presumably, according to the conceptual model of the adrenergic neuron presented above, this interneuronal norepinephrine might eventually diffuse out of the neuron and reach receptor cells, thereby overcoming the presumed deficiency. A similar mechanism may also explain the antagonism of reserpine-induced sedation with monoamine oxidase inhibitors, since there will be a replenishment of the norepinephrine deficiency initially caused by reserpine.

Lithium, one of the main agents used in the treatment of mania has also been studied with regard to its action on the life cycle of the catecholamines. Interestingly, pretreatment with lithium blocks the stimulus-induced release of norepinephrine from rat brain slices. Other investigators have suggested that lithium may facilitate reuptake of norepinephrine. If the inhibition of release observed in stimulated brain slices is due to a facilitated recapture mechanism, then the mechanism of action of lithium is the exact opposite of that of the antidepressant drugs, as would be expected according to the catecholamine hypothesis. Although a single injection of lithium may antagonize responses to norepinephrine, chronic treatment of rats leads to modest supersensitive norepinephrine responses.

As summarized in a review by Berger and Barchas, closer scrutiny of the pharmacological data cited in support of the catecholamine theory of affective disorder reveals some important discrepancies: (1) cocaine is a very potent inhibitor of catecholamine reuptake and thus, like the tricyclic antidepressants, it should increase the availability of norepinephrine at central synapses. But cocaine does not possess any significant antidepressant activity. (2) Iprandole, a tricyclic compound without any significant effect on catecholamine uptake or any influence on central noradrenergic neurons, is an effective antidepressant. Furthermore, desensitization of postsynaptic β-receptors after chronic administration of tricyclic antidepressant drugs is not entirely compatible with the proposed theory of a synaptic catecholamine deficit. (3) In laboratory studies the ability of tricyclic antidepressants to inhibit catecholamine uptake and the ability of MAO inhibitors to block MAO and elevate brain catecholamines are apparent soon after administration. Clinically, antidepressants require several weeks of continuous administration to produce therapeutic effects. (4) On the surface, the pharmacological and clinical effects of the tricyclics and lithium seem to fit nicely with the catecholamine theory of affective disorder. These agents produce opposite effects on norepinephrine disposition, and lithium is effective in treating mania while the tricyclics are useful in treating depression. The water is muddied, however, by the finding that lithium is also effective in the treatment of bipolar depressed patients.

The fact that several questions have been raised about the pharmacological data used to support the catecholamine theory of affective disorder has prompted many investigators to attempt to obtain some direct evidence of the involvement of norepinephrine systems in affective disorders. The most extensive studies have involved analysis of urinary excretion patterns of catecholamine metabolites in patients with affective disorders. The rationale has been that the urinary excretion of a particular metabolite like MHPG may be a useful reflection of central catecholaminergic processes. Despite the inherent problems in urinary catecholamine metabolite measurement, such as complications because of large contributions from peripheral sources, some interesting findings have emerged.

Findings from several clinical studies now indicate that (1) depressed patients as a group excrete less than normal quantities of MHPG; (2) diagnostic subgroups of depressed patients are particularly likely to have low urinary MHPG values; (3) patients who switch from a depressive to a euthymic or hypomanic state show a corresponding increase in urinary MHPG; and (4) pretreatment urinary MHPG values are predictive of the type of therapeutic response obtained with amitriptyline or imipramine. Although provocative and essentially consistent with the norepinephrine theory of affective disorder, these clinical findings all hinge on the issue of the degree to which urinary MHPG reflects central norepinephrine metabolism.

For the above reasons, the original hypothesis that the mechanism of action of antidepressant drugs is to increase the availability of monoamines in the brain has been updated to include the effects of long-term antidepressant treatment on monoamine receptor sensitivity. A wide array of effects of long-term treatment with antidepressants has been observed in several monoamine systems. These effects include long-term changes in receptor number and changes in physiological and behavioral sensitivity to monoamine agonists and antagonists. The most consistent findings observed following chronic administration of most of the clinically effective antidepressant drugs to experimental animals are (1) a reduction in the number of β-adrenoceptor recognition sites and a down-regulation of β-adrenoceptor functioning, (2) an increase in the sensitivity of central α-adrenoceptors suggesting an up-regulation in central α-adrenoceptor functioning, (3) similar to the observation on α-adrenoceptors, both behavioral and electrophysiological studies also point to an up-regulation in the sensitivity of central 5-HT receptors. More direct studies will be necessary, however, before it will be possible to conclude whether any or all of these changes are related to the therapeutic action of antidepressant drugs. These studies await the development of appropriate models for monitoring central neurotransmitter functioning in humans.

## SELECTED REFERENCES

Aston-Jones, G. and F. E. Bloom (1981). Norepinephrine-containing locus coeruleus neurons in behaving rats exhibit pronounced responses to nonnoxious environmental stimuli. *J. Neurosci. 1*, 887.

Bacopoulos, N. G., S. E. Hattox, and R. H. Roth (1979). 3,4-Dihydroxyphenylacetic acid and homovanillic acid in rat plasma: Possible indicators of central dopaminergic activity. *Eur. J. Pharmacol. 56*, 225.

Dahlström, A. and A. Carlsson (1986). Making visible the invisible. In *Discoveries in Pharmacology* (Vol. 3: *Pharmacology Methods, Receptors and Chemotherapy*) (M. J. Parnham and J. Bruinvels, eds.), pp. 97–125, Elsevier Science Publishers, B.V.

DiChiara, G. (1990). In vivo brain dialysis of neurotransmitters. *Trends in Pharm. Sci. 11*, 116–121.

Euler, U. S. von (1956). *Noradrenaline*. Charles C. Thomas, Springfield, IL.

Foote, S. I., F. E. Bloom, and G. Aston-Jones (1983). Nucleus locus ceruleus: New evidence of anatomical and physiological specificity. *Physiol. Rev. 63*, 844.

Foote, S. L. and J. H. Morrison (1987). Extrathalamic modulation of cortical function. *Ann. Rev. Neurosci. 10*, 67–95.

Fuller, R. W. (1982). Pharmacology of brain epinephrine neurons. *Ann. Rev. Pharmacol. Toxicol. 22*, 31–55.

Gibson, C. J. (1985). Control of monoamine synthesis by precursor availability. In *Handbook of Neurochemistry*, 2nd ed. (A. Lajtha, ed.), Vol. 8, p. 309. Plenum, NY.

Goldstein, M. and L. A. Green (1987). Activation of tyrosine hydroxylase by phosphorylation. In *Psychopharmacology: The Third Generation of Progress* (H. Y. Meltzer, ed.), pp. 75–80. Raven Press, New York.

Graefe, K.-H. and H. Bönisch (1988). The transport of amines across the axonal membranes of noradrenergic and dopaminergic neurones. In *Handbook of Experimental Pharmacology* (U. Trendelenburg and N. Weiner, eds.), Vol. 90/I, pp. 193–245. Springer-Verlag, Berlin.

Hökfelt, T., O. Johansson, and M. Goldstein (1984). Central catecholamine neurons as revealed by immunohistochemistry with special reference to adrenaline neurons. In *Handbook of Chemical Neuroanatomy* (Vol. 2, part I: *Classical Transmitters in the CNS*) (Bjorklund, A. and T. Hökfeld, eds.). Elsevier, Amsterdam.

Kelly, R. B. (1988). The cell biology of the nerve terminal. *Neuron 1*, 431–438.

Lefkowitz, R. J., W. P. Hausdorff, and M. G. Caron (1990). role of phosphorylation in desensitization of the β-adrenoceptor. *Trends Pharmacol. Sci. 11*, 190–193.

Lindvall, O. and A. Björklund (1983). Dopamine and norepinephrine containing neuron systems: Their anatomy in the rat brain. In *Chemical Neuroanatomy* (P. C. Emson, ed.). Raven Press, New York.

Maas, J. W. (ed.) (1983). *MHPG: Basic Mechanisms and Psychopathology.* Academic Press, New York.

Maas, J.W., S. E. Hattox, N. M. Geene, and D. H. Landis (1979). 3-Methoxy-4-hydroxyphenethyleneglycol (MHPG). Production by human brain in vivo. *Science 205*, 1025.

Masserano, J. M., P. R. Vulliet, A. W. Tank, and N. Weiner (1989). The role of tyrosine hydroxylase in the regulation of catecholamine synthesis. In *Handbook of Experimental Pharmacology* (U. Trendelenburg and N. Weiner eds.), Vol. 90/II, pp. 427–469. Springer-Verlag, Berlin.

Mefford, I. N. (1988). Epinephrine in mammalian brain. *Prog. Neuro-Psychopharmacol. Biol. Psychiatry 12*, 365–388.

Miller, R. J. (1987). Multiple calcium channels and neuronal function. *Science 232*, 46–52.

Moore, R. Y. and F. E. Bloom (1979). Central catecholamine neuron systems: Anatomy and physiology of the norepinephrine and epinephrine systems. *Ann. Rev. Neurosci. 2*, 113.

Nedergaard, O. A. (1988). Catecholamines: Regulation, release and inactivation. *Pharmacol. and Toxicol.* 63, 5–8, suppl. I.

O'Dowd, B. F., R. J. Lefkowitz, and M. G. Caron (1989). Structure of the adrenergic and related receptors. *Ann. Rev. Neurosci. 12*, 67–83.

Pacholczyk, T., R. D. Blakely, and S. G. Amara (1991). Expression cloning of a cocaine- and antidepressant-sensitive human noradrenaline transporter. *Nature 250*, 350–353.

Philippu, A. and H. Mattheai (1988). Transport and storage of catecholamines in vesicles. In *Handbook of Experimental Pharmacology* (U. Trendelenburg and N. Weiner, eds.), Vol. 90/I, pp. 1–42. Springer-Verlag, Berlin.

Redmond, D. E., Jr. (1987). Studies of the nucleus locus coeruleus in monkeys and hypotheses for neuropsychopharmacology. In *Psychopharmacology: The Third Generation of Progress* (H. Y. Meltzer, ed.), pp. 967–975, Raven Press, New York.

Strader, C. D., I. S. Sigal, and R. A. Dixon (1989). Structural basis of β-adrenergic receptor function. *FASEB J. 3*, 1825–32.

Stricker, E. M. and M. J. Zigmond (1986). In *Handbook of Physiology: The Nervous System IV* (P. Bloom, ed.), pp. 677–700. American Physiological Society, Bethesda, Maryland.

Sugrue, M. F. (1984). Do antidepressants possess a common mechanism of action *Biochem. Pharmacol. 32*, 1811.

Usdin, E., N. Weiner, and E. Costa (eds.) (1981). *Structure and Function of Monoamine Enzymes*, Vol. 2. Macmillan, New York.

Ward-Routledge, C. and C. A. Marsden (1988). Adrenaline in the CNS and the action of antihypertensive drugs. *Trends Pharmacol. Sci. 9*, 209–214.

Weinshilboum, R. M. (1989). Catecholamine biochemical genetics. In *Handbook of Experimental Pharmacology* (U. Trendelenburg and N. Weiner, eds.), Vol. 90/II, pp. 391–425. Springer-Verlag, Berlin.

Winkler, H. (1988). Occurrence and mechanisms of exocytosis in adrenal medulla and sympathetic nerve. In *Handbook of Experimental Pharmacology* (U. Trendelenberg and N. Weiner, eds.), Vol. 90/I pp. 43–118. Springer-Verlag, Berlin.

Ziegler, M. G. and R. C. R. Lake (eds.) (1984). *Norepinephrine: Frontiers of Clinical Neuroscience*, Vol. 2, Williams & Wilkins, Baltimore, Maryland.

Zigmond, R. E., M. A. Schwarzschild, and A. R. Rittenhouse (1989). Acute regulation of tyrosine hydroxylase by nerve activity and by neurotransmitters via phosphorylation. *Ann. Rev. Neurosci. 12*, 415–461.

# 10 | Dopamine

Dopamine is a relative newcomer to the field of monoamine transmitters in mammalian brain. Until the mid-1950s dopamine was exclusively considered to be an intermediate in the biosynthesis of the catecholamines, norepinephrine and epinephrine. Significant tissue levels of dopamine were first demonstrated in peripheral organs of ruminant species. A short time later Montagu, Carlsson and co-workers found that dopamine was also present in the brain in about equal concentrations to those of norepinephrine. The very marked differences in regional distribution of the two catecholamines, dopamine and norepinephrine, both within the CNS and in bovine peripheral tissue, led Swedish investigators to propose a biological role for dopamine independent of its function as a precursor for norepinephrine biosynthesis. Studies demonstrating that most brain dopamine is confined to the basal ganglia led to the hypothesis that it might be involved in motor control and that decreased striatal dopamine could be the cause of extrapyramidal symptoms in Parkinson's disease. The discovery of profound depletions of dopamine in the striatum of parkinsonian patients and the demonstration that L-dopa has beneficial effects in these patients substantiated the clinical relevance of this theory. These and other largely pharmacological studies were the impetus for the almost explosive developments in dopamine research during the past three decades. With the development of a fluorescent histochemical method for the visualization of catecholamines in freeze-dried tissue sections and the application of this technique to brain tissue, the anatomy of brain dopamine systems could also be described.

## Dopaminergic Systems

The central dopamine-containing systems are considerably more complex in their organization than the noradrenergic systems. Not only are there many more dopamine cells, (the number of mesencephalic dopamine cells has been estimated at about 15,000–20,000 on each side, while the number of noradrenergic neurons in the entire brain stem is reported to be about 5,000 on each side), there are also several major dopamine-containing nuclei as well as specialized dopamine neurons that make extremely localized connections within the retina and olfactory bulb. When dopamine systems were first visualized in the CNS, it was thought that all dopamine cells within the zona compacta of the substantia nigra projected to the caudate putamen nucleus. Dopamine cells in the ventral tegmental area surrounding the interpeduncular nucleus were believed to project exclusively to parts of the limbic system. This beautiful simplicity lasted a relatively short time. Soon dopamine inputs to the cortex were discovered, and within a few years, primarily through the use of retrograde tracing techniques, it became apparent that dopamine cells within the A8, A9, and A10 area form an anatomically heterogeneous population in terms of their projection areas (Björklund and Lindvall, 1984). Retrograde tracing techniques also led to another important discovery—that dopamine cells project topographically to the areas that they innervate. Thus, although there is some overlap, those dopamine cells nearest to each other in a given area are more likely to innervate a common region than are dopamine cells distant from each other.

Based on this recent progress in detailing the anatomy of the dopamine systems (Fig. 10-1), it is convenient to consider these systems under three major categories in terms of the length of the efferent dopamine fibers.

1. *Ultrashort Systems.* Among the ultrashort systems are the *interplexiform amacrine-like neurons*, which link inner and outer plexiform layers of the retina, and the *periglomerular dopamine cells* of the olfactory bulb, which link together mitral cell dendrites in separated adjacent glomeruli.

2. *Intermediate-Length Systems.* The intermediate-length systems include (a) the *tuberohypophysial dopamine cells*, which project from arcuate and periventricular nuclei into the intermediate lobe of the pituitary and into the median eminence (often referred to as the tuberoinfundibular system); (b) the *incertohypothalamic neurons*, which link the dorsal and posterior

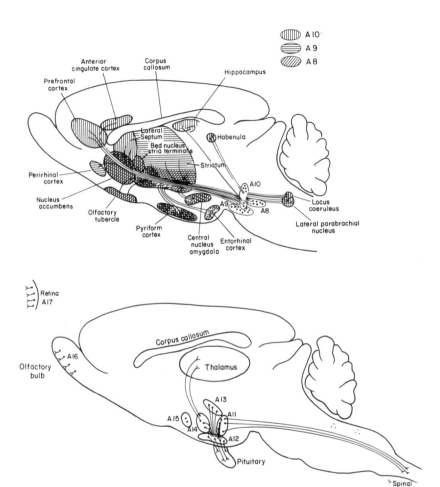

FIGURE 10-1. Schematic diagram illustrating the distribution of the main central neuronal pathways containing dopamine. The stippled regions indicate the major nerve terminal areas and their cell groups of origin. The cell groups in this figure are named according to the nomenclature of Dahlström and Fuxe (1965).

hypothalamus with the dorsal anterior hypothalamus and lateral septal nuclei; and (c) the *medullary periventricular* group, which includes those dopamine cells in the perimeter of the dorsal motor nucleus of the vagus nerve, the nucleus tractus solitarius, and the cells scattered in the tegmental radiation of the periaqueductal grey matter.

3. *Long-Length Systems.* The long-length systems are the long projections linking the ventral tegmental and substantia nigra dopamine cells with three principal sets of targets: the *neostriatum* (principally the caudate and putamen); the *limbic cortex* (medial prefrontal, cingulate, and entorhinal areas); and *other limbic structures* (the regions of the *septum, olfactory tubercle, nucleus accumbens septi, amygdaloid complex*, and *piriform cortex*). These latter two groups have frequently been termed the *mesocortical* and *mesolimbic dopamine* projections, respectively. Under certain conditions these limbic target systems, when compared to the nigrostriatal system, exhibit some unique pharmacological properties, which are discussed in detail in the latter portion of this chapter.

With regard to cellular analysis of function, almost all reported data are from studies of the nigrostriatal dopamine projection. Here most studies using the iontophoretic administration of dopamine indicate that the predominant qualitative response is inhibition. This effect, like that of apomorphine and cyclic AMP, is potentiated by phosphodiesterase inhibitors, providing the physiological counterpart to the second messenger hypothesis suggested by biochemical studies. On the other hand, the effects on the properties of caudate neurons when electrical stimulation is applied to the ventral tegmentum and substantia nigra are considerably less homogeneous, ranging from excitation to inhibition with considerable variations in latency and sensitivity to dopamine antagonism. In one study neither the excitations nor the inhibitions elicited by nigral stimulation were prevented by 6-hydroxy-dopamine-induced destruction of the dopamine cell bodies. Unambiguous pharmacological and electrophysiological analysis of the dopamine pathway thus remains to be accomplished. Although at present the bulk of the evidence favors an inhibitory role for dopamine, inquisitive students will want to examine the arguments raised by both sides and make their own evaluations of the effects reported. Important basic information is needed to rule out the spread of current to nearby nondopamine tracts and to determine accurately the latency of conduction reported for these extremely fine unmyelinated fibers.

In the last decade, it has become apparent that midbrain dopamine neurons are quite heterogeneous in terms of their biochemistry, physiology, pharmacology, and regulatory properties when compared to the prototypic nigrostriatal system in which most of the earlier studies were performed. While midbrain dopamine neurons differ in a number of important ways, their functional organization generally reflects features of transmitter dynamics that are shared by all dopamine neurons. These features have been most thoroughly studied in the nigrostriatal pathway and are summarized below (see Fig. 10-2).

*Dopamine Synthesis*

Dopamine synthesis, like that of all catecholamines in the nervous system, originates from the amino acid precursor tyrosine, which must be transported across the blood-brain barrier into the dopamine neuron. A number of conditions can affect tyrosine transport, diminishing its availability and thus altering dopamine formation. The rate-limiting step in dopamine synthesis once tyrosine gains entry into the neuron is the conversion of L-tyrosine to L-dihydroxyphenylalanine (L-dopa) by the enzyme tyrosine hydroxylase. Dopa is subsequently converted to dopamine by L-aromatic amino acid decarboxylase. This latter enzyme turns over so rapidly that dopa levels in the brain are negligible under normal conditions. Because of the high activity of this enzyme and the low endogenous levels of dopa normally present in the brain, it is possible to dramatically enhance the formation of dopamine by providing this enzyme with increased amounts of substrate. Since the levels of tyrosine in the brain are relatively high and are above the Km for tyrosine hydroxylase, under

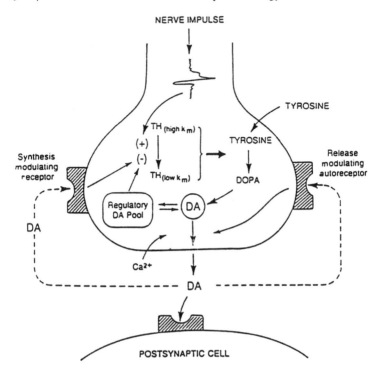

FIGURE 10-2. Schematic model of a striatal dopaminergic nerve terminal indicating mechanisms which modulate dopamine (DA) release and synthesis. Invasion of the terminal by a nerve impulse results in the $Ca^{2+}$-dependent release of DA. This release process is attenuated by release-modulating autoreceptors. Increased impulse flow also stimulates tyrosine hydroxylation, the rate-limiting step in DA biosynthesis. This appears to involve the phosphorylation of tyrosine hydroxylase (TH), resulting in conversion to an activated form with greater affinity for tetrahydrobiopterin cofactor. The rate of tyrosine hydroxylation can be attenuated by (a) activation of synthesis-modulating autoreceptors, which may function by reversing the kinetic activation of TH and (b) endproduct inhibition by intraneuronal DA, which competes with the cofactor for a binding site on TH. Release- and synthesis-modulating autoreceptors may represent distinct sites. Alternatively, one site may regulate both functions through distinct transduction mechanisms.

normal conditions it is not feasible to significantly augment dopamine synthesis by increasing brain levels of this amino acid. Since tyrosine hydroxylase is the rate-limiting enzyme in the biosynthesis of dopamine, this enzyme sets the pace for the formation of dopamine and is particularly susceptible to physiological regulation and pharmacological manipulation. Endogenous mechanisms for regulating the rate of dopamine synthesis in dopamine neurons primarily involve modulation of tyrosine hydroxylase activity. The activity of this key enzyme is subject to four major regulatory influences:

1. Dopamine and other catecholamines function as end product inhibitors of tyrosine hydroxylase (TH) by competing with a tetrahydrobiopterin (BH-4) cofactor for a binding site on the enzyme.

2. The availability of BH-4 may also play a role in regulating TH activity. Tyrosine hydroxylase can exist in two kinetic forms that exhibit different affinities for BH-4. The conversion from low- to high-affinity forms is thought to involve direct phosphorylation of the enzyme, and the proportion of TH molecules in the high-affinity state appears to be a function of the state of neuronal firing.

3. Presynaptic dopamine receptors also modulate the rate of tyrosine hydroxylation. These receptors are activated by dopamine released from the nerve terminal, resulting in feedback inhibition of dopamine synthesis. Autoreceptors can modulate both synthesis and release of dopamine and represent important sites for the pharmacological manipulation of dopaminergic function by dopamine agonists and antagonists.

4. Dopamine synthesis also depends on the rate of impulse flow in the nigrostriatal pathway. During periods of increased impulse flow, the rate of tyrosine hydroxylation is increased primarily through a kinetic activation of tyrosine hydroxylase that increases its affinity for BH-4 and decreases its affinity for the normal end product inhibitor, dopamine. Under conditions of increased impulse flow, tyrosine hydroxylation is also more susceptible to precursor regulation by tyrosine availability.

*Dopamine Release*

Calcium-dependent release of dopamine from the nerve terminal is thought to occur in response to invasion of the terminal by an action potential. The extent of dopamine release appears to be a function of the rate and pattern of firing. The burst-firing mode leads to an enhanced release of dopamine. Dopamine release is also modulated by presynaptic release-modulating autoreceptors. In general, dopamine agonists inhibit, while dopamine antagonists enhance the evoked release of dopamine.

*Dopamine Uptake and the Dopamine Transporter*

Dopamine nerve terminals possess high-affinity dopamine uptake sites which are important in terminating transmitter action and in maintaining transmitter homeostasis. Uptake is accomplished by a membrane carrier which is capable of transporting dopamine in either direction, depending on the existing concentration gradient. The dopamine transporter is a unique component of the functioning dopamine nerve terminal, which plays an important physiological role in the inactivation and recycling of dopamine released into the synaptic cleft by actively pumping extracellular dopamine back into the nerve terminal. Substantial progress has been made over the past decade in studying the dopamine transporter. Some of the psychotropic effects of cocaine may be related to its ability to block dopamine uptake in addition to its effects on other monoaminergic systems. An important advance in dopamine uptake research was the development of a new class of very potent and selective dopamine uptake inhibitors, the GBR series. Figure 10-3 illustrates the chemical structure of some of the dopamine uptake inhibitors.

With recent developments in the isolation and structural elucidation of a variety of membrane-bound receptors and the availability of several potent and selective radioligands for the dopamine uptake site, the stage is set for the isolation and molecular characterization of the dopamine transporter. At the current rate of progress on the molecular biology of receptors, it is reasonable to predict that by the time this edition is published, the dopamine transporter as well as other biogenic amine transporter systems will be cloned and sequenced. Will they all belong to a large transporter family, as is the

FIGURE 10-3. Chemical structures of some dopamine uptake inhibitors.

case with certain amine receptors? Will the recognition site of the dopamine transporter be identical in different DA systems? We shall soon see.

*Dopamine Metabolism*

Released dopamine is converted to dihydroxyphenylacetic acid (DO-PAC) by intraneuronal monoamine oxidase (MAO) after reuptake by the nerve terminal. Released dopamine is also converted to homovanillic acid (HVA), probably at an extraneuronal site through the sequential action of catechol-0-methyltransferase (COMT) and MAO. In rat brain, DOPAC is the major metabolite, and considerable amounts of DOPAC and HVA are present in sulfate-conjugated as well as free forms. In humans and other primates, however, the major brain metabolite is HVA, and only a small amount is found in the conjugated form.

The primary metabolites of dopamine in the CNS are homovanillic acid (HVA), dihydroxyphenylacetic acid (DOPAC), and a small amount of 3-methoxytyramine (3-MT). In dopamine systems, in contrast to norepinephrine systems (see Chapter 9), the acidic rather than the neutral metabolites appear to predominate. Accumulation of HVA in the brain or CSF has often been used as an index of the functional activity of dopaminergic neurons in the brain. 3-MT is also a useful index provided precautions are taken to minimize postmortem increases in this metabolite. Antipsychotic drugs, which increase the turnover of dopamine (in part because of their ability to increase the activity of dopaminergic neurons and to augment dopamine release), also increase the amount of HVA and 3-MT in the brain and CSF. In addition, electrical stimulation of the nigrostriatal pathway increases brain levels of HVA and 3-MT as well as the release of HVA into ventricular perfusates. In disease states such as parkinsonism, where there are degenerative changes in the substantia nigra and partial destruction of the dopamine neurons, a reduction of HVA is observed in the CSF. Similar changes are observed in MPTP-induced parkinsonism in humans and nonhuman primates.

In rat brain, it has been demonstrated that short-term accumulation of DOPAC in the striatum may provide an accurate reflection of activity in dopaminergic neurons of the nigrostriatal pathway. A cessation of impulse flow after the placement of acute lesions in the nigrostriatal pathway leads to a rapid decrease in striatal DOPAC. Conversely, the electrical stimulation of the nigrostriatal pathway results in a frequency-dependent increase in DOPAC within the striatum. Drugs that increase impulse flow in the nigrostriatal pathway, such as the antipsychotic phenothiazines, and butyrophenones, the anesthetics, and hypnotics, also increase striatal DOPAC. Drugs that block or decrease impulse flow, such as $\gamma$-hydroxybutyrate, 3-amino-1-hydroxypyrrolid-2-one (HA-966), apomorphine, and amphetamine, reduce DOPAC levels. Thus, there appears to be an excellent correlation between changes in impulse flow in dopaminergic neurons, which are induced either pharmacologically or mechanically, and changes in the steady-state levels of DOPAC. Unfortunately, in primates, DOPAC is a minor brain metabolite. Not only is it difficult to measure DOPAC in CSF, but in primate brain this metabolite is unresponsive to drug treatments that cause large changes in dopamine metabolism (i.e., homovanillic acid).

By means of the sensitive and specific technique of gas chromatography-mass fragmentography, it has been possible to measure accurately DOPAC, HVA, and their conjugates in rat and human plasma. Studies in rats have demonstrated that stimulation of the nigrostriatal pathway and administration of antipsychotic drugs produce an increase in plasma levels of DOPAC and HVA. Several studies in humans have also indicated that dopaminergic drugs can influence plasma levels of HVA, although the effect is quite modest in comparison to that which is observed in rodents. Thus, plasma level of these metabolites may prove to be useful indices of central dopamine metabolism in several species but probably not in primates.

*Biochemical Organization*

The synthesis and release of dopamine is influenced by the activity of dopaminergic neurons, but in the CNS these neurons do not behave in a fashion completely analogous to peripheral or central noradrenergic neurons. Nor do all dopamine systems respond identically to neuronal activity. Increased impulse flow in the nigrostriatal or mesolimbic dopamine system does lead to both an increase in dopamine synthesis and turnover and a frequency-dependent increase in the accumulation of dopamine metabolites in the striatum and olfactory tubercle. This parallels other monoamine systems where an increase in impulse flow causes an increase in the synthesis and turnover of transmitter.

Short-term stimulation of central dopaminergic neurons increases tyrosine hydroxylation, the rate-limiting step in transmitter synthesis that is mediated in part by kinetic alterations in tyrosine hydroxylase. The tyrosine hydroxylase prepared from tissue containing the terminals of the stimulated dopamine neurons has an increased affinity for pteridine cofactor and a decreased affinity for the natural end product inhibitor, dopamine. As in central noradrenergic systems, it seems that a finite period of time is necessary for this activation to occur, and once activated, the enzyme remains in this altered physical state for a short period after the simulation ends. The activation appears to involve phosphorylation of tyrosine hydroxylase.

However, if impulse flow is interrupted in the nigrostriatal or mesolimbic dopamine system, either mechanically or pharmacologically by treatment with γ-hydroxybutyrate, the neurons respond in a rather peculiar fashion by rapidly increasing the concentration of dopamine in the nerve terminals of the respective dopamine systems. Not only do the terminals accumulate dopamine by reducing release, but there is also a dramatic increase in the rate of dopamine synthesis. This increase occurs despite the steadily increasing concentration of endogenous dopamine within the nerve terminal.

The actual mechanisms whereby a cessation of impulse flow initiates changes in the properties of tyrosine hydroxylase are unclear although many experiments have suggested that they may involve a decrease in the availability of intracellular calcium. Similar changes in the activity or properties of tyrosine hydroxylase are not observed in central noradrenergic neurons or in dopamine neurons (such as the mesoprefrontal dopamine neurons) lacking synthesis-modulating autoreceptors. At present, the physiological significance of this paradoxical response of certain dopaminergic neurons to a cessation of impulse flow is unclear. However, it is conceivable that these neurons may achieve some operational advantage by being able to rapidly increase their supply of transmitter during periods of quiescence.

## Potential Sites of Drug Action on Dopaminergic Neurons

There are many sites at which drugs can influence the function of dopamine neurons. The potential sites for modulation are illustrated in Fig. 10-4 and summarized in Table 10-1. For the purpose of this discussion, drug effects can be divided into three broad categories:

1. Nonreceptor-mediated effects on presynaptic function (Fig. 10-4).
2. Dopamine receptor-mediated effects.
3. Effects mediated indirectly as a result of drug interaction with other neurotransmitter systems that interact with dopamine neurons.

The relative importance of each of these potentials sites of drug action will vary among different dopamine systems, depending on factors such as the presence or absence of autoreceptors, the efficiency of postsynaptic receptor-mediated neuronal feedback pathways and the nature of the afferent inputs impinging on the dopamine neurons in question.

## Nonreceptor-Mediated Effects

There are several stages in the life cycle of dopamine where drugs can influence transmitter dynamics, as illustrated in Figure 10-4. There are many useful pharmacological tools for modifying dopaminergic activity and manipulating dopaminergic function, but most of these agents are not very selective for dopaminergic synapses and will interact with other catecholamine (norepinephrine and epinephrine) systems—and in some cases with other monoamine (5-HT) systems as well. For example, amphetamine, cocaine, benztropine, and nomifensine interact with the presynaptic transporter that

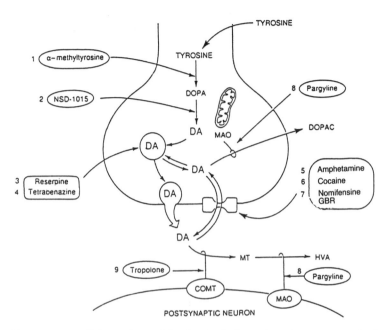

FIGURE 10-4. Schematic model of striatal dopaminergic nerve terminal. Drugs which alter dopamine (DA) life cycle include (1) α-methyltyrosine: competitive inhibitor of tyrosine hydroxylase; (2) NSD-1015: inhibitor of DOPA decarboxylase; (3) reserpine: irreversibly damages DA uptake-storage mechanisms and produces long-lasting depletion of DA; (4) tetrabenazine: also interferes with DA uptake-storage, but the effects are of shorter duration than reserpine and do not appear to be irreversible; (5) amphetamine: increases synaptic DA through a number of mechanisms, including induction of release of DA and blockade of DA reuptake; (6) cocaine: also blocks DA reuptake and induces DA release; (7) nomifensine and GBR: also block DA reuptake but lack DA-releasing ability; (8) pargyline: inhibitor of monoamine oxidase (MAO); (9) tropolone: inhibitor of catechol-O-methyltransferase (COMT). HVA, homovanillac acid; 3-MT, 3-methoxytyramine.

TABLE 10-1. Potential sites for modulating dopaminergic function

| Site | Consequences |
|---|---|
| Modulatory effects at dopamine (DA) receptors | |
| 1. Stimulate postsynaptic DA receptors | A. Enhance dopaminergic transmission |
| | B. Enhance function of neuronal feedback loops |
| Block postsynaptic DA receptors | A. Block dopaminergic transmission |
| | B. Interfere with function of neuronal feedback loops |
| 2. Stimulate presynaptic DA autoreceptors | A. Decrease DA synthesis and release |
| Block presynaptic DA autoreceptors | A. Increase DA synthesis and release |
| 3. Stimulate somatodendritic DA autoreceptors | A. Decrease firing rate and diminish DA output from nerve terminal |
| | B. Decrease somatodendritic DA turnover(?) |
| Block somatodendritic DA autoreceptors | A. Interfere with feedback regulation of firing rate and DA output from terminal |
| | B. Interfere with feedback regulation of somatodendritic DA turnover |
| Modulatory effects at non-DA receptors on DA neurons | |
| 4. Modify afferent input to cell body (i.e., block or mimic effects of transmitter released by afferent terminal) | A. Alter firing rate of DA cell and thus alter DA output from nerve terminal |
| | B. Alter somatodendritic turnover of DA (and co-localized peptides?) |
| 5. Modify afferent input to nerve terminal | A. Alter release from nerve terminal of DA (and co-localized peptides?) |

normally functions in the reuptake of released dopamine. However, these drugs also have an appreciable affinity for noradrenergic (and in some cases serotonergic) uptake sites. Recently, an uptake blocker (GBR-12935) has been characterized which appears to be highly selective for presynaptic dopamine transport complex and should prove to be a valuable experimental tool, perhaps leading to development of therapeutic agents which can selectively augment dopamine function (see Fig. 10-3).

## Dopamine Receptor-Mediated Effects

Originally, it was thought that all drugs which affect dopamine activity, including the neuroleptics, worked through nonreceptor-mediated mechanisms such as those described above. However, it is now clear that many therapeutically important drugs interact with dopamine receptors. Drugs that affect dopamine receptors can be classified into two groups (Table 10-2):

1. Receptors on non-dopamine cell types, which are usually referred to as postsynaptic receptors since they are postsynaptic to a dopamine-releasing cell.
2. Receptors on dopamine cells, which are termed autoreceptors to indicate their sensitivity to the neuron's own transmitter.

## Postsynaptic Dopamine Receptors

Postsynaptic dopamine receptors can be classified as either $D_1$ or $D_2$ receptor subtypes, based on functional and pharmacological criteria described below. Both types of receptors have been found in the projection areas of midbrain dopamine neurons, although it is unclear whether they are located on distinct subsets of dopamine-receptive cells in various projection fields. In the striatum, postsynaptic dopamine receptors regulate the activity of neuronal feedback pathways by which striatal neurons can communicate with dopamine cell bodies in the SN. This enables dopamine-innervated cells in the striatum to modulate the physiological activity of nigrostriatal dopamine neurons. In general, increased postsynaptic receptor stimulation results in decreased nigrostriatal dopamine activity.

TABLE 10-2. Biochemistry, physiology and pharmacology of $D_1$ and $D_2$ dopamine (DA) receptors

| $D_1$ Receptors Biochemical manifestations induced by receptor stimulation: - increase in cAMP formation - phosphorylation of DARPP-32 | | $D_2$ Receptors Biochemical manifestations induced by receptor stimulation: - decrease in cAMP formation or no change | |
|---|---|---|---|
| Location | Function | Location | Function |
| CNS: postsynaptic to DA neuron terminals dendrites (striatum, Nuc. Acc., Olf. tub., SN, etc.) | Enabling effect on behavioral and electrophysiological effect elicited by stim. of $D_2$ receptors. Function uncertain. | Striatum and nuc. acc., DA nerve terminals | Autoreceptors inhibit DA synthesis and release and modulate turnover |
| | | Retina | Mediate light-adaptive response of photoreceptors (↑ blink) |
| Bovine parathyroid gland | Increases parathyroid hormone release | SN and VTA: soma dendrites | Inhibits DA cell firing |

continued

TABLE 10-2. *Continued*

| | D₁ Receptors Biochemical manifestations induced by receptor stimulation: - increase in cAMP formation - phosphorylation of DARPP-32 | | D₂ Receptors Biochemical manifestations induced by receptor stimulation: - decrease in cAMP formation or no change | |
| --- | --- | --- | --- | --- |
| | Location | Function | Location | Function |
| | Vascular smooth muscle (canine renal and mesentery bed most used model system) | Vascular relaxation | Striatum: cholinergic interneurons | Inhibits acetylcholine release |
| | Vertebrate retina: in teleost, localized specifically to horizontal cells | Mediate responses of horizontal cells | Pituitary gland: anterior lobe | Inhibits cAMP and prolactin release. May also regulate Ca²⁺ channels |
| | | | Pituitary gland: intermediate lobe melanotrophs | Inhib. cAMP and αMSH release |
| | | | Chemosensitive trigger zone | Emesis |

TABLE 10-2. Continued

| | D₁ Receptors Biochemical manifestations induced by receptor stimulation: - increase in cAMP formation - phosphorylation of DARPP-32 | | D₂ Receptors Biochemical manifestations induced by receptor stimulation: - decrease in cAMP formation or no change | |
|---|---|---|---|---|
| | Location | Function | Location | Function |
| | | | Carotid body | Depresses spontaneous chemosensory discharge |
| | | | Sympathetic nerve terminals (numerous tissues) | Inhib. norepinephrine release |
| **Pharmacology** | | | | |
| Selective agonists | SKF 38393 (partial agonist); dihydrexidine (full agonist); SKF 82526 (fenoldopam) | | **LY 171555 (quinpirole); RU 24926; [+] PHNO EMD-23-448 (autoreceptor selective)** | |
| Selective antagonists | SCH 23390; SKF 83566; SCH 39166 | | (−)-Sulpiride; YM 09151-2; domperidone; raclopride | |

Following chronic exposure to dopamine agonists or antagonists, postsynaptic dopamine receptors exhibit adaptive changes. For example, chronic exposure to dopamine antagonists or chemical denervation with 6-hydroxydopamine (6-OHDA) produces an increase in the number of dopamine-binding sites measured in receptor-binding assays. This may be related to the behavioral supersensitivity to dopamine agonists that also develops as a result of chronic antagonist administration or denervation. Conversely, repeated administration of dopamine agonists decreases the number of dopamine-binding sites and produces subsensitivity to subsequent administration of dopamine agonists in behavioral as well as biochemical and electrophysiological models. Changes such as these may be relevant to understanding the state of dopamine receptors in diseases believed to involve chronic dopaminergic hyper- or hypoactivity.

*Autoreceptors*

Autoreceptors can exist on most portions of dopamine cells, including the soma, dendrites, and nerve terminals. Stimulation of dopamine autoreceptors in the somatodendritic region slows the firing rate of dopamine neurons, while stimulation of autoreceptors on the nerve terminals inhibits dopamine synthesis and release. Thus, somatodendritic and nerve terminal autoreceptors work in concept to exert feedback on dopaminergic transmission. Both somatodendritic and nerve terminal autoreceptors can be classified as $D_2$ receptors and exhibit similar pharmacological properties. Like postsynaptic receptors, somatodendritic and nerve terminal autoreceptors develop supersensitivity after chronic antagonist treatment or prolonged decreases in dopamine release, and they desensitize in response to repeated administration of dopamine agonists. Interestingly, some evidence indicates that the autoreceptors are more readily desensitized than postsynaptic dopamine receptors. This has been suggested to play a role in the 'on-off' effects observed during chronic L-dopa therapy in Parkinson's disease.

Dopamine autoreceptors can be defined functionally in terms of the events they regulate, e.g., synthesis-modulating, release-modulating, impulse-modulating autoreceptors and are therefore divided into three categories. However, it is not yet known whether distinct receptor proteins modulate each of these functions or whether the same receptor protein is coupled to each function through distinct transduction mechanisms. It is clear, however, that autoreceptor-mediated pathways for the regulation of dopamine release from the nerve terminal are distinct from autoreceptor-mediated pathways for the regulation of dopamine synthesis, since dopamine terminals in the prefrontal and cingulate cortices possess autoreceptors that regulate release but lack functional synthesis-modulating autoreceptors.

*Autoreceptors Versus Postsynaptic Receptors: Pharmacological and Functional Considerations*

Autoreceptors and postsynaptic dopamine receptors differ in several ways. The most clear-cut difference is that autoreceptors are 5–10 times more sensitive to the effects of dopamine and apomorphine than postsynaptic dopamine receptors in behavioral, biochemical, and electrophysiological models. In the low-dose range, therefore, autoreceptor-mediated effects of dopamine agonists will predominate, resulting in diminished dopaminergic function, while higher doses will also stimulate postsynaptic receptors, leading to enhanced dopaminergic function.

Autoreceptors also differ from postsynaptic receptors in their pharmacological profile. dopamine agonists have recently been synthesized which are relatively selective for autoreceptors. As would be predicted, autoreceptor-selective agonists inhibit dopamine release, synthesis, and impulse flow in dopamine neurons, and elicit behavioral responses associated with diminished dopaminergic function. These agonists are very useful experimental probes for studying dopamine receptor function and may prove useful in diseases thought to involve excessive dopaminergic activity. Most recently, dopamine antagonists that selectively block autoreceptors have also been synthesized. By blocking dopamine autoreceptors they enhance dopamine function. Some of these agents appear to have a built-in ceiling on their response since, as the dose is increased, they exert an antagonistic action on postsynaptic dopamine receptors. The structures of several of these autoreceptor-selective agents are illustrated in Fig. 10-5.

## Autoreceptor Agonists

3-(3-hydroxyphenyl)-
N-n-propylpiperidine
(3-PPP)

3-(4-(4-phenyl-1, 2, 3, 6,
-tetrahydropyridyl-1)-butyl) indole
(EMD 23-448)

## Autoreceptor Antagonists

(+)-UH232   $R_1 = R_2 =$ propyl

(+)-AJ76    $R_1 =$ propyl, $R_2 =$ H

FIGURE 10-5. Structures of some selective dopamine autoreceptor ligands.

Dopamine agonists and antagonists may act on several types of dopamine receptors to elicit biochemical changes in dopamine metabolism and alter the functional output of dopaminergic systems (Table 10-2). A drug's net effect on dopaminergic activity will depend on both its pre- and postsynaptic effects and the selectivity with which it acts at these different sites.

### Drug Interactions at $D_1$ and $D_2$ Receptors

In the preceding discussion, dopamine receptors were broadly divided into presynaptic and postsynaptic categories. A second popular dopamine receptor classification that received increasing attention in the 1980s is based on the presence or absence of a positive coupling between the receptor and adenylate cyclase activity. On the basis of biochemical, physiological and pharmacological studies, it is now well established that dopamine can act on at least two types of brain receptors, termed $D_1$ and $D_2$ receptors (Table 10-3). These two classes of receptors are clearly distinguished by their distinct biochemical characteristics. $D_1$ receptors mediate the dopamine-stimulated increase of adenylate cyclase activity. $D_2$ receptors are thought to mediate effects that are independent of $D_1$-mediated effects and also to exert an opposing influence on adenylate cyclase activity. The $D_2$ site is further characterized by picomolar affinity for antagonist, while the $D_1$ site is characterized by millimolar affinity for antagonist. The arrangement of $D_1$ and $D_2$ receptors and the nerve terminal autoreceptor are diagrammed in Fig. 10-6.

With the development of $D_1$ and $D_2$ selective agonists and antagonists, however, it has become common to rely on pharmacological characteristics when attempting to determine whether an effect is mediated by $D_1$ or $D_2$ receptors. The distinction between pharmacological and functional definitions is important because it is becoming clear that dopamine receptors with the same pharmacological characteristics do not necessarily have the same functional characteristics. For example, dopamine receptors with $D_2$ pharmacology are present in both the striatum and nucleus accumbens, but are coupled to an inhibition of adenylate cyclase only in the striatum.

TABLE 10-3. Signal transduction mechanisms associated with dopamine receptors

| $D_2$ Receptors | $D_1$ Receptors |
|---|---|
| 1. Inhibition of adenylate cyclase | Stimulation of adenylate cyclase |
| 2. Inhibition of $Ca^{2+}$ entry through voltage-sensite $Ca^{2+}$ channels | Stimulation of phosphoinositide turnover |
| 3. Enhancement of $K^+$ conductances | |
| 4. Modulation of phosphoinositide metabolism | |

FIGURE 10-6. Schematic diagram depicting the anatomical arrangement of $D_1$ and $D_2$ receptors and the nerve terminal autoreceptor. The $D_1$ site is positively coupled with adenylate cyclase via a Gs protein. The $D_2$ postsynaptic site is negatively coupled with adenylate cyclase via a $G_i$ protein, stimulation of which leads to hyperpolarization. The autoreceptors appear to exert their DA synthesis and release-modulating effects via a $G_i$ regulatory protein. DA autoreceptors are sensitive to very low (nanomolar) concentrations of DA. Although it is not known whether the $D_1$ and $D_2$ receptors are situated on the same neuron, they appear to be functionally linked, as depicted by the arrows. Innervated postjunctional dopamine receptors operate in the low-affinity state ($D_1$ low and $D_2$ low) in contrast to the $D_2$ autoreceptor, which operates in the high affinity state ($D_2$ high).

Regional differences in coupling between dopamine receptors and GTP-binding proteins have also been reported. Furthermore, many recent studies indicate that dopamine receptors can influence cellular function through mechanisms other than stimulating or inhibiting adenylate cyclase (Table 10-3). These may include direct effects on potassium and calcium channels, as well as the modulation of inositol phosphate production. It therefore seems unrealistic to expect equivalency between pharmacological and biochemical classifications of dopamine receptor subtypes.

Although $D_1$ and $D_2$ receptors can have opposite effects on adenylate cyclase activity, it is apparent that the physiological significance of their interaction is more complex. While $D_1$ and $D_2$ agonists can have opposite effects on oral movements, they also produce a synergistic increase in locomotor activity and behavioral stereotypes under certain circumstances. Electrophysiological experiments have suggested that $D_1$ receptor activation is required for full postsynaptic expression of $D_2$ effects. The interaction of the $D_1$ receptor with other neurotransmitter systems is also being explored. Most dopamine-receptive cells contain a protein, DARRP-32, whose phosphorylation is enhanced by the elevated levels of cAMP promoted through a $D_1$ mechanism. DARRP regulates the activity of a phosphatase, an enzyme that reverses the action of protein kinases. Through its effect on DARRP, the $D_1$ receptor may be able to influence the phosphorylation state of effector proteins that have been activated through calcium calmodulin or protein kinase C mechanisms.

*Dynamics of Dopamine Receptors*

Destruction of the nigrostriatal dopamine systems has clear and reproducible behavioral consequences. Unilateral lesions of this system produce rotational behavior. Behavioral studies in lesioned rats indicate that dopamine receptors in the denervated striatum are supersensitive. Administration of dopamine agonists (such as apomorphine) that selectively stimulate dopamine receptors produces rotational behavior in rats with unilateral lesions of the nigrostriatal dopamine neurons. The degree of receptor sensitivity can be quantified by measuring the amount of rotational behavior. The number of dopamine receptors in the striatum ipsilateral to the lesion increases markedly and this increase appears to correlate with the extent of the behavioral supersensitivity reflected by the rotational behavior. Thus, an increase in dopamine receptor density appears to be related to the behavioral supersensitivity observed following unilateral destruction of the nigrostriatal dopamine system.

Changes in the number of dopamine receptors are also observed in the striatum following chronic administration of dopamine antagonists. This had led to the speculation that serious side effects such as tardive dyskinesia following chronic treatment with a neuroleptic drug might be due to supersensitivity of dopamine receptors that have been chronically blocked.

Dopamine receptors have been observed to change in disease states. In schizophrenia, the density of the dopamine transporter and the $D_1$ dopamine receptor is normal. However, the $D_2$-receptor density is consistently elevated in postmortem studies of brain regions such as caudate and putamen, even in tissue obtained from neuroleptic-free individuals. Some preliminary evidence indicating abnormal $D_2$ structure as well as a reduced linkage between $D_1$ and $D_2$ receptors is available warranting a detailed study of the genes for these two receptors in schizophrenia. The loss of midbrain dopamine in Parkinson's disease is accompanied by a matching loss of the dopamine transporter and a rise in both $D_1$ and $D_2$ receptor density. These alterations are found in the caudate nucleus and putamen tissues from unmedicated patients. Long-term treatment with L-dopa appears to revert the receptor densities back toward normal levels. $D_1$ and $D_2$ dopamine receptors are decreased in the striatum of patients with Huntington's chorea, and there also appears to be a reduced or absent linkage between $D_1$ and $D_2$ receptors.

*Molecular Biology of Dopamine Receptors*

Available evidence indicates that these two classes of dopamine receptors ($D_1$ and $D_2$ are distinct molecular entities, utilize different transducing units (Table 10-3), and have a different distribution in the brain (Table 10-2).

Recent developments in molecular biology, including cloning of the cDNA and/or genes for several members of the large family of G-protein-coupled receptors, have revealed that heterogeneity in the biochemical characteristics or pharmacology of individual receptors often indicates the presence of previously unsuspected molecular subtypes (see Chapter 11). For dopamine systems, even though the $D_1/D_2$ dopamine receptor classification is widely accepted, biochemical, pharmacological, and behavioral approaches over the past few years have produced data which are increasingly difficult to reconcile with the existence of only two dopamine receptor subtypes and suggest the presence of several novel subtypes of both $D_1$ and $D_2$ dopamine receptors. In fact, recent cloning studies have already identified four subtypes of $D_2$ receptors and two subtypes of $D_1$ receptors (Table 10-4). Two forms of the $D_2$ dopamine receptor— the $D_2$ short and $D_2$ long—were identified by gene cloning and shown to be derived from alternative splicing of a common gene. These two subtypes appear to have an identical pharmacology. A third subtype of the $D_2$ receptor, termed a $D_3$ receptor, was isolated by the screening of rat brain cDNA and genomic libraries and a combination of reverse transcription and use of the polymerase chain reaction. This new $D_3$ dopamine receptor exhibits several novel characteristics. It has a different anatomical distribution, with the highest levels found in limbic brain structures, and its pharmacological profile, although similar to the $D_2S$ and $D_2L$ forms, shows some distinct differences; the $D_3$ receptor exhibits about a 100-fold increase in affinity for the dopamine agonist, quinpirol.

The fourth subtype of the $D_2$ receptor recently cloned, the $D_4$ receptor gene has high homology to the human $D_2$ and $D_3$ receptor genes. The pharmacological profile of this receptor resembles that of the $D_2$ and $D_3$ receptors, but its affinity for the atypical anti-psychotic drug clozapine is an order of magnitude higher. The $D_4$ messenger RNA has an interesting regional distribution in monkey brain with high levels observed in frontal cortex, midbrain, amygdala and medulla and lower levels detected in basal ganglia. The function of these $D_2$ receptor subtypes is presently unknown. All known varieties of the $D_2$ receptor have seven membrane-spanning domains similar to the structure originally proposed for $\beta$-adrenergic receptors. Differences in ligand binding and transduction mechanisms are presumably related to variations in the sequence of the receptor. The $D_1$ receptor of humans and rats has also been cloned, expressed, and characterized by several laboratories; this work in conjunction with other studies is consistent with the idea that other $D_1$ receptor subtypes may also exist. In fact, a gene encoding a 477-amino-acid protein has recently been cloned that has a striking homology to the

TABLE 10-4. Comparison of dopamine (DA) receptor subtypes

| Receptor isoforms | $D_1$ | $D_2$ (short) | $D_2$ (long) | $D_3$ | $D_4$ | $D_5$ |
|---|---|---|---|---|---|---|
| Brain regions enriched | C/P<br>OT<br>NA | C/P<br>OT<br>NA | C/P<br>OT<br>NA | OT<br>NA<br>IC | FCX<br>AMG<br>Midbrain | OT,NA<br>FCX<br>C/P |
| Posterior pituitary | Absent | Present | Present | Absent | — | Absent |
| Nigral DA cells | No | Yes | Yes | Yes | — | — |
| GTP regulation | Yes | Yes | Yes | No (?) | Yes | — |
| Adenylyl cyclase | Stim. | Inhib. | inhib. | No effect[a] | — | Stim. |
| Affinity for dopamine | Micromolar | High nM | High nM | Low nM | nM | High nM |
| inity for clozapine | Low | Low | Low | Low | High | Low |
| Butyrophenone potency | Micromolar | Subnanomolar | Subnanomolar | Nanomolar | Subnanomolar | Micromolar |
| Amino acids | | | | | | |
| Rat | 446 | 415 | 444 | 446 | — | 475 |
| Human | 446 | 414 | 443 | 400 | 387 | 477 |
| Amino acid sequence homology in transmembrane domains Versus $D_2$ (long) | 44% | 100% | 100% | 75% | 53% | 47% |

C/P, caudate/putamen; OT, olfactory tubercle; NA, nucleus accumbens; IC, islands of Calleja; FCX, frontal cortex; AMG, amygdala.
[a]In CHO cells.

cloned $D_1$ receptor. This $D_1$ receptor subtype, called $D_5$, has a pharmacological profile similar to that of the cloned $D_1$ receptor but displays a 10-fold higher affinity for the endogenous agonist, dopamine. Similar to the $D_1$ receptor, the $D_5$ receptor stimulates adenylate cyclase activity. This receptor is neuron specific and located primarily in the limbic areas of brain but is absent from the parathyroid, kidney and adrenal gland. An understanding of which subtypes of these DA receptors mediate particular physiological effects would facilitate the development of more specific dopaminergic agents and may lead to improved treatment of disorders thought to be related to the malfunctioning of dopamine systems. The cloning expression and characterization of the relevant DA receptor subtypes should provide the tools necessary to achieve these aims. The availability of assay systems that are based on expression of cloned receptor genes will enable the design and screening of dopamine $D_1$ and $D_2$ receptor subtype-specific compounds in the near future.

## PHARMACOLOGY OF DOPAMINERGIC SYSTEMS

### Nigrostriatal and Mesolimbic Dopamine Systems

The nigrostriatal and mesolimbic dopamine neurons appear to respond in a similar manner to drug administration (Table 10-5). Acute administration of dopamine agonists (dopamine receptor stimulators) decrease dopamine cell activity, decrease dopamine turnover, and decrease dopamine catabolism. Acute administration of antipsychotic drugs (dopamine receptor blockers) increases dopaminergic cell activity, enhances dopamine turnover, increases dopamine catabolism, and accelerates dopamine biosynthesis. The increase in dopamine biosynthesis occurs at the tyrosine hydroxylase step and is explained in part as a result of the ability of antipsychotic drugs to block postsynaptic receptors and to increase dopaminergic activity via a neuronal feedback mechanism (Table 10-1). It is also apparent that some of the observed effects are enhanced as a result of interaction with nerve terminal autoreceptors. Blockade of nerve terminal autoreceptors increases both the synthesis and the release of dopamine. These systems respond to monoamine oxidase inhibitors (MAOI)

TABLE 10-5. Pharmacology of central dopaminergic systems

| Characteristics | System response | | | | | |
|---|---|---|---|---|---|---|
| | Nigro-striatal | Meso-accumber, | Meso-prefrontal | Meso-piriform | Tubero-infundibular[a] | Tubero-hypophyseal[b] |
| Respond to DA antagonist (increase in synthesis, catabolism, and turnover) | Yes | Yes | Yes (small) | Yes | No | Yes (small) |
| Respond to DA agonists (decrease in synthesis, catabolism, and turnover) | Yes | Yes | Yes (small) | Yes | No | Yes |
| Respond to monoamine oxidase inhibitors (increase in DA, decrease in synthesis) | Yes | Yes | Yes | Yes | Yes | Yes |

| Presence of nerve terminal synthesis modulating autoreceptors | Yes | Yes | No | Yes | No | Yes |
|---|---|---|---|---|---|---|
| High-affinity DA transport | Yes | Yes | Yes | Yes | No | No |
| Respond to mild stress (increase in DA synthesis and catabolism, blocked by diazepam) | Yes | Yes? (small) | Yes | No | No | No |
| Respond to anxiogenic β-carbolines (increase in DA catabolism) | No | No | Yes | No | — | — |

[a]Cell bodies of this group of neurons are located in the arcuate and periventricular nuclei, and their axons terminate in the external layer of the median eminence.

[b]Cell bodies of this group of neurons are located in the arcuate and periventricular nuclei and their axons terminate in the neurointermediate lobe of the pituitary (posterior pituitary).

with an increase in dopamine and a decrease in dopamine synthesis, as do the other dopamine systems discussed below.

Recently it has been shown that long-term treatment with antipsychotic drugs produces a different spectrum of effects on central dopaminergic neurons. For example, following long-term treatment with haloperidol, *nigrostriatal* dopamine neurons in the rat become quiescent, and dopamine metabolite levels and dopamine synthesis and turnover in the *striatum* return to normal limits. The kinetic activation of *striatal* tyrosine hydroxylase, shown to occur following an acute challenge dose of an antipsychotic drug, also subsides following long-term treatment. These results are usually interpreted as indicative of the development of tolerance in the nigrostriatal dopamine system. In contrast (see below), tolerance to the biochemical effects observed following acute administration of antipsychotic drugs does not appear to develop in the mesoprefrontal and mesocingulate cortical dopamine pathways after chronic administration.

### Mesocortical Dopamine System

It has only become possible with the advent of more sensitive analytical techniques to measure changes in the low levels of dopamine and related metabolites in this system as well as in those discussed below. The response of the mesocortical dopamine systems to dopaminergic drugs is in most instances qualitatively similar to that of the nigrostriatal and mesolimbic systems (Table 10-5), although some notable exceptions have been recently observed. In fact, over the past few years the mesotelencephalic dopamine neurons which were once believed to be three relatively simple and homogeneous systems have been found to be an anatomically, biochemically, and electrophysiologically heterogeneous population of cells with differing pharmacological responsiveness. For example, although a great majority of midbrain dopamine neurons appear to possess autoreceptors on their cell bodies, dendrites, and nerve terminals, dopamine cells that project to the prefrontal and cingulate cortices appear to have either a greatly diminished number of these receptors or to lack them entirely. The absence (or insensitivity) of impulse-regulating somatodendritic as well as synthesis-modulating nerve terminal autoreceptors on the mesoprefrontal and mesocingulate cortical dopamine neurons may, in part, explain some of the unique biochemical, physiological, and pharmacological properties of these two subpopulations of midbrain dopamine neurons (Table 10-6). For example, the mesoprefrontal and mesocingulate dopamine neurons appear to have a faster firing rate and a more rapid turnover of transmitter than the nigrostriatal, mesolimbic, and *mesopiriform* dopamine neurons. Transmitter synthesis is also more readily influenced by altered availability of precursor tyrosine in midbrain dopamine neurons lacking autoreceptors (mesoprefrontal and mesocingulate) than in those midbrain dopamine neurons possessing autoreceptors. This may be related to the enhanced rate of physiological activity in this subpopulation of midbrain dopamine neurons making them more responsive to precursor regulation. The mesoprefrontal and mesocingulate dopamine neurons also show a diminished biochemical and electrophysiological responsiveness to dopamine agonists and antagonists. Administration of low doses of apomorphine or autoreceptor selective dopamine agonists, in contrasts to their inhibitory effect

TABLE 10-6. Unique characteristics of mesotelencephalic dopamine systems lacking autoreceptors (mesoprefrontal and mesocingulate) compared to those possessing autoreceptors (mesopiriform, mesolimbic and nigrostriatal)

1. A higher rate of physiological activity (firing) and a different pattern of activity (more bursting).
2. A higher turnover rate and metabolism of transmitter dopamine.
3. Greatly diminished biochemical and electrophysiological responsiveness to dopamine agonists and antagonists.
4. Lack of biochemical tolerance development following chronic antipsychotic drug administration.
5. Resistance to the development of depolarization-induced inactivation following chronic treatment with antipsychotic drugs.
6. Transmitter synthesis more readily influenced by altered availability of precursor tyrosine.

on other midbrain dopamine neurons, are ineffective in decreasing the activity or in lowering dopamine metabolite levels in these two cortical dopamine projections. Dopamine receptor-blocking drugs such as haloperidol produce large increases in synthesis and the accumulation of dopamine metabolites in the nigrostriatal, mesolimbic, and mesopiriform dopamine neurons, but have only a modest effect in the mesoprefrontal and mesocingulate dopamine neurons.

Heterogeneity among midbrain dopamine neurons is also found when one studies the effects of chronic antipsychotic drug administration. When classical antipsychotic drugs are administered repeatedly over time, the great majority of dopamine cells cease to fire due to the development of a state of depolarization inactivation. However, some midbrain dopamine cells appear to be unaffected by repeated antipsychotic drug administration. These dopamine cells turn out to be the neurons projecting to the prefrontal and cingulate cortices. Parallel findings are observed biochemically. Following chronic administration of antipsychotic drugs, tolerance develops to the metabolite-elevating effects of these agents in the midbrain dopamine systems that possess autoreceptors, but not in the systems that lack autoreceptors. When the atypical antipsychotic drug, clozapine (a drug which possesses therapeutic efficacy, but lacks Parkinson-like side effects and an ability to produce tardive dyskinesia) is administered repeatedly, dopamine neurons in the ventral tegmental area develop depolarization inactivation, but neurons in the substantia nigra do not. The reason for this differential effect is unknown at present. Foot shock, swim stress, or conditioned fear cause a selective (benzodiazepine-reversible) metabolic activation of the mesoprefrontal dopamine neurons without causing a marked or consistent effect on other midbrain dopamine neurons, including the mesocingulate dopamine neurons. Thus, this selective activation does not appear to be due solely to the absence of autoreceptors. The anxiogenic benzodiazepine receptor ligands such as the β-carbolines also produce a selective dose-dependent activation of mesoprefrontal dopamine neurons without increasing dopamine metabolism in other midbrain dopamine neurons.

In summary, certain mesotelencephalic dopamine systems, namely the mesoprefrontal and mesocingulate dopamine neurons, possess many unique characteristics compared to the nigrostriatal, mesolimbic, and mesopiriform dopamine systems (Table 10-6). Many of these unique characteristics may be the consequence of the lack of impulse-regulating somatodendrite and synthesis-modulating nerve terminal dopamine autoreceptors. However, some, such as the response to stress and anxiogenic β-carbolines, are clearly dependent upon other regulatory influences and not solely related to the absence of autoreceptors. These findings suggest that dopamine action at autoreceptors may be one of the important ways that dopamine cells possessing these receptors modulate their function. Since autoreceptors appear to play such an important role in regulation of the systems that possess them, future studies will need to address how midbrain dopamine systems that lack autoreceptors are regulated (role of afferent neuronal systems). In fact, some studies have suggested that a Substance P/Substance K innervation of the ventral tegmental area (A10) may influence the functional activity of mesocortical and mesolimbic dopamine neurons.

The observation that central dopamine systems are quite heterogeneous from both a biochemical and functional point of view holds promise that it will soon be possible to develop drugs targeted to modify or restore function to selective dopamine systems which are abnormal in various behavioral or pathological states. Some progress has already been achieved in developing agents which appear to have an action at selective dopamine receptor sites (Fig. 10-5). However, whether these agents will be useful in selectivity modifying the function of subsets of midbrain dopamine neurons remains to be determined.

### Tuberoinfundibular and Tuberohypophysial Dopamine Systems

The tuberoinfundibular dopamine system responds to pharmacological and endocrinological manipulations in a manner that is qualitatively different from the other three dopamine systems—nigrostriatal, mesolimbic, and mesocortical—described above (Table 10-5). The tuberoinfundibular neurons appear to be regulated in part by circulating levels of prolactin. Prolactin increases the activity of these neurons by acting within the medial basal hypothalamus, possibly acting directly on the tuberoinfundibular neurons. These neurons in turn release dopamine, which then inhibits prolactin release from the anterior pituitary. Haloperidol and other antipsychotic drugs have no effect on dopamine turnover in the tuberoinfundibular dopamine system until about 16 hours after drug administration, whereas the biochemical effects in other systems are observed within minutes and are maximal in several hours. The absence of an acute response to dopamine antagonists and agonists may be related to the lack of autoreceptors in this system. While less is known about the pharmacology of the tuberohypophyseal dopamine neurons, this system seems to respond to drugs in a manner qualitatively similar to the better-studied dopamine systems (Table 10-5).

## SPECIFIC DRUG CLASSES

### Antipsychotic Drugs (Major Tranquilizers)

Although there are at least seven major classes of antipsychotic drugs, all of which have in common the ability to ameliorate psychosis and evoke extrapyramidal reactions, the most widely used are the phenothiazines, thioxanthenes, and butyrophenones. As might be expected from the name given to chlorpromazine by the French—Largactil—the phenothiazines are notorious for their wide spectrum of pharmacological and biochemical effects. Fortunately, however, it turns out that many actions attributable to the antipsychotic phenothiazines are nonspecific properties of the phenothiazine moiety itself and do not appear to be correlated with the antipsychotic potency of the therapeutically active subgroup of phenothiazines. Along with many of their other actions, the antipsychotic phenothiazines have been shown to interact with both noradrenergic and dopaminergic neurons. However, the antipsychotic potency of these compounds appears to be best correlated with their ability to interact with dopamine-containing neurons. Much evidence has accumulated to indicate that antipsychotic drugs are effective blockers of dopamine receptors. In fact, it is believed that this reduction in dopamine activity expressed postsynaptically is responsible for the extrapyramidal side effects observed with these drugs. The ability of antipsychotic phenothiazines to block dopamine receptors on as yet chemically unidentified postsynaptic neurons may in some way also be related to the antipsychotic potency of these agents.

For many years it has been appreciated that antipsychotic drugs of both the phenothiazine and butyrophenone classes can increase the turnover of dopamine in the CNS. Since these drugs appear to have potent dopamine-receptor blocking capabilities, it has been suggested that the increase observed in dopamine turnover results from blockade of both dopamine autoreceptors and postsynaptic dopamine receptors and a consequent feedback activation of the dopaminergic neurons, presumably by some sort of neuronal feedback loop. This speculation has been verified in part by direct extracellular recording techniques.

### Antianxiety Drugs (Minor Tranquilizers)

The antianxiety drugs appear to interact with both noradrenergic and selected dopaminergic neurons. They are very effective in blocking and stress-induced increases in the turnover of both cortical norepinephrine and mesoprefrontal cortical dopamine. The actual mechanism by which these drugs exert their effects on the norepinephrine system is at the present time unknown, although in general they are believed to facilitate GABAergic transmission. Electrophysiological studies have demonstrated that many of these agents can suppress unit activity in the locus ceruleus. It has often been speculated that the relief of stress symptoms in humans is mediated by "turning off" the central noradrenergic neurons. (Noradrenergic systems were believed to be the primary monoamine system where antianxiety agents interact.) However, in view of the recent studies demonstrating an effect of stress on the mesoprefrontal dopamine system and reversal of the stress-induced activation by antianxiety drugs, it is clear that the mode of action of antianxiety drugs is an open question. Furthermore, in tests of anxiolytic action in rats, complete destruction of the telencephalic projections of the locus ceruleus fails to alter the effectiveness of benzodiazepines.

### Antidepressants

There are several major classes of antidepressant drugs, the monoamine oxidase inhibitors (MAOI), the tricyclic drugs, and the atypical agents. The MAOIs interact with both noradrenergic and dopaminergic neurons. By definition, these agents inhibit the enzyme MAO, which is involved in oxidatively deaminating catecholamines and thus cause an increase in the endogeneous levels of both dopamine and norepinephrine in the brain. At least from a biochemical standpoint, the tricyclic antidepressants appear to interact primarily with noradrenergic rather than dopaminergic neurons. The secondary amine derivatives such as desipramine are exceptionally potent inhibitors of norepinephrine uptake but have only a minimal effect on dopamine uptake. The tertiary amine derivatives are less effective in inhibiting norepinephrine uptake but are very effective in blocking serotonin uptake. The atypical antidepressants do not appear to have a selective interaction with monoamine systems when given by acute administration.

For many years it was postulated that the therapeutic action of antidepressant drugs was directly related to their uptake-blocking capability. However, since the therapeutic action of antidepressant drugs is usually delayed in onset for a week or more, the hypothesis that the rapid, acute actions of these drugs in blocking norepinephrine and serotonin reuptake are responsible for the long-term clinical antidepressant effects has been challenged. This hypothesis has been further discredited by recent investigations demonstrating that clinically effective antidepressant drugs such as iprindole and mianserin fail to significantly inhibit neuronal uptake of 5-HT and norepinephrine, while effective uptake inhibitors such as amphetamine, femoxetine, and cocaine are not effective in the treatment of depression. Current research has consequently shifted from the study of acute drug effects on amine metabolism to studies on the adaptive changes in norepinephrine and 5-HT receptor function induced by chronic antidepressant drug administration. In general, studies of this nature have revealed that chronic treatment with clinically effective antidepressant drugs causes a diminished responsiveness of central $\beta$-receptors and enhanced responsiveness of central serotonin and $\alpha_1$-receptors. The time course of these receptor alterations more closely parallels the time course of the clinical antidepressant effects in humans. At present, however, the relationship between these receptor alterations and clinical antidepressant effects is unknown.

*Stimulants*

The therapeutic usage of this class of drugs is becoming less and less common as awareness of their abuse potential increases. At the present time, in fact, their use is largely restricted to the treatment of narcolepsy and hyperkinetic children and as general anorectic agents. The principal drugs in this category are the various analogues and isomers of amphetamine and methylphenidate.

For many years it has been known that ingestion of large amounts of amphetamine often leads to a state of paranoid psychosis that may be hard to distinguish from the paranoia associated with schizophrenia. It now appears that this paranoid state can be readily and reproducibly induced in human volunteers given large amounts of amphetamine so that the drug may provide a convenient "model psychosis" for experimental study. It is of interest in this regard that antipsychotic drugs such as chlorpromazine can readily reverse the amphetamine-induced psychosis.

On a biochemical level it was no surprise to learn that amphetamine and related compounds interact with catecholamine-containing neurons, since amphetamine is a close structural analogue of the catecholamines. However, there was no clear evidence that amphetamine produced its CNS effects through a catecholamine mechanism until it was demonstrated that $\alpha$-methyl-$p$-tyrosine (a potent inhibitor of tyrosine hydroxylase) prevented most of the behavioral effects of D-amphetamine. The question as to which catecholamine, norepinephrine, or dopamine is involved in the behavioral effects of amphetamine is still an open question. But it is generally believed that the so-called stereotypic behavior in animals (i.e. compulsive gnawing, sniffing) induced by amphetamine is associated with a dopaminergic mechanism and that the increase in locomotor activity involves a noradrenergic mechanism or both.

Almost all classes of psychotropic drugs interact in one way or another with catecholamine-containing neurons. Figures 10-7 and 9-13 outline the life cycle of the transmitters of dopaminergic and noradrenergic neurons in the CNS, respectively, and indicate possible sites at which drugs may intervene in this cycle. These schematic models also provide examples of drugs or chemical agents which interfere at these various sites within the life cycle of the

FIGURE 10-7. Schematic model of a central dopaminergic neuron indicating possible sites of drug action.

Site 1: *Enzymatic synthesis*: Tyrosine hydroxylase reaction blocked by the competitive inhibitor, α-methyltyrosine and other tyrosine hydroxylase inhibitors. (See Chapter 9).

Site 2: *Storage*: Reserpine and tetrabenazine interfere with the uptake-storage mechanism of the amine granules. The depletion of dopamine produced by reserpine is long-lasting and the storage granules appear to be ir-reversibly damaged. Tetrabenazine also interferes with the uptake—storage mechanism of the granules, except that the effects of this drug do not appear to be irreversible.

Site 3: *Release*: γ-Hydroxybutyrate and HA966 effectively blocks the release of dopamine by blocking impulse flow in dopaminergic neurons. Am-phetamine administered in high doses releases dopamine, but most of the releasing ability of amphetamine appears to be related to its ability to effectively block dopamine reuptake.

Site 4: *Receptor interaction*: Apomorphine is an effective dopamine receptor-stimulating drug, with both pre- and postsynaptic sites of action. Both -3-PPP and EMD-23 (an indolebutylamine) are autoreceptor agonists. Perphenazine and haloperidol are effective dopamine receptor-blocking drugs.

transmitter substances. These numerous sorts of interactions ultimately result in an increase, decrease, or no change in the functional activity of the catecholamine neuron in question.

Only recently did it become clear exactly how various pharmacological agents alter activity in defined catecholamine neuronal systems in the brain. In most cases, the turnover of monoamines depends essentially upon impulse flow in the neuron. An increase in impulse flow usually causes an increase in turnover, and a decrease in impulse flow causes a reduction in turnover. As mentioned above, however, this is not always the case in the dopamine system, if synthesis is used as an index of turnover. Measurement of turnover has been employed to gain some insight into the activity of various types of monoamine-containing neurons during different behavioral states or after administration of different psychotropic drugs. As might be predicted, psychotropic drugs can have a variety of effects, and these effects can alter the turnover of a given transmitter substance without necessarily altering impulse flow in the neuronal system under study. For example, a drug can have a direct effect on the synthesis, degradation, uptake, or release of a given transmitter which will in turn alter the turnover of the transmitter in question but will not necessarily lead to an increase or decrease in the activity of the neuronal system which utilizes that substance as a transmitter. So it becomes clear that an alternation in turnover of a transmitter is not necessarily a clear indication that there has been

---

FIGURE 10-7. (cont.)

Site 5: *Reuptake*: Dopamine has its action terminated by being taken up into the presynaptic terminal. Amphetamine as well as benztropine, the anticholinergic drug, are potent inhibitors of this reuptake mechanism.

Site 6: *Monoamine Oxidase (MAO)*: Dopamine present in a free state within the presynaptic terminal can be degraded by the enzyme MAO, which appears to be located in the outer membrane of the mitochondria. Dihydroxyphenylacetic acid (DOPAC) is a product of the action of MAO and aldehyde oxidase on dopamine. Pargyline is an effective inhibitor of MAO. Some MAO is also present outside the dopaminergic neuron.

Site 7: *Catechol-O-methyl transferase (COMT)*: Dopamine can be inactivated by the enzyme COMT, which is believed to be localized outside the presynaptic neuron. Tropolone is an inhibitor of COMT.

a change in impulse flow in a given neuronal pathway. Therefore, the most direct way to determine if a drug alters impulse flow in a chemically defined neuronal system is to measure the activity of that system while the animal is under the influence of the drug.

It now appears that there are also a number of ways in which drugs can alter impulse flow. For example, a drug can act directly on the nerve cell body; it can act on other neurons, which then influence impulse flow in the neuron under study; or it can act at the postsynaptic receptor to cause stimulation or blockade, which then results in some sort of feedback influence on the presynaptic neuron. This feedback information could either be neuronal or perhaps transsynaptically mediated by release of some local chemical from the postsynaptic membrane. The combined histochemical-neurophysiological identification of dopaminergic and noradrenergic neurons has made possible the direct study of the effects of various drugs on the firing of these chemically defined neurons.

## Effect of Drugs on the Activity of Dopaminergic Neurons

More than a decade ago, entirely on the basis of indirect biochemical evidence, Swedish pharmacologists speculated that antipsychotic drugs, as a result of their ability to block dopaminergic receptors, caused a feedback activation of dopaminergic neurons. Direct extracellular recording experiments have validated these earlier speculations. Antipsychotic drugs of both the phenothiazine and butyrophenone classes cause a dramatic increase in the firing rate of dopamine neurons in rat brain, an action presumably mediated by a neuronal feedback loop. Phenothiazines without antipsychotic potency are completely inactive in this regard. Of course, it is still a big jump to determine whether this interesting ability of antipsychotic drugs to block dopamine receptors is in any way related to their antipsychotic properties. In fact, we already know that there is a temporal dissociation of the two actions.

A naturally occurring metabolite of mammalian brain, γ-hydroxybutyrate, also has an interesting interaction with dopaminergic neurons. When γ-hydroxybutyrate is administered to rats in anesthetic doses, this compound causes a complete cessation of impulse flow in the nigrostriatal pathway. This inhibition does not appear to be mediated via activation of a neuronal feedback loop. On the other hand, the activity of other monoamine-containing neurons such as the norepinephrine-containing neurons in the locus ceruleus or the 5-HT-containing neurons of the midbrain raphe are relatively unaffected. Thus, this drug appears to be capable of producing a reversible lesion in the nigrostriatal and mesolimbic dopamine systems. The ability of this drug to block impulse flow in dopamine neurons most likely explains its unique biochemical properties as well as why it can effectively antagonize the ability of the antipsychotic drugs to increase the accumulation of dopamine metabolites in the striatum. Whether the drug will prove useful in the treatment of certain disease or drug-induced states thought to be related to dopaminergic hyperactivity remains to be determined.

There is also compelling biochemical and behavioral evidence that amphetamine, L-dihydroxyphenylalanine, and apomorphine interact with dopamine neuronal systems in the CNS. Until recently, however, there has been no direct evidence that these drugs affect neuronal activity. Since all three drugs presumably lead either directly or indirectly to a stimulation of dopamine receptors, it has been predicted that they might show the activity of dopaminergic neurons via some sort of neuronal feedback loop. Extracellular unit-recording experiments conducted on dopamine cells in the zona compacta and ventral tegmental area have borne out this speculation for all three drugs. In doses as low as 0.25 mg/kg, D-amphetamine inhibits firing of these dopamine neurons. It appears to act indirectly through the release of newly synthesized dopamine since α-methyl-ρ-tyrosine can prevent or reverse the depression of dopamine cell firing. L-Amphetamine will also inhibit the firing of dopaminergic neurons, but is much less potent than D-amphetamine in producing this effect. L-Dihydroxyphenylalanine also inhibits firing of these neurons and appears to exert its effect indirectly by being converted to dopamine. Pretreatment with a decarboxylase inhibitor will antagonize completely the inhibitory effect of dihydroxyphenylalanine on these cells. Likewise, apomorphine appears to effectively inhibit the firing of dopamine cells, but this drug seems to act directly on dopamine receptors because its actions are not altered by inhibition of dopamine synthesis with α-methyl-ρ-tyrosine. It is also noteworthy that antipsychotic drugs have the ability to block and reverse the depressant effects of D-amphetamine, L-dihydroxyphenylalanine, and apomorphine on the firing of dopamine cells. This observation suggests that all three drugs may exert their effects on firing rate through some sort of postsynaptic feedback pathway. Other experiments indicate that apomorphine also has a direct effect on dopaminergic neurons of the nigrostriatal and mesolimbic systems. This effect is believed to be mediated by an interaction with autoreceptors on dopamine cell bodies. As indicated earlier, apomorphine acts on dopamine autoreceptors in dosages which are ineffective on postsynaptic dopamine receptors. Administered in autoreceptor-selective doses, apomorphine is ineffective influencing the activity of dopamine neurons that lack autoreceptors.

## PARKINSON'S DISEASE

Parkinson's disease (PD) is a progressive neurodegenerative disorder of the basal ganglia which is characterized by tremor, muscular rigidity, difficulty in initiating motor activity, and loss of postural reflexes. It is observed in approximately 1% of the population over age 55. It has been known for over 70 years that PD is characterized pathologically by loss of pigmented cells in the substantia nigra, but only since 1960 has it been appreciated that there is a substantial loss of dopamine in the striatum. It is now clear that PD can be defined in biochemical terms as primarily a dopamine-deficiency state resulting from degeneration or injury to dopamine neurons. The most striking degenerative loss of dopamine neurons is observed in the nigrostriatal system. Even in patients with mild symptoms, a striatal dopamine loss of 70–80% is observed, while severely impaired subjects have striatal dopamine depletions in excess of 90%. Since the dopamine transporter is heavily expressed in the terminals of dopamine neurons that are lost in PD, it is not surprising that striatal binding of agents which label this site (cocaine, nomifensine,

GBR, and mazindol) is lost in the Parkinsonian striatum. This alteration corresponds well with the loss of functional dopamine uptake visualized in vivo by position emission tomography using ($^{18}$F)-L-dopa uptake or nomifensine. Although striatal dopamine loss represents the primary neurochemical abnormality in the PD brain, typical parkinsonism is accompanied by the loss of other dopamine systems and other monoamine neurons as well. Some degeneration of dopamine-containing neurons is also apparent in the mesolimbic, mesocortical, and hypothalamic systems, norepinephrine-containing neurons in the locus ceruleus, and serotonin neurons. Nonmonoamine systems are also affected, with depletions observed in somatostatin, neurotensin, substance P, enkephalin, and cholecystokinin-8. Since many of these non-dopamine systems indirectly interact with mesotelencephalic dopamine systems, it is obvious that changes in some of them are bound to influence in a complex way the function of dopamine neurons.

The strategy for treating PD has been to restore the dopamine deficit in the brain by pharmacological means, or more recently by neural grafting of dopamine-containing cells. There are a number of theoretical strategies for drug therapy in PD, including substrate supplementation, direct and indirect dopamine agonists, metabolic inhibitors (MAO-inhibitors), and uptake inhibitors. The most successful treatment has been the use of L-dopa. Direct dopamine agonists also have some benefit in patients whose responsiveness to L-dopa is greatly reduced or erratic. So far, the only direct-acting dopamine agonist that has found extensive use in PD is bromocriptine, primarily a $D_2$ agonist. Other agents belonging to this class will no doubt prove useful in the future as supplements or alternatives to L-dopa.

In view of the behavioral and electrophysiological studies which suggest that $D_1$ receptor activation is necessary for the effects of $D_2$ receptor stimulation to be maximally expressed in normal animals as well as in animals with supersensitive dopamine receptors, the functional interaction between $D_1$ and $D_2$ receptors could have important implications in PD, where stimulation of postsynaptic dopamine receptors confers symptomatic benefit. Knowledge of the optimal ratio of relative drug activity at $D_1$ and $D_2$ receptors that is required to elicit effective stimulation of dopamine-mediated function may provide a basis for the design of new drugs. Also, as more knowledge accumulates concerning the distribution and function of various dopamine receptor subtypes, this should facilitate the development of new agents to treat dopamine deficiency states.

### *Primate Model of Parkinson's Disease*

In 1983, researchers at Stanford University identified a contaminant in a locally produced "synthetic heroin" that induced a Parkinson-like syndrome in some of the individuals who self-administered this street drug. The contaminant identified in this preparation, 1-methyl-4-phenyl-1,2-3,6-tetrahydropyridine (MPTP), exhibits a high degree of anatomical and species-specific toxicity. MPTP administered systemically in low doses to nonhuman primates produces parkinsonian symptoms and destroys nigrostriatal dopamine neurons while sparing several other brain dopamine systems. The discovery of the selective neurotoxic properties of MPTP and the development of a primate model of parkinsonism have stimulated a tremendous resurgence of inquiry into the causes and treatment of PD. The mechanism responsible for selective dopamine neurotoxic features of MPTP in primates has not been conclusively established.

MPTP appears to act as a protoxin, and MAO-B-mediated bioactivation of MPTP to MPP+ plays a critical role in the neurotoxic action of MPTP. The administration of MAO-B inhibitors, including L-deprenyl, affords full protection against the neurotoxic action of MPTP. Since dopamine uptake inhibitors such as mazindol and GBR-12909 are also able to protect against MPTP-induced neurotoxicity, it has been suggested that MPTP is oxidized to MPP+ outside the dopamine neurons, perhaps by MAO in astrocytes. MPP+ is then transported and concentrated by the dopamine uptake system in dopamine neurons. Once inside the dopamine neuron, MPP+ exerts its neurotoxic effect by acting as a mitochondrial poison through inhibition of respiration at site 1 of the electron transport chain. This postulated mechanism for MPTP's neurotoxicity in dopamine neurons is illustrated in Figure 10-8.

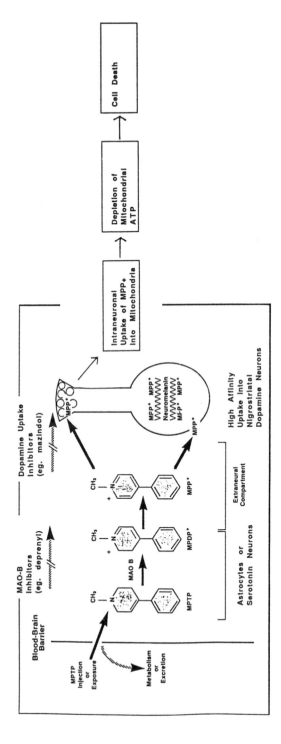

FIGURE 10-8. Hypothesized mechanisms of neurotoxicity of MPTP, which produces parkinsonism in primate species.

## DOPAMINE HYPOTHESIS OF SCHIZOPHRENIA

The growing conviction that antipsychotic agents act therapeutically by decreasing central dopaminergic transmission led to the dopamine theory of schizophrenia. This hypothesis in its simplest form states that schizophrenia may be related to a relative excess of central dopaminergic neuronal activity. Although there is a lot of data that supports the dopamine hypothesis, at present we have no direct experimental evidence of an excess of dopamine-dependent neuronal activity or an elevation of dopamine levels at central synapses in schizophrenics. Thus, the cornerstone of this hypothesis is the idea that the therapeutic effects of antipsychotic medication are due exclusively to the ability of these drugs to block central dopamine receptors and thereby reduce dopaminergic transmission.

Over the past decade experiments in animals have generated much data in support of the contention that antipsychotic drugs are effective blockers of dopamine receptors. Indirect clinical studies also suggest that antipsychotic drugs interact with dopamine neurons and effectively block central dopamine receptors. Nevertheless, it remains unclear whether dopamine receptor blockade is an essential component of the therapeutic effect of antipsychotic medication. Most behavioral, biochemical, and electrophysiological studies that demonstrate an interaction of antipsychotic drugs with dopaminergic neurons have been carried out following acute drug administration. This is a very serious drawback since it is well known that the clinical effects of antipsychotic drugs (both antipsychotic and neurological) take days, weeks, or even months to develop. Even if we are willing to agree that the pharmacological studies strongly suggest that antipsychotic agents work through blockade of central dopamine systems, the evidence that schizophrenia is caused by a defect in one or more central dopamine systems is far weaker. In fact, at the present time there is really no direct evidence implicating a defect in any of the dopamine systems in schizophrenia.

Two reasonable approaches to testing the dopamine hypothesis of schizophrenia have been the measurement of HVA in the CSF and the examination of catecholamine metabolites and related enzymes in autopsied brain obtained from controls and schizophrenics.

No significant differences have yet been demonstrated in brain or CSF levels of HVA in normal subjects and unmedicated schizophrenics. However, a significant elevation of HVA levels in the CSF of patients on antipsychotic medications has been found, and this supports the idea that these drugs interact with central dopamine neurons in human patients.

In nonhuman primates, chronic treatment with antipsychotic drugs causes tolerance to develop to the HVA increase normally observed in the putamen, caudate, and olfactory cortex after a challenge dose of an antipsychotic drug. However, in cingulate, dorsal frontal, and orbital frontal cortex, increased levels of HVA are maintained throughout the time course of chronic treatment. Similar observations have also been made in studies carried out on autopsied brain specimens obtained from human subjects. In schizophrenic patients chronically treated with antipsychotic drugs, a significant increase in HVA is found in the cingulate and frontal cortex but not in the putamen and nucleus accumbens, suggesting a possible locus for the therapeutic action of these drugs and providing the first direct experimental evidence that antipsychotic drug treatment increases the metabolism of dopamine in human brain in a regionally specific manner.

In studies examining both synthesis and degradation of dopamine in autopsied brain, no significant differences have been found between schizophrenic and control samples. There has been one report of a significant decrease in the activity of dopamine-$\beta$-oxidase in schizophrenic brain, but this observation has not been replicated in subsequent studies.

As neurochemical techniques of increasing sophistication are developed, studies of more discrete components of schizophrenic brain obtained postmortem will have greater potential for elucidating possible biochemical defects associated with schizophrenia. However, the possibility of obtaining the appropriate postmortem sample—whatever they may be—seems quite remote, especially in view of the nearly universal use of antipsychotic medication in patients who are diagnosed as schizophrenic and who are likely to be available for autopsy soon enough after death to be useful for research purposes.

Even though the evidence that synthesis, metabolism, and turnover of brain dopamine is aberrant in schizophrenia remains inconclusive, with the identification of specific brain receptors for dopamine and neuroleptic drugs it became possible to examine whether brain dopamine receptors were abnormal in schizophrenics. Dopamine receptors in postmortem schizophrenic brains have been independently reported by many groups to be increased in numbers. Increased binding was found in both the nucleus accumbens and striatum using haloperidol and spiperone as the ligand. However, neither the $D_1$ site labeled by *cis*-flupenthixol nor the so-called $D_3$-site labeled by $(H_3)$-dopamine reflected this increase. There also still remains a controversy as to whether the elevated density of dopamine receptors observed is drug induced (since most schizophrenic subjects have been drug treated) or is a cause or consequence of the disease process. This is despite the fact that two groups have independently demonstrated an increase in $H^3$-spiperone binding in brains of schizophrenics not exposed to neuroleptic drugs for over a year prior to coming to autopsy, although the observed increases were less than that usually recorded in drug-treated patients. Establishing with certainty that the elevation in dopamine receptor density is part of the disease process associated with schizophrenia would be very important for both etiological and diagnostic purposes and would serve as a possible basis for treatment strategies. The application of new noninvasive techniques such as positron emission tomography and single photon emission computed tomography to examine dopamine receptor distribution and density in schizophrenia holds promise that this may be accomplished soon.

## SELECTED REFERENCES

Andersen, P.H., J.A. Gingrich, M.D. Bates, A. Dearry, P. Falardeau, S.E. Senogles, and M.G. Caron (1990). Dopamine receptor subtypes: Beyond the $D_1/D_2$ classification. *Trends Pharmacol. Sci.* 11:231–236.

Andreasen, N.C. (1988). Brain Imaging: Applications in psychiatry. *Science* 239, 1381–1388.

Bannon, M.J. and R.H. Roth (1983). Pharmacology of mesocortical dopamine neurons. *Pharmacol. Rev.* 35, 53.

Bannon, M.J., A.S. Freeman, L.A. Chiodo, B.S. Bunney, and R.H. Roth (1986). The pharmacology and electrophysiology of mesolimbic dopamine neurons. In *Handbook of Psychopharmacology*, (X. Iverson, X. Iverson, and X. Snyder, eds.) Vol. 19, pp. 329–374. Plenum Press, New York.

Bartholini, G., B. Zivkovic, and B. Scatton (1989). Dopaminergic neurons: Basic aspects. In *Handbook of Experimental Pharmacology*, (U. Trendelenburg and N. Weiner, eds.), Vol. 90/II, pp. 277–317. Springer-Verlag, Berlin.

Björklund, A. and O. Lindvall (1984). Dopamine-containing systems in the CNS In *Handbook of Chemical Neuroanatomy, Vol. 2: Classical Transmitters in the CNS, Part I* (A. Björklund and T. Hökfelt eds.). Elsevier Science Publishers Amsterdam.

Bunney, B.S., S.R. Sesack, and N.L. Silva (1987). Midbrain dopaminergic systems: Neurophysiology and electrophysiological pharmacology. In, *Psychopharmacology: The Third Generation of Progress* (H.Y. Meltzer, ed.) pp. 113–126, Raven Press, New York.

Bunzow, J.R., H.H.M. Van Tol, D.K. Grandy, P. Albert, J. Salon, M. Christie, C.A. Machida, K.A. Neve, and O. Civelli (1988). Cloning and expression of a rat $D_2$ dopamine receptor cDNA. *Nature* 336(6201), 783–787.

Chiodo, L.A. (1988). Dopamine-containing neurons in the mammalian central nervous system: Electrophysiology and pharmacology. *Neurosci. Biobehav. Rev.* 12, 49–91.

Chiodo, L.A. and A.S. Freeman (eds) (1987). *Neurophysiology of Dopaminergic Systems: Current Status and Clinical Perspectives.* Lakeshore Publishing, Gross Pointe, MI.

Clark, D., S. Hjorth, and A. Carlsson (1985). Dopamine-receptor agonists: Mechanisms underlying autoreceptor selectivity. *J. Neural. Transm.* 62, 1.

Clark, D. and F.J. White (1987). $D_1$ dopamine receptor—The research for a function: A critical evaluation of the $D_1/D_2$ dopamine receptor classification and its functional implications. *Synapse 1*, 347–388.

DalToso, R., B. Sommer, M. Ewert, A. Herb, D.B. Pritchett, A. Bach, B.D. Shivers, and P.H. Seeburg (1989). The dopamine $D_2$ receptor: Two molecular forms generated by alternative splicing. *EMBO J. 8*, 4025–4034.

Hökfelt, T., D. Millhorn, K. Seroogy, Y. Tsuruo, S. Ceccatelli, B. Lindh, B. Meister, T. Melander, M. Schalling, T. Bartfai, and L. Terenius (1987). Coexistence of peptides with classical neurotransmitters. *Experientia 43*, 768–780.

Horn, A.S. (1990). Dopamine uptake: A review of progress in the last decade. *Prog. Neurobiol. 34*, 387–400.

Hornykiewicz, O. and S.J. Kish. (1986). Biochemical pathophysiology of Parkinson's disease. *Adv. Neurol. 45*, 19–34.

Kebabian, J.W., M. Beaulieu, and Y. Itoh (1984). Pharmacological and biochemical evidence for the existence of two categories of dopamine receptor. *Can. J. Neurol. Sci. 11*, 114.

Kuhar, M.J., M. Sanchez-Roa, D.F. Wong, R.F. Dannals, D.E. Grigoriadis, R. Lew, and M. Milberger (1990). Dopamine transporter: Biochemistry, pharmacology and imaging. *Eur. Neurol. 30*, 15–20.

Langston, J.W. (1989). Current theories on the cause of Parkinson's disease. *J. Neurol. Neurosurg. Psychiatry* (Suppl) 13–17.

Langston, J.W. I. Irwin, and G.A. Ricaurte (1987). Neurotoxins, parkinsonism and Parkinson's disease. *Pharmacol. Ther. 32*:19–49.

Lemoal, M. and H. Simon (1991). Mesocorticolimbic dopaminergic network: Functional and regulatory roles. *Physiol. Rev. 71*, 155.

Losonczy, M.F., M. Davidson, and K.L. Davis (1987). The dopamine hypothesis of schizophrenia. In *Psychopharmacology: A Second Generation of Progress.* (H.Y. Meltzer, ed.) pp. 715–726. Raven Press, New York.

Markey, S.P. N. Castagnoli, Jr., A.J. Trevor, and I.J. Kopin. (eds.) (1986). *MPTP: A Neurotoxin Producing a Parkinsonian Syndrome.* Academic Press, Orlando, FL.

Meltzer, H.Y. (1980). Relevance of dopamine autoreceptors for psychiatry: Preclinical and clinical studies. *Schizophr. Bull. 6*, 456.

Roth, R.H., M.E. Wolf, and A.Y. Deutch (1987). Neurochemistry of midbrain dopamine systems. In *Psychopharmacology: The Third Generation of Progress* (H.Y. Meltzer, ed.), pp. 81–94. Raven Press, New York.

Sedvall, G. (1990). PET imaging of dopamine receptors in human basal ganglia: Relevance to mental illness. *Trends Neurosci. 13*, 302–308.

Seeman, P. and H.B. Niznik (1988). Dopamine $D_1$ receptor pharmacology. *ISI Atlas of Science: Pharmacology* 161–168.

Sunahara, R.K., H.C. Guan, B.F. O'Dowd, P. Seeman, L.G. Laurier, G. Ng, S.R. George, J. Torchia, H.H.M. VanTol, and H.B. Niznik (1991). Cloning of the gene for a human dopamine $D_5$ receptor with higher affinity for dopamine than $D_1$. *Nature 350*, 614–619.

Strange, P.G. (1991). Interesting times for dopamine receptors. *Trends Neurosci. 14*, 43–45.

Vallar, L. and J. Meldolesi (1989). Mechanisms of signal transduction at the dopamine $D_2$ receptor. *Trends Pharmacol. Sci. 10*, 74–77.

VanTol, H.H.M., J.R. Bunsow, H.C. Guan, R.K. Sunahara, P. Seeman, H.B. Niznik and O. Civelli (1991). Cloning of the gene for a human dopamine D$_4$ receptor with high affinity for the antipsychotic clozapine. *Nature 350*, 610–614.

Wolf, M.E., A.Y. Deutch, and R.H. Roth (1987). Pharmacology of central dopaminergic neurons. In *Handbook of Schizophrenia*, Vol. 2: *Neurochemistry and Neuropharmacology of Schizophrenia*. (F.A. Henn and L.E. DeLisi, eds.), pp. 101–147. Elsevier Science Publishers, Amsterdam.

Wolf, M.E. and R.H. Roth, (1987). Dopamine autoreceptors. In *Receptor Biochemistry and Methodology* (C.J. Venter and L.C. Harrison, eds.), Vol. 8, pp. 45–96. Alan R. Liss, New York.

Wolf, M.E. and R.H. Roth (1990). Autoreceptor regulation of dopamine synthesis. *Ann. N.Y. Acad. Sci. 604*, 323–343.

Zigmond, M.J. and E.M. Stricker (1989). Animal models of parkinsonism using selective neurotoxins: Clinical and basic implications. *Int. Rev. Neurobiol. 31*, 2–60.

# II | Serotonin (5-hydroxytryptamine) and Histamine

## SEROTONIN

Of all the neurotransmitters discussed in this book, serotonin remains historically the most intimately involved with neuropsychopharmacology. From the mid-nineteenth century, scientists had been aware that a substance found in serum caused powerful contraction of smooth muscle organs, but over a hundred years passed before scientists at the Cleveland Clinic succeeded in isolating this substance as a possible cause of high blood pressure. By this time, investigators in Italy were characterizing a substance found in high concentrations in chromaffin cells of the intestinal mucosa. This material also constricted smooth muscular elements, particularly those of the gut. The material isolated from the bloodstream was given the name "serotonin," while that from the intestinal tract was called "enteramine." Subsequently, both materials were purified, crystallized, and shown to be 5-hydroxytryptamine (5-HT), which could then be prepared synthetically and shown to possess all the biological features of the natural substance. The indole nature of this molecule bore many resemblances to the psychedelic drug LSD, with which it could be shown to interact on smooth muscle preparations in vitro. 5-HT is also structurally related to other psychotropic agents (Fig. 11-1).

When 5-HT was first found within the mammalian central nervous system, the theory arose that various forms of mental illness could be due to biochemical abnormalities in its synthesis. This line of thought was even further extended when the tranquilizing substance, reserpine, was observed to deplete brain 5-HT; throughout

FIGURE II-I. Structural relationships of the various indolealkyl amines.

| Compound | Substitutions |
|----------|---------------|
| Tryptamine | $R_1$ and $R_2$ = H |
| Serotonin | Tryptamine with 5 hydroxy |
| Melatonin | 5 methoxy, $N$-acetyl |
| DMT* | $R_1$ and $R_2$ = methyl |
| DET* | $R_1$ and $R_2$ = ethyl |
| Bufotenine* | 5 hydroxy, DMT |
| Szara psychotrope* | 6 hydroxy, DET |
| Psilocin* | 4 hydroxy, DMT |
| Harmaline* | 6 methoxy; $R_1$ forms isopropyl link to $C_2$. |
| 5-MT | 5-methoxytryptamine |
| 5,6 DHT | 5,6 dihydroxytryptamine |
| 5,7 DHT | 5,7 dihydroxytryptamine |

*Psychotropic or behavioral effects.

the duration of the depletion, profound behavioral depression was observed. As we shall see, many of these ideas and theories are still maintained, although we now have much more ample evidence on which to evaluate them.

## BIOSYNTHESIS AND METABOLISM OF SEROTONIN

Serotonin is found in many cells that are not neurons, such as platelets, mast cells, and the enterochromaffin cells mentioned above. In fact, only about 1–2% of the serotonin in the whole body is found in the brain. Nevertheless, because 5-HT cannot cross the blood-brain barrier, it is clear that brain cells must synthesize their own.

For brain cells, the first important step is the uptake of the amino acid tryptophan, which is the primary substrate for the synthesis. Plasma tryptophan arises primarily from the diet, and elimination

of dietary tryptophan can profoundly lower the levels of brain serotonin. In addition, an active uptake process is known to facilitate
the entry of tryptophan into the brain, and this carrier process is
open to competition from large neutral amino acids including the
aromatic amino acids (tyrosine and phenylalanine), the branch-chain
amino acids (leucine, isoleucine, and valine), and others (i.e., methionine and histidine). The competitive nature of the large neutral
amino-acid carrier means that brain levels of tryptophan will be
determined not only by the plasma concentration of tryptophan but
also by the plasma concentration of competing neutral amino acids.
Thus, dietary protein and carbohydrate content can specifically influence brain tryptophan and serotonin levels by effects on plasma
amino-acid patterns. Because plasma tryptophan has a daily rhythmic
variation in its concentration, it seems likely that this concentration
variation could also profoundly influence the rate and synthesis of
brain serotonin.

The next step in the synthetic pathway is hydroxylation of tryptophan at the 5 position (Fig. 11-2) to form 5-hydroxytryptophan
(5-HTP). The enzyme responsible for this reaction, tryptophan hydroxylase, occurs in low concentrations in most tissues, including
the brain, and it was very difficult to isolate for study. After purifying the enzyme from mast cell tumors and determining the characteristic cofactors, however, it become possible to characterize this
enzyme in the brain. (Students should investigate the ingenious
methods used for the initial assays of this extremely minute enzyme
activity). As isolated from brain, the enzyme appears to have an
absolute requirement for molecular oxygen, for reduced pteridine
cofactor, and for a sulfhydryl-stabilizing substance, such as mercaptoethanol, to preserve activity in vitro. With this fortified system
of assay, there is sufficient activity in the brain to synthesize one
$\mu$g of 5-HTP per gram of brain stem in an hour. The pH optimum
is approximately 7.2 and the $K_m$ for tryptophan is $3 \times 10^{-4}$M.
Additional research into the nature of the endogenous cofactor, tetrahydrobiopterin, yielded a $K_m$ for tryptophan of $5 \times 10^{-5}$M,
which is still above normal tryptophan concentrations. Thus, the
normal plasma tryptophan content and the resultant uptake into

FIGURE 11-2. The metabolic pathways available for the synthesis and metabolism of serotonin.

brain leave the enzyme normally "unsaturated" with available substrate. Tryptophan hydroxylase appears to be a soluble cytoplasmic enzyme, but the procedures used to extract it from the tissues may greatly alter the natural particle-binding capacity. Investigators examining the relative distribution of particulate and soluble tryptophan hydroxylase have reported that the particulate enzyme may be associated with 5-HT-containing synapses, while the soluble form is more likely to be associated with the perikaryal cytoplasm. The particulate form of the enzyme shows the lower $K_m$ and bears an absolute requirement for tetrahydrobiopterin.

Purified tryptophan hydroxylase has a molecular weight of 52,000–60,000. It is a multimer of identical subunits that can be activated by phosphorylation, $Ca^{2+}$ phospholipids and partial proteolysis.

The cloning and sequencing of cDNAs for tryptophan hydroxylase have recently been reported. Comparison of the rabbit tryptophan hydroxylase sequence with the sequences of phenylalanine hydroxylase and tyrosine hydroxylase demonstrates that these three pterin-dependent aromatic amino acid hydroxylases are highly homologous, reflecting a common evolutionary origin from a single primordial genetic locus. The pattern of sequence homology supports the hypothesis that the carboxyl-terminal two-thirds of the molecules constitute the enzymatic activity cores and the amino-terminal thirds of the molecules constitute domains for substrate specificity.

The tryptophan hydroxylase step in the synthesis of 5-HT can be specifically blocked by $p$-chlorophenylaline, which competes directly with the tryptophan and also binds irreversibly to the enzyme. Therefore, recovery from tryptophan hydroxylase inhibition with $p$-chlorophenylalanine appears to require the synthesis of new enzyme molecules. In the rat, a single intraperitoneal injection of 300 mg/kg of this inhibitor lowers the brain serotonin content to less than 20% within 3 days, and complete recovery does not occur for almost 2 weeks.

Considerable attention has been directed to the overall regulation of this first step of serotonin synthesis, especially in animals and humans treated with psychoactive drugs alleged to affect the serotonin systems as a primary mode of their action. These studies have made an important general point that seems to apply, in fact, to the brain's response to drug exposure in many other cell systems as well as to serotonin: because transmitter synthesis, storage, release, and response are all dynamic processes; the acute imbalances produced initially by drug treatments are soon counteracted by the built-in feedback nature of synthesis regulation. Thus, if a drug acts to reduce tryptophan hydroxylase activity, the nerve cells may respond by increasing their synthesis of the enzyme and transporting increased amounts to the nerve terminals.

Mandell and colleagues have provided evidence, for example, that short-term treatment with lithium will initially increase tryptophan uptake, resulting in increased amounts being converted to 5-HT. After 14–21 days of chronic treatment, however, repetition of the measurements shows that while the tryptophan uptake is still increased, the activity of the enzyme is decreased, so that normal amounts of 5-HT are being made. In this new equilibrium state, the neurochemical actions of drugs like amphetamine and cocaine on 5-HT synthesis rates are greatly reduced, as are their behavioral actions (see below). In this way the 5-HT system, by shifting the relationship between uptake and synthesis during Li exposure, can be viewed as more "stable." This factor may be more fully appreciated when one considers that in the treatment of manic-depressive psychosis a minimum of 7–10 days is usually required before the therapeutic action of Li begins, a period during which the reequilibration of the 5-HT synthesizing process could be undergoing restabilization.

### Decarboxylation

Once synthesized, 5-HTP is almost immediately decarboxylated to yield serotonin. The enzyme responsible for this was presumed to be identical with the enzyme that decarboxylates dihydroxyphenylalanine (dopa). This information was gained mainly by the study of decarboxylase activities partially purified from liver or kidney and of the regional distribution of enzyme activity. More recent studies permit a reconsideration of this viewpoint. When the decarboxylating step is examined in brain homogenates, the activity for dopa differs widely from 5-HTP with respect to pH, temperature, and substrate optima; and within brain homogenates, the two activities become enriched in different subfractions—5-HTP decarboxylase being mainly associated with the synaptosomal and dopa-decarboxylase with the soluble or microsomal fraction. Finally, the case for two separate enzymes is supported by the observation that treatment of animals with intracisternal 6-hydroxydopamine (see Chapters 9 and 10) reduces dopa-decarboxylase activity but not 5-HTP decarboxylase activity. On the other hand, immune sera raised against the decarboxylase purified from kidney cross-react with both decarboxylases from the brain, perhaps indicating that many common antigenic determinants are shared. Since this decarboxylation reaction occurs so rapidly, and since its $K_m$ ($5 \times 10^{-6}$M) requires less substrate than the preceding steps, tryptophan hydroxylase would appear to be the rate-limiting step in the synthesis of serotonin, providing the added tryptophan is available in the controlled state. Because of this kinetic relationship, drug-induced inhibition of serotonin by interference with the decarboxylation step has never proven to be particularly effective.

### Catabolism

The only effective route of continued metabolism for serotonin is deamination by monoamine oxidase (MAO). The product of this reaction, 5-hydroxyindoleacetaldehyde can be further oxidized to 5-hydroxyindoleacetic acid (5-HIAA) or reduced to 5-hydroxytryptophol depending on the $NAD^+$/NADH ratio in the tissue. Enzymes have been described in liver and brain by which 5-HT could be catabolized without deamination through formation of a 5-sulfate ester. This could then be transported out of brain, possibly by the acid excretion system handling 5-HIAA.

Brain contains an enzyme that catalyzes the N-methylation of 5-HT using S-adenosylmethionine as the methyl donor. An N-methylating enzyme which uniquely preferred 5-methyl tetrahydrofolate (5MTF) as the methyl donor has been described. Subsequent work by several other groups revealed this reaction to be an artifact of the in vitro assay system (see also Chapter 9) in which the 5-MTF is demethylated, releasing formaldehyde that then condenses across the amino-N and the C-2 of the indole ring to form the cyclic compound tryptoline. Like other derivatives of the 5-HT metabolic product line, the intriguing possibility that one such molecule might be psychotogenic has contributed to as yet unrewarded efforts to find these abnormal metabolites in human psychotics.

## Control of Serotonin Synthesis and Catabolism

Although there is a relatively brief sequence of synthetic and degradative steps involved in serotonin turnover, there is still much to be learned regarding the physiological mechanisms for controlling this pathway. At first glance, it seems clear that tryptophan hydroxylase is the rate-limiting enzyme in the synthesis of serotonin, since when this enzyme is inhibited by 80%, the serotonin content of the brain rapidly decreases. On the other hand, when the 5-HTP decarboxylase is inhibited by equal or greater amounts, there is no effect upon the level of brain 5-HT. These data could only be explained if the important rate-limiting step were the initial hydroxylation. Since this step also depends upon molecular oxygen, the rate of 5-HT formation could also be influenced by the tissue level of oxygen. In fact, it can be shown that rats permitted to breathe 100% oxygen greatly increase their synthesis of 5-HT. It is also of interest that 5-hydroxytryptophan does not inhibit the activity of tryptophan hydroxylase.

If the situation for serotonin were similar to that previously described for the catecholamines, we might also expect that the concentration of 5-HT itself could influence the levels of activity at the hydroxylation step. However, when the catabolism of 5-HT is blocked by monoamine oxidase inhibitors, the brain 5-HT concentration accumulates linearly to levels three times greater than controls, thus suggesting that end-product inhibition by serotonin is, at best, trivial. Similarly, if the efflux of 5-HIAA from the brain is blocked by the drug probenecid (which appears to block all forms of acidic transport), the 5-HIAA levels also continue to rise linearly for prolonged periods of time, again suggesting that the initial synthesis step is not affected by the levels of any of the subsequent metabolites. Two possibilities, therefore, remain open: the initial synthesis rate may be limited only by the availability of required cofactors or substrate such as oxygen, pteridine, and tryptophan from the bloodstream; or the initial synthesis rate may be limited by the other more subtle control features, more closely related to brain activity. In fact, evidence is beginning to accumulate to suggest that impulse flow may, as in the catecholamine systems, initiate changes in the physical properties of the rate-limiting enzyme, tryptophan hydroxylase. Several mechanisms have been postulated for the physiological regulation of tryptophan hydroxylase induced by alterations in neuronal activity within serotonergic neurons. The majority of evidence currently supports the involvement of calcium-dependent phosphorylation in this impulse-coupled regulatory process.

## PINEAL BODY

The pineal organ is a tiny gland (1 mg or less in the rodent) contained within connective tissue extensions of the dorsal surface of the thalamus. While physically connected to the brain, the pineal is cytologically isolated for all intents, since, as one of the circumventricular organs, it is on the "peripheral" side of the blood permeability barriers (see Chapter 2) and its innervation arises from the superior cervical sympathetic ganglion. The pineal is of interest for two reasons. First, it contains all the enzymes required for the synthesis of serotonin plus two enzymes for further processing serotonin, which are not so pronounced in other organs. The pineal contains more than fifty times as much 5-HT (per gram) as the whole brain. Second, the metabolic activity of the pineal 5-HT enzymes can be controlled by numerous external factors, including the neural activity of the sympathetic nervous system operating through release of norepinephrine. As such, the pineal appears to offer us a potential model for the study of brain 5-HT. The pineal also appears to contain many neuropeptides, however, and thus its secretory role remains as clouded as ever.

Actually, the 5-HT content of the pineal was discovered after the isolation of a pineal factor, melatonin, known to induce pigment lightening effects on skin cells. When melatonin was crystallized and its chemical structure determined as 5-methoxy-*N*-acetyltryptamine, an indolealkylamine, a reasonable extension was to analyze the pineal for 5-HT itself. The production of melatonin from 5-HT requires two additional enzymatic steps. The first is the *N*-acetylation reaction to form *N*-acetylserotonin. This intermediate is the preferred substrate for the final step, the 5-hydroxy-indole-$O$-methyl-trans-ferase reaction, requiring $S$-adenosyl methionine as the methyl do-nor.

The melatonin content, and its influence in supressing the female gonads, is reduced by environmental light and enhanced by dark-ness. The established cyclic daily rhythm of both 5-HT and me-latonin in the pineal is driven by environmental lighting patterns through sympathetic innervation. In animals made experimentally blind, the pineal enzymes and melatonin content continue to cycle, but with a rhythm uncoupled from lighting cycles. The adrenergic receptors of the pineal are of the β-type, and—as is characteristic of such receptors—their effect on the pineal is mediated by the postjunctional formation of 3'−5' adenosine monophosphate (cyclic AMP). Elevated levels of cyclic AMP occur within minutes of the dark phase, and lead to an almost immediate activation of the 5-HT-$N$-acetyl transferase. The same receptor action also appears to be responsible on a longer time base for tonic enzyme synthesis. Thus, the proposed use of pineal as a model applicable to brain 5-HT loses its luster, since this regulatory step does not seem to be of functional importance in the CNS. Furthermore, the "adrenergic" sympathetic nerves also can accumulate 5-HT (which leaks out of pinealocytes) just as they accumulate and bind norepinephrine (NE). It remains to be shown whether this is a functional mistake (i.e., secretions of an endogenous false transmitter) or is simply a case of mistaken biologic identity. It seems likely, however, that it is the NE whose release is required to pass on the intended communica-tions from the sympathetic nervous system, since only NE activates the pinealocyte cyclase to start the enzyme regulation cascade.

### Localizing Brain Serotonin to Nerve Cells

While some of these pineal curiosities may prove to be useful for the study of brain 5-HT, they are no substitute for data derived directly from the brain. Although most early neurochemical phar-macology assumed the brain 5-HT was a neurotransmitter, more than 10 years elapsed before it could be established with certainty that 5-HT in the brain is actually contained within specific nerve circuits. Based on lesion and subcellular fractionation studies, 5-HT content was first related to specific neuronal elements on a very coarse scale. With the introduction of the formaldehyde-induced fluorescence histochemical methodology by Falck and Hillarp, however, it became possible to observe the 5-HT-containing processes directly. Nevertheless, the mapping work has proceeded slowly because the 5-HT fluorophore develops with much less efficiency than that yielded by the condensation with catecholamines and also fades rapidly while viewed in the fluorescence microscope. Although the cell bodies can be seen with relative ease, direct analysis of the nerve terminals of these cell bodies has, until recently, required extreme pharmacological measures such as combined treatment with MAO inhibitors and large doses of tryptophan; these methods do not lend themselves to discrete mapping of the projections. The situation has been greatly improved for the 5-HT mapping studies, as it has for most other neurochemically defined systems, through the combined application of immunohistochemistry (directed first toward partially purified tryptophan hydroxylase and most recently to the direct localization of 5-HT itself), of orthograde axoplasmic transport of radiolabeled amino acids microinjected into cells identified as containing 5-HT by fluroescence histochemistry, and of retrograde tracing back to known 5-HT cells from suspected terminal fields. (see Chapter 2).

As a result of these extensive efforts by many groups, serotonin-containing neurons are known to be restricted to clusters of cells lying in or near the midline or raphe regions of the pons and upper brain stem (Fig. 11-13). In addition to the nine 5-HT nuclei ($B_1$–$B_9$) originally described by Dahlström and Fuxe, recent immunocytochemical localization of 5-HT has also detected reactive cells in the area postrema and in the caudal locus ceruleus, as well as in and around the interpeduncular nucleus. The more caudal groups, studied by electrolytic or chemically induced lesions project largely to the medulla and spinal cord. The more rostral 5-HT cell groups (raphe dorsalis, raphe medianus, and centralis superior, or $B_7$–$B_9$ [Fig. 11-4] ) are thought to provide the extensive 5-HT innervation

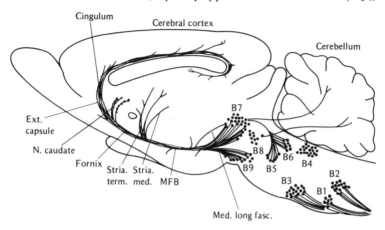

FIGURE 11-3. Schematic diagram illustrating the distribution of the main serotonin-containing pathways in the rat central nervous system. (Modified from G. Breese, *Handbook of Psychopharmacology*, Vol. 1, 1975)

of the telencephalon and diencephalon. The intermediate groups may project into both ascending and descending groups, but since lesions here also interrupt fibers of passage, discrete mapping has required the analysis of the orthograde and retrograde methods. The immunocytochemical studies also reveal a far more extensive innervation of cerebral cortex, which unlike the noradrenergic cortical fibers, is quite patternless in general.

In part, these studies could be viewed as disappointing, in that most raphe neurons appear to innervate overlapping terminal fields, and thus are more NE-like than DA-like in their lack of obvious topography. Exceptions to this generalization are that the $B_8$ group (raphe medianus) appears to furnish a very large component of the 5-HT innervation of the limbic system, while $B_7$ (or dorsal raphe) projects with greater density to the neostriatum, cerebral, and cerebellar cortices, and thalamus (Fig. 11-5).

In the past, attempts to localize 5-HT-containing terminals relied primarily on the uptake of reactive 5-HT analogues or radiolabeled 5-HT. The use of labeled 5-HT, electron-dense analogues, or 5-HT-selective toxins (like the dihydroxytryptamines) depended for

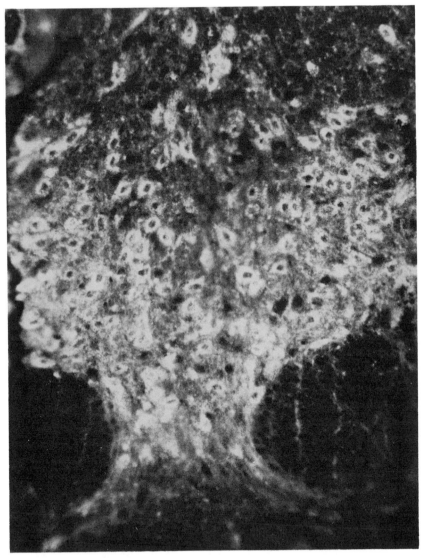

FIGURE 11-4. Fluorescence micrograph of raphe cell bodies in the midbrain of the rat. This rat was pretreated with L-tryptophan (100 mg/kg) 1 hour prior to death. (Courtesy of G. K. Aghajanian).

specificity on the selectivity of the uptake process. This situation has been rectified by immunocytochemistry of endogenous 5-HT (Figs. 11-5 and 11-6).

## CELLULAR EFFECTS OF 5-HT

From the biochemical and morphological data above we can relatively certain that the 5-HT of the brain occurs not only within the nerve cells but within specific tracts or projections of nerve cells. We must now inquire into the effects of serotonin when applied at the cellular level. (See Chapter 2.) In those brain areas in which microelectrophoretically administered 5-HT has been tested on cells that exhibit spontaneous electrical activity, the majority of cells decrease their discharge rate. The effects observed typically last much longer than the duration of the microelectrophoretic current. How-

FIGURE 11-5. Photomicrograph of the serotonergic neurons of the caudal portion of the dorsal raphe. Section was stained using an antibody directed against serotonin. The serotonergic innervation of the dorsal tegmental nucleus (DTN) can also be seen. (Courtesy of A. Y. Deutch)

FIGURE 11-6. Darkfield photomicrograph illustrating the serotonergic innervation of the bed nucleus of the stria terminalis, as revealed by immunohistochemical staining with antibody directed against serotonin. The innervation of the bed nucleus of the anterior commissure (BAC) can also be seen above the anterior commissure (AC). LV marks the lateral ventricle. (Courtesy of A. Y. Deutch)

ever, in other regions, 5-HT also causes pronounced activation of discharge rate.

Recent electrophysiological analyses of 5-HT have focused on neurons of the facial motor nucleus (cranial nerve VII) where the innervation by 5-HT fibers has been well documented. With intracellular recordings from these cells, 5-HT is found to produce a slow, depolarizing action accompanied by a modest increase in membrane resistance. As might then be anticipated on biophysical grounds, the combination of depolarization and increased membrane resistance facilitates the response of these neurons to other excitatory inputs. In a rigorous sense, such effects are not exactly in keeping with the emerging characteristics of modulatory actions (see Chapter 2), since here iontophoretic 5-HT changes both membrane potential and resistance on its own. It will be of interest to determine if activation of a 5-HT pathway to these cells at levels, which do not in themselves directly change membrane properties, will nevertheless modify responses of the target cells to other inputs, analogous to effects described for noradrenergic connections.

Several specific 5-HT-containing tracts, investigated electrophysiologically, indicate that 5-HT produces mainly, if not exclusively, inhibitory effects. While the pathways do conduct slowly, as would be expected for such fine-caliber axons, the synaptic mediation process appears to be relatively prompt.

*Characterization of* 5-HT Receptors

The existence of multiple receptors for serotonin in the central nervous system has been suggested by physiological studies. Radioligand binding studies demonstrating that $H^3$-5-HT and $H^3$-spiperone label separate populations of high-affinity binding sites for 5-HT, termed $5\text{-}HT_1$ and $5\text{-}HT_2$, respectively, have also provided evidence for multiple receptors in brain tissue. A high correlation between the potencies of 5-HT antagonists in displacing the binding of $H^3$ spiperone and inhibiting serotonin-induced behavioral hyperactivity, coupled with a lack of such a correlation of $H^3$-5-HT binding sites, has led to the proposal that inhibition and excitation induced by serotonin are mediated at $5\text{-}HT_1$ and $5\text{-}HT_2$ receptors, respectively. Recent binding studies have further subdivided the $5\text{-}HT_1$ class of recognition sites into $5\text{-}HT_{1A}$ and $5\text{-}HT_{1B}$ subtypes and compounds selective for these "receptor subtypes" have been identified. Autoreceptors for 5-HT appear to fall into the category of $5\text{-}HT_{1A}$ receptor subtypes. Drugs such as 8-OH DPAT and long-chain substituted piperazines appear to have selective $5\text{-}HT_{1A}$ binding activity and these 5-HT autoreceptor agonists are effective in inhibiting midbrain raphe neurons. Ketanserin is a new agent that blocks 5-HT receptors that apparently belong to the $5\text{-}HT_2$ category without having any significant effect on $5\text{-}HT_1$ receptors. Because of this discrimination, it has been described as a selective $5\text{-}HT_2$ blocker. However, it is important to note that ketanserin is nonspecific in the sense that it has appreciable affinity for both $\alpha_1$-adrenergic receptors and histamine $H_1$ receptors as well. It does have the advantage that its action on 5-HT receptors is as a pure antagonist.

## 5-HT Receptors

It is more than three decades since Gaddum and Picarelli (1957), basing their work on the pharmacological properties of serotonin agonists and antagonists, reported evidence for two separate serotonin receptors in peripheral smooth muscle preparations studied in vitro. One they named the "D" receptor because it was blocked by dibenzyline, and the other they called the "M" receptor because the indirect contractile response to 5-HT mediated by the release of acetylcholine from cholinergic nerves in the myenteric plexus could be antagonized by morphine. The advent of receptor-binding studies in the 1970s revealed the existence of multiple binding sites. But while a correlation existed between the pharmacological profile of the $5\text{-HT}_2$ binding site and the D receptor originally described by Gaddum, no such correlation existed between the $5\text{-HT}_1$ receptor subtypes identified by receptor-binding techniques and the M receptor. Since the M receptor originally described in the nerves of the guinea pig ileum is pharmacologically distinct from the $5\text{-HT}_1$ and $5\text{-HT}_2$ receptors and their numerous subtypes, it was renamed the $5\text{-HT}_3$ receptor. With the recent introduction of several extremely potent and highly selective $5\text{-HT}_3$ antagonists, much attention has been refocused on this receptor and its possible functions in both the periphery and the CNS, as well as the therapeutic potential for these newly developed $5\text{-HT}_3$ compounds.

At present, some eight sub-types of serotonin receptors in brain tissue have been defined and characterized, based on radioligand binding studies. As noted in Chapter 5, it is premature to characterize as a receptor a binding site defined in this manner. Nevertheless, the majority of the original speculations about serotonergic receptor subtypes generated from radioligand binding experiments appear to have been substantiated by many other types of experiments, including, most recently, the cloning of three of these subtypes. Table 11-1 lists the characteristics of these 5-HT receptor subtypes.

## TABLE 11-1. Characteristics of 5-HT receptor subtypes

| | 5-HT$_1$ Receptors | | | | 5-HT$_2$ Receptors | | 5-HT$_3$ Receptor |
| | 5-HT$_{1A}$ | 5-HT$_{1B}$ | 5-HT$_{1D}$ | 5-HT$_{1C}$ | 5-HT$_{2A}$ | 5-HT$_{2B}$ | 5-HT$_3$ |
|---|---|---|---|---|---|---|---|
| Molecular biology | Cloned | ? | ? | Cloned | ? | Cloned | ? |
| High-density regions | Raphe nuclei Hippocampus | Substantia nigra Globus pallidus | Basal ganglia | Choroid plexus | Layer IV Cortex | Layer IV Cortex | Peripheral neurons Entorhinal cortex Area postrema |
| Potent pharmacologic agents | | | | | | | |
| **Selective** | 8-OH-DPAT Ipsapirone Buspirone | No agents avail. | No agents avail. | No agents avail. | DOB DOI | No agents avail. | Zacopride Granisetron Ondanserton |
| **Non-selective** | RV 24969 d-LSD (−)Pindolol | RV 24969 (−)Pindolol | Metergoline | Metergoline | Ketanserin Ritanserin Spiperone | Metergoline Ketanserin Spiperone | ? |
| Second messenger | Inh. of adenylate cyclase | — | — | PI turnover | ? | PI turnover | ? |
| Membrane effects | Hyperpolarization via opening K channels | ? | ? | Depolarization via opening of Ca$^{++}$ channel | ? | Depolarization | Depolarization |
| Other functional correlates | Basilar artery Thermoregulation Hypotension Sexual behavior 5-HT Syndrome (Somato-dendritic) autoreceptor | Autoreceptor (Release Modul.) | Autoreceptor (Release Modul.) | ? | ? | Vascular contraction Platelet aggregation Paw edema Head twitches | Transmit. release von Bezold-Jarisch reflex |

Source: Modified from Schmidt and Peroutka, 1989.

*Molecular Biology*

Within the past 3 years, cDNA or genomic clones have been isolated for three 5-HT receptor subtypes ($5HT_{1A}$, $5HT_{1C}$, and $5HT_2$). Although the $5\text{-}HT_{1A}$ receptor was the first 5HT receptor to be successfully cloned, its identity remained unknown until mid-1988. All three cloned receptors are single subunit proteins and members of the G protein receptor superfamily. This family of receptors is characterized by the presence of seven transmembrane domains and by the ability to activate G protein-dependent processes such as activation or inhibition of adenylate cyclase activity, activation of phosphonositide turnover and direct activation of ion channels. The amino acid sequence of these membrane-spanning domains shows the least amount of variability compared with the other cloned biogenic amine receptors. The third cytoplasmic loop that is thought to interact with the G protein shows the greatest variability. Of these cloned 5-HT subtypes there is a very close structural homology between the $5\text{-}HT_{1C}$ and $5\text{-}HT_2$ receptors; the $5\text{-}HT_{1A}$ receptor is a more distant cousin of these two subtypes. The structural homology between the $5\text{-}HT_{1C}$ and the $5\text{-}HT_2$ receptors is exemplified by the similar pharmacology exhibited by the two receptor types (see Table 11-1).

Progress in our knowledge of the primary structure of at least some of the subtypes of serotonin receptors in recent years has been rapid; it is likely that this pace will continue and that before long, the sequences of all the subtypes will be known. Knowledge of the primary structure will validate the concept that these receptor subtypes are indeed distinct proteins mediating specific second-messenger functions and having discrete pharmacological profiles and perhaps even specific physiological functions.

*Behavioral Aspects of Serotonin Function*

In view of the extraordinarily widespread projections and highly regulated pacemaker pattern of activity that is characteristic of serotonin neurons, a broad homeostatic function has been suggested for serotonergic systems. By exerting simultaneous modulatory effects on neuronal excitability in diverse regions of the brain and spinal cord, the serotonergic system is in a strategic position to coordinate complex sensory and motor patterns during varied behavioral states. Single-unit electrophysiological recordings from serotonergic neurons in unanesthetized animals have shown that serotonergic activity is highest during periods of waking arousal, reduced in quiet waking, reduced further in slow-wave sleep, and absent during rapid-eye-movement sleep. An increase in tonic activity of serotonergic neurons during waking arousal would serve to enhance motor neuron excitability via descending projections to the ventral horn of the spinal cord. A suppression of sensory input, conversely, would serve to screen out distracting sensory cues. A cessation of serotonergic neuronal activity during rapid-eye-movement sleep would tend to impede motor function in this paradoxical state in which internal arousal is associated with diminished motor output. Altered function of serotonergic systems has been reported in several psychopathological conditions, including affective illness, hyper-aggressive states, and schizophrenia. There is mounting evidence for impaired serotonergic function in major depressive illness and suicidal behavior. In this connection, it is interesting that several effective antidepressant drugs appear to act by enhancing serotonergic transmission.

*Neurochemistry*

Only recently has it been possible to examine the mechanisms of signal transduction in central 5-HT receptors systems, and evidence is emerging that the two major transducing systems are linked to different 5-HT receptors in mammalian brain. The two systems that carry the extracellular signal or receptor activation across the plasma membrane are the adenylate cyclase/cyclic AMP cascade and phospholipase C/phosphoinositide hydrolysis. These signals modify cellular systems largely through the common mechanism of phosphorylation. The second messenger for the $5\text{-HT}_{1A}$ receptor subtypes is linked to the modulation of adenylate cyclase, while the $5\text{-HT}_{1C}$ and $5\text{-HT}_2$ receptor subtypes appear to be linked to phosphoinositide hydrolysis.

Recent data suggest that 5-HT$_3$ receptors are coupled to an ion channel, probably a calcium channel. Thus, the 5-HT$_3$ receptors share more similarities with the nicotinic cholinergic receptor than with the 5-HT$_1$ or 5-HT$_2$ receptor families. The direct demonstration that 5-HT$_3$ receptors in guinea pig submucosal plexus are ligand-gated ion channels implies a role for 5-HT (and perhaps for other biogenic amines) as a "fast" synaptic transmitter. At present, no information is available on the molecular biology of 5-HT$_3$ receptors.

*Physiology*

Neurophysiological and behavioral studies have benefited from the development and characterization of selective agents for 5-HT receptors. Electrophysiological studies have clearly demonstrated that 5-HT$_{1A}$ receptors mediate inhibition of the raphe nuclei. The firing of serotonergic neurons is tightly regulated by intrinsic ionic mechanisms (e.g. a calcium-activated potassium conductance), which accounts for the well-known tonic pacemaker pattern of activity of these cells. The intrinsic pacemaker is modulated by at least two neurotransmitters: (1) norepinephrine acting through adrenergic receptors accelerates the pacemaker; and (2) 5-HT acting through somatodendritic 5-HT$_{1A}$ autoreceptors slows the pacemaker. In the hippocampus, which is another anatomical structure containing a high density of 5-HT$_{1A}$ sites, 5-HT$_{1A}$ agonists hyperpolarize CA$_1$ pyramidal cells by opening potassium channels via a pertussis toxin-sensitive G protein. Electrophysiological studies carried out in *Xenopus* oocytes that express the 5-HT$_{1C}$ receptor reveal that application of 5-HT causes a detectable inward current which is blocked by mianserin. Activation of the 5-HT$_{1C}$ receptor apparently liberates inositol phosphates, raising intracellular Ca$^{2+}$ levels and leading to the opening of Ca$^{2+}$-dependent chloride channels. In mammalian systems, two specific neurophysiological effects have been attributed to activation of the 5-HT$_2$ receptor. 5-HT facilitates the excitatory effects of glutamate in the facial motor nucleus, an action that is antagonized by 5-HT$_2$ antagonists. Similar data were obtained from intracellular studies which showed that the activation of 5-HT receptors caused a slow depolarization of facial motor neurons and increased input resistance, leading to an increased excitability of the cell, probably through a decrease in resting membrane conductance to potassium. These data suggest that 5-HT$_2$ receptors mediate the 5-HT-induced excitation of facial motor neurons.

It has also been shown that 5-HT causes a slow depolarization of cortical neurons that is associated with decreased conductance. The effect can be desensitized by repeated applications of 5-HT and blocked by the selective 5-HT$_2$ antagonist ritanserin. Thus, the effect of 5-HT on cortical pyramidal neurons share many similarities to the depolarizing effects observed in the facial motor nucleus and appear also to be mediated by 5-HT$_2$ receptors.

5-HT$_3$ receptors in peripheral nervous tissue mediate excitatory responses to 5-HT and are involved in modulating transmitter release. These receptors are also found in the CNS, where they are present in high density in the entorhinal cortex and area postrema. Recent experiments demonstrate that the release of endogenous dopamine by stimulation of 5-HT$_3$ receptors in the striatum occurs in a calcium-dependent fashion. Even though the physiological function of 5-HT$_3$ receptors in the CNS is unclear, the observation that selective 5-HT$_3$ antagonists possess central activity in rats and primates in anxiolytic and antidopaminergic-like behavioral models has generated considerable excitement and speculation about the potential therapeutic use of 5-HT$_3$ antagonists and agonists. From animal experiments it has been speculated that these compounds may be useful in treating schizophrenia, pain, anxiety, drug dependence, and cytotoxic drug-induced emesis; but so far only the analgesic and antiemetic effects have been demonstrated in humans.

## Cellular Pharmacology of Brain Serotonin

Let us first consider whether or not a dynamic reuptake and turnover of serotonin occurs in a fashion similar to that described above for the catecholamines. If we attempt to use the same techniques, namely, to place a small amount of radioactive serotonin into the ventricle to label the endogeneous stores of serotonin and to follow the decline in specific radioactivity of serotonin in the brain, we find that the serotonin half-life is very long, on the order of 4–5 hours after the initial acute drop is over. When this ventricular labeling technique is verified by fluorescence histochemistry or light-microscopic or electro-microscopic autoradiography, the majority of the uptake is seen to be into those nerves that normally contain serotonin; but the labeling is mainly over terminals and axons with very little labeling within the cell-body area. Therefore, we know, initially, that the labeling of the serotonin pool by these injection techniques is not complete and that the decline in radioactivity does not reflect total brain 5-HT. Furthermore, if we use any of the other methods for estimating turnover, such as inhibiting monoamine oxidase and following the rate of rise of serotonin or inhibiting the efflux of 5-HIAA from the brain, we find that the biochemical estimate of this turnover is considerably faster than that determined by the labeling with radioactive 5-HT.

There would seem to be at least two explanations for this kinetic discrepancy. One would be that the uptake for serotonin is, in some respect, less selective or specific than that for the catecholamines. However, the uptake system appears to be similar in that it is energy dependent, that is, it is much more active at 37°C than at 0°C, it requires both glucose and oxygen, and it can be inhibited by ouabain, dinitrophenol, or iodoacetate. Furthermore, the uptake system for 5-HT can be partially inhibited by the same types of drugs that inhibit the uptake of catecholamine into catecholamine-containing nerve endings, such as desmethylimipramine, chlorpromazine, or cocaine, when evaluated in brain slices. However, the tertiary tricyclics appear to be more effective in blocking 5-HT uptake, and one such drug—Cl-imipramine—is very selective for 5-HT uptake.

On the other hand, when the turnover rates of brain serotonin (i.e., complete whole-brain serotonin) are estimated by using precursor labeling (i.e., tryptophan) and determining specific activity changes with time, results are mainly compatible with the fast rather than the slow turnover time of serotonin. The logical tentative conclusion to be reached, then, is that the pool of neuronal serotonin, which the ventricular injection most readily labels, consists mainly of the excess or storage form of serotonin; whereas total endogenous serotonin, in terms of synthesis and utilization, is turned over much more rapidly. These findings would suggest that a great deal of serotonin (which is probably true for other transmitters as well) resides in the storage form, patiently awaiting the call to action. For many years, virtually the only specific pharmacologic tool available for studying the role of 5-HT in the brain was p-chlorophenylalanine. In the pursuit of additional specific pharmacological tools, however, it was discovered that 5,6-dihydroxytryptamine can produce a selective long-term destruction of 5-HT axons and terminals in the brain, similar to the effects of 6-OHDA on the catecholamines. 5,6-DHT is more toxic and produces less extensive destruction, and so far it has found its greatest utility after local microinjections and for fluorescence and electron microscopy. Recently, there has been a reawakening of interest in p-chloroamphetamine, which for reasons that remain unclear, produces long-lasting 5-HT depletions.

### Behavioral Effects of 5-HT Systems

One of the first drugs found empirically to be effective as a central tranquilizing agent, reserpine, was employed mainly for its action in the treatment of hypertension. In the early 1950s when both brain serotonin and the central effects of reserpine were first described, great excitement arose when the dramatic behavioral effects of reserpine were correlated with loss of 5-HT content. However, it was soon found that NE and DA content could also be depleted by reserpine and that all these depletions lasted longer than sedative actions. The brain levels of all three amines remained down for many days while the acute behavioral effects ended in 48–72 hr. Hence, it became difficult to determine whether it was the loss of brain catecholamine or serotonin which accounted for the behavioral depression after reserpine.

More extensive experiments into the nature of this problem were possible when the drugs that specifically block the synthesis of catecholamines or serotonin were discovered. After depleting brain serotonin content with parachlorophenylalanine, which effectively removed 90% of brain serotonin, investigators observed that no behavioral symptoms reminiscent of the reserpine syndrome appeared. Moreover, when *p*-chlorophenylalanine-treated rats, which were already devoid of measurable serotonin, were treated with reserpine, typical reserpine-induced sedation arose. These results again favor the view that loss of catecholamines could be responsible for the reserpine-induced syndrome. Furthermore, when α-methyl-*p*-tyrosine is given and synthesis of norepinephrine is blocked for prolonged periods of time, the animals are behaviorally sedated and their condition resembles the depression seen after reserpine. Students will find it profitable to review in detail the original papers describing the results just summarized, and the other theories currently in vogue.

## Hallucinogenic Drugs

One of the more alluring aspects of the study of brain serotonin is the possibility that it is this system of neurons through which the hallucinogenic drugs cause their effects. In the early 1950s the concept arose that LSD might produce its behavioral effects in the brain by interfering with the action of serotonin there as it did in smooth muscle preparations, such as the rat uterus. However, this theory of LSD action was not supported by the finding that another serotonin blocking agent, 2-bromo LSD, produced minimal behavioral effects in the central nervous system. And, in fact, it was subsequently shown that very low concentrations of LSD itself—rather than blocking the serotonin action—could potentiate it. However, none of these data could be considered particularly pertinent since all the research was done on the peripheral nervous system and all the philosophy was applied to the central nervous system.

Shortly thereafter Freedman and Giarman initiated a profitable series of experiments investigating the basic biochemical changes in the rodent brain following injection of LSD. Although their initial studies required them to use bioassay for changes in serotonin, they were able to detect a small (on the order of 100 ng/gm, or less) increase in the serotonin concentration of the rat brain shortly after the injection of very small doses of LSD. Subsequent studies have shown that a decrease in 5-HIAA accompanies the small rise in 5-HT. Although the biochemical effects are similar to those that would be seen from small doses of monoamine oxidase inhibitors, no direct monoamine oxidase inhibitory effect of LSD has been described. This effect was generally interpreted as indicating a temporary decrease in the rate at which serotonin was being broken down, and it could also be seen with higher doses of less effective psychoactive drugs. In related studies by Costa and his co-workers, who estimated the biochemical turnover of brain serotonin, prolonged infusion of somewhat larger doses of LSD clearly promoted a decrease in the turnover rate of brain serotonin.

The next advance in the explanation of the LSD response was made when Aghajanian and Sheard reported that electrical stimulation of the raphe nuclei would selectively increase the metabolism of 5-HT to 5-HIAA. This finding suggested that the electrical activity of the 5-HT cells could be directly reflected in the metabolic turnover of the amine. Subsequently, the same authors recorded single raphe neurons during parenteral administration of LSD and observed that they slowed down with a time course similar to the effect of LSD. Thus, following LSD administration both decreased electrical activity of these cells and decreased transmitter turnover occur.

Of the several explanations originally proposed for this effect, the data now support the view that LSD is able to depress directly 5-HT-containing neurons at receptors that may be the sites where raphe neurons feed back 5-HT messages to each other through recurrent axon collaterals or dendrodendritic interactions; at these receptive sites on raphe neurons, LSD is a 5-HT agonist. In other tests on raphe neurons, iontophoretic LSD will antagonize activity of raphe neurons that show excitant responses to either NE or 5-HT. However, at sites in 5-HT terminal fields, when LSD is evaluated as an agonist or antagonist of 5-HT, its effects are considerably weaker than on the raphe neurons. These observations have led Aghajanian to suggest that LSD begins its sequence of physiological and neurochemical changes by acting on 5-HT neurons. In this view, the psychedelic actions of LSD must entail a primary or perhaps total reliance upon decreased efferent activity of the raphe neurons.

As Freedman has indicated, however, several points need further clarification before the description of LSD-induced changes in cell firing and cell chemistry can be incorporated in an explanation of the pharmacological and behavioral effects of LSD. If the effects of LSD could be "simply" equated with silencing of the raphe and subsequent disinhibition of raphe synaptic target cells, then many aspects of LSD-induced behavioral changes should be detectable in raphe-lesioned animals, but they are not. Typical LSD effects are also seen when raphe-lesioned animals are administered LSD. When normal animals are pretreated with $p$-Cl-phenylalanine (in dose schedules that antagonize raphe-induced synaptic inhibition) and give LSD, the effect is accentuated. In further contrast to the predictions of the 5-HT silencing effect, the LSD response is further accentuated with concomitant treatment with 5-HTP. The physiologic manipulation that most closely simulates behavioral actions of LSD is stimulation of the raphe, leading to decreased habituation to repetitive sensory stimuli. These data are difficult to reconcile with the view that LSD-induced behavior results from inactivation of tonic 5-HT-mediated postsynaptic actions. An important aspect to be evaluated critically in the continued search for the cellular changes that produce the behavioral effects is the issue of tolerance: LSD and other indole psychotomimetic drugs show tolerance and cross-tolerance in humans, but these properties have not been seen in animal studies at the cellular level.

The student must realize that it is extremely difficult to track down all of the individual cellular actions of an extremely potent drug like LSD and to fit these effects together in a jigsaw puzzlelike effort to solve the question of how LSD produces hallucinations. Similar jigsaw puzzles lie just below the surface of every simple attempt to attribute the effects of a drug or the execution of a complex behavioral task like eating, sleeping, mating, and learning (no rank ordering of author's priorities intended) to a single family of neurotransmitters like 5-HT. While it is clearly possible to formulate hypothetical schemes by which divergent inhibitory systems like the 5-HT raphe cells can become an integral part of such diverse behavioral operations as pain suppression, sleeping, thermal regulation, and corticosteroid receptivity, a very wide chasm of unacquired data separates the concept from the documentary evidence needed to support it. The gap is even wider than it seems since we do not at present have the slightest idea of the kinds of methods that can be used to convert correlational data (raphe firing associated with sleeping-stage onset or offset) into proof of cause and effect. While previous editions of this guide to self-instruction in cellular neuropharmacology have attempted superficial overview of the behavioral implication of 5-HT neuronal actions, we now relinquish that effort until the cellular bases become more readily perceptible.

*Actions of Other Psychotropic Drugs*

Subsequent studies by Aghajanian and his colleagues have indicated that other drugs which can alter 5-HT metabolism can also disturb the discharge pattern of the raphe neurons. Thus, monoamine oxidase inhibitors and tryptophan, which would be expected to elevate brain 5-HT levels, also slow raphe discharge; while clinically effective tricyclic drugs (antidepressants such as imipramine, chlorimipramine, and amitriptyline) also show the raphe neurons and could elevate brain 5-HT levels locally by inhibition of 5-HT reuptake. At the present time it remains unclear whether these metabolic changes in 5-HT after psychoactive drugs are administered reflect changes in the cells that receive 5-HT synapses or in the raphe neurons themselves. A large question is whether these circuits mediate the therapeutic responses of the drugs or are the primary pathologic site of the diseases the drugs treat. One etiologic view of schizophrenia, for example, might be based on the production of an abnormal indole, such as the hallucinogenic dimethyltryptamine, a compound that can be formed in human plasma from tryptamine. Some evidence indicates that schizophrenic patients have abnormally low monoamine oxidase activity in their platelets, which could permit the formation of abnormal amounts of plasma tryptamine and con-

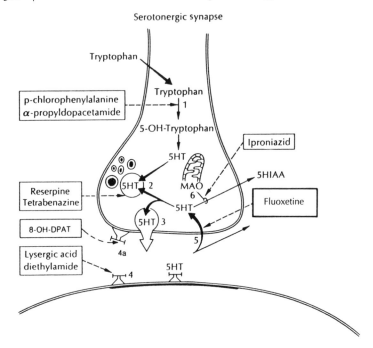

FIGURE 11-7. Schematic model of a central serotonergic neuron indicating possible sites of drug action.

Site 1: *Enzymatic synthesis*: Tryptophan is taken up into the serotonin-containing neuron and converted to 5-OH-tryptophan by the enzyme tryptophan hydroxylase. This enzyme can be effectively inhibited by *p*-chlorophenylalanine and α-propyldopacetamide. The next synthetic step involves the decarboxylation of 5-OH-tryptophan to form serotonin (5-HT).

Site 2: *Storage*: Reserpine and tetrabenazine interfere with the uptake-storage mechanism of the amine granules, causing a marked depletion of serotonin.

Site 3: *Release*: At present there is no drug available which selectively blocks the release of serotonin. However, lysergic acid diethylamide, because of its ability to block or inhibit the firing of serotonin neurons, causes a reduction in the release of serotonin from the nerve terminals.

Site 4: *Receptor interaction*: Lysergic acid diethylamide acts as a partial agonist at serotonergic synapses in the CNS. A number of compounds have also been suggested to act as receptor-blocking agents at serotonergic synapses, but direct proof of these claims at the present time is lacking.

sequently abnormal amounts of dimethyltryptamine as well. Figure 11-7 summarizes possible sites of drug interaction in a hypothetical serotonin synapse in the CNS.

In this chapter we have encountered one of the more striking examples of an intensively studied brain biogenic amine, and there is every reason to believe that it is an important synaptic transmitter. Still to be determined are the precise synaptic connections at which this substance accomplishes the transmission of information and the functional role these connections play in the overall operation of the brain with respect to both effective and other multicellular inter-neuronal operations. The central pharmacology of serotonin, while intensively investigated, remains poorly resolved. Specific inhibition of uptake and synthesis are possible, but truly effective and selective postsynaptic antagonists remain to be developed.

## HISTAMINE    *p. 367-378*

Since the beginning of this century, when Henry Dale demonstrated that histamine is an endogenous tissue constituent and a potent stimulator of a variety of cells, this substance has been thought to act as a transmitter or neuromodulator. However, direct evidence in support of this idea has accumulated relatively slowly.

The challenge posed by histamine to neuropharmacologists has

---

FIGURE 11-7. (cont.)

Site 4a: *Autoreceptor interaction*: Autoreceptors on the nerve terminal appear to play a role in the modulation of serotonin release. 8-Hydroxy-di-proplaminotetraline (8-OH-DPAT) acts as an autoreceptor agonist at serotonergic synapses in the CNS.

Site 5: *Re-uptake*: Considerable evidence now exists to suggest that serotonin may have its action terminated by being taken up into presynaptic terminal. The tricyclic drugs with a tertiary nitrogen such as imipramine and amitryptyline appear to be potent inhibitors of this uptake mechanism.

Site 6: *Monoamine oxidase. (MAO)*: Serotonin present in a free state within the presynaptic terminal can be degraded by the enzyme MAO, which appears to be located in the outer membrane of mitochondria. Iproniazid and clorgyline are effective inhibitors of MAO.

led to a vigorous chase across meadows of enticing hypotheses surrounded by bogs of confusion and dubious methodology. At last, more than 60 years after its isolation from pituitary by J. J. Abel, the role of histamine in the brain seems to be approaching a resolution that this amine occurs in two types of cells: mast cells and as yet unidentified hypothalamic neurons.

Most of what has been known about the synthesis and degradation of histamine in the brain was based on attempts to simulate in brain tissue data obtained from more or less homogeneous samples of peritoneal mast cells (Fig. 11-8). But since mast cells were not supposed to be found in healthy brains, and since histamine does not cross the blood-brain barrier, it had long been assumed that histamine could also be formed by neurons and hence be considered as a neurotransmitter. In fact, attempts to develop drugs which were histamine antagonists, in the mistaken belief that battle field shock was compounded by histamine release, were a key to the subsequent development of antipsychotic drugs. Furthermore, as every hayfever sufferer knows, present-day antihistamine drugs clearly produce substantial CNS actions such as drowsiness and hunger. Finally, we should realize that in retrospect the increased content of histamine found in transected degenerating sensory nerve trunks was likely to be an artifact of mast cell accumulation, rather than a peculiar form of neurochemistry. Viewing the other data on CNS histamine through that same retrospectroscope, as they have been illuminated by the innovative experiments of Schwartz and his associates, we now have a rather compelling case that histamine qualifies as a putative central neurotransmitter in addition to the role the same amine plays in mast cells.

The major obstacle in elucidating the functions of histamine in brain has been the absence of a sensitive and specific method to demonstrate putative histaminergic fibers in situ, the lack of suitable methods to measure histamine and its catabolites and problems in the characterization of histamine receptors in the nervous system. Some progress has been made in recent years to overcome these impediments and evidence has accumulated to support the hypothesis made more than two decades ago that histamine functions as a neurotransmitter in the brain.

*Histamine Synthesis and Catabolism*

Because histamine penetrates the brain from blood so poorly, brain histamine arises from histamine synthesis in situ from histidine. Active transport of histidine by brain slice has been demonstrated and because histidine loading has been shown to elevate brain histamine, histidine transport could be a controlling factor in brain histamine synthesis.

Two enzymes are capable of decarboxylating histidine in vitro: L-aromatic amino acid decarboxylase (i.e., dopa decarboxylase) and the specific histidine decarboxylase. The pH optimum, affinity for histidine, effects of selective inhibitors, and the regional distribution of histamine-synthesizing activity indicate that the specific histidine decarboxylase is responsible for histamine biosynthesis in brain (Fig. 11-8). The instability of histidine decarboxylase and its low activity in adult brain have precluded purification of the enzyme from this source, but fetal liver histidine decarboxylase has been purified to near homogeneity. Studies of the pH optimum, cofactor (pyridoxal phosphate), requirements, inhibitor sensitivity, and antigenic properties have demonstrated that the brain and fetal enzyme have similar properties. Antibodies to histidine decarboxylase have been used to map for the distribution of this enzyme in brain by employing immunohistochemical techniques.

The estimates of the $K_m$ of histidine for brain histidine decarboxylase are much higher than the concentration of histidine in plasma or brain, suggesting that this enzyme is not saturated with substrate in vivo and consistent with the observations that administration of L-histidine increases brain histamine levels.

There are surprisingly few selective inhibitors of histidine decarboxylase. Most of the effective inhibitors act at the cofactor site and, although they reduce histamine formation, they also inhibit other pyridoxal-requiring enzymes.

Recently, a selective inhibitor of histidine decarboxylase, α-fluoromethylhistidine (FMH), has been identified. This agent acts selectively and irreversibly by formation of a covalent linkage with the serine residue at the active site of the enzyme. FMH is more selective and potent than other decarboxylase inhibitors and does

FIGURE 11-8. Metabolism of histamine. (1) Histidine decarboxylase. (2) Histamine methyl transferase. This is the major pathway for inactivation in most mammalian species. (3) Monoamine oxidase. (4) Diamine oxidase (histaminase). (5) Minor pathway of histamine catabolism.

not inhibit dopa and glutamate decarboxylase or other histamine-metabolizing enzymes such as histamine N-methyltransferase and N-acetyl-histamine deacetylase. This agent may prove useful for manipulating in vivo actions of histamine.

Histamine is metabolized by two distinct enzymatic systems in mammals. It is oxidized by diamine oxidase to imidazoleacetalde-hyde and then to imidazoleacetic acid and is methylated by histamine methyl transferase to produce methyl histamine. Mammalian brain lacks the ability to oxidize histamine and nearly quantitatively methylates it. Methyl histamine undergoes oxidative deamination by either diamine oxidase or monoamine oxidase. The affinity is higher for diamine oxidase, but in brains which lack diamine oxidase, methyl histamine is oxidized primarily by monoamine oxidase type B.

The major route of catabolism of orally injested histamine is via N-acetylation of bacteria in the gastrointestinal tract to form N-acetylhistamine.

*Histamine-Containing Cells*

Although there are fluorogenic condensation reactions that can detect histamine in mast cells by cytochemistry, the method has never been able to demonstrate histamine-containing nerve fibers or cell bodies. Because the histamine content of mast cells is quite substantial, however, it has been possible to use the cytochemical method to detect mast cells in brain and peripheral nerve. From such studies, Schwartz has estimated that the histamine content of brain regions and nerve trunks that show about 50 ng histamine/gm (i.e., every place except the diencephalon) could all be explained on the basis of mast cells. Moreover, the once inexplicable rapid decline of brain histamine in early postnatal development can also be attributed to the relative decline in the number of mast cells in the brain during development.

Mast cell histamine shows some interesting differences from what we shall presume is neuronal histamine: in mast cells, the histamine levels are high, the turnover is relatively slow, and the activity of histidine decarboxylase is relatively low; moreover mast cell hista-mine can be depleted by mast cell-degranulating drugs (48/80 and polymyxin B). In brain, only about 50% of the histamine content can be released with these depletors, and for that which remains, the turnover is quite rapid. The activity of histidine decarboxylase is also much greater. Even better separation of the two types of cellular histamine dynamics comes from studies of brain and mast cell homogenates. In the adult brain, a significant portion of the histamine is found in the crude mitochondrial fraction that is enriched in nerve endings and is released from these particles on hypoosmotic shock. In cortical brain regions and in mast cells, most histamine is found in large granules that sediment with the crude nuclear fraction, and this histamine, unlike that in the hypothalamic nerve endings, has the slow half-life characteristic of mast cells.

Despite the encouraging result that histamine may be present in fractions of brain homogenates containing—among other broken cellular elements—nerve endings, it is difficult to parlay that information into a direct documentation of intraneuronal storage. More promising steps in that direction were taken in studies where specific brain lesions were made. The student will recall that lesions of the medial forebrain bundle region produced a loss of forebrain norepinephrine and 5-HT along a time course parallel to nerve fiber degeneration, in experiments that were done at a time when our understanding of CNS monoaminergic systems was not so far along as it is for histamine today. When such lesions were placed unilaterally and specific histidine decarboxylase activity followed, a 70% decline in forebrain histidine decarboxylase activity was found at the end of one week. The decline was not due to the concomitant loss of monoaminergic fibers, since lesions made by hypothalamic injections of 6-OHDA or 5,7-dihydroxytryptamine did not result in histidine decarboxylase loss. The most reasonable explanation would be that the lesion interrupted a histamine-containing diencephalic tract; the histamine and decarboxylating activity on the ipsilateral cortex was reduced only about 40%, suggesting that the pathway may make diffuse contributions to nondiencephalic regions. However, subsequent studies of completely isolated cerebral cortical "islands" show a complete loss of histamine content. As mentioned earlier, antibodies to histidine decarboxylase have also been utilized to map the distribution of this enzyme in rodent brain by immunohistochemical techniques. Steinbusch and co-workers have developed an immunohistochemical method for the visualization of histamine in the central nervous system using an antibody raised against histamine coupled to a carrier protein. Results obtained with this technique are in general agreement with studies on the immunohistochemical localization of histidine decarboxylase. The highest density of histamine-positive fibers are found in brain regions known to contain high histamine levels, such as the median eminence and the premammillary regions of the hypothalamus.

Lesion and immunohistochemical studies indicate the presence of a major histamine-containing pathway emanating from neurons in the posterior basal hypothalamus and reticular formation and ascending through the medial forebrain bundle to project ipsilaterally to broad areas of the telencephalon (Fig. 11-9). A descending pathway originating from the hypothalamus and projecting to the brain stem and spinal cord has also been suggested. The precise mapping of the histamine projections has not been possible due to the limited sensitivity of the immunohistochemical methods.

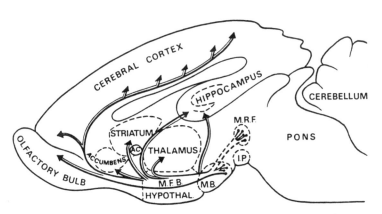

FIGURE 11-9. Schematic illustration of the distribution of histamine-containing neurons in brain. M.R.F., mesencephalic reticular formation; M.B., mammillary bodies; M.F.B., medial forebrain bundle. (Modified from Schwartz et al., 1986)

*Histamine Receptors*

Detailed studies of histamine receptors on smooth-muscle preparations have revealed that they exist in two forms: an $H_1$ receptor, with which the well-known histamine blockers interact, and an $H_2$ receptor, where these classical antagonists do not work but other antagonists do (such as metiamide and burimamide) (Figs. 11-10 and 11-11). These two classes of histamine receptors also reveal themselves by their differential responses to a number of histamine-like agonists. For example, 2-methylhistamine preferentially elicits responses mediated by $H_1$ receptors; whereas 4-methyl histamine and dimaprit have preferential effects mediated through $H_2$ receptors. The structures of some of these histamine agonists are illustrated in Figure 11-12.

Attempts to characterize the electrophysiological effects elicited by histamine on neurons in the central nervous system by employing selective histamine antagonists have been hampered by the local

$H_1$-RECEPTOR BLOCKING DRUGS

Diphenhydramine

Chlorpheniramine

Tripelennamine

Promethazine

Cyclizine

FIGURE 11-10. Representative $H_2$-receptor blocking drugs.

$$H_3C \underset{N \diagdown\!\!\!\diagup N}{\boxed{\phantom{xx}}} CH_2-S-CH_2CH_2NH-\underset{\underset{S}{\|}}{C}-NH-CH_3$$

Metiamide

$$\underset{N \diagdown\!\!\!\diagup N}{\boxed{\phantom{xx}}} CH_2CH_2CH_2CH_2NH\underset{\underset{S}{\|}}{C}-NH-CH_3$$

Burimamide

$$CH_3 \underset{N \diagdown\!\!\!\diagup N}{\boxed{\phantom{xx}}} CH_2SCH_2CH_2NH\underset{\underset{N-C\equiv N}{\|}}{C}-NH-CH_3$$

Cimetidine

FIGURE 11-11. Representative $H_2$-receptor blocking drugs.

anesthetic properties of histamine–$H_1$ antagonists and the ability of $H_2$ antagonists themselves to depress the spontaneous firing rate of neurons. However, electrophysiological studies reveal that stimulation of histamine receptors can cause stimulation or inhibition of subpopulations of neurons in the CNS. In general, the excitatory actions of histamine are most often related to an interaction with $H_1$ receptors; whereas the inhibitory actions appear to be related to $H_2$ receptors. Most recently, a histamine-sensitivity adenylate cyclase has been described in both rat and guinea pig brain. This receptor is, by pharmacological criteria, an $H_2$ receptor; the response to adenylate cyclase is most pronounced in the neocortex and hippocampus, but is not seen in hypothalamus. The ability of histamine to activate metabolic processes in the neocortex by a presumed cyclic AMP-mediated activation of glycogenolysis further supports a histaminergic physiology.

A third histamine receptor ($H_3$) was only recently discovered and differs from the other two histamine receptors in its pharmacology and localization (Table 11-2). $H_3$-receptors are exquisitely sensitive to histamine and to the chiral agonist, (R) α-methylhistamine, which is active at nanomolar concentration. Stimulation of $H_3$-receptors results in an inhibition of depolarization-induced release and syn-

FIGURE 11-12. Structure of histamine and histamine agonists that act at $H_1$ and $H_2$ receptors.

thesis of histamine. Thus, $H_3$ can be characterized as an autoreceptor. Recently, with the design of selective brain-penetrating $H_3$ receptor ligands, it has been shown that $H_3$-receptors modulate histamine synthesis and release in vivo. For example, the $H_3$ antagonist, thioperamide, markedly increases histamine turnover in brain; whereas (R) α-methylhistamine has an inhibitory effect. It is of interest that similar pharmacologic responses also occur in the lung, where histamine is believed to be stored largely in mast cells. These observations are consistent with the possibility that activation of $H_3$ receptors might inhibit the synthesis and release of histamine and possibly other mediators of inflammation and allergy.

At present, none of the histamine receptors has been purified or cloned. The second messenger or associated channel of the $H_3$ re-

TABLE 11-2. Pharmacology of histamine receptors

| Nomenclature | $H_1$ | $H_2$ | $H_3$ |
|---|---|---|---|
| Selective agonists | 2-Thiazolyl-ethylamine | Dimaprit Impromidine (also an $H_3$ antagonist) | (R)-α-methylhistamine |
| Selective antagonists | Mepyramine Triprolidine | Ranitidine Tiotidine | Thioperamide |
| Effector pathways | IP$_3$/DG | cAMP | |

ceptors has not yet been identified. While the second messengers of the $H_1$ and $H_2$ receptors are known, details concerning the intracellular mechanisms they trigger are still poorly understood.

In summary, there is compelling evidence that histamine, in addition to its presence in mast cells, exists in neurons where it probably functions as a neurotransmitter in the CNS. Brain has a similar non-uniform distribution of histamine, a specific histidine decarboxylase, and methyl histamine (the major metabolic of brain histamine). The cerebellum has the lowest levels, whereas the hypothalamus is most enriched. Hypothalamic synaptosomes contain histamine and histidine decarboxylase suggesting a localization in nerve endings. Depolarization of hypothalamic slices causes a calcium-dependent release of histamine, although histamine release from neurons has not been convincingly demonstrated in *in vivo*. The turnover of brain histamine is quite rapid, as with other biogenic amine transmitters.

The actions of histamine in the CNS appear to be mediated by three classes of receptors. These three types, $H_1$, $H_2$, and $H_3$, can be distinguished in the CNS by their pharmacology, their localization, and the intracellular responses they mediate.

Neuropharmacological studies of brain histaminergic systems have been hampered by the lack of appropriate pharmacological agents. In the last few years, parenterally active drugs, $H_2$ antagonists, $H_3$ agonists, and antagonists have become available and their effects on behavioral, neuroendocrine, and vegetative functions are being studied in animals. Parenterally active $H_1$ and $H_2$ agonist have yet to be developed.

Lesions of the midbrain or caudal hypothalamus cause a progressive reduction in forebrain histamine and histidine decarboxylase consistent with the existence of an ascending histamine-containing system, which has now been directly visualized by employing immunohistochemical techniques. Continued application of these immunohistochemical techniques for visualization of histidine decarboxylase-like and histamine-like activity in brain should provide detailed maps of histamine-containing neuron systems in the brain in the near future. However, we are still far from being able to speak with conviction of specific histaminergic circuits and their relation to behavior, and thus the functions of histamine in brain are highly speculative.

The high levels of histamine and the presence of histamine receptors in the hypothalamus, together with the known ability of histamine to alter food and water intake thermoregulation, autonomic activity, and hormone release, indicate a possible role for histamine in these vegetative functions. Also, because of the presence of ascending histamine-containing fibers originating from the reticular formation, coupled with the sedative nature of $H_1$ antagonists and the activation effects of histamine on some brain cells, a possible role for histamine in arousal has been suggested.

SELECTED REFERENCES
*Serotonin*

Aghajanian, G.K., J.S. Sprouse, and K. Rasmussen (1987). Physiology of the midbrain serotonin system. In *Psychopharmacology: The Third Generation of Progress* (H.Y. Meltzer, ed.) pp. 141–150. Raven Press, New York.

Aghajanian, G.K. and C.P. Vandermaelen (1986). Specific systems of the reticular core: Serotonin. In *Handbook of Physiology*, Vol. 4, Sec. 1: *Neurophysiology* (V.B. Mountcastle, F.E. Bloom, and S.R. Geiger, eds.), pp. 237–256. American Physiological Society, Bethesda, Maryland.

Boadle-Biber, M.C., J.N. Johannessen, N. Narasimhachari and T.-H. Phan (1986). Tryptophan hydroxylase: Increase in activity by electrical stimulation of serotonergic neurons. *Neurochem. Int.* 8(1):83–92.

Charney, D.S., J.H. Krystal, P.L. Delgado, and G.R. Heninger (1990). Serotonin-specific drugs for anxiety and depressive disorders. *Annu. Rev. Med. 41*, 437–46.

Chuang, D.M. (1989). Neurotransmitter receptors and phosphoinositude turnover. *Annu. Rev. Pharmacol. Toxicol. 29*, 71–110.

Derkach, V., A. Surprenant, and R.A. North (1989). 5-HT$_3$ receptors are membrane ion channels. *Nature 339*, 706–709.

Fozard, J.R., (ed) (1989). *The Peripheral Actions of 5*-Hydroxytryptamine. Oxford University Press, New York.

Frazer, A., S. Maayani, and B.B. Wolfe (1990). Subtypes of receptors for serotonin. *Annu. Rev. Pharmacol. Toxicol. 30*, 307–348.

Fuller, R.W. (1988). The pharmacology and therapeutic potential of serotonin receptor agonists and antagonists. In *Adv. Drug Res. 17*, 349–380.

Hartig, P.R. (1989). Molecular biology of 5-HT receptors. *Trends Pharmacol. Sci. Rev. 10*, 64–69.

Hoyer, D. (1988). Functional correlates of serotonin 5-HT$_1$ recognition sites. *J. Recept. Res. 8*, 59–81.

Osborne, N.N. and M. Hamon, (eds.) (1988). *Neuronal Serotonin.* Wiley & Sons, New York.

Sanders-Bush, E. (ed.) (1988). *The Serotonin Receptors.* Humana Press, Clifton, New Jersey.

Sanders-Bush, E. and P.J. Conn (1987). Neurochemistry of serotonin neuronal systems: Consequences of serotonin receptor activation. In *Psychopharmacology: The Third Generation of Progress* (H.Y. Meltzer, ed.), pp. 95–103. Raven Press, New York.

Schmidt, A.W. and S.J. Peroutka (1989). 5-Hydroxytryptamine receptor "families." *FASEB J. 3*, 2242–2249.

Steinbusch, H.W.M. and A.H. Mulder (1984). Serotonin-immunoreactive neurons and their projections in the CNS. In *Handbook of Chemical Neuroanatomy, Classical Transmitters and Transmitter Receptors in the CNS*, Vol. 3, Part II (A. Björklund, T. Hökfelt, and M. Kuhar, eds.). Elsevier, Science Publishing, New York.

*Histamine*

Arrang, J.M., M. Garbarg, J.C. Lancelot, et al. (1987). Highly potent and selective ligands for histamine H$_3$-receptors. *Nature (Lond) 327*, 117–23.

Hill, S.J. (1990). Distribution, properties, and functional characteristics of three classes of histamine receptor. *Pharm. Rev. 42*, 45–83.

Hough, L.B. (1988). Cellular localization and possible functions for brain histamine: Recent progress. *Prog. Neurobiol. 30*, 469–505.

Hough, L.B., J.K. Khandelwal, and J.P. Green (1986). Inhibition of brain histamine metabolism by metoprine. *Biochem. Pharm.* 35, 307–310.

Prell, G.D. and J.P. Green (1986). Histamine as a neuroregulator. *Ann. Rev. Neurosci.* 9, 209–54.

Schwartz, J-C., M. Garbarg, and H. Pollard (1986). Histaminergic transmission in the brain. In *Handbook of Physiology*, Vol. 4, Sect. 1, *The Nervous System Intrinsic Regulatory Systems of the Brain.* (Mountcastle V.B., F.E. Bloom, S.R. Geiger eds.), pp. 257–316. American Physiological Society, Philadelphia.

Schwartz, J., J.C. Arrang, J.M. Garbarg, H. Pollard, and M. Ruat (1991). Histaminergic transmission in the mammalian brain. *Physiol. Rev.* 71, 1.

Steinbusch, H.W.M. and A.H. Mulder (1984). Immunohistochemical localization of histamine in neurons and mast cells in brain. In *Handbook of Chemical Neuroanatomy*, Vol. 3, Part II, *Classical Transmitters and Transmitter Receptors in the CNS*. (A. Bjorklund, T. Hokfelt, and M.J. Kuhar, eds.), pp. 126–140. Elsevier Science Publishing, New York.

Wamsley, J.K. and J.M. Palacios (1984). Histaminergic receptors. In *Handbook of Chemical Neuroanatomy*, Vol. 3, Part II, *Classical Transmitters and Transmitter Receptors in the CNS* (A.S. Björklund, T. Hökfelt, and M. Kuhar, eds.), p. 386. Elsevier Science Publishing, New York.

# 12 | Neuroactive Peptides

Neuropeptides continue to be a very active research area in neuro-pharmacology and a very compelling target for speculation—both in the possibilities for peptide functions and their drug manipulation, and in the companies that may some day make these drugs. The rapid advances in molecular biological understanding of gene structure, regulation of gene expression, and the determination of peptide sequences by deduction from nucleic acid sequences (see Chapter 3) are among the many enticements, giving an impression that all the open questions in peptide signaling may soon be solved. Alas, this appearance is misleading. As in most of the fields discussed in this book, better data beget better and more complex questions. Nevertheless, for readers interested in testing their comprehension of what it takes to identify a neurotransmitter and to characterize the role of the circuits that contain it, neuropeptides pose many important challenges.

A very large number of peptides made by neurons have now been shown to affect specific target cells of the central and peripheral nervous systems: neuronal, glial, smooth muscle, glandular, and vascular. Although the number of known endogenous peptides already exceeds several dozen, with no obvious end in sight, the actual molar concentrations of any given peptide in the brain is maximally two to three orders of magnitude lower than that of the monoamines, acetylcholine, and amino acids and have potencies at correspondingly lower concentrations. The specific signaling advantages that peptides may hold for the operation of neuronal circuits is not yet obvious. Furthermore, no specific peptides have yet been linked selectively to a given functional system in the brain, nor correlated in any exclusive manner with any pathological states. Thus, the challenge of devising new drugs for neurological or psychiatric disorders based on these peptides is considerably more difficult than *just* designing potent congeners that can act as their agonists or antagonists. Nevertheless, there are strong implications that the biologic properties evoked by peptide-mediated signals will influence future pharmacological development.

## SOME BASIC QUESTIONS

### What's Different about Peptides?

Peptide-secreting neurons differ in their biology from neurons using amino acids and monoamines in ways other than the molecular structure of their transmitter. The amino acid or monoamine transmitters are formed from dietary sources by one or two intracellular enzymatic steps; the end product of these enzymatic actions is the active transmitter molecule which is then stored in the nerve terminal until release. After release, the transmitter (or choline in the case of ACh) can be reaccumulated back into the nerve terminal by the energy-dependent active reuptake property, thus conserving the requirement for de novo synthesis. Peptide-secreting cells employ a somewhat more formidable approach: Synthesis directed by mRNA can take place only on ribosomes and thus only in the perikaryon or dendrites of a neuron. Furthermore, all known peptides arise from larger prohormone forms (inactive precursors). The biologically active, secreted form is cleaved from these prohormones by the actions of selective proteolytic enzymes.

Thus, the process for peptides starts with ribosomal synthesis of the prohormone, which is then packaged into vesicles in the smooth endoplasmic reticulum, and transported from the perikaryon to the nerve terminals for eventual release. These steps in the molecular processing of a neuropeptide are described in greater detail in Chapter 3.

Insofar as present data reveal, peptide-releasing neurons share certain basic properties with all other chemically characterized neurons: transmitter release is Ca-dependent and some of the postsynaptic effects may be mediated by directly altering ion channel conductances or indirectly regulating ion channels through second messengers such as $Ca^{2+}$, cyclic nucleotides or inositol triphosphates (see Chapter 6). Furthermore, like the monoamines, peptides identical to those extracted from the nervous system are often made by nonneural secretory cells in endocrine glands and the mucosa of the hollow viscera. Some observers of the peptide scene would like to emphasize characteristics of neuropeptide action which are extrapolations from the actions of endocrine peptide hormones: targets that are distant from release sites, release into portal or other circulatory systems, higher potency and a longer time course of effects. Although it is clear that endocrine hormones, peptides, or amines can often act in concentrations in the nanomolar range or below, it remains to be determined how time course and thresholds vary when the same neuropeptides act on their target cells in the brain or ganglia. In amphibian autonomic ganglia, at least one peptide does act in such a local endocrine, or *paracrine*, fashion, producing synaptic potentials that last for hundreds of milliseconds. These effects of an endogenous peptide that is very similar to hypothalamic luteinizing hormone-releasing hormone are produced on a nonsynaptic neuronal target by diffusing at least 10–100 μ from preganglionic synaptic release sites, without apparently acting at all on the immediate postsynaptic neuron. Whether these particular paracrine properties are ways around the simple amphibian autonomic anatomy or a prototype for all central and peripheral peptide actions remains debatable.

*How Are New Peptides Found?*

Before considering the interesting relationships among the many known peptides, we can anticipate future events by examining the recurrent pattern of events that seems to underlie every wave of peptide discovery and characterization. From this historical overview, the student can see that new peptides do not just happen into existence. The primary necessity for the discovery of a new peptide has classically been the recognition of a biological function controlled by an unknown factor; this biological action is then employed as the bioassay for the subsequent steps of the discovery process. Although this approach was used for the characterization of gastrointestinal peptide hormones in the 1940s and 1950s, the process was perfected and greatly increased in power by Guillemin and Schally and their teams during the 1960s and 1970s, as they pursued the hypophysiotrophic hormones by which the hypothalamus regulates the secretion of adenohypophysial (anterior pituitary) hormones for control of the major peripheral endocrine tissues. The starting bioassay is used as a screen for chemical manipulations of tissue extracts, and through chemical manipulations of the extract (i.e., differential extractions, molecular sieves, etc.) the active factor is enriched and ultimately purified. For some factors, the purification of nanograms of active peptide has required hundreds of thousands of brains. The peptidic nature of the purified material is inferred by the loss of biological activity after treatment with peptidases (carboxypeptidases or endopeptidases). The cleaved peptide fragments are then sequenced and the entire factor is eventually reconstructed.

When a sequence has been achieved and matched against the amino acid composition of the pure factor, it is then necessary to synthesize the peptide and determine if the synthetic replicate matches actions and potencies with the purified natural factor. Only when the replicate's properties match those of the factor can the natural peptide be considered to have been "identified." At this point the factor is given a name which reflects its actions in the original bioassay.

However, this is far from the end of the discovery process. When the chemical structure of a peptide has been identified and synthetically replicated, two new opportunities arise: large amounts of the synthetic material can be prepared for examination of physiological and pharmacological properties; at the same time, antibodies can be prepared against the synthetic material. The antibodies are used for radioimmunoassay and for immunocytochemistry. The quantitative measurements made possible by the radioimmunoassay and the qualitative distribution of the peptide assessed by microscopic cytochemical localizations then frequently reveals that the peptide has a much broader distribution, and, therefore, ostensibly has a much more general series of actions than was originally presumed. Autoradiographic mapping of ligand binding sites for peptides, generally the last step in the molecular and cellular characterization, are then defined. Curiously, these ligand binding maps show a flagrant disregard for the cellular distribution of the recognized forms of the endogenous peptides; this mismatch strengthens in some minds the concept of paracrine diffusion for peptide actions. Thereafter, the endogenous peptide or an analog of it is ordinarily proposed to be the cause or cure of a major mental illness. In many of the more recent reports, it is frequently observed that the peptide isolated and found to be active is, in fact, not the only active form contained in the tissue: In many cases better extraction methods confirmed by radioimmunoassay reveal larger molecules with full or even greater potency. Although the general rule is that active peptides are synthesized from larger precursor hormones, processing can sometimes lead to active larger peptides that (then) cannot really be viewed as "precursors," since they have potent activity in their own right.

As more and more peptides have been identified within the nervous system and from other sources, their internal structural similarities allow us to consider them as members of one or another family grouping of peptides. The family groupings are useful because they indicate that certain sequences of amino acids have had considerable evolutionary conservation, presumably because they provide unambiguous signals between secreting and responding cells.

Two aspects of peptide family groupings deserve recognition: (1) families in which separate propeptide genes or mRNAs sharing one or more short peptide sequences are expressed by different cell groups in the same species; (2) families in which the peptides expressed by homologous cell groups share generally identical peptide sequences with minor to moderate variation. The first category, exemplified by the opioid peptide and the tachykinin peptide families, implies that the natural ligand's receptors may diverge into subtypes that can discriminate the fine differences in peptide sequences. Although some individual peptides have already earned their own receptor subtypes (vasopressin, somatostatin), in other cases, such as the tachykinins and the opioid peptides, the multiple receptor subtypes predicted the later definition of multiple natural ligands. In those cases in which the propeptide form may give rise to multiple different agonists, it is possible—but by no means yet broadly supported—that more than one peptide messenger is released from the possible array. Some dreamy-eyed pundits have theorized that different branches of a neuron might have the option of changing the mix of cleavage products available for release.

The latest additions to the list of neuroactive peptides have been discovered by strategies that depart from the classical bioassay strategy purification schemes and instead rely either on specific common general features, such as a C-terminally amidated sequence, or on the detection of potential cleavage fragments when the propeptide sequence has been deduced by molecular cloning of the mRNA or gene. Although these historical discovery cycles are individually entertaining stories, the punch lines—determining what the peptides do and how to make drugs based upon these actions—still remain elusive.

### Transmitters or Not?

In Chapter 3 we considered the kinds of evidence needed to demonstrate that a substance found in nerve cells is the transmitter that those cells secrete at their synapses. To recapitulate, it must be shown that the substance is present within the nerve cell and specifically in its presynaptic terminals, that the nerve cell can make or accumulate the substance, and that it can release that substance when activated; when the substance is released, it must be shown to mimic in every aspect the functional activity following stimulation of the nerves that released it, including the magnitude and quality of changes in postsynaptic membrane conductances. A criterion especially pertinent to the objectives of this book is that drugs which can simulate or antagonize the effects of nerve fiber activation must have an identical influence on the effects of the substance applied exogenously to the target cell.

In the case of peptides, the opportunities for supplying these data would at first glance seem better than they are with the many categories of small molecules we have discussed in previous chapters.

Once the peptide has been isolated and its structure determined, immunocytochemical localization of the peptide usually follows promptly, as does the demonstration that with the right sensitive assay, the peptide can be shown to be released from brain slices by a $Ca^{2+}$-dependent, depolarization process. The development of a suitable synthetic ligand helps define receptor distribution, possible actions on presumptive synaptic targets, and on potential mechanisms of cellular regulation, and in a few cases, the development of receptor subtype-specific antagonist analogs. In several peptide families, synthetic agonist and antagonist peptide analogs have been employed to document behavior-altering actions of the exogenous forms, and, by inference, a role of the endogenous form in behavior and possibly in disease states. Although these molecular tools have accelerated the early partial fulfillment of transmitter criteria for peptides generally, there are as yet no cases within the CNS in which the complete array of neuronal actions transmitted by a peptide-containing circuit have been shown to be completely attributable to the peptide. There are important reasons for this unsatisfying state of peptide transmitter documentation, and lack of effort is not one of them.

## They Are Not Alone

Earlier editions of this book were organized according to a then-prevalent concept in neuropharmacology: a given neuron operated by one and only one transmitter. According to this concept, one aspect of a neuron's phenotype, as classic as its size, shape, location, circuitry, and synaptic function, was its neurochemical designation as "GABA-ergic" or "cholinergic" or "adrenergic" or whatever. All card-carrying pharmacologists knew that autonomic neurons came in only two color-coded categories: adrenergic and cholinergic. And then a curious finding began to repeat itself: Neuroactive peptides started showing up in autonomic neurons where there was no need for additional transmitters. Initially viewed by many as an oddity, the idea of coexisting peptides in central as well as peripheral neurons that are already occupied by an amino acid or monoamine or even another neuropeptide has now gained wide acceptance (see Table 12-1).

The notion of coexistence of other transmitters with peptides leads one to ask whether there is any such thing as a truly "peptidergic" neuron, or rather only neurons in which the peptide that is there simply expands the armamentarium of messenger molecules available

TABLE 12-1. Neuroactive peptides coexist with other transmitters

| Transmitter | Peptide | Location |
| --- | --- | --- |
| GABA | Somatostatin | Cortical and hippocampal neurons |
| | Cholecystokinin | Cortical neurons |
| Acetylcholine | VIP | Parasympathetic and cortical neurons |
| | Substance P | Pontine neurons |
| Norepinephrine | Somatostatin | Sympathetic neurons |
| | Enkephalin | Sympathetic neurons |
| | NPY | Medullary and pontine neurons |
| | Neurotensin | Locus ceruleus |
| Dopamine | CCK neurotensin | Ventrotegmental neurons Ventrotegmental neurons |
| Epinephrine | NPY | Reticular neurons |
| | Neurotensin | Reticular neurons |
| Serotonin | Substance P | Medullary raphe |
| | TRII | Medullary raphe |
| | Enkephalin | Medullary raphe |
| Vasopressin | CCK, dynorphin | Magnocellular hypothalamic neurons |
| Oxytocin | Enkephalin | Magnocellular hypothalamic neurons |

for transmitting an *enriched* message that requires more than one type of transmitter for its fully refined signal content. Although the latter concept is far from a neuroscientific consensus, the data in hand are certainly compatible, recognizing the enormous void in our knowledge in which the majority of neurons have not yet had either their peptidic or nonpeptidic transmitters identified.

Such a revolutionary concept then forces us to ask: If the peptide is not the sole signaling molecule, but rather a minor, fractional percent of messenger-signaling capacity of the nerve terminal, how might peptides affect signals transmitted by the coexisting amino acid or monoamine? The honest answer now is "We don't know," at least for the CNS. However, in the autonomic nervous system, where Tomas Hökfelt and his peptide liberation team have managed to find at least one peptide in every sympathetic, parasympathetic, or enteric neuron they have studied, some solid peptide–monoamine interactions are emerging. Vasoactive intestinal peptide (VIP), released when cholinergic nerves discharge at high frequency, augments parasympathetic control of salivation by increasing glandular blood flow. Neuropeptide Y (NPY), found in many sympathetic neurons, sensitizes smooth muscle target cells to adrenergic signals. Thus, peptide agonist or antagonist actions might well alter neuronal information flow by disturbing the normal symbiotic relationships between the signals.

Other peptide actions, although not necessarily on coexisting amino acid or monoamine transmitters, have been reported with irregularity: increasing or decreasing the amount of transmitter released by a given stimulus, or enhancing or diminishing the response of a common target cell (in either amplitude or duration or both) to combined transmitter signals. For example, VIP greatly accentuates the response of cortical neurons to subthreshold doses of norepinephrine as indicated by the amount of cyclic AMP generation and the potency on altering neuronal activity. VIP and some other peptides have been reported to alter the affinity of postsynaptic receptors for their nonpeptidic ligands.

One way to recast these players in the proper perspective might be to consider that a peptide usually embellishes what the primary transmitter for a neuronal connection seeks to accomplish. Such an effect may be to strengthen or prolong the primary transmitter's actions, especially when the nerve is called upon to fire at higher than normal frequencies. The peptide may provide a part of the intraneuronal signal to alter the rate of production of the primary transmitter, and there may still be places in which the peptide itself can fulfill all of the effects of a primary transmitter.

Accepting this concept for the moment, several other important concepts for pharmacology emerge: the anticipated effects of peptide-directed drugs will not only depend on the location of the receptors and their actions, but on the context of the signals with which the peptides normally cooperate. Thus, the pharmacology of NPY or neurotensin may be most appropriately understood as a part of the total picture of central noradrenergic pharmacology, given the degree to which these two peptides may participate in that monoaminergic neuron's transmission. Furthermore, one may imagine a relatively modest number of response mechanisms on which peptide messengers may operate (e.g., direct regulation of Na, K, or Ca channels, or second messenger-mediated regulation of those or other channels), but with a great enrichment of signaling possibilities attainable through the interplay between frequency-dependent and diffusion-dependent release and response sites. However, before we all grow obese on the meringue of what may only be a lemon pie-in-the-sky, there are some facts worth having. The rest of this chapter reviews pharmacologically relevant data for the grand peptide families (oxytocin/vasopressin, the tachykinins, glucagon-related peptides, pancreatic polypeptide-related peptides, and opioid peptides,) and for a few individual peptides (CCK, somatostatin, angiotensin, calcitonin-gene-related peptide, and CRF). Future editions will certainly require an expansion of this roster.

In terms of the development of drugs active on the nervous system, research on the peptides has given us a humbling view of the riches that may await mining in the inner depths of the brain.

*Emerging Trends in Neuropeptide Research*

Observers of the active peptide parade may find it useful to monitor certain recurring themes in several of the brain and autonomic peptide systems. They illustrate potential principles that could apply to peptide signaling systems generally.

*Peptides are dynamically regulated.* In the past few years, reliable methods have been developed for assessing the dynamic synthesis and catabolism of neuropeptides; these may help identify the functional conditions under which the brain increases or decreases its rate of utilization of the specific peptide. The turnover of the peptide under such conditions is best estimated by measuring simultaneously mRNA, the precursor propeptide, and the signaling form. Such triple measurements place important constraints on the interpretation of conditions previously measured simply in terms of more or less peptide per unit brain volume. These studies have helped clarify the effects on peptides of drug treatments that diminish or increase the levels of the coexisting amines in a given class of neurons. Furthermore, examination of the genes for some neuropeptides has revealed regulatory genetic elements that make gene transcription sensitive to gonadal hormones (oxytocin, vasopressin, and proenkephalin) or to intracellular second messengers (vasoactive intestinal polypeptide, corticotropin releasing hormone, and prosomatostatin). Such data help to establish even more securely that the nature of functional regulation for peptides may not reflect that of its coresident small transmitter or other peptide partners.

*Post-release cleavage products may provide different signals.* Based on the absence of any specific data, it had been assumed that despite the enormous logistical prelude to constructing a propeptide and then cleaving and storing the active form, its secretion was the end of the line. In several peptide systems, however, pharmacological evidence suggests that catabolic forms of the secreted peptide may have real signal value, both on the neuron that secreted the full peptide and on the postsynaptic neuron. The data suggest that such shorter forms may participate in fine-tuning the levels of interaction between the peptides and other coexisting transmitters.

*Nonpeptidic drugs may yet be possible.* The third emerging trend is less an example of peptide physiology than an expression of appreciation for the achievements of medicinal chemists in synthesizing rigid nonpeptidic molecules that can act as agonists and (experimentally more important) as antagonists of the peptide's receptors.

While it was clear that mother nature could do this in the form of the basic morphine molecule by making an agonist for opioid peptide receptors, extension of this principle to other peptides was slow in coming. However, new molecules are coming forth and as nonpeptidic antagonists are created for peptide systems, the ability to dissect out their functional roles will almost certainly be improved.

## THE GRAND PEPTIDE FAMILIES

### Vasopressin and Oxytocin

These two highly similar nonapeptides (see Fig. 12-1) with internal 1,6 disulfide bridges are the original mammalian peptide "neurohormones": They are synthesized in the neuronal perikarya found in the large neurons of the supraoptic and paraventricular nuclei, and they are stored in the axons of these neurons in the neurohypophysis, from which they are released into the bloodstream. Each peptide is synthesized as part of a larger propeptide (see Chap. 3) with which it is stored and released and from which it is cleaved as part of the release process. In the periphery, vasopressin (also known as antidiuretic hormone) facilitates distal tubular water reabsorption, while oxytocin stimulates epididymal and uterine muscle contraction. In the hypothalamus, the neurons of the supraoptic and paraventricular nuclei have been found to give off axon collaterals that project within the nuclei, between the nuclei, and to the median

FIGURE 12-1. Molecular sequence of oxytocin and vasopressin, in which amino acid names are symbolized by the standard single letter symbols, and * indicates an amidated C-terminus. (Key to amino acid single letter symbols: A = Ala; R = Arg; N = Asn; D = Asp; B = Asparagine; C = Cys; Q = glutamine; E = Glu; G = Gly; H = His; I = Ile; L = Leu; K = Lys; M = Met; F = Phe; P = Pro; S = Ser; T = Thr; W = Trp; Y = Tyr; V = Val.).

eminence. When these so-called "magnocellular" neurons are recorded from and identified on the basis of antidromic stimulation of their axons in the neurohypophysis, a recurrent inhibition is seen. Tests with antagonists of all other presumed neurotransmitters fail to explain the chemical mediator of this inhibition, and since both oxytocin and vasopressin were found to have potent inhibitory actions on neurons projecting to the neurohypophysis, Nicoll and Barker proposed that the same peptide released from the pituitary into the blood might also function as the transmitter for the recurrent pathway. If this could be demonstrated convincingly, that would considerably defuse the sham conflict between neurohormones and neurotransmitters. Some parvocellular neurons of the supraoptic and paraventricular nuclei also contain oxytocin or vasopressin. Their circuits project either to the median eminence, where at least vasopressin acts as a coreleasing hormone of ACTH, or to other distant targets in the diencephalon, pons, and spinal cord, including the locus ceruleus, and the nucleus of the solitary tract. Additional vasopressin-containing neurons have been identified outside of the hypothalamus in the anterior pro-optic area, and these may be the source of the minute quantities of vasopressin and oxytocin reported within the limbic system.

The behavioral actions of vasopressin are quite impressive, although the mechanisms accounting for them remain unclear. These effects are described in greater detail in Chapter 13.

Analogs of vasopressin and oxytocin have now been developed with selective agonist or antagonist properties; these molecules, often shorter and more stable than the native peptide, should make useful pharmacological probes. Based on the selective actions of vasopressin analogs that act as agonists or antagonists, two subtypes of peripheral receptors have been characterized: the $V_1$ receptors mediate responses of some analogs on arteriolar walls, and the $V_2$ receptors mediate the effects of other analogs on the real tubules. A $V_1$ receptor agonist form of AVP has been reported to maintain the long-term potentiation that can be induced in neurons of the lateral septal nucleus by high-frequency stimulation of the fimbria, a two-way pathway between the septum and the hippocampal formation (see

Chapter 13). The dynamic regulation of OXY and AVP expression is sensitive to gonadal steroids, thus providing a gender-specific neuronal expression pattern that is turned on at puberty and that can be further regulated through reproductive function. Novice neuropeptide researchers have an opportunity left behind by the marauding peptide pioneers: what is the function of oxytocin in the male brain?

The effects of vasopressin analogs on either memory or learning behaviors or on secretory responses mediated through the median eminence do not adhere to either receptor class and may indicate that more subtypes will be characterized.

### The Tachykinin Peptides

In 1931, von Euler and Gaddum discovered an unexpected pharmacologically active substance in extracts of brain and intestine, which they later named Substance P, because it was present in the dried acetone powder of the extract. Although studied intermittently through bioassays, Substance P remained somewhat shaded in obscurity until almost 40 years later, when Leeman and her co-workers purified a sialogogic peptide from hypothalamic extracts, while looking for the still-elusive corticotropin-releasing factor. This sialogogic peptide turned out to have an amino-acid content and pharmacological profile identical to Substance P, and when finally purified, sequenced, and synthesized, it was identified as Substance P, an undecapeptide (Fig. 12-2). The knowledge of the structure and the availability of large amounts of the synthetic material permitted the development of radioimmunoassays and immunocytochemical tests that were then used to map the brain and assay its Substance P content. Substance P is present in small neuronal systems in many parts of the CNS, and on subcellular fractionation it is found in the vesicular layer. It is especially rich in neurons projecting into the substantia gelatinosa of the spinal cord from the dorsal root ganglia and has even been proposed as the transmitter for primary afferent sensory fibers. While it is very potent as a depolarizing substance in direct tests of spinal cord excitability (about 200 times stronger

## The TACHYKININ Peptides

R P K P Q Q F F G L M *   Substance P

D V  P K S  D Q F V G L M *   Kassinin

H K T  D S F V G L M *   Neurokinin A

pE  P S K  D A F I  G L M *   Eledoisin

D M H  D F F V G L M *   Neurokinin A

FIGURE 12-2. Structural homologies between the peptides of the tachykinin family, presented according to the schema of Figure 12-1. pE indicates pyroglutamate.

on a molar basis than GLU), its long duration of action prompted caution in accepting Substance P as the primary sensory transmitter. Other peptides have also been identified in dorsal root ganglion cells, and GLU released from cultures of these cells can also produce a prompt, powerful excitatory action on spinal dorsal horn neurons. If GLU and Substance P were cotransmitters for some sensory fibers, Substance P could be viewed as prolonging and intensifying the transmission into the cord.

Radioimmunoassays and immunocytochemistry also show brain regions other than the spinal cord to be rich in Substance P, especially the substantia nigra, caudate-putamen, amygdala, hypothalamus, and cerebral cortex. Tests with iontophoretic application in these regions generally indicate excitatory actions, again with a long duration. The presence of high levels of Substance P in the striato-nigral fiber system and its disappearance there after interruption of the system have led to the proposal that Substance P is the transmitter for this pathway. This nearly accepted view came into question when maps of autoradiographically localized Substance P binding sites showed no presumptive receptors in the substantia nigra, but many binding sites in parts of brain with much lower content of Substance P. This was taken as another example of a mismatch between endogenous ligand maps and ligand binding site maps, and proved to be a log on the fire of those favoring peptide actions through diffusion. In the human neurologic disease, Huntington's chorea, characterized by profound movement disorders and psychological changes, Substance P levels in the substantia nigra are considerably reduced. Substance P coexists with 5-HT in some raphe neurons projecting to the spinal cord, but there is no 5-HT in the dorsal root ganglia.

Based on smooth muscle bioassays of N-terminally shortened Substance P analogs and early antagonist analogs, an initial subtyping of receptors suggested a P-type, where Substance P was as potent or more potent than other nonmammalian analogs (see Fig. 12-2), and an E-type receptor where one such amphibian peptide, *eledoisin*, was potent, and another *kassinin*, was an even more potent agonist. The search for kassinin-like peptides, using such smooth muscle receptor subtypes as a bioassay, revealed two forms that were clearly not Substance P and have been termed Substance K, and neuro-medin K.

Tachykinin research has been one of the windfall areas benefitting from the application of the molecular biological methods. The cloning of the precursor forms of the three main tachykinin peptides in the mammalian CNS and their first receptor subtypes has helped to clarify their relationships to each other and to other neurotransmitters. There are two mammalian tachykinin genes: The neurokinin A gene (on human chromosome 7) can produce three forms of mRNA through alternative splicing of its many exons; the least prevalent form encodes only substance P, and the other two forms encode both Substance P and neurokinin A (the term the tachykinin nomenclature committee prefers for the peptide previously called Substance K). In general, tissue and cellular distributions of Substance P and neurokinin A have been similar. A second tachykinin gene (located on human chromosome 12) encodes the neurokinin B precursor, and the peptide previously called neuromedin K has been designated neurokinin B. The receptors for all three peptides have been cloned, and their sequence suggests they are all members of the 7-transmembrane domain, G-protein, regulatory type (see Chapter 6).

## Neurotensin

Strictly speaking, neurotensin is not part of the tachykinin family of peptides. However, there is a tenuous historical relationship in that Leeman and co-workers isolated and sequenced the tridecapeptide immediately after their success with Substance P while still looking for the corticotropin-releasing factor. When injected intracisternally, the synthetic neurotensin lowers body temperature, accentuates barbiturate sleeping time, and stimulates the release of growth hormone and prolactin. Again, the availability of large amounts of the synthetic material has provided radioimmunoassays and immunocytochemistry which indicate that the largest amounts of this peptide are to be found in the anterior and basal hypothalamus, in the nucleus accumbens and septum, and in the spinal cord and brainstem within small interneurons of the substantia gelatinosa and motor trigeminal nucleus. Neurotensin colocalizes to some dopamine and some adrenergic neurons. When dopamine stores are depleted by reserpine treatment, immunocytochemically defined neurotensin-containing fibers increase in number visually; however, since neurotensin synthesis is not increased under these conditions, the effect may be explained as decreased release of the coexistent peptide. Neurotensin selectively alters ethanol-induced anesthesia in Long Sleep and Short Sleep lines of mice.

Cellular tests of neurotensin action suggest it may produce excitation, but the mechanisms are not yet defined. In the various peripheral, whole-animal bioassays, the blood pressure receptors and the hyperglycemia receptors appear to read the Arg-Arg dipeptide near the middle of neurotensin. Neurotensin produces diminished responsiveness to painful stimuli and hypothermia after central injection. Studies in humans and dogs show marked increases in neurotensin-like material circulating in plasma after fatty meals.

## Glucagon-related Peptides

Vasoactive intestinal polypeptide (VIP), a peptide composed of twenty-nine amino acids, was originally isolated from porcine intestine and named for its ability to alter enteric blood flow. Establishment of its sequence revealed marked structural similarities to glucagon, secretin, and another peptide of gastric origin which inhibits gastric muscular contraction (GIP). These structural similarities constitute the basis of what is presumed to be a peptide family (see Fig. 12-3). The development of synthetic VIP for preparation of immunoassays and cellular localization revealed that VIP exists independently of its cousins in gut and pancreas and showed that VIP was prominent in many regions of the autonomic and central nervous system. In parasympathetic nerves to the cat salivary gland, VIP coexists with acetylcholine and is apparently released with ACh as part of an integrated command to activate secretion and to increase blood flow through the gland. In the CNS, VIP-reactive neurons are among the most numerous of the chemically defined cells of the neocortex, and they exhibit there a very narrow radial orientation, suggesting that they innervate cellular targets located wholly within a single cortical column assembly. (See Fig. 12-4.) In peripheral structures, VIP-reactive nerves innervate gut, especially sphincter regions, as well as lung and possibly even the thyroid gland. Preliminary tests on neuronal activity suggest that VIP excites; biochemical tests show that it is able to activate synthesis of cyclic AMP, an action that in the gut is blocked by somatostatin. A very

## GLUCAGON-RELATED PEPTIDES

| | |
|---|---|
| **H S D A V F T D N Y T R L R K O M A V K K Y L N S I L N**≢ | V I P |
| **H A D G V F T S D F S R L L G Q L S A K K Y L E S L I**∗ | P H I 27 |
| **H A D G V F T S D F S K L L G Q L S A K K Y L E S L M** ∗ | P H M 27 |
| Y A D I F T N S Y R K V L G Q L S A R K L L Q D --- | G H R H$_{1-24}$ |
| **H S Q G T F T S D Y S K Y L D S R R A Q D F V Q W L M N T** | Glucagon |
| **H S D G T F Y S E L S R L R D S A R L Q R L L Q G L V**∗ | Secretin |

FIGURE 12-3. The glucagon-related peptide family represented by their single-letter amino acid symbols. The sequences of PHI-27, PHM-27, growth hormone-releasing hormone 1−24, and glucagon and secretin that match those of VIP are indicated in bold letters. For an interesting exercise, the reader may wish to construct a complementary table in which matches to glucagon are highlighted.

FIGURE 12-4. Ultrastructural immunoperoxidase localization of vasoactive intestinal polypeptide in neurons of the rat cerebral cortex. At left, immunoreactivity is seen at the perimeter of a small dendrite of the cortex that can clearly be seen receiving synaptic contacts from several nonreactive axon terminals. At right, immunoreactivity in the cortex can also be seen within two axon terminals; the upper one is making a symmetrical synaptic junction on a large, nonimmunoreactive dendrite, presumably of a pyramidal neuron. Calibration bars = 0.5 μ in both micrographs. (Unpublished micrographs from Battenberg and Bloom, Scripps Clinic)

pernicious gut cancer that actively secretes VIP has been described, but no other known disease states involving this peptide have yet been documented.

Additional members were added to this important family of peptides when Guillemin and colleagues isolated the long-sought growth hormone-releasing hormone (GHRH) peptide and recognized the homologous shared amino acid sequences. The latest members of the family are termed PHI-27 and PHM-27, names that reflect their size, 27 amino acids long, and the one-letter initials of their N-terminal (H = Histidine) and C-terminal (isoleucine or methionine) peptides (where P stands for "peptide," not proline). PHI-27 was initially isolated by Mutt and associates from gut extracts while searching for other C-terminally amidated peptides, a property all active members of this family share. PHM-27 was identified from the deduced sequence of the pro-VIP mRNA in cloning experiments. GHRH has a relatively limited neuronal distribution concentrated in the hypothalamus and median eminence. No cellular maps for PHI or PHM in brain have yet been reported.

To reverse a trend, molecular cloning of the mRNA for the precursor of secretin, another member of this peptide superfamily, indicates that this specific peptide is not actually found in the brain, as had been proposed based on immunocytochemistry with polyclonal antibodies some years ago.

## Pancreatic Polypeptide-related Peptides

The pancreatic polypeptides were recognized in extracts of pancreatic islets in the mid-1970s, and those from pigeon, pig, and human pancreas were all found to be highly homologous 36-residue peptides with amidated C-termini (see Fig. 12-5). Antisera against these peptides recognized cells and fibers in the autonomic and CNS, but these immunocytochemical observations were rightly qualified as "pancreatic polypeptide-like immunoreactivity," because when the same sera were used in their highly dilute form for radioimmunoassay, only scant extractable material was detected. When Mutt and Tatemoto implemented their chemical isolation strategy centered on the detection of novel C-terminally amidated gut and brain peptides, they soon were able to announce the amino-acid sequences of two more members of this family. The first one, found in gut, was given the name PYY (a neuropeptide with tyrosine (single-letter amino acid symbol "Y") residues at both the N- and C-termini). However, the one found in brain also had the same length, and the same N- and C-terminal tyrosines, with slight internal amino acid substitutions, and has been termed NPY. In rapid order, this peptide's distribution was described in rodent and human brains, and

## PANCREATIC POLYPEPTIDES

| | |
|---|---|
| **Y**PSKPDNPGEDAPAE DLAR**Y**YSA LRHYINL ITRQR**Y**ᕼ | NPY |
| **Y**PA KPEAPGQN AS PQQLS RYYAS LRH**Y**LNLVTRQR**Y**ᕼ | PYY |
| G P SQP T**Y** PGDDAP**V**EDLI RF**Y**DN LQQ**Y**LN**V**VTRHR**Y**ᕼ | APP |
| AP L EP V**Y**PGD N AT PEQMAQ**Y**AAD LRR**Y**INM**L**TRPR**Y**ᕼ | HPP |

FIGURE 12-5. The pancreatic polypeptide family represented by their single-letter amino acid symbols. The sequences of peptide YY (PYY), avian pancreatic polypeptide (APP), and human pancreatic polypeptide (HPP) that match those of NPY are indicated in bold letters.

its regional content was quantified, showing NPY to form one of the most extensive of the peptide systems, with very high amounts in the hypothalamus, limbic system, and neocortex—not to mention some loosely correlated losses in some schizophrenics. In many places, including the autonomic nervous system, NPY coexists with either norepinephrine or epinephrine. NPY increases the sensitivity of sympathetically innervated smooth muscle to norepinephrine and is one of the most potent natural vasoconstrictors known.

Neuropeptide Y, especially in the autonomic nervous system, also exhibits the phenomenon of postrelease signals arising from shortened versions of the secreted peptide. Two types of NPY receptors have been defined; the N-terminally shorter form of NPY reacts exclusively at the $Y_2$ site, which has been found to be enriched presynaptically where it may impose constraints on the release of coexisting norepinephrine.

### Opioid Peptides

An "endorphin" is any "endogenous substance" (i.e., one naturally formed in the living animal) which exhibits pharmacological properties of morphine. When this term was first coined in mid-1975, it was a useful abstraction to cover "morphine-like factors," from brain extracts and spinal fluids that were active in opiate ligand-displacement assays or opiate-sensitive smooth muscle assays. Within a year, a highly competitive effort resulted in the purification, isolation, sequencing, and synthetic replication not only of one but of nearly a half-dozen peptides that deserved the term endorphin. Subsequent research has greatly clarified the molecular and genomic relationships between the three major branches of the opioid peptide greater family (see Fig. 12-6): the proopiomelanocortin (POMC)-derived peptides, the proenkephalin-derived peptides, and the prodynorphin-derived peptides. Other structurally related natural pep-

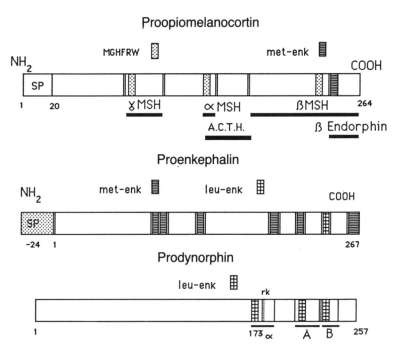

FIGURE 12-6. Structural relationships among the pro-hormone, precursor forms of the three major branches of the opioid peptides, depicted as a bar diagram, whose length in amino acid residues is indicated by the small number at the corresponding C-termini. The location of the repeating peptide sequences are indicated. Basic amino-acid sequences that constitute consensus cleavage sites for processing are indicated as single or double vertical lines within the bar. Proopiomelanocortin and proenkephalin have consensus signal peptides indicated at their N-termini.

tides lack opioid receptor activity (such as the invertebrate cardioac-celeratory peptide FMRF-amide); furthermore, some opioid-acting peptides have been found "exogenously" in milk and in plant proteins and have been called "exorphins." These developments have lead activists in the field to give the entire group of structures a more general name, such as endogenous opioid peptides. This also spares those who prefer to study enkephalin and dynorphin peptides from the burden of seeming to carry the endorphin banner.

The incredible explosion of work on this class of peptides began with attempts to isolate and characterize the receptor to opiates as part of a molecular biological approach to the question of narcotic addiction. When specific binding assays were developed, substantial evidence was accumulated to indicate that a high-affinity binding site in synaptic membranes showed stereo-selective opioid recognition properties. The receptor showed Na-sensitive allosteric-like affinity shifts (i.e., in the presence of Na, agonists show reduced affinity) but was not altered in number or affinity during narcotic dependence or withdrawal.

A whole new approach to neurotransmitter identification took shape when Hughes, Kosterlitz, and their colleagues in Aberdeen demonstrated that extracts of brain contain a substance that can compete in the opiate receptor assays and show opioid activity in in vitro smooth-muscle bioassays. In late 1975, this endogenous opioid activity was attributed to two pentapeptides, named enkephalins, which shared a common tetrapeptide sequence, YGGF, varying only in the C-terminal position: hence, they were called Met$^5$-enkephalin and Leu$^5$-enkephalin. Perhaps even more dramatic than the announcement that the brain contained not one but two opioid peptides was the realization that the entire structure of Met$^5$-enkephalin is contained within a 91-amino-acid pituitary hormone, β-lipotropin (β-LPH), whose isolation and sequence was reported several years earlier by C. H. Li, but whose function was never really very clear.

Several groups then reported isolation, purification, chemical structures, and synthetic confirmation of three additional endorphin peptides: α-endorphin (β-LPH$_{61-76}$), γ-endorphin (β-LPH$_{61-77}$) and β-endorphin (β-LPH$_{61-91}$; also called "C-fragment"). Numerous claims and counterclaims were parried across the symposium stages for several months as to one person's peptide being another person's artifact or precursor. Eventually, this was clarified.

CHEMICAL AND CELLULAR RELATIONSHIPS AMONG THE OPIOID PEPTIDES

1. *The proopiomelanocortin (POMC) peptides* are expressed independently in the anterior pituitary, the intermediate lobe of the pituitary, and one main cluster of neurons in the area of the arcuate nucleus of the hypothalamus. The major endorphin agonist produced from POMC is the 31-amino-acid C-terminal fragment, β-endorphin, the most potent of the natural opioids. N-terminal fragments of β-endorphin are much less potent, and analogs with no N-terminal tyrosine (so-called des-Tyr versions) lose all opioid activity, although in some hands, such des-Tyr peptides are reputed to be active behaviorally. In the corticotropin-secreting cells of the anterior pituitary, POMC is processed largely to corticotropin and to an inactive form of β-endorphin; whereas in intermediate lobe cells and arcuate neurons, the same precursor is processed to α-MSH and active β-endorphin. A third MSH-containing heptapeptide component, discovered during the cloning and sequencing of the POMC mRNA, suggests that yet another end product may be possible.

2. *The enkephalin pentapeptides*, Met$^5$-enkephalin and Leu$^5$-enkephalin are expressed in wholly separate neuronal systems from the POMC neurons and are much more pervasively distributed throughout the central and peripheral nervous systems, including the adrenal medulla and enteric nervous system. The cloning and sequencing of the mRNA for the proenkephalin, starting with mRNA from adrenal medullary tissue, produced an unexpected dividend in that the precursor exhibits multiple copies of the two peptides in almost exactly the 6:1 ratio of Met$^5$- to Leu$^5$-enkephalins that had been described in regional brain and gut assays: this solved the mystery of the two similar peptides.

3. *The prodynorphin peptides* consist of C-terminally extended forms of Leu$^5$-enkephalin arising from a different gene and from a different mRNA that encodes for production of four major peptides, termed dynorphin A, dynorphin B, and two neoendorphins, α and β. These C-terminally extended peptides all act as potent opioid agonists without cleavage down to the enkephalin pentapeptide form, and on mapping they were found to represent a third separated series of rather generally distributed central and peripheral neurons.

Each of the separate classes of neurons containing β-endorphin, enkephalin, or dynorphin peptides have distinct morphological features (see Fig. 12-7). The β-endorphin-containing neurons are long projection systems that fall within the general endocrine-oriented systems of the medial hypothalamus, diencephalon, and pons. The proenkephalin-derived peptides and the prodynorphin-derived peptides are generally found in neurons with modest to short projections, groups of which are widespread. In some regions the enkephalin-derived and dynorphin-derived peptides show intriguing relationships. For example, enkephalin-containing neurons project from the entorhinal cortex to the molecular layer of the dentate gyrus of the hippocampus, while dynorphin-containing-neurons project from the dentate gyrus to the CA$_3$ pyramidal cells. In the spinal cord, intrinsic interneurons contain dynorphin peptides, while descending long axons from the pons and medulla contain enkephalin peptides. In addition, all these peptide systems presumably contain other nonpeptidic transmitters that have not yet been rigorously identified as well as some peptides that have (see Table 12-1). The most clearcut evidence suggests functional relationships between opioid peptide systems and catecholamines in the medullary systems regulating cardiovascular function (see Fig. 12-7).

*Cellular Effects*

Given these twists and turns at the molecular level, analysis of the effects of synthetic endorphins at the cellular level may well be expected to be preliminary, since it remains unclear just which pep-

FIGURE 12-7. An ultrastructural basis for functional interaction between central opioid-containing neurons and central catecholamine neurons is provided by this dual label, autoradiography and immunocytochemistry. Nerve terminals exhibit Leu-enkephalin immunoreactivity (immunoperoxidase reaction around many small lucent vesicles in terminals labelled LE-T), and one also exhibits tyrosine hydroxylase immunoreactivity (small autoradiographic grains; terminal labeled LE+TH-T). The latter is making a symmetric synaptic contact on a dendrite (TH-D) bearing many autoradiographic grains, indicating extensive tyrosine hydroxylase content. Scale bar lower right = 0.5m. (Modified from Milner, Pickel, and Reis, *J. Neurosci.* 9, 2114–2130, 1989)

tides should be tested on which target cells. Currently, there are at least four schemes of endorphin–receptor classifications based on the comparative actions of morphine or of morphine-like drugs with mixed agonist–antagonist actions on the dog spinal cord (the μ, κ, and σ scheme of Martin and Gilbert), or on the relative effects of endogenous and synthetic opioids on various smooth muscle in vitro assays (the μ and δ scheme of Kosterlitz, or the μ, δ; and ε scheme of Herz), or on, alternatively, GTP-modifiable ligand binding. One of the most remarkable of these features of the partially characterized endorphin "receptor" schemes is how poorly they equate with the endorphin or enkephalin-like peptide circuits, and how little any of them are affected by chronic exposure to morphine.

The best concordance between receptor subtypes and opioid peptide systems stems from the studies of dynorphin-derived peptides by Goldstein and Chavkin, which emphasized the ability of these peptides to act on the κ type of opioid receptor site. This is most apparent in studies of the gut receptors, but is supported by studies on central neurons as well. Naloxone, the workhorse antagonist for all opioid receptors, has far more potent ability to reverse μ and δ opioid actions, but at 10-fold higher doses it will also antagonize κ sites. When the prodynorphin-derived peptides found within the hippocampus are evaluated for their relative content and potency, the most potent are the least prevalent and vice versa. Although none of the receptors has yet been purified completely, a 500-fold enrichment of the μ-receptor from rat brain membranes discriminates its macromolecular properties from the δ-receptor.

A minor disappointment in the field of opioid peptide research has been its failure to deliver on the promise of providing insight into the nature of drug dependence. Despite many attempts, little significant change in the concentrations of any of the opioid peptides or their receptors could be detected with drug dependence. Again, molecular biological methods have been helpful; more recent studies of morphine-dosed animals show initial increases in β-endorphin mRNAs, followed by a new equilibrium at levels near normal. The added β-endorphin gene product found under these conditions is a C-terminally shortened form that may be either a very weak agonist or, more interestingly, an opioid antagonist. Indeed, synthetic versions of the peptide, β-endorphin 1-27, identified on the basis of molecular sizing and radioimmunoassays, does antagonize morphine analgesia. Chronic naltrexone treatments, which upregulate ligand binding sites for the shorter opioid peptides, also increase their mRNAs by several-fold in the rat striatum and to lesser degrees in other opioid-sensitive brain regions; however, the concentration of peptides encoded by the mRNAs is not changed.

The membrane mechanisms underlying the activation of the various classes of opioid receptors are not well understood. Some studies suggest they may block the activation of adenylate cyclase, and that such effects may underlie the chronic tolerance that develops with repeated dosing. Intracellular recordings of myenteric ganglionic neurons and of locus ceruleus neurons in vitro indicate that these cells respond by hyperpolarization to acute administration of opioids mediated by an increased $K^+$ conductance that secondarily depresses Ca-dependent spike activity. In the dorsal horn, neither membrane potential nor conductance are impressively altered, but responsiveness to depolarizing synaptic potentials is reduced.

Iontophoretic tests with enkephalins and β-endorphin suggest that neurons throughout the CNS can be influenced by these peptides at naloxone-sensitive receptors; in general, responses tend to be depressant, except in the hippocampus where excitatory actions are so profound that hippocampal seizures can be induced. However, the mechanism of this excitation is the exception which proves the rule, as it is based on inhibition on *inhibitory* interneurons and produces excitation by disinhibition. In such tests, all endorphins show qualitatively equivalent effects and similar onset of actions; effects of β-endorphin appear to be more potent and longer lasting, which may be due to its slower hydrolysis. Analogs in which cleavage of the N-terminal dipeptide bond is delayed by substitution of a D-Ala are more long lasting, while peptides with no N-terminal Tyr are much weaker.

*Behavioral Effects*

It is in terms of behavior that the effects of these peptides have attracted growing attention. Early efforts were made to answer the question of morphine substitution and were somewhat disappointing in showing that the enkephalins produced only transient analgesia after direct intracerebroventricular injection; in such tests β-endorphin is 50–100 times more potent than morphine on a molar basis. In mice, β-endorphin produces some significant analgesia after intravenous injection, but the dose required is about 1,000 times that needed on central injection, and the duration of effect after peripheral injection is much shorter.

Morphine-dependent rats show cross-tolerance to all opioid peptides; similarly, animals given continuous injections of endorphin or enkephalin show tolerance and also show withdrawal signs when given naloxone. The fact that blood-borne peptides do not penetrate into the brain well or survive the gauntlet of peptidases to which they are exposed in the process has spurred the search for more effective analogs. However, the real power of such analogs may not be realized until the cellular mechanisms of the several opioid peptide-containing systems are better evaluated.

The sheer number of whole animal effects that have been interpreted as endorphinergic physiology on the basis of naloxone effects has grown considerably but remains open to more comprehensive analysis. Among the proposed physiological properties that may be regulated by one or another of the endorphin substances are blood pressure, temperature, feeding, sexual activity, and lymphocyte mitosis, along with pain perception and memory. All this seems like a lot to ask of one peptide. But then, who are we to ask what a peptide may—or can—do for us? As we said before, don't blink or you'll miss the next blazing development.

INDIVIDUAL PEPTIDES WORTH TRACKING

We conclude this chapter with brief comments on a few of the other neuroactive peptides that are under active investigation. Around those we have selected, bodies of research are consolidating and the neuropharmacological implications seem strong.

*Somatostatin (Somatotropin Release-inhibiting Factor)*

In 1971, workers began to look for other goodies in their hard-won hypothalamic extracts. Vale, Brazeau, and Guillemin tried their extracts for potency in releasing growth hormone from long-term cultured anterior pituitary cells and found to their amazement a factor that inhibited even basal growth hormone release in minute amounts. They named this factor somatostatin. Isolation and purification studies eventually culminated in the characterization of this molecule as a tetradecapeptide with disulfide bridge between $Cys^3$ and $Cys^{14}$ (Fig. 12-8). Radioimmunoassays, immunocytochemistry, and whole-animal tests of the synthetic peptide made it clear that somatostatin was doing more than "just" inhibiting growth hormone release. Somatostatin was found to be widely distributed in the gastrointestinal tract and pancreatic islets, localized in the latter tissue to the delta cells by immunocytochemistry. Somatostatin in islets can apparently suppress the release of both glucagon and insulin, and in diabetic humans, who have no insulin, suppression of glucagon can be an important element in determining insulin requirements. The mechanisms of this suppression are not known but may be similar to the effect of somatostatin on growth hormone release from pituitary, an action accompanied by suppression of TSH release.

FIGURE 12-8. Structure of the prohormone form of somatostatin, with the location and sequence of the 28-amino-acid residue form at the C-terminus, and the relative sequences and locations of the different forms of somatostatin indicated.

When somatostatin is injected intracerebroventricularly, animals show decreased spontaneous motor activity, reduced sensitivity to barbiturates, loss of slow wave and REM sleep, and increased appetite. Radioimmunoassays and immunocytochemistry of rat brain regions show that somatostatin is largely concentrated in the mediobasal hypothalamus, with much smaller amounts present in a few other brain regions (see Fig. 12-9). Immunocytochemical studies led to the surprising finding that somatostatin-reactive cells and fibers are also present in dorsal root ganglia, in the autonomic plexi of the intestine, and in the amygdala and neocortex. Avian and amphibian brains contain considerably more somatostatin than mammalian brains: physiological tests on the isolated frog spinal cord suggest that it

FIGURE 12-9. Ultrastructural immunoperoxidase localization of somatostatin in a nerve terminal making synaptic contact with an unreactive small dendritic spine in the rat neocortex. Calibration bar = 0.5 μ. (Unpublished micrographs from Battenberg and Bloom, Scripps Clinic)

may facilitate the transmission of dorsal root reflexes after a long latent period. Iontophoretic tests on rat neurons indicate a relatively common depressant action that is brisk in onset and termination. At the level of cellular electrophysiology, somatostatin hyperpolarizes neurons in a potent manner and can dynamically open the so-called "M" current channel that cholinergic muscarinic receptors open in order to excite hippocampal and other neurons. The net result of somatostatin's actions in the intact brain is to enhance responsiveness to acetylcholine. The important missing datum is what somatostatin does to the responses to GABA, its frequent but not universal co-existence partner.

An endogenous large somatostatin, extended at the N-terminus by an additional 14 amino acids also exists in both brain and gut, and shares equipotency for many somatostatin actions. In rodent and primate neocortex, the N-terminally extended forms reveal a far more extensive neuronal density, which at least overlaps with the intrinsic GABA-ergic cortical neurons. In early-onset Alzheimer's disease, cortical somatostatin content is depleted, and somatostatin-28 immunoreactive neuritic processes are involved in the formation of the hallmark Alzheimers lesion, the plaque. Cysteamine, a drug developed to treat the metabolic disorder known as cystinosis, will selectively deplete somatostatin-14 without altering brain levels of somatostatin-28 or somatostatin-28 [1–12], suggesting that these peptides may be stored in separable subcellular compartments.

Although somatostatin was an unexpected by-product of the race to identify the positive regulators of anterior pituitary release, its pharmacological and diagnostic potentials promise an important future. Somatostatin deficits in cerebrospinal fluid have been linked to affective disorder and to Alzheimer's disease. Long-lasting analogs of somatostatin have already been clinically applied in the control of pituitary hypersecretion of growth hormone. The widespread distribution of somatostatin in the brain strongly suggests that it may be difficult to influence receptors in a selective manner for disorders based on regional alterations; but, then, whoever said it would be easy to make a good new drug?

*Cholecystokinin (CCK)*

Among the gut hormones with the longest histories are gastrin and cholecystokinin (CCK). Subsequently, when their molecular structures were determined, a striking homology was revealed between the C-termini (Fig. 12-10). After some confusing interludes, it became recognized that the gastrinlike material extractable from nervous tissue was caused by antisera cross-reacting with the C-terminal octapeptide of CCK, whose tyrosine version is sulfated. Although the exact species of the peptide present in brain is still in some chaos, much evidence favors the view that the C-terminal octapeptide exists as a separate entity and is released from nerves. CCK-like material coexists with dopamine in nerve cells of the ventrotegmental area and in their terminals in the nucleus accumbens. A minimum amount of data exist as to cellular action which generally causes responsive cells to fire more rapidly. Immune staining patterns also reveal this peptide to exist within numerous small GABA-containing intracortical neurons. Because CCK is released from distended intestines, a minor controversy has developed around its ability to reduce appetite in experimental animals and its possible role in gut and in cortex to regulate eating. Although the picture is yet far from complete, it is of interest that the "satiety" effects of peripherally injected

SQEPPISLDLTFHLLREVLEMTKADQLAQQAHSNRKLDIA    C R F (OVINE)
SEEPPISLDLTFHLLREVLEMARAEQLAQQAHSNRKMEII    C R F (RAT)
pEGPPISIDLSLELLRKMIEIEKQEKEKQQAANNRLLDTI    SAUVAGINE


SCNTATCVTHRLAGLLSRSGGVVKDNFVPTNVGSEAF*    "C G R P"

DYMGWMDF*    CCK$_8$

FIGURE 12-10. The homologies between ovine and rodent corticotropin-releasing factor and sauvagine are indicated by bold single-letter amino acid symbols. Below are indicated the amino acid sequences of calcitonin gene-related peptide (CGRP) and of the C-terminal octapeptide of cholecystokinin, with a sulfated tyrosine at position 2. pE indicates pyroglutamate.

CCK are blocked when the vagus nerve is cut below the diaphragm. While an alternative drug approach to dietary control is clearly a desirable goal, it has not yet become clear how these data fit that need. Two interesting, but as yet unexplained, pharmacological interactions deserve continued monitoring. In iontophoretic tests on spontaneously active hippocampal pyramidal cells, CCK-8 shows a potent ability to activate firing, an action that is compatible with the CCK contained within the dentate granule cell mossy fiber synapses to these neurons. Low doses of systemic or iontophoretically administered benzodiazepines selectively block CCK-induced activation without altering the excitatory effects of enkephalin or acetylcholine. In separate lines of investigation, largely at the behavioral level, systemic CCK proved to have opiate antagonistic actions depressing opiate analgesia, but without any direct effects on opioid receptors. When rats were actively immunized against CCK, exogenous opiates had an enhanced initial potency, but tolerance still developed with repeated doses of opiates. Although pain researchers have yet to be convinced that the opposing relationships between CCK and opioid actions are physiologically interesting, it is already clear that the new, potent nonpeptide inhibitors of CCK are useful in potentiating responses to opiate drugs.

*Angiotensin II*

Present evidence suggests that we should keep an open mind as to just which roman numerals are used to refer to the "naturally stored" and "naturally released" forms of this peptide, whose metabolism comes across as a shaggy dog story yet vividly illustrates the mode in which at least one group of active peptides is synthesized and released. Until a few years ago, the role of angiotensin was thought to be mainly the peripheral modulation of blood pressure. Angiotensin (Fig. 12-11) was the name given to a vasoconstricting decapeptide formed in blood from an $\alpha$-2 hepatic globulin by the proteolytic enzyme renin; as its name suggests, renin is made and secreted by specialized cells of the kidney. However, the decapeptide, now termed Angiotensin I, is converted to an octapeptide,

Angiotensinogen (liver)

D R V Y I H P F H L L V Y S (Protein)

Renin ↑ (kidney)

Angiotensin I

D R V Y I H P F H L

Angiotensin–Converting ↑ (plasma, liver,

Enzyme              nerve)

Angiotensin II

D R V Y I H P F

↑ Aspartate Amino Peptidase

Angiotensin III

R V Y I H P F

FIGURE 12-11. The angiotensin family and the relationships between specific cleavage enzyme actions and derived peptide products.

Angiotensin II, with a similar pharmacological profile of higher intrinsic activity through a "converting enzyme" that selectively cleaves off the C-terminal dipeptide. Subsequently, Angiotensin III (a natural N-des-Asp Angiotensin II) was identified; it is even more potent and may more readily traverse biological membranes. All of the substrates and enzymes needed for these conversions of angiotensin have been described as occurring in the brain. Radioimmunoassays, immunocytochemistry, and receptor displacement studies all indicate the presence of neural systems containing or responding to one or another of these peptides. The angiotensin system appears to be relatively concentrated in the periventricular zone, and the specialized innervated organs that characterize this zone—the area postrema, pineal, subfornical, and subcommisural organs, as well as the intermediate lobe of the pituitary, and others. These organs lie within the recesses of the brain but are on the blood side of the blood—brain barrier.

Circulating Angiotensin II can indeed modify blood pressure and induce secretion of aldosterone. With the development of angiotensin-converting enzyme inhibitors, scientists have been able to realize one of the major ambitions of future drug development, namely, computer modeling drugs to fit the active catalytic pockets of purified peptide-processing enzymes. This class of drugs has been shown to be very effective, alone or with low doses of diuretics, in regulating hypertension through direct vascular actions. The central effect that has generally caught the attention of pharmacologists is its ability to produce profound drinking behavior when injected in physiological (i.e., picomol) amounts into the third ventricle. Although angiotensin can elicit drinking, it is probably not the "drinking" hormone since circulating levels do not correlate with drinking activity. Iontophoretic studies have shown that angiotensin excites the neuronal-like cells of the subfornical organ. Neurons in the supraoptic nucleus are also excited by Angiotensin II, which may in part explain how central or peripheral administration of angiotensin can result in vasopressin release from the neurohypophysis. In the long-term nephrectomized rat and dog, immunocytochemically detectable Angiotensin II is present in small amounts throughout the diencephalon, pons, and brain stem, but the possible role these presumed neurons may have in central cardiovascular regulation or other functions has only recently been suggested on the basis of long-acting inhibitors of angiotensin-converting enzyme. An amazing development in the saga of how angiotensin controls the cells that respond to it was the recognition that in cell lines expressing the mas oncogene, Angiotensin II is such a potent activator of this protein's ability to phosphorylate specific protein substrates that it has been interpreted as the most probable natural regulator of the normal cellular proto-oncogene.

## Calcitonin Gene-related Peptide

Calcitonin is a 32-amino-acid peptide hormone secreted by special cells in the thyroid gland whose function is to oppose parathormone and increase the urinary excretion of $Ca^{2+}$ and $PO_4$. The cells that make this hormone, the C cells, are embryologically regarded as arising from neural crest. However, this ancestral lineage would not have merited inclusion of the hormone in this edition were it not for the results of studies originally carried out on a very undifferentiated thyroid carcinoma as part of a plan to characterize the genomic relationships between the segments of DNA encoding the calcitonin prohormone. Under certain conditions of growth in culture, the thyroid carcinoma cells were observed to produce additional mRNA forms that contained part of a series of amino acids encoded by the procalcitonin mRNA, but that differed at their carboxy terminus where the calcitonin occurs. Analysis of the genomic relationship between the exons encoding the segments of the mRNA revealed that the new form of the calcitonin gene-related prohormone contained a potentially novel peptide, termed calcitonin gene-related peptide (CGRP), which bore no significant structural similarity to calcitonin. Antisera were then raised to a synthetic version of the predicted 37-amino acid-long peptide (see Fig. 12-10). The antisera as well as the cDNA forms of the CGRP mRNA were then used to determine whether this previously unexpected peptide was actually expressed in normal tissues. Tests on the hypothalamus and on the trigeminal sensory ganglion were positive, just as they were in other neuronal systems when the rat nervous system was mapped more completely. The exact mechanisms of mRNA processing by which the same primary RNA transcript of the calcitonin CGRP gene can give rise to calcitonin in thyroid C cells and to CGRP in neurons remain unclear. However, the concept of "alternative" RNA processing may underlie one part of the peptide coexistence puzzle and clearly represents a mechanism by which a limited number of peptide-encoding gene sequences can be variably arranged into different end products in different cell types. Early physiological tests of CGRP indicate that it is an extremely potent direct vasodilator (at femtomolar doses) but inactive on calcitonin-responsive peripheral cells. No actions on central neurons have yet been reported.

### Corticotropin-releasing Factor

The search for the corticotropin-releasing factor ended in 1981 when Wylie Vale and colleagues completed the purification and sequence analysis of the peptide taken from extracts of sheep hypothalamus. Thus ended a three-decade-long search for a mystery factor that put the secretion of corticotropin and other anterior pituitary hormones under neuronal control and allowed the brain to replace the pituitary as the master gland of the body. The remaining member of the original four horsemen of the hypophysiotrophic hypothalamic control system was lassoed a year later when Vale and Roger Guillemin independently reported the isolation, sequencing, and synthetic replication of growth hormone-releasing hormone. Nonparticipants in this highly competitive struggle probably had mixed emotions when these quests ended, since along the way the world of neuropeptide discovery was at least triply blessed first by Substance P, then somatostatin, and eventually neurotensin, all of which were discovered by teams intent on CRF.

When CRF was in hand, it turned out to be an interesting 41-amino-acid peptide (see Fig. 12-10) structurally related to a rather obscure frog skin peptide, sauvagine, and to another peptide, termed *urotensin*, obtained from an obscure peripheral organ, the urohypophysis of certain fish. The cellular origin of the mammalian CRF was traced to that portion of the paraventricular nucleus that projects to the median eminence, but not into the posterior pituitary. Later, these and other CRF-containing circuits were identified as innervating a very extensive group of neurons in the pons and medulla, perhaps representing a stress-related circuitry. CRF is an extremely potent ACTH secretogogue, but its effects are significantly augmented by vasopressin (produced by the adjacent magnocellular paraventricular neurons) and by norepinephrine and angiotensin.

In addition to its premier action in regulation of corticotropin secretion, synthetic CRF has equally potent effects on neurons in vitro and in vivo, increasing the frequency of action potentials in cells that fire in bursts, such as the hippocampal pyramidal cells. Even modest doses of the peptide can induce seizurelike activity within the limbic system. At still smaller doses given intracerebroventricularly, CRF is a potent activator of spontaneous locomotion, and can also produce an "anxiogenic" response (opposite to the effects of antianxiety drugs like benzodiazepines and ethanol) in different behavior tests. Clearly, the complete physiological effects of CRF at the pituitary and at other neuronal sites represent a much more comprehensive basis for the mobilization of bodily systems during stress. The Vale group has now developed a very potent CRF antagonist in the form of an N-terminally shortened CRF 9-41. The ability of this peptide, on intracerebral administration, to reverse many of the locomotor, thermoregulatory, and autonomic effects of CRF has already established the utility of this approach and greatly extended the use of antibodies to CRF as tentative antagonists within the extracranial circulation. More extended examinations of the role of stress-related phenomena indicate that CRF may well be one of the most overworked of the brain's potent peptides, and a fair target for still more selective drug development.

## A Reader's Guide to Peptide Poaching

Until more is learned about the functions, sites, and mechanisms of action of any one peptide, we will have trouble formulating even tentative roles for these substances in neurotransmitter-neurohormonal regulation of central drug actions.

As the story of neuroactive peptides unfolds (the sheer number of peptides available for pursuit makes the going slower owing to the division of the available work force), interested students should be alert for answers to the following questions: Are there general patterns of circuitry? Are specific peptidases amenable to selective pharmacological intervention, or do neuronal and glial peptidases read only the dipeptides, whose bonds they are about to cleave? Do the peptides act presynaptically, postsynaptically, or at both sites? How are peptidases specifically activated either to release neuroactive peptides from precursors or to terminate the activity of the peptide? Can the peptides modulate the release or response to transmitters of other neurons or those with which they coexist in a given neuron? Can the promise of peptide chemistry deliver useful antagonists to prove identity of receptors with nerve pathway stimulation? Does the presence of receptors to other centrally active drugs indicate that still more endogenous peptides should be sought?

An endogenous peptide ligand has now been extensively described that can displace benzodiazepine from its binding sites on brain membranes and has, surprisingly, the pharmacological profile of an inverse agonist (that is, causes actions that are pro-conflict, pro-seizure, and anti-GABA, in contrast to the classical pharmacology of benzodiazepines). At least three different genes seem capable of expressing this peptide segment, and the nature of the family emerging here may well hold still more surprises. The success of this latest application of the "why is there such a selective receptor for this drug?" approach that spawned opioid peptides and now the brain's own benzodiazepine displacer has whetted appetites for an endogenous ligand for the PCP receptor.

Another trend sure to provide provocative claims—if not actual hard data—in the near future is the constant hinting about a molecular exchange between the immune system and the nervous system. Existing data document that regulatory peptides that were first discovered in neurons also work within some of the complex regulatory cascades in the immune system. Furthermore, some peptide signals of the immune system may also be expressed by neurons; for the moment, this renders arguments about cross-talk between immune cells and neurons less appealing than the idea of a universal system of peptide-mediated molecular events that serve to fine-tune function within the cells that compose many of the body's complex regulatory networks. Stay tuned, the data flow fast.

## SELECTED REFERENCES
### General Sources

Bloom, F. E. (1990). Peptides: Regulators of cell function in brain and beyond. In: *FIDIA Research Foundation Neuroscience Award Lectures*, Vol. 4, pp. 229–268. Raven Press, New York.

Hökfelt, T., O. Johansson, A. Ljüngdahl, J. M. Lundberg, and M. Schültzberg (1980). Peptidergic neurones. *Nature 284*, 515–521.

Hökfelt, T., Fuxe, K., and Pernow, B. (eds.) (1986). Vol. 68. Coexistence of neuronal messengers—A new principle in chemical transmission. In *Advances in Brain Research*. Elsevier Science Publishing, New York.

Krieger, D. T., M. J. Brownstein, and J. B. Martin, eds. (1983). *Brain Peptides*. Wiley, New York.

Mocchetti, I. and E. Costa (1987). In vivo studies of the regulation of neuropeptide stores in structures of the rat brain. *Neuropharmacology 26*(7B), 855–62.

Sherman, T. G., H. Akil and S. J. Watson (1989). The molecular biology of neuropeptides. *Disc. Neurosci.* 6, 1–58.

Tuominen, M. and J. Leppaluoto (1987). Peptides and neurotransmission in the central nervous system. *Med. Biol.* 65, 137–42.

### Angiotensin II

Chiu, A. T., J. V. Duncia, D. E. McCall, P. C. Wong, W. A. Price, M. J. M. C. Thoolen, D. J. Carini, A. L. Johnson, and P. B. M. W. M. Timmermans (1989). Nonpeptide angiotensin II receptor antagonists. III Structure-function studies. *J. Pharmacol. Exp. Ther.* 250, 867–874.

Ferrario, C. M., K. L. Barnes, C. H. Block, K. B. Brosnihan, D. I. Diz, M. C. Kohosla, and R. A. Santos (1990). Pathways of angiotensin formation and function in the brain. *Hypertension* 113–119.

Fitzsimons, J. T. (1975). The renin-angiotensin system and drinking behavior. *Prog. Brain Res.* 42, 215.

Ganong, W. F. (1989). Angiotensin II in the brain and pituitary: Contrasting roles in the regulation of adenohypophyseal secretion. *Horm. Res.* 31, 24–31.

Phillips, M. I., J. Weyhenmeyer, D. Felix, and D. Ganten (1979). Evidence for an endogenous brain renin angiotensin system. *Fed. Proc.* 38, 2260–2266.

### Oxytocin and Vasopressin

Buijs, R. M. (1990). Vasopressin and oxytocin localization and putative functions in the brain. *Acta Neurochir.* [*Suppl.*] *(Wien)* 47, 86–9.

de Wied, D. (1983). The importance of vasopressin memory. *Trends Neurosci.* 7, 62–64.

Gash, D. M. and G. J. Thomas (1983). What is the importance of vasopressin in memory processes? *Trends Neurosci.,* 6 197–198.

Hagler, A. T., D. J. Ogusthorpe, Dauber- Osguthorpe, and J. C. Hempel (1985). Dynamics and conformational energetics of a peptide hormone: Vasopressin. *Science* 227, 1309–1315.

Kasting, N. W. (1989). Criteria for establishing a physiological role for brain peptides. A case in point: The role of vasopressin in thermoregulation during fever and antipyresis. *Brain Res. Rev.* 14, 143–153.

Koob, G. F., R. Dantzer, F. Rodriguez, F. E. Bloom, and M. Le Moal (1985). Osmotic stress mimics the effects of vasopressin on learned behaviour. *Nature* 315, 750–752.

Miller, F. D., G. Ozimek, R. J. Milner, and F. E. Bloom (1989). Regulation of neuronal oxytocin mRNA by ovarian steroids in the mature and developing hypothalamus. *Proc. Natl. Acad. Sci. U.S.A. 86*, 2468–2472.

Simerly, R. B. and L. W. Swanson (1987). The distribution of neurotransmitter-specific cells and fibers in the anteroventral periventricular nucleus: Implications for the control of gonadotropin secretion in the rat. *Brain Res. 400*, 11–34.

Swanson, L. W. and P. E. Sawchenko (1983). Hypothalamic integration: Organization of the paraventricular and supraoptic nuclei. *Ann. Rev. Neurosci. 6*, 269–324.

van den Hoof, P., I. J. A. Urban, and D. de Weid (1989). Vasopressin maintains long term potentiation in rat lateral septum slices. *Brain. Res. 505*, 181–186.

### Neurotensin

Bean, A. J., M. J. During, A. Y. Deutsch, and R. H. Roth, (1989). Effects of dopamine depletion on striatal neurotensin: Biochemical and immunohistochemical effects. *J. Neurosci. 9*, 4430–4438.

Carraway, R. and S. E. Leeman (1975). The amino acid sequence of a hypothalamic peptide, neurotensin. *J. Biol. Chem. 250*, 1907–1912.

Ju, G., L. W. Swanson, and R. B. Simerly (1989). Studies on the cellular architecture of the bed nuclei of the stria terminalis in the rat: II. Chemoarchitecture. *J. Comp. Neurol. 280*, 603–21.

Kobayashi, R. M., M. Brown, and W. Vale (1977). Regional distribution of neurotensin and somatostatin in rat brain. *Brain Res. 126*, 584–590.

### Tachykinin Peptides

Kotani, H., M. Hoshimura, H. Nawa, and S. Nakanishi (1986). Structure and gene organization of bovine neuromedin K precursor. *Proc. Nat. Acad. Sci. (USA) 83*, 7074–7078.

Lundberg, J. M., A. Saria, E. Brodin, S. Rosell, and K. Folkers (1983). A substance P antagonist inhibits vagally induced increase in vascular permeability and bronchial smooth muscle contraction in the guinea pig. *Proc. Nat. Acad. Sci. (USA) 80*, 1120–1124.

Maggio, J. E. (1988). Tachykinins. *Ann. Rev. Neurosci. 11*, 13–28.

Nawa, H., H. Kotani, and S. Nakanishi (1984). Tissue specific generation of two preprotachykinin mRNAs from one gene by alternative RNA splicing. *Nature. 312*, 729–734.

Nicoll, R. A., C. Schenker, and S. E. Leeman (1980). Substance P as a transmitter candidate. *Ann. Rev. Neurosci. 3*, 227–268.

Nilsson, G., T. Hökfelt, and B. Pernow (1974). Distribution of Substance P-like immunoreactivity in the rat central nervous system as revealed by immunohistochemistry. *Med. Biol. 52*, 424–448.

Substance P in the nervous system (1982). *Ciba Foundation Symposium 91.* Pitman Publishers, London.

Vaught, J. L. (1988). Substance P antagonists and analgesia: A review of the hypothesis. *Life Sci. 43*, 1419–1431.

Yanaihara, N., C. Yanaihara, T. Zhang, M. Hoshino, K. Iguchi and T. Mochizuki (1989). Recent advances in brain-gut hormones. *Arch. Histol. Cytol. 54* (Review), 1–45.


*Glucagon-related Peptides*


Everitt, B. J., T. Hökfelt, L. Terenius, K. Tatemoto, V. Mutt, and M. Goldstein (1985). Neuropeptide Y-, substance P- and VIP-immunoreactive nerves in cat spleen in relation to autonomic vascular and volume control. *Cell Tissue Res. 239*, 9–18.

Fahrenkrug, J. and P. C. Emson (1982). Vasoactive intestinal polypeptide: Functional aspects. *Br. Med. Bull. 38*, 265–70.

Guillemin, R., P. Brazeau, P. Bohlen, F. Esch, N. Ling, and W. B. Wehrenberg (1982). Growth hormone releasing factor from a human pancreatic tumor that caused acromegaly. *Science 218*, 585–587.

Lundberg, J. M., B. Hedlund, and T. Bartfai (1982). Vasoactive intestinal polypeptide enhances muscarinic ligand binding in cat submandibular gland. *Nature 295*, 147–149.

Magistretti P. J. and M. Schorderet (1985). Norepinephrine and histamine potentiate the increases in cyclic adenosine $3':5'$-monophosphate elicited by vasoactive intestinal polypeptide in mouse cerebral cortical slices: mediation by $\alpha 1$-adrenergic and $H_1$-histaminergic receptors. *J. Neurosci. 5*, 362–368.

Morrison, J. H., P. J. Magistretti, R. Benoit, and F. E. Bloom (1984). The distribution and morphological characteristics of the intracortical VIP-positive cell: An immunohistochemical analysis. *Brain Res. 292*, 269–282.

Rivier, J., J. Spiess, M. Thorner, and W. Vale (1982). Characterization of a growth hormone releasing factor from a human pancreatic islet tumor. *Nature 300*, 276–278.

Said, S. I. (1984). Vasoactive intestinal polypeptide (VIP): Current status. *Peptides. 5*, 143–50.

Tatemoto K. and V. Mutt (1981). Isolation and characterization of the interstitual peptide porcine PHI (PHI-27), a new member of the glucagon-secretin family. *Proc. Nat. Acad. Sci. (USA) 78*, 6603–6607.

*Pancreatic Polypeptide-related Peptides*

Allen, Y. S., T. E. Adrian, J. M. Allen, K. Tatemoto, T. J. Crow, S. R. Bloom, and J. M. Polak (1983). Neuropeptide Y distribution in the rat brain. *Science 221*, 877–879.

Mutt, V. (1983). New approaches to the identification and isolation of hormonal polypeptides. *Trends Neurosci.* 6, 357–360.

Sheikh, S. P., R. Hakanson, and T. W. Schwartz (1989). Y1 and Y2 receptors for neuropeptide Y. *FEBS Lett. 245*, 209–14.

Wahlestedt, C., R. Ekman, and E. Widerlov (1989). Neuropeptide Y (NPY) and the central nervous system: Distribution effects and possible relationship to neurological and psychiatric disorders. *Prog. Neuropsychopharmacol. Biol. Psychiatry. 13*, 31–54.

*Opioid Peptides*

Bloom, F. E. (1983). The endorphins: A growing family of pharmacologically pertinent peptides. *Ann. Rev. Pharmacol. Toxicol. 23*, 151–170.

Bronstein, D. M., R. Przewlocki, and H. Akil (1990). Effects of morphine treatment on pro-opiomelanocortin systems in rat brain. *Brain. Res. 519*, 102–11.

Costa, E., I. Mocchetti, S. Supattapone, and S. H. Snyder (1987). Opioid peptide biosynthesis: Enzymatic selectivity and regulatory mechanisms. *FASEB J. 1*, 16–21.

Ebadi, M. and Y. Hama (1988). Dopamine, GABA, cholecystokinin and opioids in neuroleptic-induced tardive dyskinesia. *Neurosci. Biobehav. Rev. 12*, 179–87.

Fischer, E. G. (1988). Opioid peptides modulate immune functions. A review. *Immunopharmacol. Immunotoxicol. 10*, 265–326.

Gall, C. M. (1988). Localization and seizure-induced alterations of opioid peptides and CCK in the hippocampus. *NIDA Res.* (Monogram) *82*, 12–32.

Gallagher, M. (1988). Behavioral significance of opioid peptides in relation to hippocampal function. *NIDA Res.* [Monogram] *82*, 118–32.

Goldstein, A., S. Tachibana, L. I. Lowney, and L. Hold (1979). Dynorphin—(1–13), an extraordinarily potent opioid peptide. *Proc. Nat. Acad. Sci. (USA) 76*, 6666–6670.

Herkenham, M. and S. McLean (1988). The anatomical relationship of opioid peptides and opiate receptors in the hippocampi of four rodent species. *NIDA Res.* (Monogram) *82*, 33–47.

Hughes, J., T. W. Smith, H. W. Kosterlitz, L. A. Fothergill, G. A. Morgan, and H. R. Morris (1975). Identification of two related pentapeptides from the brain with potent opiate agonist activity. *Nature 258*, 577.

Nakanishi, S., A. Inoue, T. Kita, A. C. Y. Chang, S. Cohen, and S. Numa (1979). Nucleotide sequence of cloned cDNA for bovine corticotropin-β-lipotropin precursor. *Nature* 257, 238–240.

Nicoll, R. A., G. R. Siggins, N. Ling, F. E. Bloom, and R. Guillemin (1977). Neuronal actions of endorphins and enkephalins among brain regions: A comparative microiontophoretic study. *Proc. Nat. Acad. Sci. (USA)* 74, 2584.

Price, M., M. A. Gistrak, Y. Itzhak, E. F. Hahn, and G. W. Pasternak (1989). Kappa opiate receptor multiplicity: Evidence for two U50,488-sensitive kappa 1 subtypes and a novel kappa 3 subtype. *J. Pharmacol. Exp. Ther.* 251, 461–8.

Tempel, A., J. A. Kessler, and R. S. Zukin, (1990). Chronic naltrexone treatment increases expression of preproenkephalin and preprotachykinin mRNA in discrete brain regions. *J. Neurosci.* 10, 741–747.

## Somatostatin

Beal, M. F. and J. B. Martin (1986). Neuropeptides in neurological disease. *Ann. Neurol.* 20, 547–65.

Benoit, R., N. Ling, B. Alford, and R. Guillemin (1982). Seven peptides derived from prosomatostatin in rat brain. *Biochem. Biophys. Res. Commun.* 107, 944–950.

de Lima, A. D. and J. H. Morrison (1989). An ultrastructural analysis of somatostatin-immunoreactive neurons and synapses in the temporal and occipital cortex of the macaque monkey. *J. Comp. Neurol.* 283, 212–227.

Effendic, S. and R. Luft (1980). Somatostatin: A classical hormone, a locally active polypeptide, and a neurotransmitter. *Ann. Clin. Med.* 12, 87–94.

Iversen, L. L. (1988). Test models and new directions in dementia research. *Psychopharmacol (Series 5)*, 196–203.

Johansson, O., T. Hökfelt, and R. P. Elde (1984). Immunohistochemical distribution of somatostatin-like immunoreactivity in the central nervous system of the adult rat. *Neuroscience* 13, 265–339.

Moore, S. D., S. G. Madamba, M. Joëls, and G. R. Siggins (1988). Somatostatin augments the M-current in hippocampal neurons. *Science* 239, 278–280.

Reichlin, S. (1983). Somatostatin. *N. Engl. J. Med.* 309, 1495–1501, 1556–1563.

Rubinow, D. R., C. L. Davis, and R. M. Post (1988). Somatostatin in neuropsychiatric disorders. *Prog. Neuropsychopharmacol. Biol. Psychiatry 55* (Review).

Tran, V. T., M. F. Beal, and J. B. Martin (1985). Two types of somatostatin receptors differentiated by cyclic somatostatin analogs. *Science 228*, 492–494.

### Cholecystokinin

Albus, M. (1988). Cholecystokinin. *Prog. Neuropsychopharmacol. Biol. Psychiatry 21* (Review).

Baile, C. A., C. L. McLaughlin, and F. M. A. Della (1986). Role of cholecystokinin and opioid peptides in control of food intake. *Physiol. Rev. 66*, 172–234.

Beinfeld, M. C. (1985). Cholecystokinin (CCK) gene-related peptides: distribution, and characterization of immunoreactive pro-CCK, and an amino terminal pro-CCK fragment in rat brain. *Brain Res. 334*: 351–355.

Dourish, C. T., D. Hawley, and S. D. Iversen (1988). The novel CCK antagonist L364,718 abolished caerulein- but potentiates morphine-induced antinociception. *Eur. J. Pharmacol. 152*, 163–6.

Lotti, V. J., R. G. Pendleton, R. J. Gould, H. M. Hanson, R. S. Chang, and B. V. Clineschmidt (1987). In vivo pharmacology of L-364,718, a new potent nonpeptide peripheral cholecystokinin antagonist. *J. Pharmacol. Exp. Ther. 241*, 103–9.

Rehfeld, J. F., N. R. Goltermann, L.-I. Larsson, P. M. Emson, and C. M. Lee (1979). Gastrin and cholecystokinin in central and peripheral neurones. *Fed. Proc. 38*, 2325–2329.

White, F. J. and R. Wang (1984). Interactions of cholecystokinin octapeptide and dopamine on nucleus accumbens neurons. *Brain Res. 300*, 161–166.

Zetler, G. (1985). Neuropharmacological profile of cholecystokinin-like peptides. *Ann. N.Y. Acad. Sci. 448*, 448–69.

### Calcitonin Gene-related Peptide

Brain, S. D., T. J. Williams, J. R. Tippins, H. R. Morris, and I. MacIntyre (1985). Calcitonin-gene related peptide is a potent vasodilator. *Nature 313*, 54–56.

Rosenfeld, M. G., J.-J. Mermod, S. G. Amara, L. W. Swanson, P. E. Sawchenko, J. Rivier, W. W. Vale, and R. M. Evans (1983). Production of a novel neuropeptide encoded by the calcitonin gene via tissue-specific RNA processing. *Nature 304*, 129–135.

Rosenfeld, M. G., S. G. Amara, and R. M. Evans (1984). Alternative RNA processing: determining neuronal phenotype. *Science 225*, 1315–1320.

*Corticotropin-releasing hormone*

Berridge, C. W. and A. J. Dunn (1989). CRH and alpha-helical-CRH modulate behavioral measures of arousal in monkeys. *Pharmacol. Biochem. Behav. 32*, 919–26.

Kobayashi, K., J. Tamaoki, N. Sakai, T. Kanemura, A. Chiyotani, T. Shibasaki, and T. Takizawa (1989). Potentiation of acoustic startle by corticotropin-releasing factor (CRF) and by fear are both reversed by alpha-helical CRF (9-41). *Neuropsychopharmacology 2*, 285–92.

Koob, G. F., B. K. Thatcher, A. Tazi, and M. M. Le (1988). Behavioral pharmacology of stress: Focus on CNS corticotropin-releasing factor. *Adv. Exp. Med. Biol. 245*, 25–34.

Nemeroff, C. B. (1988). The role of corticotropin-releasing factor in the pathogenesis of major depression. *Pharmacopsychiatry 21*, 76–82.

Vale, W., J. Spiess, J. Rivier, and C. Rivier (1981). Characterization of a 41-residue ovine hypothalamic peptide that stimulates secretion of corticotropin and beta-endorphin. *Science 213*, 1394–1397.

Vale, W., C. Rivier, M. R. Brown, J. Spiess, G. Koob, L. Swanson, L. Bilezikjian, F. Bloom, and J. Rivier (1983). Chemical and biological characterization of corticotropin releasing factor. *Rec. Progr. Horm. Res. 39*, 245–270.

Vale, W. and M. Greer (1985). *Corticotropin Releasing Factor*—A conference report. *Fed. Proc. 44*, 145–263.

Valentino, R. J. (1988). CRH effects on central noradrenergic neurons: Relationship to stress. *Adv. Exp. Med. Biol. 245*, 47–64.

# 13 | Cellular Mechanisms in Learning and Memory

In other chapters of this edition, we have noted specific behavioral changes that correlate either with biochemical differences in specific transmitters or with functional changes in the activity of biochemically defined neuronal systems. This level of correlation avoids the more difficult question of just what role the specific systems play in initiating, maintaining, or terminating the behavior. Now we return to an issue ignored by us for the past decade, an issue that represents one of the most complex behavioral achievements of nervous systems—the ability to learn and remember.

When we last discussed this topic, in the third edition, we observed that "unequivocal causal relations between a change in cell structure or function and learning still remain to be demonstrated," and concluded that this subject probably did not yet merit intellectual investment by neuropharmacologists. Since then, however, the frontiers of neuroscience have moved into this void. Although we cannot yet provide inquiring minds with certified maps to today's Holy Grail in drug development—the cognitive enhancer designed to delay or reverse the ravages of Alzheimer's disease—there are now definite leads.

Part of our problem in presenting the neuropharmacology of learning and memory has been that there were no data establishing that a change in a specific neurotransmitter action at a specific synaptic location was necessary and sufficient for a behavioral change in a living organism. The experimental and theoretical reports that make such claims fall into four large classes:

1. *Cellular and molecular* research which seeks to attribute the changes in cell-cell interactions to specific molecular events in their trans-synaptic operations;

2. *Neuronal process* research which seeks to define either the functional changes in a brain network or the set of neural pathways that are necessary and sufficient to account for the behavioral changes observed in an experimental learning paradigm;

3. *Behavioral* research in which intracerebral or parenteral drug treatments or other perturbations of brain structure and function are used to disrupt the ability of an animal to modify its behavior in a predictable way in specific environmental settings;

4. *Model systems* research in which the object is to determine, from simulations of neurobiological events, the minimum number of hypothetical operations required to explain an equally abstractly defined memory or learning phenomenon; this model network of hypothetical "neurons" is then used to predict either how brains work or how better computers ought to.

These lines of research more or less independently address the issues of learning and memory by setting their questions *within* one of the main hierarchical levels of the neuroscience enterprise: molecular, cellular, multicellular, or behavioral (see Chapter 1). The complex interactions between these levels make it difficult and often misleading to connect small changes at one end of this hierarchy with changes at the other. Over the last decade, however, some new data have appeared which relate the abstract and essentially behaviorally-defined operations of memory and learning in whole animals to specific synaptic events. It is these lines of experimental evidence that emphasize a vertically connected series of data between molecules, cells, and behavior that we now take as our starting point.

## FORMULATING EXPERIMENTS IN MEMORY AND LEARNING

Biological analysis of memory and learning typically requires two parallel lines of work: a *behavioral* component in which the subject is trained, given a training recess of variable intervals, and then tested for retention of the trained response and a *functional, structural,* or *biochemical* component intended to define the essential changes, sites, or molecular sequelae underlying these events. Such two-track experiments thus offer—in our view—a better approach than earlier studies in which the biological substrates for the learning were inferred from the effects of systemic drug treatments (from protein synthesis inhibitors to hormone antagonists) between the learning and testing phases.

Scientists working in this field commonly distinguish two categories of learning: "non-associative" and "associative." Non-associative learning describes the functional changes that ensue when an organism interacts with a single form of stimulus. For example, the decreased responses that occur when the same sensory stimulus is repeated sequentially, termed "habituation," is a non-associative form of learning, as is the reversal of the habituated response, termed "sensitization," by a different intensity or quality of the stimulus. Associative learning, as the name implies, is the form of learning in which the subject associates a previously neutral stimulus with a response normally generated by another cue, the sort made famous by Pavlov's classic experiments that triggered dog salivation with a bell instead of raw meat.

An exciting prospect for such work has been opened by the development of experimental test systems in invertebrates—and more recently in vertebrates as well—to show that the behavioral performance of the organism depends on synaptic events in specific locations, and then to define the changes that occur at these locations as the organism learns and performs. Such possibilities for molecular and cellular explanations exist, it should be recognized, only because of the extensive data that have been obtained over this same interval.

The great neurocytologist, Ramón y Cajal, held strongly to the view that learning was a synaptic event. He regarded the synapse as the primary site of interneuronal communication. The subsequent advances in biochemistry, anatomy, and physiology that are emphasized in this text led to the notion that drugs should be able to regulate the critical sites of synaptic transmission. Given this premise, the manipulations of memory processes by specific drugs used as tools for dissecting the roles played by specific transmitters and defined sites should not only illuminate the underlying process, but also provide a means towards eventual therapeutic interventions.

## CELLULAR MODELS OF LEARNING IN INVERTEBRATE NERVOUS SYSTEMS

Studies carried out in the visceral ganglia of invertebrates, particularly the marine mollusc, *Aplysia*, have already provided information on molecular mechanisms of the cellular and synaptic changes that accompany simple forms of behavior modification, such as habituation and sensitization. Sensitization is the ability of nonspecific but strongly arousing sensory stimulation to enhance the effectiveness of synaptic transmission in other neuronal pathways. When the gill-withdrawal reflex is studied for this effect, strong electrical stimulation of the connections between the visceral ganglion and the head ganglion facilitates the withdrawal. The strong stimulation also diminishes habituation of the reflex if tested with identical repetitive sensory stimuli. As judged by the analysis of postsynaptic potentials, the facilitating stimulation increases the amount of transmitter released by the afferent limb of the withdrawal reflex (i.e., the sensory nerves). Once initiated in the *Aplysia* ganglion, the effects of the sensitization can last from several minutes to hours.

Further pursuit of the presynaptic mechanism of the enhanced release became possible when it was found that the sensitizing stimulation also increased the ganglionic content of cyclic AMP and that exposure of the ganglion both to serotonin (known to activate cyclic AMP production in the ganglion) and to cyclic AMP (applied to the whole ganglion or injected intracellularly into the sensory nerve cell) replicated the effects of the sensitizing stimulation. In this case, the molecular mediation sequence of the second messenger hypothesis (see Chapter 6) suggests that a serotonin-secreting interneuron is activated by the sensitizing stimulation, leading to increased pre-synaptic levels of cyclic AMP and a consequent enhancement of the sensory transmitter release.

Subsequent studies have shown that the short-term memory for sensitization of the *Aplysia* gill- and siphon-withdrawal reflex is in fact distributed across at least four sites of circuit modification. Each of these invokes a slightly different circuitry and a different type of synaptic modification (presynaptic facilitation, presynaptic inhibition, post-tetanic potentiation, and increased tonic firing rate), all of which result in facilitation. Nevertheless, all four of these mechanisms seem to be mediated by a common modulatory transmitter (serotonin), to utilize the same cyclic AMP-mediated second messenger system, and to require a phosphorylation event (affecting either intravesicular proteins or ion channels) to enhance transmitter release. These short-term changes, lasting from minutes to hours, do not require protein synthesis.

More recently, Kandel and associates have reported that the same modulatory neurotransmission processes involved in the short-term memory changes can also lead, through the same or alternative second messenger systems, to more prolonged intercellular modifications that can account for longer-term (i.e., several days) associative changes in *Aplysia*. Although beyond the scope of this survey, Alkon and associates have observed that very similar processes underlie associative learning of visual responses by the marine snail *Hermissenda*.

The scientific search for the cellular and molecular basis of learning was launched by Kandel, Tauc, Gershenfeld, Strumwasser, Alkon, Levitan, Kaczmarek, and other pioneers of invertebrate psychobiology. They thought these smaller nervous systems could be fathomed, and they set themselves the task of working out the rules of connectivity by which these systems adapt to environmental conditions. Their meticulous descriptive work has given us a logical, consistent and compelling account of the cellular changes accompanying behavioral modification and the molecular basis of these changes.

When similar claims regarding the role of a single transmitter in learning and memory were made for mammalian systems, they required the identification of the specific 5-HT-mediating interneuron that is activated by and directly involved in the behavioral process. In fact, very recent findings from Kandel and associates have documented that the 5-HT neuron which modulates the critical presynaptic and postsynaptic intraganglionic connections enables the *Aplysia* (or at least its abdominal ganglion) to learn to associate the withdrawal reflex with a novel sensory stimulus. However, they also found that a functionally identical pathway can produce this effect without using 5-HT. The experiments on molluscan ganglia clearly confirm the possibility that prolonged, possibly permanent changes in the relationship of transmission between one or more cells in a critical circuit can be correlated with the behavioral modification.

The monoamine hypothesis of memory and learning in mammals advanced by Kety in the late 1960s could now be viewed as anticipating, in a more primitive mechanistic way, the serotonin and cyclic AMP-mediated presynaptic facilitation model derived from the studies of invertebrate sensitization. Kety's model called for a brain system that could mediate the ability of arousal to consolidate experiences into adaptive behavioral mechanisms. To reconcile the two situations, we must first substitute the mammalian transmitter norepinephrine (NE) for the role played by 5-HT in the invertebrate. The central NE neurons and their synapses have now been well mapped, and electrophysiological recordings in behaviorally responding rats and monkeys have established that the NE cells fire when novel sensory events occur in the external environment. These data are logical and internally consistent with a role of NE neurons in mediating arousal. Furthermore, the severity of Alzheimer's dementia seems to be more profound in those patients who show the greatest loss of the noradrenergic (and cholinergic) projections to the cortex. The problem with such correlations is that other transmitters not included in the model are also often deficient. Earlier cholinergic hypotheses of memory based exclusively upon the ability of cholinergic antagonists to disrupt memory performance failed to yield convincing evidence because it was not possible to specify where and how such effects took place. It is also likely that learning and memory events in mammalian brain function—as in the invertebrate—are too critical to rely on only one transmitter system.

## THE RABBIT NICTITATING MEMBRANE REFLEX AND ASSOCIATIVE LEARNING

We turn next to a mammalian neuronal system, the rabbit's nictitating membrane, that has provided another molecular and cellular model for memory and associative learning. This system permits the direct observation of an animal's performance during tests of learning and memory and also the direct determination of exactly where in the circuitry the learning events have occurred.

The basic studies, largely done independently by John Harvey's and Richard Thompson's groups, showed that the rabbit blink reflex could be associatively conditioned. Rabbits will normally blink (i.e., cover their cornea with the nictitating membrane) every time a puff of air is directed at the cornea. Repeated presentation of a loud tone just before the air puff conditioned the rabbits to blink in response to the tone. Eventually the rabbits will blink every time they hear the tone, with no air puff being required.

At this point, chemical and electrolytic lesions as well as microstimulations were used to define the pathways that relay the unconditional (air puff-induced) blink and the conditional blink triggered by the tone (see Fig. 13-1). The air puff stimulus travels through the sensory fibers of the trigeminal nerve to activate motor neurons of the abducens nucleus, retracting the eye into the orbit, and then causing the nictitating membrane to extend over the eye. The acoustic stimulus travels through the cochlear nucleus to the pontine nucleus, and seems quite separate at its early stages from the corneal sensory pathway. However, the researchers also noted that even before the rabbits learned to associate the sound with the blinking, the acoustic stimulus which was rather loud could often cause an increased response amplitude to the normal air puff stimulus. This suggested that the acoustic stimulus could perhaps also sensitize the unassociated air puff stimulus.

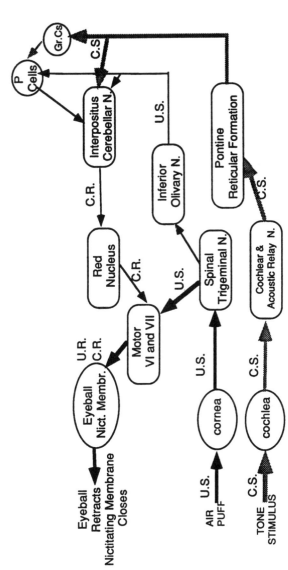

FIGURE 13-1. Schematic diagram of the sensory and motor circuitry for the rabbit nictitating membrane model of cellular mechanisms in associative learning. Pathways marked as U.S. participate in the elicitation of the unconditional reflex response (U.R. components) in which a puff of air to the cornea will always provoke a blink by closing the nictitating membrane. The auditory pathways that carry the tone information that can become associated with the air puff-induced blink are indicated as the C.S. (conditional stimulus) or C.R. (conditional response) components. When the animal has been well trained, the tone C.S. will now evoke the C.R. even without a U.S.

Based upon comparisons of rabbits in which discrete lesions were made along the known anatomical paths within the two systems of sensory processing, the critical site for producing the association seems to be located in the interpositus nucleus, one of the deep cerebellar nuclei. The efferent limb of the motor reflex then courses through the red nucleus directly to the abducens nerve, where it activates the eyeball retraction reflex (see Fig. 13-1).

Since most of the transmitters operating in these hierarchical controlling chains have not yet been defined, it would seem that the model was not quite ready for transmitter-specific pharmacology to be a useful analytical tool. The only sites that have been probed so far are the synapses within the interpositus and red nuclei; here the GABA antagonists bicuculline and picrotoxin will block the conditional reflex. However, Harvey and colleagues have used this associative eye blink model to show that low doses of amphetamine as well as LSD will enhance this form of learning, while a wide range of drugs from pimozide to atropine and scopolomine, as well as agonists for kappa and sigma opioid receptors, will decrease acquisition at doses that do not affect the basic reflex. Because these latter drugs were all given systemically, however, it was not clear where (within the cranial nerve-cerebellar circuitry or elsewhere) they were acting to produce these effects.

In more recent experiments, forebrain regions traditionally viewed as participating in memory and learning functions have also been implicated in the nictitating membrane associational reflex. For these experiments, the rabbits received "classical conditioning" of the nictitating membrane response; the tone stimulus and the air puff were separated by a pause (or "trace") of 500 msec. The short interruption made the simple learning task just a bit more complicated. The extra time delay allowed the investigators to distinguish nonspecific arousal—possibly sensitizing the reflex—from more specific interactions.

Thompson and colleagues found that lesions of the hippocampus or cingulate/retrosplenial cortex would disrupt acquisition of the interrupted conditioned response but that neocortical lesions did not. Neither lesion affected the acquisition of the noninterrupted pairing of tone and air puff. When animals with hippocampal or cingulate/ retrosplenial cortex lesions were switched to a standard delay paradigm in which the conditioned stimulus and the unconditioned stimulus were given at the same time, rabbits acquired the association in about the same number of trials as naïve animals.

In the interrupted protocol, however, macroelectrode recordings showed substantial increases of multi-unit activity in the CA1 region of the hippocampus that began during the tone and persisted through the trace interval, even before the rabbit showed consistent association. As the rabbit's performance in responding to the tone stimulus improved, the hippocampal activity shifted to later and later in the trace interval.

These data thus directly relate behavioral demonstration of associational learning with discrete neuronal circuitry. Such an experimental system should eventually lend itself to pharmacological and electrophysiological analysis of the changes within the critical neurons that alter synaptic function. Student volunteers are welcome.

## LONG-TERM POTENTIATION: A VERTEBRATE MODEL OF SYNAPTIC PLASTICITY

Next we turn to an increasingly popular form of mammalian forebrain synaptic plasticity in which electrophysiological changes at the synaptic level have been probed extensively by drugs to identify the transmitter systems responsible for discrete transductive mechanisms. The term "long-term potentiation" (LTP) refers to a long-lasting (10 minutes to days, depending on the conditions) enhancement of synaptic transmission. The effect is measured as increased amplitudes of excitatory postsynaptic potentials (or the currents generated by these potentials) in specific circuits after high-frequency, high-intensity activation of these same circuits or other discrete paths. Because the phenomenon was originally described with macroelectrode recordings in the hippocampus of intact animals, it has been a candidate to link learning and cellular changes in vivo. However, the most intense recent studies have more often involved analysis of the pertinent connections in vitro in the now classical slice preparations of the hippocampus or neocortex.

This special form of enhanced synaptic transmission was first demonstrated by brief, high-frequency stimulation of the entorhinal cortex, through the perforant path (see Fig. 13-2), to enhance activation of granule cells of the hippocampal dentate gyrus by subsequent single stimuli of the perforant path. In awake cats, guinea pigs, and rats this enhanced transmission could be seen for periods of days to weeks. The transmitter for this pathway is now thought to be glutamate (GLU) or possibly aspartate (ASP), although the role—if any—of coexisting peptides, such as the pro-enkephalin-derived opioid peptides, remains to be established.

Long-term potentiation has also been observed at two other sites within the hippocampal formation: (1) at the synapses between the dentate granule cells and the targets of their mossy fiber synapses, the CA3 pyramidal neurons, and (2) between the Schaffer collaterals of CA3 pyramidal neurons, as well as associational fibers from the contralateral hippocampus, and the CA1 pyramidal neurons (see Fig. 12-3). The transmitter for these two pathways is thought to be ASP, GLU, or possibly homocysteate; coexisting peptides (prodynorphin-derived, as well as CCK) remain an unsolved part of the action here at least for the mossy fiber connection to CA3 pyramidal neurons. Although the basic phenomenon of long-term potentiation after a high-frequency, high-intensity period of afferent pathway activation is similar in all three synaptic sites, the relative importance of specific transmitters and their responsible transductive mechanisms differ on a site-by-site basis.

The essential pharmacological advance came with the recognition that the N-methyl-D-aspartic acid (NMDA) subtype of excitatory amino acid (EAA) receptor (see Chapter 7) was responsible for the induction phase of the long-lasting synaptic enhancement. Antagonists of this form of EAA receptor (such as aminophosphovaleric acid) will prevent LTP induction without interfering with previously potentiated transmission or with normal low-frequency transmission in the pathway under study. The critical link established by Nicoll and colleagues is that the required high-frequency, high-intensity

FIGURE 13-2. The synaptic circuits of the rodent hippocampal slice preparation in which long-term potentiation (LTP) can be elicited are indicated in the upper panel, while the neurotransmitters associated with these circuits or with the target cells capable of expressing the LTP response are shown in the lower panel. Each of the three major hippocampal circuits (entorhinal cortex to dentate, dentate to CA3, and CA3 to CA1) shows a generally similar LTP, but the pharmacology of the modification varies with the specific location and pathways. Glutamate-mediated synaptic events figure prominently, as indicated in the text.

stimulation acts via the NMDA receptor to couple the depolarization with the increased $Ca^{2+}$ entry. This combined response is then thought to depolarize the small dendritic domains that are the site of convergent afferents in the pathway under study and to increase their subsequent transmission. In the perforant path-to-dentate circuit, drugs that block μ-opioid receptors or β-adrenergic receptors will also block LTP. The latter antagonists are also very effective in blocking LTP of CA3 neurons, although not that of CA1 neurons. These drug effects coincide nicely with the regional patterns of monoamine innervation of the hippocampal formation (see Fig. 13-2).

The NMDA receptor has been accepted as a critical step in initiating LTP, as well as in a related intrahippocampal process called long-term depression that has so far received much less scientific examination. However, the NMDA-regulated step alone does not seem to be adequate for the long-term maintenance of the enhanced transmission. The pharmacological analysis of the LTP maintenance phase is emerging towards consensus, but the available tools are far from specific, preventing resolution of even a tentative final picture. One simplified version of the present "bottom-line" is that the NMDA-induced Ca influx activates Ca-dependent protein kinases, such as the Ca-calmodulin-regulated kinase (CamKinase II) and the Ca-phospholipid-dependent protein kinase (protein kinase C, see Chapter 6). Once these kinases are activated—either presynaptically, postsynaptically, or both—they "switch" to activator-independent forms. In this state, the activated enzymes could be expected to maintain the end responses of increased presynaptic transmitter release, increased sensitivity of the postsynaptic receptors to the released transmitter, and decreased electrical resistance within the postsynaptic dendritic spines. The pharmacology of these kinases is still being written, and perturbers of their responses, such as phorbol esters, sphingosine, and "H-7," all appear to have other effects in addition to regulation of the kinase. Thus, much remains to be accomplished with this system, including the demonstration that such events within single pathways of the hippocampal formation are necessary and sufficient for the animal or the hippocampus to "learn" something.

Readers intrigued by these memory model synaptic systems should consult the selected bibliography for two other models in which the circuitry has been spelled out and awaits the application of creative pharmacological analysis: the olfactory memory pathways studied by Lynch and associates in rodents and the long-term depression of cerebellar units that may be a critical component of the vestibulo-ocular pathway, as described by Ito and colleagues.

## ARE THERE ANY NATURAL MEMORY DRUGS?

Back in the third edition, in our last outing onto the sea of memory modulators, we mentioned the growing literature on the ability of natural hormones such as vasopressin and adrenocorticotropin (ACTH), as well as "endocrinologically inert" fragments derived from them, either to repair learning deficiencies in hypophysectomized rats or to delay or accelerate the extinction of a previously learned performance. Unfortunately, as the pathways containing these peptides were more clearly defined in their projections to targets other than the posterior pituitary, and as the known barriers to diffusion of these peptides from the blood stream into the brain were shown to apply to all of them, this once-promising area became a source of contention. However, this body of research remains an important case study for scholars of the neuropharmacology of behavior. Extended analyses of the behavioral responses regulated by systemic peptide hormones have demonstrated that visceral afferent nerves can influence the brain even if the peptides are excluded by the blood-brain barrier. Furthermore, there is a strong possibility that secrets leading to the development of memory-enhancing drugs may be discovered among the intracerebral pharmacologic effects of what were once considered to be exclusively endocrine peptides.

Therefore, despite the murky nature of this particular research strategy, students should persist. For example, several studies have shown that "low doses" of subcutaneously administered vasopressin can enhance acquisition of a behavioral response, such as maze running, or extinction of active avoidance in a shuttle box. Since vasopressin was named for its potent ability to increase blood pressure, it is not surprising that while "low" in dose weight, the behaviorally active systemic doses of vasopressin also cause systemic hypertension. Moreover, vasopressin analogs that block the peripheral vascular receptors will also block the "memory performance" effects of the hormone. Koob has concluded that all behavioral effects of vasopressin have been blocked by antagonists of the vascular receptor, and that the apparent central effect is indirectly mediated by an arousal secondary to the inappropriate hypertension. On the other hand, deWied and his colleagues report that substituted and truncated versions of vasopressin lacking any vascular activity can still alter memory performance. Since the latter demonstrations of effectiveness have been obtained with memory tasks driven by aversive stimuli, their interpretation is still open.

Regardless of the arguments as to how or where the peripherally injected vasopressin acts, still smaller doses of vasopressin (1/1,000th the systemic dose) have similar effects on memory performance when given intracerebroventricularly or intracerebrally. These low-dose (nanogram or picomolar) central effects are also reduced or prevented by central administration of the peripheral vascular vasopressin antagonist. Furthermore, opposite effects, (i.e., memory performance impairment) have been reported in some tasks after central administration of vasopressin antagonists that are thought to act at "vascular" receptors. This result would suggest that somewhere within the central vasopressin-containing pathways is a circuit whose release of vasopressin is critical in eliciting proper performance and which has a receptor highly similar to those on blood vessels. Whether this means that the vascular receptor is also present on the central targets, or that the central targets are actually on the blood side of the blood-brain barrier, is an unanswered question.

The concept that vasopressin is a simple natural memory hormone has been seriously challenged by recent studies of the Brattleboro rat, whose genetic defect produces a defective messenger RNA which cannot be translated into a secretable vasopressin. Although initially reported as being memory deficient, the Brattleboro rat has supporters who regard its memory ability as normal, especially when salt and water balance are maintained by oral or systemic loading.

Furthermore, humans with diabetes insipidus (the human disease of vasopressin deficiency) are not reported to have significant memory impairment.

Without some rigorous identification of the precise cellular sites and specific receptor transductive mechanisms on which either blood-borne or cerebrospinal fluid-borne vasopressin acts, this line of work faces difficulties. The possibility that vasopressin-derived subfragments (whose informational value has been suggested but never defined) can influence neuronal operations critical to the acquisition or retention of the memory tasks that have been studied remains ripe for further study. Future research will probably establish the superficiality of such interpretations as the following: (1) vasopressin acts directly on "memory processes"; (2) vasopressin can be an aversive hormone that when given at non-physiological doses arouses the animal, who then learns better. We await eagerly the answers to this mind-drug-behavior puzzle, but they may not be found in the next edition, either.

## Approaching the Neuropharmacology of Human Memory

In the selected animal models reviewed here, several key ingredients were required for the partial resolution of how selective drugs could modify the process of memory and learning: well-defined and relatively simple memory tasks, well-defined neuronal circuits whose transmitters and transmitter receptors were identified, and drugs that could be administered in ways that restricted their access to the sites being observed. An ultimate goal of such studies would be to develop a specific neuropharmacology to improve human memory function, either in normal subjects or in those in the early stages of dementing illnesses such as Alzheimer's disease or AIDS. Until recently, almost none of the essential facts were in place. Furthermore, the prospects of inferring from noninvasive techniques which sites in a human's brain were participating in memory-related functions or how systemically administered drugs with multiple sites of interaction affected these events seemed dim (see Judd et al., 1987).

However, dealing with memory processes in humans or even non-human primates has recently become far more attractive, partly because of the ability of methods such as positron emission tomography to reveal very brief shifts in blood flow within the brain while humans perform complex cognitive processing, thereby indicating which locations were active with specific kinds of higher mental activities (see Posner et al., 1988). These methods, combined with experimental neurosurgical approaches to the rapidly unfolding description of cortical circuits in the monkey brain, have helped clarify a long-studied area of human memory research, namely, the amnesias that follow discrete toxic or traumatic lesions of the human brain. These combined strategies have allowed investigators to return to a point made earlier in the chapter (namely, that memory functions in more complex brains are likely to involve multiple systems), to ask how the primate brain is organized for memory functions, and to determine which neuronal systems are involved.

From this body of work has emerged the hypothesis that information processing is partly tied to the specific processing areas of the brain that are engaged during learning and that these "memory" events are stored within the same neural systems that also participate in the processes of perceiving, analyzing, and processing the sensory information (see Squire et al., 1990). Thus, in the visual system, the temporal cortical region involved in analyzing complex visual patterns (like faces) seems also to be involved in processing the information and in storing it. These and other examples of complex sensory systems suggest that some aspects of learning can be localized to specific subtasks, but that many parts of the brain are involved with the overall process through intricate parallel-distributed neuronal circuits.

Other sites in the brain seem to be important for the process of remembering and learning without playing any direct roles in memory storage. This point is made especially well by human amnesia victims in whom past memories and overall intellectual abilities are retained, but in whom no new memories can be formed (anterograde amnesia) following structural damage specifically to the hippocampal formation. This type of selective and severe loss of new memory ability can thus be cleanly distinguished from the more subtle forms of memory disability associated with normal aging. An indication of future prospects are recent efforts to bolster short-term memory abilities in aged rhesus monkeys (see Arnsten et al., 1988). Memory capacity was assessed by a moderately complex task that required the animal to remember information over short time intervals and to update this information on every trial. Through impressive structure activity comparisons of a series of $\alpha_2$ adrenergic agonists, two forms of memory-related actions could be defined: hypotensive, sedating, and memory-impairing effects at one type of site and the memory-enhancing effects at another $\alpha_2$ receptor site. In low doses the $\alpha_2$ adrenergic agonist, guanfacine, improved memory without inducing hypotension or sedation, offering hope for the treatment of at least some memory disorders in man.

On this hopeful note, we await with the student of such research the long awaited "future developments."

## Selected References

Abrams, T. W. and E. R. Kandel (1988). Is contiguity detection in classical conditioning a system or a cellular property? Learning in *Aplysia* suggests a possible molecular site. *Trends Neurosci.* *11*, 128–135.

Alkon, D. L. (1988). *Memory Traces in the Brain*. Cambridge University Press, Cambridge.

Arnsten, A. F., J. X. Cai, and P. S. Goldman-Rakic (1988). The alpha-2 adrenergic agonist guanfacine improves memory in aged monkeys without sedative or hypotensive side effects: Evidence for alpha-2 receptor subtypes. *J. Neurosi.* *8*, 4287–4298.

Baudry, M. and G. Lynch (1988). Properties and substrates of mammalian memory systems. In *Psychopharmacology: The Third Generation of Progress* (H. Y. Meltzer, ed.), pp. 449–462. Raven Press, New York.

Brown, T. H., P. F. Chapman, E. W. Kairiss, and C. L. Keenan (1988). Long-term synaptic potentiation. *Science* *242*, 724–728.

Frost, W. N., G. A. Clark, and E. R. Kandel (1988). Parallel processing of short-term memory for sensitization in *Aplysia*. *J. Neurobiol.* *19*, 297–334.

Glanzman, D. L., S. L. Mackey, R. D. Hawkins, A. M. Dyke, P. E. Lloyd, and E. R. Kandel (1989). Depletion of serotonin in the nervous system of *Aplysia* reduces the behavioral enhancement of gill withdrawal as well as the heterosynaptic facilitation produced by tail shock. *J. Neurosci.* *9*, 4200–4213.

Goelet, P., V. F. Castellucci, S. Schacher, and E. R. Kandel (1986). The long and short of long-term memory—a molecular framework. *Nature 322*, 419–422.

Haley, D. A., R. F. Thompson, and J. IV Madden (1988). Pharmacological analysis of the magnocellular red nucleus during classical conditioning of the rabbit nictitating membrane response. *Brain Res. 454*, 131–139.

Harvey, John A. (1987). Effects of drugs on associative learning. In *Psychopharmacology: The Third Generation of Progress* (H. Y. Meltzer, ed.), pp. 1485–1491. Raven Press, New York.

Ito, M. (1987). Long-term depression as memory process in the cerebellum. In *Synaptic Function* (G. M. Edelman, W. E. Gall, and W. M. Cowan, eds.), pp. 431–447. Wiley-Interscience, New York.

Judd, L. L., L. R. Squire, N. Butters, D. P. Salmon, and K. A. Paller (1987). Effects of psychotropic drugs on cognition and memory in normal humans and animals. In *Psychopharmacology: The Third Generation of Progress* (H. Y. Meltzer, ed.), pp. 1467–1476. Raven Press, New York.

Linden, D. J. and A. Routtenberg, (1989). The role of protein kinase C in long-term potentiation: A testable model. *Brain Res. Rev. 14*, 279–296.

Mishkin, M. and T. Appenzeller (1988). The anatomy of memory. *Scientific American*, 80–89.

Posner, M. I., S. E. Petersen, P. T. Fox, and M. E. Raichle (1988). Localization of cognitive operations in the human brain. *Science 240*, 1627–1631.

Posner, M. I., S. E. Petersen, T. Fox, and M. E. Raichle (1988). Localization of cognitive operations in the human brain. *Science 240*, 1627–1631.

Solomon, P. R., E. R. Vander-Schaaf, R. F. Thompson, and D. J. Weisz (1986). Hippocampus and trace conditioning of the rabbit's classically conditioned nictitating membrane response. *Behav. Neurosci. 100*, 729–744.

Squire, L. R. and S. Zola-Morgan (1988). Memory: brain systems and behavior. *Trends Neurosci. 11*, 170–175.

Squire, L. R., M. Mishkin, and A. Shinamura eds. (1990). Learning and memory. *Disc. Neurosci. 6*, 15–124.

Thompson, R. F. (1986). The neurobiology of learning and memory. *Science 233*, 941–947.

# Index